SHIPTON

AND

TILMAN

The Great Decade of Himalayan Exploration

Jim Perrin

arrow books

Published by Arrow Books 2014

2 4 6 8 10 9 7 5 3 1

Copyright © Jim Perrin 2013
Foreword © Nick Shipton 2013

First published in Great Britain in 2013 by Hutchinson

Arrow Books
Random House, 20 Vauxhall Bridge Road,
London SW1V 2SA

www.randomhouse.co.uk

Addresses for companies within The Random House Group Limited
can be found at: www.randomhouse.co.uk/offices.htm

The Random House Group Limited Reg. No. 954009

A CIP catalogue record for this book
is available from the British Library

ISBN 9780099505082

The Random House Group Limited supports the Forest
Stewardship Council® (FSC®), the leading international
forest-certification organisation. Our books carrying the FSC
label are printed on FSC®-certified paper. FSC is the only
forest-certification scheme supported by the leading
environmental organisations, including Greenpeace.
Our paper procurement policy can be found at:
www.randomhouse.co.uk/environment

Typeset by SX Composing DTP, Rayleigh, Essex
Printed and bound by CPI Group (UK) Ltd, Croydon, CR0 4YY

To Bill Bowker, Martin Boysen, Paul Ross, Tony Shaw,

climbing friends of my youth.

And for another companion of memorable days on the rock

Ken Wilson

who has done more than anyone to keep Shipton's and Tilman's names current over the last thirty years.

Thanks to all of you for the times and projects we have shared.

'Of what avail are forty freedoms
without a blank spot on the map?'

Aldo Leopold

Contents

Illustrations

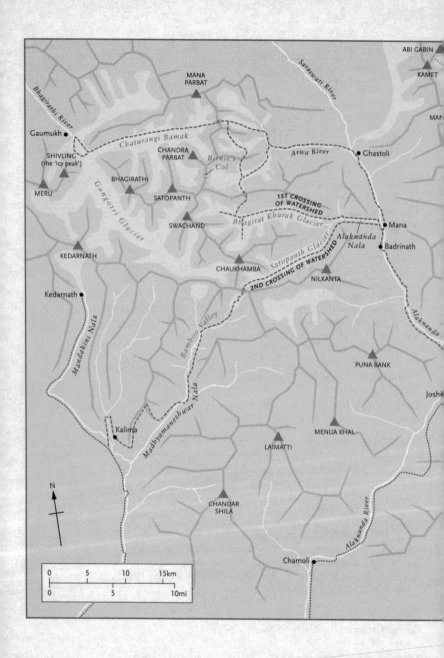

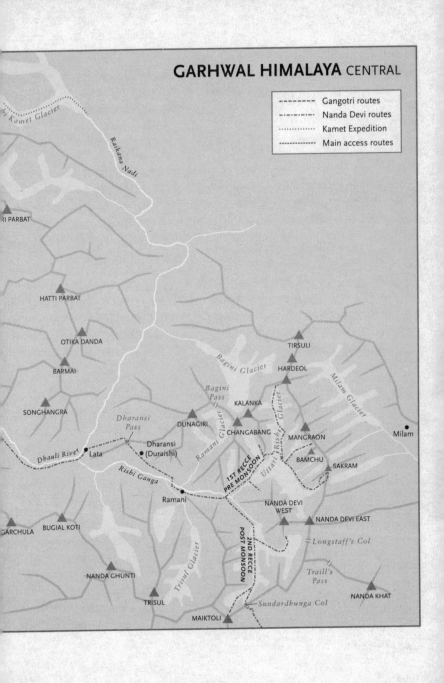

GARHWAL HIMALAYA CENTRAL

- – – – – Gangotri routes
- – · – · – Nanda Devi routes
- · · · · · · · Kamet Expedition
- · · · · · · · Main access routes

Kamet Glacier

Raikana Nadi

RI PARBAT

HATTI PARBAT

OTIKA DANDA

BARMAI

SONGHANGRA

Dhauli River   Lata

GARCHULA   BUGIAL KOTI

Dharansi
Pass

Dharansi
(Duraishi)

Rishi Ganga

Ramani

NANDA GHUNTI

TRISUL

Trisul Glacier

MAIKTOLI

Bagini Glacier

Bagini
Pass

DUNAGIRI

Ramani Glacier

KALANKA

CHANGABANG

1ST RECCE
PRE MONSOON

2ND RECCE
POST MONSOON

NANDA DEVI
WEST

TIRSULI

HARDEOL

Milam Glacier

Uttari Rishi Glacier

MANGRAON

BAMCHU

SAKRAM

Milam

NANDA DEVI EAST

Longstaff's Col

Traill's
Pass

Sundardhunga Col

NANDA KHAT

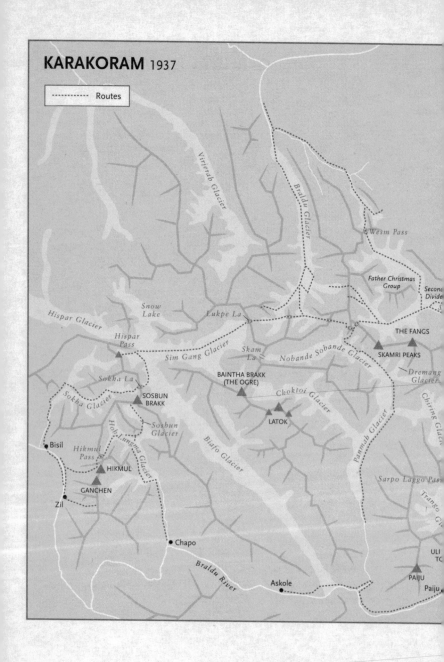

KARAKORAM 1937

-------- Routes

Virjerab Glacier

Braldu Glacier

Wesm Pass

Father Christmas Group

Second Divide

Snow Lake

Lukpe La

THE FANGS

Hispar Glacier

Hispar Pass

Sim Gang Glacier

Skam La

Nobande Sobande Glacier

SKAMRI PEAKS

Dremang Glacier

Sokha La

BAINTHA BRAKK (THE OGRE)

Choktoi Glacier

Chiring Glac

Sokha Glacier

SOSBUN BRAKK

LATOK

Panmah Glacier

Hoh Lungma Glacier

Sosbun Glacier

Bisil

Hikmul Pass

Biafo Glacier

Sarpo Laggo Pass

HIKMUL

Zil

GANCHEN

Tranxo G

Chapo

ULI TO

Braldu River

PAIJU

Askole

Paiju

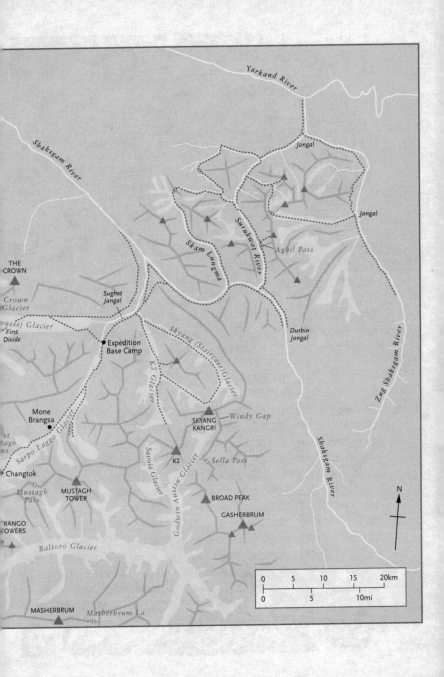

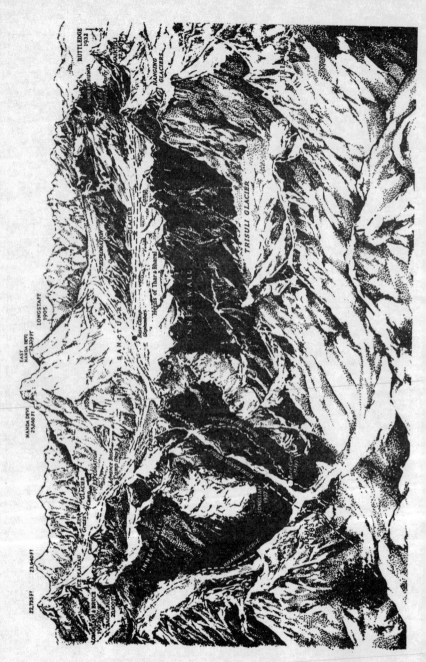

Nanda Devi Sanctuary: an artist's impression (1934)

Foreword

by Nick Shipton

Jim Perrin's researches reveal a lot to me that I did not know about my father, and explode some of the myths about him in which I had believed. As surprised as I am about Jim's assertions, for the most part he is on to something. My father was not always who he appeared to be. Then again, who is? His childhood and adolescence were certainly atypical, but not as deprived as I had been led to believe. His facility with written language always surprised me for a man who claimed serious dyslexia.

The character of the man my father spent so much time with is also clearer to me now from Jim's research. My mother did not talk much about H.W. Tilman, except to dismiss him as a misogynist. My brother sailed with him in the 1970s and my stepfather in the 1950s, only to jump ship with other crew members in Gibraltar due, it was claimed, to harsh treatment and bad food! In the accounts of many, Tilman was a difficult person. Somehow my father was able to get on with difficult characters. I wonder if that was a speciality of his, or a factor in male relationships in interwar Britain?

In describing the development of my father's emphasis on exploration over pure mountain 'conquest', Jim shows that his early notoriety was based on the ability to impress his contemporaries with spectacular achievements. In the small world of British climbers he gained a remarkable reputation very young. He certainly took risks, but in a way that would impact only on himself, with the agreement of his companions. He remained responsible for his own actions.

Eric Shipton was certainly a man of his time. The life he chose to lead was perfectly suited to his era. Being British, he had privileged access to many parts of the globe. Communication was fast enough for his reputation to reach fellow enthusiasts but slow enough for him to travel unmolested and in isolation for long periods of time. Let's not forget that these advantages came from colonialism. The pervasive attitude was that the world was made for the use of the colonisers and that indigenous people lacked the knowledge, curiosity or sophistication needed to make the best use of their heritage. Today, most of us would find these attitudes unacceptable.

My father certainly had a deep curiosity about country and, maybe to a lesser extent, people. He used the assets that imperialism afforded but was able to relate to and respect the strengths and motivations of local people. He used the terrain and what it provided rather than trying to carry England with him on the backs of porters. Throughout my father's writings, I sense his consciousness that actions taken with respect and awareness are permissible where the same actions taken for fame, hubris or profit are not. Certainly his Himalayan journeys show him becoming increasingly aware of this. He treated the people he met with respect and an openness that was unusual in an explorer of his time. I remember him telling me that one reason for his secondment to the diplomatic post in Kashgar was his frequent invitation of Indian officers, *havildars* or even sergeants, to the officers' mess. His Indian Army commanding officer's irritation hastened his move. His interest in people seems to have overridden his interest in conformity.

Eric Shipton developed a style of travel that left a minimum of environmental or cultural debris. Using local resources and knowledge enabled his lightweight style, and implies a respect for indigenous ways of being. Ideas of conservation and ecology in the main came after his time. I suspect that he would have embraced them in ways that suited him. The single-mindedness he showed in so much of his travelling may have meant, however, that his priorities from today's perspective could be questionable. Faced with the fjords of southern Patagonia, he did not baulk at carrying a rubber dinghy into places where a motor had never been heard – though the carrying was often on his own back. His enthusiasm for the Pinochet regime may have been the rightward shift of an older man, but I hope it had more to do with keeping in with his Chilean navy contacts, who facilitated access to Tierra del Fuego and its archipelago. This, after all, was the man who encouraged his sons to piss over the border into Franco's Spain while on holiday in the French Pyrenees in the late 1950s.

Over the last seventy-five years attitudes towards the natural environment have changed. Since my father's era, many have come to appreciate and understand the complexities of ecology. Our actions, we see, have unlooked-for consequences. In remote areas such as those my father moved in, the damaging effects of unconsidered intervention can be so obvious. A tourist, traveller, explorer is, by definition, transient and often has little interest in what they might leave behind.

I cannot imagine how a young Eric Shipton would express himself in a world of instant communication, GPS navigation and travel restrictions. I would love to have the opportunity now to discuss with him the implications of treading in areas that were untrodden, and opening lands up to exploitation that were previously overlooked. Having pushed open the gate to some unique parts of the globe, does he bear some responsibility for the long-term effects of the following masses? Small, lightweight, low-impact – phrases always associated with my father – have even more importance today. It seems to me that if travellers to the Himalayas, Patagonia, Xinjiang and other remote areas can behave in those same ways, there is more chance of them remaining unspoiled. His responsibility for blazing trails now falls on the shoulders of those who follow.

Nick Shipton
Bristol, August 2012

Preface

By a neat irony, given the attitude of Eric Shipton in particular towards "Everest", this book first appeared amid all the brouhaha leading up to the celebration of the diamond jubilee of what was still all too frequently termed the 'British conquest of Everest'. Faced with this nonsense, the sardonically inclined might have pointed out, among other things, that neither of the two men who first reached the summit in 1953 was British; that the mountain has a perfectly good indigenous name, which many find preferable to the colonial relic long foisted upon it (that of a singularly unpleasant and tyrannical Victorian surveyor-general); and that the notion of 'conquest' is one inimical to the spirit and best traditions of mountain exploration and ascent, the use of which betrays a lack of understanding of these activities.

Those holding to these purist notions would doubtless also have found much to ponder in the widely reported April 2013 incident on the Lhotse Face and at Everest Base Camp, in which three European mountaineers – authentic ones, not the more numerous guided and cosseted versions – were stoned by Sherpas for impinging on the latter's commercial activities. This state of affairs would have baffled and saddened Shipton and Tilman – two of the first westerners to befriend the Sherpas and travel with them in many respects as equals. How had it come to this?

What's certain in answer to that question is that Shipton and Tilman approached their mountains with a purer, more amused and curious attitude than the egotistical, acquisitive and status-fixated one that now holds sway with regard to the highest peaks of the world. The editor of the *Alpine Journal*, reviewing the first edition of this book in the *Independent*, noted how it 'pokes a timely stick into the conscience of 21st-century mountaineering, with all its commercialism and celebrity'. Whether or not that was my intention in writing, it's certainly true that the insouciant, ragamuffin, adventurous style of my two subjects appeals to me far more than all the siege expeditions and guided ascents in a sphere where high adventure is now open to all who have the means and the contacts to pursue their self-enhancing dreams – a democracy of the affluent.

In writing primarily of the 1930s, with a few brief glances before and after, I was attempting to bring into focus the styles that were evolving in that fascinating decade, and the implicit debate that focused around them then and which has continued down to the present day. Much lip-service has been paid to the admirable, low-impact austerities of the Shipton/Tilman style at the same time as much lucre has been expended on ensuring that western mountaineers attain their summits and life-goals. The dialectic essentially resolves into one between pure motive and public acclaim, and to seek out the latter is to enter into a devil's pact where incidents like that on the Lhotse Face become ever more likely – money doesn't talk; it swears!

All this is matter for the future historians of mountaineering. My concern was to present the characters and achievements of my two subjects, of whom I have been most fond for many years. Climbing has been of enormous importance in my life, both as one of the most demanding and sensuous physical activities imaginable, and also as a paradigm. What you bring to a climb can reflect and instruct in how you approach a life. The interplay here has long fascinated me, as it did the subject of my first climbing biography, Menlove Edwards.

In a world that grows increasingly literal-minded and dis-educated, I wished to keep that view alive by presenting two characters to whom it was also palpably precious and meaningful. Keeping company with them, as I have done in some sense throughout the greater part of my life, has been a joyful and humorous experience. A sense of real fun is the hallmark of all those who dance their way through dangers. These two, prankster and sly straight-man, demonstrate that maxim to perfection. Something far more subtle than comedy-club gag and guffaw is at work in their relationship. Follow the bent of their satires and anti-Establishment sallies and you glimpse a saner world in the making. I love them both for that.

A biographer should always take leave of his subjects regretfully, aware of his own shortcomings in their treatment and fretful at what might have been left out of the portrait, what might have been missed. Within weeks of this work rolling off the presses I was alerted, by Mr William Holgate of Holme in Yorkshire – a curmudgeon after my own heart – to the existence of a book published in Australia under the title *A Walk Through Blue Poppies: The Letters of Eric Shipton to Margaret Bradshaw 1934–1974*, edited by Jane Allen. Through the good offices of an Australian friend, Andrew Long of Arapiles Mountain Books, I came by a copy. Diligently edited by her daughter, it comprises the correspondence between Shipton and a woman he met on the boat sailing home from the 1933 Everest expedition. Its main interest lies outside the area of the present book, and where it overlaps, generally it repeats, and rather less intimately, the material in the extraordinary letters to his mother from which I quote extensively.

The Bradshaw correspondence does provide a few pieces of new information – that the Norway lectures of 1934 were in Oslo and Bergen, and the names of various boats on which he voyaged – and also gives a sense of Shipton's manner of conducting his various and numerous flirtations (this being a safe one since Margaret Bradshaw was newly married). Growing more intimate as the years pass, and giving interesting insights into his marriage to Diana and his relationship with Phyllis Wint, the letters will certainly be useful to Shipton biographers, though they don't leave me with a sense of despair at not having come across them in time.

Tony Smythe's excellent biography of his father Frank, published late in 2013, also gave food for thought about Smythe's influence on Shipton, whilst confirming my sense that the former's legacy has been unjustly marked down by recent generations of mountain enthusiasts whose views were shaped by Graham Brown's protracted calumniation of Smythe. As Tony points out, the similarities between Smythe and Shipton, and the difficulties they both faced in the mountain culture of their time, are marked.

I hope there will be future books on Shipton and Tilman. Their place in the history of mountain exploration is assured and revered, and the style in which they undertook their expeditions still seen as a benchmark. It seems to me that, far from becoming less relevant, their example is of increasing value as the spirit of adventure sadly becomes devalued, commercialised and misunderstood. I wrote my book in order to remedy certain misconceptions about my subjects, and hope that any new understanding it may have brought will result in more and better interpretations of their characters and the remarkable examples they set. Both of them fully deserve such attention. In a misinformed world that increasingly feasts on the phoney, contents itself with the ersatz, and sates itself on celebrity, Shipton and Tilman come across as the authentic article. From both of them we may still learn much.

Jim Perrin, Ardudwy, October 2013

Prologue

At the Cow's Mouth

Dry, writhing branches of resinous, sweet-scented deodar spit and fume on a raised fire-slab in the dhaba. Spurts of yellow flame illuminate the shadows within. The wood has been carried here along a thrilling path through the gorge for twenty kilometres from forest-slopes above Gangotri, on porters' backs in huge lashed bales. Alongside the stone and canvas shelter in its wilderness of rocks these now lie stacked, to be used most sparingly. There are government regulations, environmental prohibitions on gathering fuel around this holiest site of Hindu pilgrimage. Soldiers are a frequent patrolling presence here. They beat with heavy *latis* any hill people who transgress. Little enough grows in all conscience across this wide acreage of blanched boulders, sparse grazing and bare gravel.

I sit on a rough bench in the primitive tea shop at one of the most revered and magnificent places on earth and watch blue smoke swirl up and curl out of the open doorway to gauze an upward view towards Shivling and the Bhagirathi peaks. Here the founding myths of Hinduism are enshrined in spectacular features of landscape. Two or three hundred yards away from where I rest is Gaumukh – the Cow's Mouth. Out of the grimy snout of the Gangotri glacier, the Bhagirathi river – main headwater stream of the sacred Ganges – bursts forth milk-white and roaring, a terrifying weight and released energy of water that races down-valley and past the temple steps at Gangotri to pour into gorges thousands of feet deep, heading on by way of Uttarkashi and Tehri to Devprayag. There it merges with the Alaknanda river, into which flow the tributaries that drain the high easterly peaks of Garhwal, Nanda Devi and Kamet among them. And so it becomes the holy river of all India – personified as the goddess Ganga, daughter of Himavan king of the mountains, flowing through Rishikesh and down on to Varanasi and the hot plains of India before seeping out beyond Calcutta along a thousand delta-channels into the Bay of Bengal.

Sky-clad, trident-brandishing and ash-smeared devotees of Shiva watch as sadhus stand thigh-deep in the out-rush from hideous caverns of grey ice, waiting to immerse brave and faithful pilgrims who, searching for short cuts to Nirvana, wade out to them. I take my own chance on soul survival and avoid the chilling ritual. Chandra the tea shop proprietor tosses a sparse handful of twigs on to the fire under a blackened kettle, takes a pinch of boiled potato from a pan and kneads it into a clunch of dough that he rolls out across an oiled skillet and sears above the flames. Soon I'm handed a grimy earthenware cup of sweet milky *chai*, poured straight from the kettle – no crook of the little finger and request for more sugar here. He hands across on a battered enamel plate the *aloo paratha*, singed and blackened, glistening with ghee, with a small spoonful of fiery lime pickle dabbed on to it. I tear a piece off, touch it to the pickle and chew. The texture is gritty. Washed down with a sip of *chai*, it's the most delicious food and drink I've ever tasted.

There are a scant couple of hours of daylight left. Up here at above 12,000 feet, once the sun moves away the temperature plummets. Already the far wall of the valley is losing its detail, densening into shadow. I look across at my heavy rucksack, stuffed with cabbage and garlic and onions, and think of continuing on my way. The four-stone sack of potatoes I bought in the market along the alley leading to the temple in Gangotri this morning is on the back of a porter with whom I bargained to carry it up to Tapovan, giving him money to rest and eat tonight at Bhojbasa and promising him more if he arrives with his load at our Tapovan base camp on the high meadow under Shivling tomorrow. I have promised to make it there tonight, and it is time to move.

For the last month I've been camping with a group of friends at Tapovan as the last of the monsoon drifts away. The members of our team, if you can call it that, have formed alliances, fallen ill, fallen out, wandered to and fro on their own enterprises, established and provisioned high camps on Shivling. Some have come to take keenly anticipated pleasure in each day's unvarying diet of cabbage curry, rice and dhal, chapattis and stuffed parathas. Others have sulked in their tents in solitude, cooking on little mountain gaz-stoves freeze-dried and processed expedition food the thought of which makes me feel bilious. Mere sight of the foil packets with their clotted-grease contents reminds me of Tilman's snarling strictures to Charlie Houston about the food the Americans brought from Harvard to Nanda Devi in 1936: 'Bloody chemicals – might as well eat a boiled shirt!' I liked Tilman, found him a friendly and humorous man, agreed with him on most things and argued amiably and enthusiastically on others. This packaged stuff hasn't improved in sixty years. You would eat it if you were starving, and never otherwise. As to what to do with that foil packaging on a mountain, most people's answer lies plain to see. A host of ills engender here, a tainting lack of mindfulness robbing us of the world's beauty, and its former purity too. The Sanctuary is closed to us now, and you cannot but think that it is rightly so.

Tapovan, where we made our base camp, is magnificent, sublime – within the same landscape as Gaumukh, but removed from the grey ruin of the glacier, its perspectives finer, the immediate texture exquisite in its detail. At two thousand feet higher than the Cow's Mouth, and a thin-aired fourteen and a half thousand above sea-level, it's a meadow that stretches for two or more miles behind the high lateral moraine above the west bank of the Gangotri ice-stream. 'Grassy flats brilliant with flowers and watered by meandering streams' is how Shipton describes it in *Nanda Devi* – surely the most enjoyable and exciting of all books about mountain exploration, and beyond question one of the happiest and most modest. Fireweed and sparse lemon-coloured grasses cover Tapovan's floor, a stream winds through sand flats. Each dawn its margins are crystalline with ice. One afternoon I watch as an avocet stalks past on coppery-blue legs, upturned bill probing the silt for food, and think that I have seen the bird of paradise. Ranged in a row beyond the glacier to the south-east are the Bhagirathi peaks – soaring pinnacles of rock with delectable ridges and overhanging walls that both excite and disquiet the imagination of the climber. Above our camp is Shivling, one of the world's defining mountains, an icy pyramid of perfect proportions and irresistible allure first climbed by an Indian expedition in 1974, but known long before then as the epitome of savage mountain beauty. The play of light and cloud across it continually entrances. You can scarcely take your eyes off it. Even in the darkness, by starlight it glimmers, a felt presence. Across this meadow of Tapovan move flocks of bharal, traversing continually among the screes. All around my tent one

morning were the unmistakable pug-marks of a snow leopard, that
had stopped and sniffed, only a thin layer of nylon between it and
where I lay sleeping, its muzzle inches from my face.

The hardier pilgrims make their way up here to spend time at
primitive huts where Mama Ji and Om Giri run their ashrams and
instruct needy sophisticates in the art of simple living, asserting
rigorous ritual and practice and the simplest of diets – inner laundry
to remove the stains of society from brain and gut. These novices
are taught to chant in counterpoint to wind and stream. Avalanches
and falling seracs provide the timpani. Stones sent slithering by the
bharal add in a snare drum. Trekkers who have walked up from
Gangotri and beyond to Gaumukh sometimes find their way to
this paradise-place. One of them is Sylvia, a woman from Dresden,
statuesque and clear-hazel-eyed, a former East German Olympic
swimmer with a logical and humorous take on life. When it's
time for her to start out on a journey to south India she asks me
to accompany her down to the road-head at Gangotri. I go, not
only at her request but also to reprovision our camp with fresh
food. She and I walk laughing down the arduous trail; balance
across torrents and cliff walkways; drink mango juice that trickles
stickily down our chins at the dhabas; find a room in a quiet house
across the river from the temple with the water surging beneath,
the continual rumble of boulders carried along in its fierce flow,
bells tolling through the night and prayers chanted in the dawn.
I watch her dress on our last morning in lorn appreciation of this
gift of closeness and time. Her skin has a pearly lustre as she moves
around the room with the grace of a dancer in the dawn light. To
come to this softness from a world of stone! We wave as she departs
down-gorge on the ramshackle pilgrim bus that slithers and grinds
over boulder fields and through mud. I head for the market to buy
the provisions, and race back up the long valley pursued by regret.

At the dhaba by the Cow's Mouth, Chandra rolls a last cigarette
for us to share and urges on me the need for caution when crossing
the glacier. I heft the rucksack on my back and set off lightly, without
anxiety, something of the night gathering around the peaks. The
slope beyond Gaumukh to gain the ice is on the east side of the
valley, raked by stone-fall, and all the more so at this time of day
when a westering sun warms the snowfields on a twenty-thousand-
foot ridge-gable south of the Raktraran glacier. Stones whir through
the air, shatter on bluffs in their descent, send shrapnel spraying

across the traverse line. I hitch the rucksack high on the left shoulder to protect my head, crab across out of the fall-zone and on to the first ice. Rough paths marked by a confusion of cairns jag away in all directions. The need is to cross the ice-stream at right angles, then turn right to pick up the path climbing a loose lateral moraine alongside the outfall from the Tapovan stream. None of the myriad cairned ways seem to lead in anything like that direction. From out of a side valley in the left wall of the mountains ahead rolls a bank of dense mist, and it speeds towards me. An exhilarating calm fright upon me, I take note of landscape features in the desired direction. Within the space of a few short minutes they are annihilated. Bare feet in trekking sandals grow cold.

We think of glaciers as places of clean ice and snow and white simplicity, pure even, flagging up their crevassed dangers by wrinkle and rent, seldom deceiving us. The Gangotri glacier, one of the largest in the Himalaya, is not that kind of place. It resembles nothing so much as a huge and hideous motorway construction site, mounds of broken rock and piled-up gravel scattered across its surface, hideous rifts lipped with dull grey gravelly ice opening up on every side. I steer through the mist by hopeful instinct, following leads and brief disjunctive paths. Half an hour of nerve-racking progress with a sense filtering through of the light's thickening and dwindling brings me to the edge of a huge chasm. It plunges down for hundreds of feet. From its depths comes the constant roaring of water. There is no way round.

A sudden breeze parts the mist. I see the Bhagirathi peaks high above, disconnected somehow. Beyond the monstrous crevasse is a lateral moraine guarding access to the little alp of Nandavan, a mile away from Tapovan on the opposite side of the main glacier. To my left, a long valley, the one out of which the mist streamed, leads away to the east. I've arrived at the convergence of the Chaturangi with the Gangotri glacier – have stumbled heedless and unwitting into a torment of grinding and fractured streams of infinitely slow-moving ice, crushed and tortured in gravity's inexorable pull through generations. And I remember that Shipton and Tilman, Ang Tharkay, Pasang and Kusang have been here before me, had encountered this astonishing elemental disorder and calmly, competently had found their way through it: '... if the merit acquired is proportionate to the energy expended, ours must have been great. There was no lateral moraine on our side, and we toiled

by devious ways through chaotic hills and valleys of ice strewn
with gigantic boulders.'[1]

I sit down on a flat boulder, take a little carton of mango juice
out of the sack, and search among the folds of mist that are now
scouring away up the Chaturangi glacier. What I am searching for
is the subject of this book. In 1934, rattling down the gruesome
glacier in high spirits came the five men I've just mentioned, whose
mountain travels that summer are the finest expression of what
Eric Shipton defined as 'delight in the purely aesthetic nature of the
quest'. The passage above is how he described this exact place. But
he also captures its magic, as here when he tells of seeing Shivling
from Nandavan:

> '. . . we woke to a fine morning and looking out of the tent-
> flap we saw a sight which fairly made us spring from our
> bags. West across the Gangotri floated, high up, a silvery spire,
> graceful as that of Salisbury, and sparkling in the early sun. It
> seemed poised in mid-air, for the base on which it rested was
> momentarily hidden by the mists writhing upwards from the
> valley.'[2]

Remember Salisbury spire, for we will come back to it. With his
four companions Shipton had just made the first crossing of the
watershed between the Alaknanda and Bhagirathi rivers. I have come
here to get some sense of the nature of the ground they travelled that
momentous summer. The impression it has made will never leave
me. As if on cue, as if in recognition of those five men and the nature
and style of their achievement, Shivling's white sheering ridges across
the glacier begin to glow, suffused with an ever-deepening red. 'As
the sun sank the ice became rosy, reflecting the light in the sky; the
distant Downs too were tinted the same colour.'[3]

I roll myself a little cigarette the better to appreciate the fantastic
loveliness of it all. And laugh at the memory of coming across
an account in a letter passed on to me of how Shipton himself,
in his later years, had been supplied with *charas* from the hills of

---

[1] Eric Shipton, *Nanda Devi* (3rd edition, Hodder & Stoughton, 1939), p.198.
[2] Shipton, *Nanda Devi*,. p.199.
[3] Richard Jefferies, *Bevis: The Story of a Boy* (1910. Dent, 1981), p.418. File this
away with the Salisbury reference, for re-examination in Chapter Two.

Himachal Pradesh by a woman with whom he enjoyed a long, close friendship. Did he and the Sherpas, I wonder, round their juniper fire and over their dishes of wild rhubarb gathered from the lovely alps alongside the glacier, share this aesthetically intensifying aspect of the Himalayan experience? Did he and Tilman crumble it into their ever-present pipes? As a writer you can be allowed a degree of mischievous speculation when you're fond of your subjects, in possession of salient facts about them and desirous of defending them against the taint of being Establishment figures.

But then Shipton and Tilman were never that. Their impulse was too wayward, the manner of their achievement too rigorously uncompromised ever to align easily with all the suspect attitudes, vainglorious posturings and required show that societal authority and its corrupt mouthpiece of the press report requires. What's admirable to me is for how long they managed to get away with the simple integrity of being themselves before the climbing establishment, in its slow and glacial way, finally realised what they were about and, in the case of Shipton – the undoubted ringleader, play-master and Lord of Misrule – sidelined him, and regressed for a sad generation or so to its own regimented code. And how Shipton and Tilman, again through being themselves, had bequeathed to their successors as initiates in the direct and unpolluted joyful engagement in mountain experience a philosophy, and a bold example. Far from fading, these have gathered force and lustre over the decades between their time and ours, so that the Shipton & Tilman style and not the martially named 'siege approach' is the one now seen as exemplary. They have become, in the American mountaineer David Roberts's fine phrase, 'retro-active heroes of mountaineering's avant-garde'. From the oddest of friendships came the paradigm against which all informed participants in mountain activity now assess ambition and enterprise.

This book explores that revolutionary, mutually enhancing and inspiring friendship, with its lasting legacy. At heart, it's a study of *homo ludens* in the mountain context; it's about the recognition and winning through to acceptance of what Shipton and Tilman, and the approach in which they so fortuitously balanced and enabled each other, gave to the worldwide activity of mountaineering. So, having arrived at the resolution to struggle with that theme, and saluted the wraiths retreating back into the mist, I must now extricate myself from a dreamy torpor, the alpenglow brilliant on the superlative phantom spire above, cross a mile of tortured and perilous ice, and deliver a sack of cabbage and garlic and onions to base camp before the freezing onset of a rapidly encroaching dark.

Introduction:

Their Ordinary Selves

A decade that began with the Great Depression and ended with the outbreak of the Second World War – and that has become synonymous with deprivation, austerity, migrant poverty and the social problems that contributed to the rise of fascism in Germany and Italy (and to a lesser degree in England through Oswald Mosley's Mussolini-inspired British Union of Fascists) – might not be thought one of the happier times in any sphere of human activity. For British mountaineering, however, the 1930s were halcyon days. They saw the establishment of an ethical paradigm that has remained the sport's gold standard to this day, proudly adopted and proclaimed by its leading contemporary practitioners worldwide, from former Soviet Bloc countries such as Poland, the Czech Republic and Slovenia to the Americas; and from Britain and the Continent to the East. That this should have been so is in large measure through the achievements and example of Eric Shipton and H.W. Tilman, and the shared philosophy of adventure they expressed in bodies of written work that include what many acknowledge as *the* major classics of mountain literature. They were both English, one of them from a colonial background, the other of Liverpool's rising mercantile stock. Shipton was the younger by nine years, already feted as one of the outstanding young British alpinists when he met the Great War veteran Tilman in Kenya colony at the decade's outset. Tilman at the time was a novice climber, whose stature had grown by the end of the decade to the extent that he was appointed leader for Britain's last pre-war attempt on Everest. The names of these two men are indissociably linked in mountain culture – the 'Shipton/Tilman style', with its qualifying tag of 'lightweight', its eschewing of quasi-militarism in tackling ascents, its dialectical insistence on local diet, 'living off the land', and keeping expeditionary scale appropriate to the interests of indigenous mountain communities, is now a set formula for all that is most admirable in exploratory activity among the world's great mountain ranges.

A friendship is implied by the collocation of their names, and a relationship based on respect and interdependence and leavened with a teasing humour certainly existed between the two men. Shipton even dedicated his first book to his most frequent mountain companion. Yet the very lack of intimacy and mutual knowledge in their friendship almost debars it from any definition of the term that we might recognise. There was, for example, none of the frisson of Cambridge and Bloomsbury homosexuality that followed George Leigh Mallory around wherever he chose to climb. The whole province of emotion remained unexplored between Shipton and Tilman, only that of action being relevant. This was not a friendship as we know it in the importunate and disclosing manner of the twenty-first century. Nor was it merely a connection based in expediency and convenience. For a few short years – surprisingly few, given how ubiquitous their influence has become – Shipton and Tilman orbited around each other in enabling balance, achieving much that was and is still seen as radical together, despite differences in character vast as the landscapes they traversed. To the lay observer, perhaps all mountaineers assume a standard identity. The impression, if taken thus, is a false one, and viewed as caricature by performers from within the range of activities that constitute the sport. Published commentary on mountaineering in recent years has tended to the external, and often fails to grasp the essence of the matter. If there were an annual 'Bad Climbing' award to parallel the 'Bad Sex' award, the candidates would be many, few of them from within the sport. What participants for the most part understand is that there is a rich complexity of national and local traditions within the history of approaches to mountains and rocks.

Shipton's and Tilman's grand project and their main achievements are not characterised by technical accomplishment or advances in achieved difficulty. Neither man was among the virtuoso performers of his day on rock or ice, however much the 1930s English mountaineering establishment sought to talk up the talents of those they wished to claim as their own. Here's Hugh Ruttledge, for example, leader of the 1933 and 1936 Everest expeditions, writing in the foreword to Shipton's *Nanda Devi*: 'Those who read this book with understanding will realise the number of tight places this party got into, where nothing but the most brilliant technical competence could have got them out alive.'[1] Good-hearted this assuredly is; decent old buffer Ruttledge certainly was; it remains nothing but bluster. Shipton and Tilman were admirable in many different ways, but no one should think to promote 'brilliant technical competence' as among their distinguishing qualities. The claim is one resulting from the external view mentioned above, that has bedevilled so much writing on mountains over the decades. Elsewhere Shipton himself bridled at this kind of ignorant hyperbole[2] and the actual language used here. What both of this book's subjects did develop – and Shipton in particular – was a solid, all-round competence on mountains, and a fine instinct for the best route that may well be the most important and useful of all qualities for the exploratory mountaineer. For their ambitions, which in the main were outside the usual parameters of acquisition and 'conquest', this was enough.

Had they been put alongside the foremost French or Italian ice-climbers, Bohemian[3] or even British rock-climbers and judged on technical skills alone, they would not have been distinguished by their expertise in these aspects of mountain-craft. For all that, and for differing reasons, their names today are ranked within mountaineering history as high as or higher than other climbing stars of the 1930s: Comici and Cassin, Charlet and Gervasutti, Heckmair and Kirkus, Menlove Edwards and Frank Elliott – all these were outstanding performers within their own mountain disciplines, yet none have quite the world-wide cachet of Shipton and Tilman. On the north faces of the Eiger or the Matterhorn, Les Courtes, the Walker Spur or the Cima Ovest, Tilman and Shipton would have been hopelessly out of their depth. The harder climbs of the period on Clogwyn Du'r Arddu or Dow Crag, at Helsby Hill, Bärenbrünnerhof or Scafell were far beyond their grasp. But mountaineering is a broad church, and these venues were not where

[1] In Eric Shipton, *Nanda Devi* (3rd edition, Hodder & Stoughton, 1939), p.xii.
[2] See the discussion of his views on leadership in Chapter Seven of the present book, for example.
[3] The achieved standards of rock-climbing on outcrops in the Elbsandsteingebirge, south of Dresden along the border between Germany and the Czech Republic (in the region known as Bohemia along the river Elbe), was by far the highest in the world in the period between 1920 and 1960, and was not paralleled elsewhere probably until the late 1960s or early 1970s, when Britain and the USA began to establish a brief hegemony in the sport through a handful of rare talents – Henry Barber, John Bachar, Jim Bridwell, Ron Fawcett, John Allen and so on.

their interest lay; nor did they give scope for the approach at which they did excel. Which was other, and larger. After their initial forays together among the mountains of Africa, the Himalaya – greatest of all mountain ranges – became for the rest of the 1930s and beyond the focus of their activity. If it is erroneous to assume a single identity for mountaineering tradition, so too is it a mistake to look on the Himalaya as a single mountain range. This formidable physical barrier where all the world's highest peaks are located, that lies between Russia and China and what was until 1947 British India, is immensely varied in its localities, atmospheres and land forms – unsurprising, given that it stretches for over 1,800 miles (if the eastern and northern extensions of the Karakoram and the Hindu Kush are, as is generally the case, included). The thorough exploration of these mountains, and the making of alliances with the states into which history had divided them, was a political necessity and a geographical obsession of the British for well over a century.

The necessity was because of inexorable Russian expansion into central Asia, and the threat thus posed to India, the most valuable and valued of all British colonies, upon which Napoleon himself had cast covetous eyes. The early history of Himalayan exploration,[4] then, is an important subtext to that of the Great Game – the struggle for supremacy in the region lying between Russia and India. It takes in subjects as diverse as the history of the Survey of India, which had been founded in 1767, and the Great Trigonometric Survey inaugurated in 1802, as well as the fascinating accounts of the pundit explorers – men like Kinthup, who was sold into slavery whilst trying to establish the source of the Brahmaputra river; and Hari Ram, who made his way along the Bhote Khosi and around Mount Everest in 1871–2; and Nain Singh Rawat, who visited Lhasa in 1865, met the Dalai and Panchen Lamas, and was awarded a gold medal for his efforts by the Royal Geographical Society. Each of these resolute and highly intelligent native hill men faced great danger in carrying out work for the Survey of India, travelling disguised, with maps and papers concealed in their prayer wheels

---

[4] The two crucial books to read for detailed accounts of this period are John Keay's *When Men and Mountains Meet* (John Murray, 1977) – not to be confused with Tilman's work under the same Blakeian title; and Peter Hopkirk's *The Great Game* (John Murray, 1990), which is as exciting as any thriller. John Keay's *The Great Arc* (HarperCollins, 2000) is an invaluable and fascinating account of the early years of the Survey of India.

and calibrated bead necklaces to mark off distances on their charts. They laid impeccable foundations for the early ventures into the Himalaya by Western explorers. Around the turn of the nineteenth century, travellers, mountaineers and soldiers – a hundred years of ever-increasing activity having rendered the mountains of Europe as familiar as the streets of the metropolis – were probing regularly into the fastnesses of the highest of all the world's mountain ranges.

It was with this generation that the practical and philosophical basis for Shipton's and Tilman's great Himalayan exploratory project of the 1930s was laid down. If we look for their forebears, among the names that come to mind are those of the Schlagintweit brothers of Munich, who travelled extensively in the Himalaya, Karakoram and Kunlun in the 1850s; of Martin Conway, eminent art historian and, in 1892, discoverer of the so-called 'Snow Lake' (Lukpe Lawo) – the supposed mother lode of all Karakoram ice streams; of A. F. Mummery, Victorian author of one of the most stylish and well-loved mountaineering chronicles, *My Climbs in the Alps and Caucasus*, who went to Nanga Parbat on a lightweight expedition with Professor Norman Collie in 1895, and with his two Gurkha companions perished in an avalanche on the Rakhiot face of the mountain; of Francis Younghusband and his journey from Beijing to India in 1887 – a more fragrant memory, this, than his massacre of Tibetan monks at Guru in 1904 on the Mission to Lhasa; or most directly of all, that of Tom Longstaff, whose knowledge of Garhwal, Kumaon and the Tibetan border regions, gained in extensive mountain travels throughout the first decade of the twentieth century, was a crucial underpinning to that of Shipton and Tilman in 1934, and a clear model for the style they adopted. You will hear much of Longstaff and his resolute and adventurous spirit in the narrative that follows.

From the distinctly odd nature of their friendship, their relationship to the traditions and practice of mountaineering, and their possible antecedents, we might move on to consider the scale of what Shipton and Tilman achieved in the decade to which I have, with due allowance for a few glances before and after, restricted this book. The first ascent of the West Ridge of Mount Kenya, completed by them in 1930, was the high point of Shipton's technical achievement, and comparable with the hardest alpine rock ridges of the time. Even set against those, it was more remote and at substantially higher altitude. The adventure quotient here was enormous. It was also Tilman's first real climb, which speaks volumes for Shipton's confidence in his companion. Shipton's ascent of Kamet with Frank Smythe, Raymond Greene and others in 1931 established a summit altitude record that was only broken five years later by Tilman's and Odell's ascent of Nanda Devi – a record that itself lasted for fourteen years. Yet where our subjects are concerned, talk of successful ascents is more or less incidental, and the use of that word 'conquest' – loathsome in a mountain context – is wholly inadmissible. There is far more to these two than that.

There were the various pre-war Everest expeditions – 1933, 1935, 1936, 1938 – in which the pair were individually or jointly involved, and which were always augmented by adventurous reconnaissances into adjacent massifs. There was the season of 1934 – to my mind the most exciting story in the whole saga of mountain discovery – that saw them, with three Sherpa companions, make their way up the Rishi gorge into the Nanda Devi Sanctuary, and hence solve one of the long-standing problems of Himalayan geography. There was Shipton's growing interest in mapping and surveying, that led to the extraordinary Shaksgam and Karakoram venture of 1937 in which they were both involved, and which brought a significant third party into their pioneering arrangements – the poet's brother and flamboyant character Michael Spender, through whom Shipton was linked in to an entire 1930s London cultural coterie. At the very end of the decade there was Tilman's tragic probe into Assam, and Shipton's vastly ambitious continuation of the 1937 *Blank on the Map* journeys – a project that was a summary of their work through the entire decade, to which the onset of war brought a premature close.

When the seminal French film director Jean-Luc Godard was asked by an interviewer for the meaning of his chaotic black comedy *Weekend* (1967), he responded with '*Le Moral? C'est le Travelling.*' So too with Shipton and Tilman, and not just the travelling, but the entire insouciant, happy-go-lucky, minimal and self-reliant style of their mountain vagabondage. These men were exemplars wholly at odds with the consumerist bent of their own or even more markedly of our time. For that reason they are still admired, studied, praised, occasionally copied and in some quarters almost revered. We give our notional assent to their way of doing things in a way that we do to few others in the sphere of adventure. For us, they stand for something entirely authentic, stimulated by a real curiosity about the physical world around us, wholly disconnected from the modern celebrity ills of egotism, self-aggrandisement, the illusory and the making of money.

Also, our two subjects – and I will not call them heroes, whatever my personal feelings about them, that term being so debased – were both possessed of one of the finest and most levelling of human qualities: a sense of humour. In this again they differed markedly, but both of them, when I read and consider what they wrote, how they recorded what they did and what went on around them, tease a smile out of me continually. It's a subtle humour too. Fifty or more years ago, when I was beginning my own climbing career on the gritstone outcrops of the north of England, and starting to read about mountain exploits, their texts were regarded as simple record. They were not seen as expressions of style, of elaborate fun. How the stiff were duped! How Shipton and Tilman made such monkeys of the members of that establishment along the margins of which they variously played! I love them still for the sly mischief of all that.

I have been a devotee of their writings throughout my own involvement in climbing. Thirty years ago, working as editor on the Diadem imprint for the publisher Ken Wilson, compendium volumes of their mountain titles were the first projects I argued for and saw back into print, where they have remained without a break in Britain and America[5] to this day, sustaining and augmenting their authors' long influence. I might now modify in a few small details the arguments I put forward for both men in the critical introductions to those collections. The general sense, however, would remain unchanged. My enthusiasm for the work and the example has only increased with the passage of years.

Several reasonably competent, more-or-less adequate[6] biographies have been published – one for Shipton and two for Tilman (whose life in exploration carried on in the 1950s and beyond to embrace an entirely new area of interest, which was the sea, his writings about which won him a different audience, and a new kind of notoriety every bit as admirable as the old, of the austerity and simplicity of which it was a logical extension). This present book in no sense

---

[5] Under The Mountaineers imprint, of Seattle.
[6] Critically speaking, the term is Matthew Arnold's, the implications of whose use of it are well worth weighing in this context.

should be seen as *competition* for these, though it does occasionally seek to correct a few of their points. It pleads the subjects' case in partisan fashion as mountaineers and as writers; it is not a straight and formal biography, though the element of life-writing in it is strong. This is how their favoured activity is best done, it argues, implicitly, through the medium of its subjects' lives. Insofar as it traces the entire outline of both lives, it does so in plan, its emphasis deliberately placed on that single decade of Shipton's and Tilman's most significant mountain-exploratory achievements. This decision to limit the scope was taken for three main reasons. First, I wished to focus on the crucial climbs and journeys made between 1930 and 1939, because – affection for the decade apart – here, I felt, was encapsulated the essence and summation of their philosophy of mountain exploration.

Second, over the years I have collected a good deal of original material – notebooks, correspondence and the like, especially by Shipton – which relates particularly to this time. Much of this is of exceptional quality, previously unpublished or even unknown. I have quoted extensively from it here and there in the chapters that follow. To have held and read through the small journal Shipton carried with him on the first journey into the Nanda Devi Sanctuary had a feeling for me akin to the handling of a religious relic or icon. Here was the simplicity of encounter, the beauty and wonder of first experience, the central values and the directness of response – all expressed in slant, purple-pencil, legible scrawl that filled every scrap of available space. The transcriptions from that notebook alone to my mind are justification enough for this book.

Third, and perhaps most significantly, it has seemed to me that for all the interest bestowed upon Shipton and Tilman over the thirty-five years since their deaths, there has been a ghost at this feast – that of a friendship never fully addressed, which was the major enabling factor in their crucial climbing and journeying. Even where these were not jointly accomplished, its effect particularly upon Tilman – junior in mountain experience, senior in age, the durable rock to whom Shipton was anchored for most of the decade – is palpable. So this book is essentially about a friendship and its relevance to a sphere of activity. It's about that friendship's inception, its testing and inquisition, and ultimately the slow natural transference of allegiance away from it, though mutual respect endured lifelong on both sides.

The book also forms the third part of a biographical mountain trilogy on which I have worked over very many years. This began with *Menlove* (1985) about Menlove Edwards, the major figure from British rock-climbing in the 1930s and finest of all essayists on his sport; it moved on to *The Villain* (2005), a consideration of Don Whillans, the celebrated northern mountaineer from the 1950s; and it now concludes with the present volume, which is the story of a relationship, its achievements and its implications. My aim throughout the sequence has been to present the nature of various facets of mountain experience and affect through looking closely at individual subjects, their responses and their achievements. With the Menlove Edwards book, the psychological dimension particularly of rock-climbing was what interested me. The study was one of alienation, and its outcome was tragic. The Don Whillans biography by contrast provided objects for scrutiny in climbing's (and by extension society's) mythopoeic tendencies, the associated reasons for engagement in the sport, and their potential for destructive effect. The outcome here too in a sense was tragic.

Having experienced my own portion of the dark side in the years since the writing of that book, it was heartening for me to turn to a story of how the mountain environments and the activities they engaged in there, as well as their companionship, proved wholly ameliorative in the lives of Shipton and Tilman, repairing the damage that society had inflicted upon them, and making good. Here then is a happy story at last, and a good-humoured one, that places its faith in simple and timeless values and implicitly adduces through both characters a spiritual dimension to balance the psychological and temperamental ones of the earlier works. A clear expression of this is provided by the Trappist monk – Tilman would surely have related well to him, particularly given their shared taste for beer – and twentieth-century Christian mystic, Father Thomas Merton, who writes in *The Wisdom of the Desert* of how the 'simple men who lived their lives out to a good old age among the rocks and sand only did so because they had come into the desert to be themselves, their *ordinary* selves, and to forget a world that divided them from themselves.'[7]

It would have been all too easy for Shipton and Tilman to have divided from themselves by celebrity and public acclaim at

---

[7] Thomas Merton, *The Wisdom of the Desert* (New Directions, 1960) pp. 22–3.

many stages in their lives. Had Shipton kept the leadership of the successful 1953 Everest expedition to which he was appointed – and it is beyond reasonable discussion or doubt that his leadership, buttressed by the presence as deputy leader of Charles Evans,[8] would have put climbers on the summit – the consequent celebrity would have placed him in grave jeopardy. The pay-offs would have been too lavish. The quirks and foibles of his character would have been ruthlessly exposed by the intrusive press even of a more principled and private age. The mutual susceptibility between himself and women – that desire for softness to redeem the harshness of stone – would have gained him notoriety. Thank heavens, then, for the 'unworthy device' (to use Charles Evans's accurate term) by which the poisoned chalice was taken from him and passed to the politic Brigadier John Hunt, who craved and welcomed it, was innately decent, suffered no devastating harm by its possession, and used it tirelessly pro bono publico. All this matter is beyond the scope of the present book, and I am glad of it. Its absence leaves me free to concentrate on example, and not the corrupting values implicit in the reception of success. Thomas Merton again: '. . . to leave the world, is, in fact, to help save it in saving oneself.'

Merton carries on to provide a gloss for this statement on the exemplary, that reflects in its turn on the exploratory paradigm Shipton and Tilman created for the community of mountaineering.

> This is the final point, and it is an important one. The . . . hermits who left the world as though escaping from a wreck, did not merely intend to save themselves. They knew that they were helpless to do any good for others as long as they floundered about in the wreckage. But once they got a foothold on solid ground, things were different. Then they had not only the power but even the obligation to pull the whole world to safety after them.
>
> Perhaps this is their paradoxical lesson for our time . . .[9]

The resonance here is huge, and yet the longer I have thought

---

[8] Two years later, Charles Evans was to lead the lightweight expedition two members of which, Joe Brown and George Band, made the first ascent of the much more difficult peak of Kanchenjunga – at 28,169 feet the third highest in the world.

[9] Merton, *Wisdom of the Desert*, p.23.

upon them, the more it seems to me to emanate out from what Shipton and Tilman were, and thought, and wrote, and did. They lived in a time when the potential wreckage of the world was apparent to all – another reason for restricting this book's chronological span to the 1930s. For as long as they could, throughout that time Shipton and Tilman pursued an active course of curiosity and knowledge and hope; of fellowship; of considered values and shared experiences, their emphasis not on material gain but on heuristic and knowledge-enhancing action.

> These monks insisted on remaining human and 'ordinary'. This may seem to be a paradox, but it is very important. If we reflect a moment, we will see that to fly into the desert in order to be extraordinary is only to carry the world with you as an implicit standard of comparison. The result would be nothing but self-contemplation . . .[10]

Our modern, sponsored, media-hyped so-called explorers and adventurers might take heed of those words. Shipton and Tilman did not go to the mountains to be considered extraordinary. They went out of simple curiosity, and they moved through them in the least intrusive manner possible, with indigenous people they regarded and treated not as underlings, but as friends. So much of what they did and how they did it comes across now as strikingly modern, and informed by an evolving environmental consciousness of real integrity. Their ordinary selves have become our best examples.

A few technical points may be useful for what follows. As with the Whillans biography, I have made extensive use of footnoting rather than chapter notes or endnotes. A few readers of the Whillans book picked up on the purpose of these, which was to provide an alternative discourse in which a social history of post-war British rock-climbing was given. The footnoting in this book is not quite so extensive, its main function simple contextualisation or explanation, and if some readers are irritated by it, they are cordially invited to ignore it. I have not seen fit to provide an extensive bibliography – footnote references for quoted texts surely obviate the necessity for this, and my feeling anyway is that the device of the many-pages-long

---

[10] Merton, *Wisdom of the Desert*, p.22.

bibliography has become, in non-academic works, an assertive and inauthentic boast, and one frequently used to mask essential ignorance.

Finally, references to mountain heights, place names,[11] weights and measures: these are generally given in a manner my protagonists would have approved and understood, in Imperial nomenclature or the safe hands of the British Weights and Measures Act of 1824. No slight is intended here on any country's right to self-definition – we are simply talking historicity. Conversion tables are readily available for those who need or insist upon them for the old system of measures. The world as it was between 1930 and 1939 was rather less standardised than it is now – a subject on which, no doubt, Shipton and Tilman would have had their views. Whether or not you share them, I hope you enjoy their adventurous, invigorating and eccentric company through the next few hundred pages.

Ariège, August 2012

---

[11] I would have preferred throughout to have used the name Chomolungma instead of 'Mount Everest' – an unfortunate attribution to an unpleasantly self-righteous and tyrannical nineteenth-century Indian Surveyor-General. But the name has now become almost too deeply embedded in our consciousness for such an act of cultural resistance, and I leave others to fight this worthy cause.

Surveying the Landscapes
of these Lives

There is an intricate balance of personal authority between our two protagonists to be considered in due course, but a point to be borne in mind from the outset is that Shipton, the younger man by almost a decade, was for much of the early history of his association with Tilman the dominant and senior partner certainly in mountaineering terms, his older friend cast in a supportive role to Shipton's ambitions. So it is with the origins of Shipton's mountaineering that we must at some point near the beginning of this narrative concern ourselves, and they will be considered in Chapter Three. For this, even though the purpose of the present book is not primarily biographical, we will need some biography. It might be thought that both our subjects have been well served in this area, though closer scrutiny fails to bear this out.

A brief survey of the field will be useful here. Tilman's life has been written twice.[1] The first attempt was by a former *Guardian* journalist, J. R. L. Anderson, best known for a popular 1970 book on the psychology of risk called *The Ulysses Factor*, in which Shipton figured large. Anderson's 1980 life of Tilman, *High Mountains & Cold Seas*, was a sterling and solid effort, all the more so in view of its author's failing health, the book being completed during Anderson's terminal illness. It remains a useful record of the life's events, though failing perhaps to convey the elusive element of its

---

[1] At the time of writing (June 2012), I hear that publication of *Tilman: The Enduring Legacy of the Great British Explorer* by David Glen is imminent. From the publicity material I've seen this finely illustrated and designed collector's edition looks to be an affectionate and admiring brief account of Tilman's life, based on interviews with many who knew him. I wish it well.

subject's personality in any more than general terms. The attention is heavily focused on simple factual chronology to the exclusion of what James Boswell, speaking of the paintings of Sir Joshua Reynolds, called the speck that gives life to the eye.[2]

In Tilman's case, that 'speck' might be defined as his pervasive humour, growing more ironic and detached with the passing of time, and ever more sombre too, as a sardonic tone took over from the earlier 'jaunts and jollities' vein. He saw too much of man's destructive nature through the course of his life to remain light-hearted.

More recently, Tim Madge called his 1995 biography *The Last Hero: Bill Tilman*. This latter was a curious book, heavily indebted to Anderson's earlier and better work. It was little appreciated by the redoubtable Tilman apologist and former *Baroque*[3] crew-member Andrew Craig-Bennett, a witness in whose testimony I have implicit faith. Madge has informed points from the conventional safety standpoint to make about sailing in general, and some controversial ones about Simon Richardson and the loss at sea of his converted tugboat *En Avant*, in which Tilman sailed on his last voyage. The extent of Madge's knowledge of mountaineering is apparent. Crucially, Tilman would have flinched at and recoiled from the *title* of the book for two reasons: on account of its grandiosity, for he was the most modest and self-effacing of men; and for its familiarity – something that may be more difficult for our later generations to understand. Very few people of his acquaintance would have thought to call Tilman 'Bill'. It would have offended his reticence, his formality. Even though I could count him as a friend I shall not do so in this book.

On board his boats, some variant on the term 'skipper' was the norm, though on his last voyage, as an ordinary crew-member of Simon Richardson's boat, the crew apparently reverted to the

---

[2] The exact quotation, from one of Boswell's late-1770s 'Hypochondriack' columns for the *London Magazine*, runs thus: 'By how small a speck does the painter give life to an eye!'

[3] *Baroque* was third, after *Mischief* and *Sea Breeze*, in the sequence of ancient Bristol Channel pilot cutters in which Tilman made his momentous voyages north and south between 1954 and 1977, after retiring from Himalayan mountaineering in the early 1950s. Eric Shipton's younger son John sailed in *Baroque* on Tilman's penultimate exploratory voyage – an attempt to reach Ellesmere Island in the High Arctic during 1975.

affectionate and rather charming term of address 'Tilly', by which
he had been known among his fellow artillerymen during the Great
War – and 'Tilly' for once, having considerable respect for the young
man who was the skipper and for the rest of his crew, enjoyed the
familiarity. His favourite niece Pam Davis, incidentally, called him
'Willy' (as he refers to himself in his journals at times), but no one
else would have presumed do that. I called him 'you crotchety old
bugger' once, which raised a wry smile of assent. It was on top of a
Welsh mountain, Cader Idris, across the estuary of the Mawddach
from his home at Bodowen. I'd arrived up the north side with my
dog[4] by way of an interesting and wintry grade two gully that led
directly to the summit, and was sheltering in the hut near the top
when a solid and alert-looking man in his seventies, shabbily dressed
in ancient and worn outdoor clothing and carrying a frayed canvas
rucksack, slid in to join me across the snowdrift that guarded the
entrance. I shared my flask with him, about the contents of which,
despite a liberal lacing of whisky, he was justifiably ungallant. His
opening sally was that he'd hoped this was one place he might
have had to himself on a day like this, to which my response was
as above. I knew who he was instantly, and had long been of the
opinion, unfashionable at the time, that his writing was the best
thing in the whole of mountaineering literature (about Shipton's I
was initially less convinced – probably from having started off with
the wrong books, the quality of his published work being notably
uneven). My dog, ever hopeful of food, rolled her brown eyes at
the new arrival and cosied up to him. There was no risk of the
jibe being deemed insubordination, and every indication that I'd
taken his assumed grumpiness exactly the right way. Also, he liked
dogs, and was gratified when I came out with Frederick the Great's
famous maxim by way of counter to his jokey[5] misanthropy: 'The
more I see of humanity, the more I love my dog.'

For the most part, though, those of us who did not sail with him

---

[4] This characterful black Labrador was with me for fifteen years. I would quite
often take her up easy winter climbs when she was in her prime, tying her into a
special harness roped to mine, towing her behind me up the steeper passages, and
letting her romp past with her built-in crampons on the easier-angled sections.
Her enjoyment of this was palpable, though no doubt well-meaning observers
would report me for cruelty to animals these days, or to the Health and Safety
Executive for dangerous mountain behaviour.

[5] Freud on jokes needs to be borne in mind here.

and who regarded him a friend – as I came to quite soon after this
first meeting, after taking up his invitation and regularly visiting
his house – would address him, however old-fashioned it might
sound to the contemporary ear, as 'Major Tilman', or even as 'sir',
which felt when used towards him in no way abject. It was a way
of showing a respect which was his due, and he was comfortable
with it in a way that he was not with casual modern assumptions
of intimacy.

The story that Shipton tells, and which has attained widespread
currency, about asking Tilman whether after seven months of
being continually together in the Himalayas he might bring himself
to call him 'Eric', and Tilman hanging his head in embarrassment
and supposedly responding that 'it sounds so damned silly', I think
is inherently unlikely[6] and needs to be taken with the usual dose
of Shiptonian salt. (There were in fact a few people among his
contemporaries and mountaineering companions who did call him
'Bill': Shipton himself, Peter Lloyd, Charles Evans – the list speaks
for itself.) But the point Shipton is making through the anecdote in
his habitual vein of sly humour is to do with the way Tilman's innate
shyness – still present even in his eightieth year when I last saw him
just before he sailed away south to his death – found expression
through reticence and formality. These two came to know each other
very well, and at the same time hardly at all. This theme of constant
underlying jocularity and teasing will be a recurrent one in discussing
the relationship between the two men and their differing ways of
presenting themselves particularly through their writing to the world.

To turn briefly to how Shipton has been dealt with biographically,
Peter Steele's useful 1998 volume, *Eric Shipton: Everest and Beyond*,
is for the most part commendably affectionate towards its subject,
and fairly thorough in its treatment of some of the crucial phases
of the mountaineering career, though the more critical reader may
regard a scant five pages allotted to the first twenty-one years of
Shipton's life as parsimonious. You might even describe it as obtuse

---

[6] For one thing, this would have been quite a rude response, and I never found
Tilman to be other than unfailingly polite and courteous. Although it was well
after the event, it is worth noting the familiar way in which Tilman calls Shipton
'Eric' throughout in his obituary notice for the latter in the *Himalayan Journal*.
He appears to have used this form of address quite naturally from an early stage
in their friendship, though in the more formal sphere of the written word he is
much more reticent.

if you take the Wordsworthian/Rousseau-istic view that sees the child as father of the man[7] – a viewpoint more than usually apposite in the case of Shipton, who gives us both clue and permission to approach from this angle in his first and in some ways his best book, *Nanda Devi*, which describes the Garhwal journeys of 1934 and was published in 1936. This is certainly not to dismiss some of his later titles – *That Untravelled World*, for example, is an exceptionally accomplished, dignified and convincing piece of autobiographical writing – but rather to marvel at the assured, simple quality of his first effort. I am increasingly drawn, after studying much manuscript material, to the notion that editing of his writing, particularly by his long-term lover from the 1930s, Pamela Freston – a process in which a degree of academic insecurity led him perhaps too easily to acquiesce – changed its tone in places and contrary to received opinion may at times have diminished rather than enhanced its quality.

There is a connected matter here, and a vexed, emotive and complex one that needs to be discussed at the outset and at some length, since it has taken root and come to be regarded as a given, invariably repeated in articles about the man. It is that of Shipton's supposed dyslexia. As if to underline the point, in *That Untravelled World* the word itself is misspelt. When I first came across this I was inclined to suspect a case of the sly Shiptonian humour at work, but on checking the passage against the hand-written manuscript of the book, the term Shipton used was the old-fashioned one of 'word-blindness', from which he believed he 'must have suffered'; so perhaps his editor, whilst asserting herself, was having a bad day, as they occasionally do.

Peter Steele, in his workmanlike way and with a frequently assumed medical hat on, rather fixates around the dyslexia, neglecting to consider that this was a self-diagnosis argued up to the status of unassailable fact[8], and even intruding it into his account

---

[7] 'My heart leaps up when I behold/A rainbow in the sky:/So was it when my life began;/So is it now I am a man;/ So be it when I shall grow old,/ Or let me die!/ The Child is father of the Man;/ I could wish my days to be/Bound each to each by natural piety.' William Wordsworth, 'The Rainbow' (1802).

[8] A very human tendency, extreme manifestations of which – and Shipton's was not one of these – are known by the name of Munchausen's syndrome, a psychological condition to which those who suffer from poor self-image and low self-esteem are particularly prone.

of Shipton's lone and near-fatal descent in a storm to Camp Five on Everest in 1933. To bolster his view, he also allots to a general practitioner's standard account of the condition one of those five sparse pages covering the years from family background and birth to attainment of the then age of majority.

I find all this extremely puzzling. What Shipton's own analysis from *That Untravelled World* graphically provides is a detailed description of intense distress consequent on mockery and punishment for his incompetence in the routine requirement to read aloud during morning service at what sounds to have been, throughout the time that Shipton was a pupil there (it seems to have improved considerably in later years), an extremely unpleasant Home Counties preparatory school – markedly so even by the frequently dismal standards of those establishments at the time. To give a modern perspective on the condition, and one which is helpful in considering whether Shipton actually did suffer from it, it's worth quoting Lawrence Ives's summary article on dyslexia from the *Oxford Companion to the Mind*[9]. Dr Ives makes inter alia the following points – we might bear them calmly in mind through discussion of what can at times be an inflammatory topic:

> The diagnosis of this condition in children has led to much controversy, and views range from neurologists who postulate a 'developmental dyslexia' said to be the consequence of a neurological delay in development which is of constitutional origin, to psychologists who doubt whether such a syndrome, with a specific underlying cause and specific symptoms, has been identified.

Dr Ives makes a further point which will bring us right back to Shipton's case when he states that the term is one used 'to describe a severe disability which reveals itself initially in difficulty in learning to read, and subsequently by erratic spelling and deficits which affect written as opposed to spoken language'.

Note the 'subsequently' and 'written' there. Peter Steele, in his biography, proceeds to a firm diagnosis of dyslexia that is based entirely on Shipton's own slightly jumbled account from *That Untravelled World* of how his behaviour and performance were

---

[9] Ed. R. L. Gregory (10th impression, revised, 1997).

significantly affected by viciously insensitive and prolonged pedagogical ill treatment. My first response to Steele is to ask for the proofs on which he bases his retrospective diagnosis. In the light of the supposed condition, did he closely consider the very extensive holograph material on which he had to draw – letters, some from an early age; journals, diaries, manuscripts? According to Dr Ives's definition, which is authoritative and based on decades of thorough professional research, evidence for dyslexia ('subsequently by erratic spelling and deficits which affect written as opposed to spoken language'), must have been present here had Shipton's late and tentative self-diagnosis been correct.

It is, however, to all intents non-existent – right from the earliest letters written to his mother from his prep school, the spelling is near-flawless, the syntax entirely competent, the handwriting perfectly legible even when set down under the most trying and arduous circumstances. You are hard pressed to find even the slightest confusion, word omission, mirror writing or spelling error, all of which would inevitably survive into adulthood as base-level indices of the condition had Shipton actually suffered from it rather than having merely suggested to his readers the possibility.[10]

Not only that, but close attention to the texts particularly of Shipton's books and journal articles from the 1930s will also reveal a frame of reference that indicates wide reading. He may have been a late developer as a reader – far from uncommon with many who become fine and celebrated writers (Martin Amis is a good modern case in point here, as *Experience* – his exceptional volume of autobiography – makes very clear) – but once he had started, he

---

[10] The full extent of what he writes in *That Untravelled World* (p.14) is as follows: 'I believe I must have suffered from a condition now known to child psychologists as dislexia [sic].' Note, however, that the mis-spelt term is an editorial import, and not Shipton's own, which was 'word blindness'. It is only fair to point out that John Shipton disagrees with me in this argument, pointing to recurrence of the condition within the family and citing his father's very slow reading as evidence for his opposing view.

The only place in the whole of the very extensive holograph material to which I've had access where Shipton's spelling does become occasionally erratic – and even here the errors are infrequent and slight – is in the sequence of letters written to his mother from Sar in 1935 (see Chapter Eight, below). That this was a time of considerable stress, as he led his first official expedition and had to contend with the intransigence of Tibetan authority and the misbehaviour of his favourite Sherpa Ang Tharkay and its consequences, cannot but be relevant, and again points us away from dyslexia as the cause.

made up the ground impressively. I think it safe to conclude that
if Shipton was 'dyslexic' at all – and we should be quite clear that
there was no formal diagnosis of this by an educational psychologist
or any other appropriate authority; all we have is that tentative self-
diagnosis which is of a piece with the defensive persona his writings
carefully construct – it was the mildest of cases, surely consequent on
severe distress and punishment, which had entirely self-adjusted by
the time he had reached adolescence. I have the hovering suspicion
that we are back in the very complicated territory of Shipton the
joker here, busily manipulating authorial persona and purposively
fashioning a defensive image in time-honoured writerly fashion –
much in the way that his mountain-writing mentor from the 1930s,
Frank Smythe, did. Aspects of this, apparently so tangential to the
mountaineering, will reflect interestingly through his later career in
exploration. So we had perhaps better escape for the moment all its
complexity, which puts us in danger of irritating those readers who
were expecting a straightforward tale of mountain derring-do, and
return to that extraordinary book *Nanda Devi*.

At what is surely the crucial point in the whole story, the one at
which, after nine days of uncertain, risky and arduous struggle, the
small party of Shipton, Tilman and their three Sherpa companions
finally enter the terrain – completely untrodden by human foot – of
the Nanda Devi basin and its inner sanctuary, following on from
recounting the mysterious thrill this experience of wholly unknown
country gave him and communicating his excited anticipation of
what every small part of the place might yield up, Shipton uses a
strangely disjunctive and reflexive statement to explain the depth
of its appeal: '*My most blissful dream as a child* was to be in some
such valley, free to wander where I liked, and discover for myself
some hitherto unrevealed glory of Nature.' Having assured us that
the reality now encountered was in no way less entrancing than
the until now half-forgotten dream, he asks 'of how many *childish
fancies* can that be said, in this age of disillusionment?'[11]

The italics are mine. He was still in his twenties when this
passage was written. Similar references to childhood and youth
recur throughout his writing. As with the comparison of Shivling
to Salisbury Cathedral spire quoted in the prologue, there is a lost
landscape of early experience, a significant place, hovering here

---

[11] Eric Shipton, *Nanda Devi* (3rd edition, Hodder & Stoughton, 1939), p.131.

around the new intensity of moments in his adult life. Indeed, the remarkable nature of the adult life can be viewed as a prolonged attempt to recapture that early intensity. Here it is once more, again from *Nanda Devi*:

> Before us, rising out of a misty shadow-lake of deepest purple, stood the twin summits of Nanda Devi, exquisitely proportioned and twice girdled by strands of white nimbus. This was backed by a liquid indigo, changing to mauve as it approached the south-west, where the icy pyramid of Trisul stood in ghostly attendance. Then, after passing through every degree of shade and texture, the colour died, leaving the moon to shed her silver light over a scene of ravishing loveliness, and *to revive within me childish fancies, too easily forgotten in the materialism of maturer years*.'[12]

The style police would not, of course, allow you to write in this manner these days. Deadly accusations of 'poeticism' and 'rhapsodic prose' would be levelled by those who have never faced the quandary of how to communicate the effect on the human consciousness of direct encounters with the most sublime and powerful scenes of natural beauty (and for that matter, have never read Richard Jefferies,[13] the rich lexis and rapturous prose rhythms of whose late work echo here – but more of this soon). For purposes of comparison, and in order to understand Shipton's communicative intent in working up this passage for publication, it's worth giving the original account, written as he was experiencing the scene. It comes from the small, cloth-bound beige notebook secured with a

---

[12] Shipton, *Nanda Devi*, pp. 160–1.

[13] Richard Jefferies (1848–87) is perhaps the most versatile of English writers on nature, and the great generalist within the genre. Mrs Leavis thought his *Round About a Great Estate* of 1880 'one of the most delightful books in the English language' (Q.D. Leavis, 'Lives and Works of Richard Jefferies', in F. R. Leavis, ed. *A Selection from Scrutiny*, 2 vols. Cambridge University Press 1968, II. 206). The influence of Jefferies' later works – particularly *Bevis: The Story of a Boy* (1882), *The Story of My Heart* (1883) and the poignant last essays collected in *The Life of the Fields* (1884), *The Open Air* (1885) and the posthumously published *Field and Hedgerow* (1889) – on writers such as Mary Webb, Henry Williamson and D. H. Lawrence, who followed him in using natural settings and writing on themes from nature, was fruitful and immense. Edward Thomas was also a devotee, and wrote what is still the standard biography (*Richard Jefferies: His Life and Work*, Hutchinson, 1909).

broad band of black elastic – on the front of which, perfectly spelt and in fading ink, is written 'First Rishi Ganga Expedition, May 21–July 2, 1934' – mentioned in the introduction. Here's the entry for 22 June that parallels the version from *Nanda Devi*:

> Camp in Valley no. 5 at 18,100. This is the best evening we have had. We got here at 1 and after sweltering in the sun were hailed upon heavily. Towards sunset it cleared and we have been having the most heavenly impressions of N[anda] D[evi] through streaks of coloured clouds backed by blue and mauve sky with the half moon above. Then Trisul would suddenly appear to the right looking like a ghostly Arctic peak and wonderfully aloof. We are lying in the open lazily contemplating this most wonderful display of nature while night closes in upon us. It is now too dark to write more, for which I am thankful – and now for more blissful contemplation of this wonderland.

The way in which these immediate impressions, intensely effective in their own way, have been selected and revised into the finished version is very telling. Although he edits out much detail that certainly gives immediacy to the journal extract – the sweltering in the sun, the hail, the dark making it impossible to write more, the sleeping in the open – Shipton's stratagem in the published account of relating the effect of the scene to the intensity of childhood experience is instinctive, successful and astute. It brings us back in short order to biography – to the consideration of where exactly were these scenes of a formative natural aesthetic which were to have so powerful and lasting an effect. To this as well you will recall that Shipton has given us the clue: 'West across the Gangotri floated, high up, a silvery spire, graceful as that of Salisbury, and sparkling in the early sun.' Within sight of Salisbury Cathedral, then, and we should also take into account the pulsing reminders of Richard Jefferies' novel of 1882, *Bevis*, particularly throughout this earliest of Shipton's books. *Bevis* – and indeed Jefferies' writing as a whole – may now languish unread, but very few boys of Shipton's generation would have been unacquainted with or unaffected particularly by the novel.[14] Nor by

---

[14] I would argue that Jefferies is the single most important literary influence on Shipton. ubiquitous and pervasive in his writing. You see it particularly

Shelley, who provides title and epigraph to Shipton's first attempt at autobiography, *Upon That Mountain*; nor by George Borrow, polymath, traveller, pugilist, gypsy-lover, proto-Sebaldian raconteur extraordinaire; a now wholly unread great Victorian miscellaneous – or indeed uncategorisable – prose writer, quotations from whom are slipped in unobtrusively to our supposedly dyslexic author's *Nanda Devi*, to certain recognition by the great majority of his contemporary and educated readers in the 1930s.

There is another intellectual sleight of hand here too, that illuminates Shipton's sense of humour. As with Borrow, you must not take his statements on self entirely at face value. You have to be on your guard for authorial agendas and the construction of a persona, which latter will serve him both as defence against the Establishment of his time and its values, and as an individualist critique of that too. We do well to remember, when Shipton is presenting himself here and there in his autobiographical writing as the uneducated simpleton, that this is the man who walked away from the possibility that was his for the taking of a place at a Cambridge college with the climbing elite of his time, and chose to plough – more or less literally – his own furrow in East Africa. But we are running ahead of ourselves, fascinating though all this material may be, and it is time to track down more closely those scenes of his childhood that had so lasting an effect.

---

in the reflective principle, close to the nature mysticism Jefferies expresses in *The Story of My Heart* (1883 – a book that in some ways is a philosophical gloss on *Bevis*, published the previous year), which Shipton can carry off with great poise and delicacy at times, avoiding the pitfalls of bathos or inflation, examples of which we shall be coming to in due course. There is a satisfying irony in suggesting an affinity with mysticism for Shipton, given that he professed agnosticism throughout his adult life. Even if only for the joy of argument – which was one of the pleasures of his social life – he would probably have rejected the contention. Yet perhaps his disclaimer of religious belief was akin to that of Simone Weil, concealing and containing a sense of divine mystery within the universe. Certainly a recurrent point of interest in Shipton's writings is the tension between practical preoccupation with physical phenomena, and frequent lapsing into quietistic modes of thought. (Note here that 'mysticism' is not being used in the vague and inaccurate reproachful and pejorative sense, but the precise philosophical one to do with oneness in all things perceived through ecstatic contemplation of nature or divinity.)

2

Shipton in Bevis-land

Eric Earle Shipton was born in Kandy in the Central Highlands of what is now Sri Lanka and was then Ceylon – a British colony – on 1 August 1907. He was the second child (an elder sister, Marjorie, generally known as Marge, preceded him by two years) of Cecil Shipton and his elegant wife, the former Miss Isobel Earle – hence his second name. There is surviving testimony to the effect that his parents' union was passionate and mutually devoted, and there is support for the existence of that state of bliss in a letter, the preservation of which was surely significant, written by Cecil to his wife-to-be on their wedding morning:

'The Wedding Day
10 a.m.

My own Darling,

As they won't let me see you this morning I feel I must just write you a few lines. I got back safely last night and found the best man sitting up for me – we went to bed about half past one but I could not get to sleep for hours, thinking of you – I think it must have been because I did not kiss you good night. I had a sudden fit of shyness when I said 'Good night Darling' to you last night. I felt I must kiss you, but could not with so many strangers looking on. I am just going round to Dr Joy's to see if everything is all right. I don't know how I am to pass the hours until we meet at the church – sweetheart-mine I love you – may God bless you angel mine.

From your ever loving
Cecil

Dr Joy indeed! The modesty and the simple statements of affection here incline us to like the man, though his nervous self-abnegations might not be thought good auguries in achieving conjugal balance.

Cecil Shipton, a tea-planter, had been born, also in Kandy, on 16 September 1869, the son of John Shipton, a doctor, and Kate Hoyle his wife. These two – Eric Shipton's paternal grandparents – had been married in 1864 in the parish church of Kimberworth, just west of Rotherham in south Yorkshire, and had shipped out to Ceylon shortly thereafter. In *That Untravelled World*, Eric Shipton records that his father died before he was three, and goes on to tell us that his mother, about whom early biographical detail is frustratingly sketchy, 'was extremely reserved and never encouraged intimate discussion'. A thick file of correspondence from his Kashgar years yields very little information about her, though it highlights the extent even in wartime of her incessant and restless travelling and indicates a lively, intellectually engaged, warm and surprisingly close relationship between them at that time. He does tell us that she never mentioned her late husband, and that he himself well into his early manhood felt little curiosity about his father, though he did later discover that Cecil had been a devoted spouse whose passion was ornithology. He also records that his mother's 'views were even more strait-laced than most women's of her generation'.[1]

Two points to be made here are that his mother's refusal – or perhaps more properly inability – to talk about her late husband even, or perhaps especially, to their children could be seen as one of the more frequent manifestations of extreme grief.[2] If you consider Shipton's account from *That Untravelled World* of his early childhood and his mother's behaviour after his father's death, the effect on her is abundantly clear – as how could it not be? What he describes of her in that book is the early, restless, searching phase of the journey through grief – a journey the characteristic stages of which, aside from variations in the intensity with which they are individually experienced, are remarkably recurrent from

---

[1] Eric Shipton, *That Untravelled World* (Hodder & Stoughton, 1969), p.94.
[2] From personal experience, I find it very hard still, eight years after his death, to talk about my son Will, perhaps the finest British adventure climber of his generation, who took his own life in 2004 at the age of twenty-four. With an emotional wound as deep as this (itself forcing you to ponder how much deeper was Will's to lead him to his action), sometimes your only recourse is to close up around it and allow the psychological scar tissue to manifest in whatever way it will.

person to person: 'For several years after my father's death we were constantly on the move, travelling between England and Southern India and Ceylon . . . We were never in one place for long and had no settled home, which is generally thought to be essential for the psychological welfare of children.'[3]

The second point is that his father did not, as stated in *That Untravelled World*, die before Eric was three. Confirmation of this – and obviously getting any information out of either the present authorities in Sri Lanka or the British Foreign Office is a task doomed to frustration, however good your contacts may be – comes from what is in itself a very interesting source, and one worth quoting at some length as giving an insight into the milieu of Shipton's early life, and the personalities who inhabited it:

Colombo Club, 17th August 1910

Dear Mrs Shipton,

I do hope to hear that your cold is alright and that you had a pleasant journey up, – 'naughty Nellie' may perhaps have forgotten her troubles for once, – nobody loves her more than I, – but you do allow her to be too selfish where you are concerned though of course it is entirely due to her thoughtlessness. However I trust you were taken proper care of for once.

'Not wholly in the busy world or quite beyond it lies the garden that I love' – and there, many years ago, one idle summer day, amidst old world flowers, trim yew hedges and the quiet song of the bees I absorbed the first book of Virgil. It is full of immortal lines, and if their beauty is once appreciated they cannot be forgotten, – but your gracious kindness has made them flame for me with a clearer and more brilliant light than ever. Now please don't sit in the seat of the scornful but know that my gratitude is sincere.

When do Marjorie and Sonny have their birthday party, – and I would fancy it more strenuous than a Surf Club Ball.

With kind regards to Mr Shipton.

Yours sincerely,

M. H. Haly

---

[3] Shipton, *That Untravelled World*, p.10.

The hyperbolical Mr Haly, you might think, is trying very hard to impress, and you could be forgiven for wondering what Mr Shipton made of the letter, if he ever saw it. It was followed three weeks later by another interesting missive:

Colombo Club, 7th September 1910

Dear Mrs Shipton,

I wonder if you realise how much I enjoy myself at Coldstream, – if you do you will understand it is impossible for me to be sufficiently grateful for your kindness. My return journey was uneventful, – we made Shatton with one wheel usually in the ditch – no sleeping berths available but pleasant thoughts rendered one unnecessary.

As you asked me I am posting you *Amitié Amoureuse,*[4] and you will pardon me 'if some random chord your fine female sense offends'. The characters really lived and were known to a friend of mine. Personally I think it is one of the most artistic books I have ever read. Imagine these peoples' lives treated by stupid and vulgar savages like V.C. and E. Glynn [sic][5] – it makes me shudder. Tilson Young, Meredith and possibly Thomas Hardy might have done well with them, and I think Henry James and Lucas Malet.[6] I hope you will enjoy it – keep it as long as ever you like, it is not a book to lend in a hurry. I send it to you without care – since I send it to my friend, – and should there be any trace of my own life in it – treat them as part of the book, – if you are anxious, – but they are confidences.

---

[4] Title of the 1896 book by Hermine Oudinot Lecomte du Noüy – a publishing sensation of its time. The title – dangerously ambiguous and, being French, distinctly complex – can be translated as 'loving friendship', though this far from covers it.

[5] Not sure to whom V.C. refers. Elinor Glyn was a turn-of-the-century-and-later green-eyed erotic novelist of immense popularity, famous in her day for serial sexual relationships with British aristocrats, who seemed to have queued up to oblige her. ('Would you like to sin/With Elinor Glyn/On a tiger skin?/Or would you prefer/ To err with her/On some other fur?' is how a popular verse of the day had it, assuming the desire was in no doubt, only the place of its consummation.) She is credited with the re-invention of Gloria Swanson and the coining of the term 'it' in reference to sexual matters – 'it' being something she clearly enjoyed, scandalous though this may have been for women of the time.

[6] All of them popular late-Victorian novelists, some of them still well known. Though not necessarily well read.

With kind regards to all at Coldstream and very many thanks,

Yours sincerely.

M. H. Haly

P.S. I am so sorry I have forgotten to look up that remark of Goethe's for your mottos.

If this letter were a car, I'd think it in danger of overheating. The element of potential *amoureuse* certainly outstrips the professed *amitié*. It appears to have gone unanswered – it would certainly have been unsurprising had Mrs Shipton felt compromised by it, and I doubt she would have wished her husband to see it.

Two months later Mr Haly tried his luck again:

Empire Hotel, Kuala Lumpur, 9th November 1910

Dear Mrs Shipton,

I wonder if you could possibly find time to send me a few lines very soon. I am badly in need of a tonic, – for never in my life have I felt so utterly helpless, which is very much like hopeless.

The voyage was a nightmare, but I had the good fortune to sit at the Captain's table opposite the most charming and interesting person in the ship. In the intervals I lost at bridge, talked rubber, entered for a gymkhana and got severely reprimanded by various savage ladies for not turning up for the events. I escaped ashore the next day without damage.

Our mysterious Mr Haly then took another ship down to Port Swettenham,[7] on which outpost of progress he makes some scabrous and condescending comments quite at odds with the aesthetic affectations of his earlier letters before reassuring Mrs Shipton of 'how happy I am to have the privilege of writing to you. This is the first letter I have written and as of all my friends I always think first of you, it goes to you.'

At Coldstream, however, despite his good wishes, all was far

---

[7] On the east side of the Straits of Malacca and now known as Klang, this port built on a mangrove swamp is chiefly famous as the location where a link between mosquitoes and malaria was first established. In 1910 it had a polo club and a high mortality rate (the two not necessarily connected).

from well. The correspondence dwindled, and by the time Haly next wrote to Mrs Shipton, over a year later on 9 December 1911, her situation had changed radically. At some time during those thirteen months, Mrs Shipton had lost a husband, and her children their father. Mr Haly, in a peculiarly solipsistic way, seemed set on pressing home the advantage circumstance had bestowed:

'My dear Mrs Shipton,
    News of you at last, I see you do not leave Ceylon until next April. If I am very lucky I may possibly be able to get over to Ceylon before then and I shall certainly try very hard to if you will only say that I may come and see you. May I?'

This is an extraordinary beginning to a letter addressed to a recently bereaved widow. On application of the I-count[8] – that very elementary test of where the primary concern of the writer lies – it fails dismally. By the beginning of the second paragraph Mr Haly does briefly bring himself to remember in what respect a proper concern should be displayed, before immediately launching once again into his habitual sententiousness: 'Dear lady, I do not forget the closing year has been a most unhappy one for you, but you have courage, and with that great gift life always contains possibilities.' Among which latter, no doubt, she might consider the great good fortune of being able to count Mr Haly. He continues:

For myself I am in very serious difficulties which, if I surmount successfully, will give me assurance to stand upright in your gracious presence. I am worn out with overwork and worry. I wonder if you have the remotest idea how eagerly I turn to the recollection of the kindness I have so frequently met with from you which enables me to struggle on from one weary day to another. Recollect, you asked me to succeed, – the possibility never occurred to me before and the attainment is as far away as ever, but I have reason for trying, in the absence of which I would long since have gone under. How shy you were. I wondered if you feared your words, or me. Did you think I did not, would not understand, that I should doubt your sincerity or attribute it to anything but a wish that your friend should

---

[8] A simple count of recurrence of first- or second-person pronouns.

be happy. It is no use pretending that I did not desire more, but I knew to retain your friendship it was necessary that I schooled myself to be content with all that you could give. What you could give you gave freely, generously, as became you. Charm is not of beauty but of breeding, and where the breeding is perfect there is beauty – a beauty which grows and grows stifling all foul things until one learns Heaven is on Earth, and here before there was only Hell.

Dear fragrant memory.

H.

This was written, remember, to a woman recently widowed with two young children to care for. If the letter strikes you as odd in the circumstances under which it was written, consider then the next, sent three weeks later:

Kuala Lumpur, 28th Dec. 1911

Dear Lady,

12 o'clock but I must reply to your letter just received. Did you get mine addressed to the Survey Bungalow, Galle [the letter quoted above]? Never mind. Your letter does recall you and – happiness. The gentle irony I knew and loved so well. – Just like the glow of the setting sun on the iceberg wandering and wondering in strange seas.

Small wonder Mrs Shipton felt inclined to exercise irony against her fulsome admirer. He continues, and in a disturbing vein.

You smile – how can a poem appreciate the spirit which animates it? Well I could have fallen in love with Mrs C. if you had not been there. Imagine then – the position – she was open to criticism – you were beyond my thoughts – but [illegible] comparison was a necessity and I was saved. Circumstance, often intolerable, often compels wisdom or at least saves from folly. Is this folly? Then I love it – and would not be saved. A learned judge was my host tonight *à deux* and the morality of the world and Pommard preserved us through dinner. He had a cold, but preserved the dignity of the bench and the Oxford manner. We discussed your sex from the hights [sic] of Olympus and I heard weird tales from Hongkong to Aden.

How he lied, and how interestingly because he told the truth.
This is not a paradox. I rely on imagination for the hiatus as is
necessary hence the lie.

But may I see you again? Yes.

H.

Lucky Mrs C.! Not so lucky Mrs Shipton, however. I doubt I'm alone
in the involuntary shudder Haly's letters induce in me, or the concern
they engender around this man's likely effect on Mrs Shipton's two
children. She resisted the blandishments of her bibulous Olympian
admirer for a while, went off to England and the South of France,
but by 1914 she was back in the Nilgiri Hills of Kerala, where she
became Mrs Haly – the name she bore for the rest of her life.

In 1915 the newly ordered family left the wooded gorges of the
Nilgiris and made their way across the Gulf of Mannar to Ceylon,
where they eventually found passage, despite the alarms of war and
the growing U-boat menace, on board the SS *Kashgar*[9] for England.
There they found a London flat near Kensington Gardens. A
governess was initially employed, to educate the children and walk
them in the Gardens each day, passing by Sir George Frampton's
famous 'Peter Pan' statue of 1912 – 'a circumscribed life' is how
Shipton characterises it in his autobiography, and so it must have
been after his previous experiences, adding that he began increasingly
to inhabit a dream world and relate less and less to other people. He
also offers the opinion that his sister 'was a gregarious little girl . . .
kind and affectionate towards me'. The following summer, that of
1916, they holidayed at Alverstoke, on the Solent by the entrance to
Portsmouth Harbour – no better places for encouraging restlessness
than where the great ships are forever coming and going past your
windows.

'Uncle Haly', as his new honorific had it, in that terrible time
when the German army had nearly broken through at Ypres and
Zeppelins were bombing London, had responded early in 1916 to
Kitchener's plea to augment the regular army through the famous
exhortation that 'Your country needs you'. He joined the Second
Hampshire Regiment of the British Expeditionary Force, the
formation of which was a turning-point stratagem in the Great War.

[9] Where Shipton was later to serve as HM Consul General – extraordinary, the
patterns of recurrence and suggestion in a life.

After basic training, he was promptly sent to France. No letters back to his new wife survive, but there are some, written from France, that indicate he was taking his new role as stepfather more seriously than those disturbingly odd letters of courtship might have led us to expect. Perhaps he had simply been young and was now growing up – the jejune tone and constant attempts to claim seniority suggest that; though traces of insecurity in these uncertainly pitched letters to his stepchildren remain:

4th August 1916
Somewhere in ———

My darling little Marjorie,

Thanks so much for your letter – it was very kind of you to write and must have taken such a long time. I can *parlez* like anything now. I do hope you like Alverstoke and that you and Eric are having an awfully good time and taking the greatest care of mother. This place is not as bad as it might be, but I must not tell you what it is like [because of the censor]. There are a lot of Huns and they are always shooting at Uncle Haly. They are very brave when they are a long way off and can't be seen, but I think we give them terrible frights sometimes.

Did Eric get a prize and do you mind the beach being stony very much.

There are such a lot of great fat cats swanning about.

Much love to everybody and kiss mummy for me. It is difficult to write here.

Mind at the end of its tether? He wrote again to Marjorie from France on 25 August – a very strange letter, stress of the front line upon it:

My dear little Marjorie,

So many thanks for your letter. How much was the poor bird nearly eaten only half or quite a quarter – and which liked it most the cat or the bird, or the kitten or can't kittens like yet. How is Eric getting on – can he sing well now and has the doctor operated on his throat. Did you both like the Victory[10] – she must have had a fine fight. I have not done any fighting

---

[10] Nelson's flagship from Trafalgar, preserved at Portsmouth.

for a week – but I expect to soon again – perhaps tomorrow night – and if I get killed you must take great care that she is not too sorry, because you know she is the sweetest and best and most beautiful mother any little girl has ever had so you will take the greatest care of her won't you and see she is always as happy as possible.

Much love to you and Eric,

Uncle Haly

On 6 of September it was Eric's turn for a letter:

My dear Eric,

Thanks very much for your letter. I was very glad to get it – but you must be able to swim fast now to beat a wave. Mother says Marjorie has not been very well but I hope she is alright now. How many tons of sea water have you swallowed? I hope it will help you win a prize next term – mother would be so pleased and so would I, so you will try – is mother quite well and happy – it is your business to take the greatest care that she is. I was digging a nasty muddy wet trench last night and got in such a mess. There is a lot of water in the trenches now and the Germans always shoot at us but they hardly ever hit anybody. Would you ask mother to tell the Army & Navy stores to send me the long white waterproof boots we saw at the A & N stores and not to pay for them till I tell her. Ask her to tell the stores to put them in a bag that I can sling over my shoulders otherwise I shan't be able to carry them. I should like them soon as my feet get so cold and wet and dirty. We are living in cellars with every home in the town knocked down – all in ruins – our artillery is much stronger than the Germans and are always shooting at them – a frightful uproar. Sometimes the Germans send a few shells when we make them angry but they seldom hit anybody. I have had a very exciting time which I will tell you all about if ever I get home again – if I don't – mind you always take the greatest care of mother and make her happy whatever happens. Tell mother I am quite well. Much love to you all.

Uncle Haly

He would not be coming home, though. Something of the terrible fear that must have permeated the trenches seeps through into this correspondence, and for a contemporary reader perhaps tempers its manipulations. The last surviving letter he wrote to his stepchildren gives a glimpse into conditions on the Western Front, and an inevitable sense of foreboding hovers behind its forced gaiety – hard not to have a sense of mortality when the fragility of life, of the human body, was everywhere apparent:

> Tuesday 19-9-16, dull, occasional sunshine
> My dear Marjorie and Eric,
>   Thanks so much for the chocolate you sent me – it was very good – I have not finished it yet – but shall eat the rest when I go up the line next time. How are the kittens and do they like each other and you? & how can you tell? We are in a wood now and fairly safe as very few shells come this way and bullets and other nasty things – of which there are lots – can't come this way so far. We have a band playing and the men are getting clean after being covered in mud for days.
>   I expect you are in London now and I hope you had a jolly good holiday and will be able to learn quite a lot now because there are a good many things you must know about and how to do if you are to take care of mother properly.
>   I hope I shall be able to get a bath today – I have not had a bath for 12 days – isn't it awful!
>   I expect you will take a long time to read this letter because I write so ill.
>   Much love to you all,
>   Uncle Haly

The family was indeed back in the London flat, together again and once more leading the circumscribed life for a few weeks. Eric fought battles with his toy soldiers and followed the progress of the war. In his autobiography half a century later, he dismissed the role his stepfather had played in his life with a few unemotional lines: 'My step-father was not with us for long, as he joined the Army soon after the outbreak of war and was sent to France; so I suppose I regarded him as just another adult who came and went like the rest. He was killed in action in 1917.'[11]

---

[11] Shipton, *That Untravelled World*, p.11.

The sad and confused figure of 'Uncle Haly' passes thus from the family record, with not a clue as to whether anyone lamented him, or had cause to do so. Eric, meanwhile, as Uncle Haly's letter to him implies, had been sent to a boarding preparatory school in 1916, to which he returned after the summer vacation in Alverstoke. The school was at Heronsgate, between Rickmansworth and Chorleywood in Hertfordshire (Tilman had very recently left his boarding school at Berkhamsted, six miles to the north-west, for the Royal Military Academy in Woolwich, when Shipton arrived in Heronsgate – strange, somehow, to think of Britain's two greatest mountain explorers being Hertfordshire boarding-school boys at the same period). It was called Beaumont House, and it occupied a large late-Victorian bay-windowed building at the southern end of Nottingham Road South, with extensive gardens and grounds, outbuildings scattered among them.

You can still see the schoolhouse if you go there today, divided into two private dwellings now, former drill hall and laundry ramshackle behind them, lying half a mile from Junction 17 on the M25 London Orbital motorway, the roar of which is ever audible. In 1916 this was a peaceful, semi-rural place of large houses and large gardens, chiefly famous for having been the location of O'Connorville – the great Chartist leader Feargus O'Connor's benevolent and doomed experiment of 1847 in social living, the former dwellings of which lay all around the school. Though not exactly one of those innumerable nameless and ephemeral institutions which through the great good fortune of twentieth-century educational progress have disappeared without trace or record, Beaumont House's history was not particularly long. It had been in existence for a little over ten years when the nine-year-old Shipton arrived, and it continued to operate until 1973. Kim Philby the spy placed his son here.

Shipton's earliest extant letter was sent from school in the summer of 1916, perfectly spelt, and pencil-written in a round, robust and childish hand the only hesitancy in which is over how many loops to give an 'M' and an 'N'.

Beaumont House, Heronsgate

My dear Mummy,
     I hope you are all right. I was so pleased you could come to see the sports yesterday. When can you come again? Can you

come not the next Saturday, but the next? I am afraid I can't
write much as I want to write two letters.
  With love
  from
  Eric
  xxxxxxxxxx

In the period after the Second World War, under the efficient
headship of Peter Vesey, Beaumont House was quite highly regarded,
a successful feeder-institution for the better public schools, and it
still has a thriving old boys' association whose members – healthy
and prosperous-looking to a man – keep its memory and its motto
(*'Cum sapientia veritas'*) alive with annual dinners at the Sloane
Club and the House of Lords, visits to the battlefields of the Somme,
rounds of golf and amiable barbecues at each other's houses. At
least one of its masters in the post-Second World War period had
been there in Shipton's time. Vernon Birds, a classicist, had been
invalided out of the army after being severely wounded and lying
out thus in the field day-long during the advance on Beaumont
Hamel in the Battle of the Somme, on 1 July 1916 – the day that
huge Allied mines had gone up under the German observation post
of Hawthorn Redoubt. Benign and enthusiastic Mr Birds may have
been – though perhaps a little ineffectual or even neurasthenic when
faced by a classroom of Latin-resistant boys – but he seems to have
been an exception to the general tenor of the school in the closing
years of the Great War and on to beyond the end of the decade. If
we are to read between the lines of Shipton's accounts, and pick
up on its effect on his personality, the reality sounds to have been
brutal and perverted. The school was run at that time, he tells us,
by a Mr Gifford and his wife. The name clearly held no pleasant
associations for him in later life. The flogging was excessive, and
Shipton the most regular recipient, the ritual involving removal of
shorts, rolling up of shirt tails, and lying face down on the Giffords'
marital bed. Mrs Gifford, *en déshabille*, received all the boys each
morning whilst taking breakfast in this same bed on which they
suffered their thrashings, and recorded in a register their bowel
movements, administering cod liver oil where required.

These days the likes of Mr Gifford obtain their pleasure by other
no doubt equally unsavoury but rather more private means, or they
are sent to gaol. Eric, unsurprisingly in the face of this sustained

sadism, failed the Common Entrance examination that would have gained him a place at Harrow, for which his name had been put down. In *That Untravelled World* he gives a remarkable account of how he coped with the inappropriate and vicious treatment accorded him, and in doing so affords an insight into his later air of calm unflappability as a mountaineer. Psychologically, this is surely a key passage:

> Gradually I acquired a reputation for being quite unperturbed by flogging, a delusion I was careful to foster for reasons of pride. In fact, I was always terrified; I cared nothing for the humiliation and feared only the pain, which was always worse than I had expected. But the most unpleasant thing about those beatings was that they were never executed on the spot; we had to wait for several days, even as much as a week, for the dread summons. By then one was often in the company of other victims who formed a queue outside the bedroom, counting the strokes and listening to the wails of their fellows.[12]

The sustained vileness of Gifford's behaviour had the single positive outcome of developing an emotional control – perhaps even the classic place-of-safety of the mind that some abused children manage against all odds to create – that would serve Shipton well as mountaineer.[13] However that may be, at the age of fourteen, after six long and damaging years at Beaumont House, a stroke of good luck did befall him. It came in the shape of a former Harrow master, Dr Crawford, who in 1918 had opened a school in the rolling, wooded country of Cranborne Chase in south Wiltshire. For its premises, Dr Crawford's new school leased Pyt House, a fine south-facing Palladian mansion dating from 1725, with a severely graceful Ionic portico in grey ashlar. It looked down beyond the ha-ha on to ninety-five acres of parkland. The fourteen-year-old Eric Shipton arrived here in January 1922. The educational regime proved to be

---

[12] Shipton, *That Untravelled World*, p.14.
[13] The sheer ghastliness and sadism of the English preparatory and public school system also had its part to play in the ethos which could so willingly and stoically accept the horrors of the Great War. Wade Davis's monumental, unfortunately titled *Into the Silence: The Great War, Mallory, and the Conquest of Everest* (Bodley Head, 2011) – a book admiration for which seems to me to be in inverse proportion to its readers' involvement with mountaineering – is suggestive on this topic.

as amiable as the surroundings, and he prospered, was encouraged, began to find his interests and his stride. Most of his fellow pupils were dropouts from the great public schools who had arrived here to acquire the necessary qualifications to join a regiment or go to university. One of them was Arnold Haskell, the balletomane and dear friend of Ninette de Valois, who later became headmaster of the Royal Ballet School. Few others attained distinction; but they drove cars, did as much or as little as they needed to, gently mocked the masters in every inoffensive way, and generally established an atmosphere of benign anarchy that shaped Shipton's sense of humour, defined his attitude to authority, and – after the terrors and despondencies of the Gifford establishment – redeemed his young life.

If there was discipline in the school at all, it was far from draconian. There was one occasion when Shipton found himself in trouble. He had been raiding the school larder late one night with his particular friend Jim Horsfall. They had carried their booty back to Shipton's room and were sitting innocently in bed together having scoffed it when footsteps sounded down the corridor and stopped by the door. It opened and a torch shone into the room. Jim dived under the bedclothes. The master – a retired army captain with the odd soubriquet of 'The Bum Skipper' – came in and asked amiably enough whether they were having a good time.

'Yes, sir,' the two boys piped up in all innocence. They were enjoined to report after prayers next morning, by which time reports of the incident had done the rounds and the less innocent senior boys had intimated the conclusions that could be drawn from their artless response. So next morning they made a full and frank admission of their larcenous but far-from-lubricious behaviour, and were punished with no more than five hundred lines each. Even for that oppression, Shipton received a very belated apology:

June 8 '70

My Dear Eric,

Thank you very much indeed for sending me your auto-biography. I am not upset by the Pyt House part! In fact, I am much amused! I feel I was illogical to give you 500 lines; having accepted your explanation was tantamount to saying you had not committed any wrong, so why inflict 500 lines? Typical soldier's attitude! I have reached the chapter on the

Karakoram in your book; I find it and – for that matter –
everything most interesting. It was very nice to see you again.
I should have known you, I think, anywhere by your eyes.[14]

Please bring Malcolm Campbell to see us, but come yourself
anyway. Give me a day or so's notice to ensure finding us . . .

Patricia and I send best regards,

Yours very sincerely,

Aubrey Hill

Nearly fifty years on, both the tone of this letter and the fact
that Shipton had taken the trouble to maintain or reinstate contact
speak volumes. He had certainly stepped into an educational
establishment where the benign was the rule, but this is only a
part of the story, and probably the least important one. Not only
was the school a decent and friendly place where he made marked
progress academically and began to read and master the subjects
he would need for the future; the surroundings of the place were
heaven-sent too – he had crash-landed in Bevis-land, the Richard
Jefferies original for which lay twenty or so miles to the north
around Coate in Wiltshire, the county where, in E. M. Forster's
view, 'the fibres of England unite'.[15] In Shipton's case, they did so
to healing effect. The character, the atmosphere of Jefferies's novel
on the themes of boyhood friendship and adventures afloat and
on foot, its realm of exploration and imagination, the potential for
its playful re-enactments, its emulation, lay all around in Wardour
vale within sight of Salisbury's lofty spire. It's worth mentioning
at this juncture that *Bevis* was one of the books that Shipton was
encouraged to read at Dr Crawford's, and its influence both on his
subsequent career and on his prose style was obvious and lasting.

This region of ancient Wiltshire was a place to which he was
drawn back throughout his life, and in which he ended his days,
after being rescued from a dark basement flat in Chelsea and
taken in and cared for in her home at Ansty manor house by a
dear friend and gracious woman, Aileen Fisher-Rowe, during his
last illness:[16]

---

[14] The eyes – disconcertingly blue and direct, with a reserve about them at the
same time – were remarked upon by all who knew him. His sons have inherited
the disconcertingly direct quality, if not the exact colouring.

[15] E. M. Forster, *The Longest Journey* (Harmondsworth, 1960), p.132.

[16] See Epilogue, note 19.

In our ample spare time we were free (within the limits imposed by common law) to do as we pleased and go wherever we liked. As Pyt House was in the heart of one of the loveliest parts of rural England, surrounded by great stretches of woodland and with many lakes near by, this freedom was specially valuable and I was not slow to appreciate it.[17]

This is hardly to overstate the case. Nowadays, and rightly so, it is designated as an Area of Outstanding Natural Beauty – an AONB – one of the largest in England. Salisbury spire rises ever-present easterly out of the plains where the valleys of the Wylye and the Nadder converge. Shaftesbury – Hardy's old-fashioned place of Shaston – is just to the west. Woods and wolds lie along each horizon. Extravagant ruins like the gothic novelist William Beckford's bizarre and jerry-built Fonthill Abbey,[18] with its extensive and beautifully planted grounds, and the unique fourteenth-century Wardour Old Castle add interest to the scene. This Wiltshire/Dorset border country was one of the most perfectly beautiful versions of English pastoral, and to some extent still is, though it has changed in the thirty years I've known it.

The destruction of the former rural communities by the ingress of second-home-owners and metropolitan escapees has ensured that no one would now be able to tell Shipton and his friend Jim, as a friendly farmer of their time did – one as vested in long rural tradition as a yeoman out of Hardy – about the local tradition of a tunnel running from Wardour Castle into the woods near Pyt House by which a lady from a Royalist family of Cromwell's day had escaped from the besieging Parliamentary forces that left the fortified building in its present ruinous state. Here was an adventure then, and Shipton and Jim set to exploring. For weeks they searched high and low – mostly low – and eventually came across the likeliest lead, in the grounds of Pyt House. A hole in what Shipton describes as a hut in the woods – it had been used by the gardeners as a latrine – dropped into a dark and evil-smelling chasm beneath, into which he lowered himself on a rope, destroying the latrine seat in

---

[17] Shipton, *That Untravelled World*, p.19

[18] Hazlitt's summary verdict on this grand folly is well worth quoting: 'a glittering waste of industrious idleness'. It collapsed in 1825, less than thirty years after being put up.

the process. I went to Pyt House a quarter of a century or so ago, to soak up the atmosphere – however putrid it might prove on occasion – of this phase in Shipton's boyhood. By this time it was being run as a retirement home by the Country Houses Association (the cost of upkeep eventually proved too great, the necessary fees rose too high, and it became a private house again). On the glorious autumn day of my visit, old gentlemen in wheelchairs, wheeled out to sun themselves on the terrace, nodded amiably in my direction. A distinguished-looking person of upright bearing who was obviously in charge strolled over to enquire politely after my business. I told him Shipton's story of the gardeners' latrine. He chuckled – nothing an old gent likes better than a touch of cloacal humour – held up a finger in a gesture of recognition and bade me follow him. We walked across to the west side of the house and into a shrubbery. 'Lo!' he exclaimed, with a theatrical sweep of his hand towards an igloo-shaped building of a kind I had never seen before. A domed entrance led to a tunnel through the thick stone walls.

'Go in, mind your head, and watch out for the hole in the floor.'

I did as I was invited and came out into a hemispherical chamber with a large round hole in its floor. This gave on to a lower version of the chamber I was in, the drop being about ten feet as far as I could judge in the cave-like gloom. 'So what on earth is that?' I quizzed as I emerged once more into daylight.

'Well I can assure you it's not the gardeners' latrine any more – your precious Health and Safety, damn them and all their works, would certainly have something to say about that. No, it's the old ice-house – all the grand places had them two hundred years ago. But what a jape, your friend getting himself down there. I doubt very much there's any truth in the story about a tunnel from Wardour, incidentally. Too far for that sort of thing. I expect you'll be going there next, after you've joined us for a cup of tea?'

Which latter is exactly what I did, having been seated at a table on the lawn, brought tea and Victoria sponge cake, and been royally entertained and introduced to most of the nodding gentlemen – not one of whom at a guess would have been under the age of eighty. I heard their stories, and explained to them my presence there. One remarkable thing was that every one of them, my host included, knew of Eric Shipton and regarded him with great admiration. I went on my way that beautiful autumn afternoon with the strongest sense of how the benevolence that comes through in Shipton's descriptions of his life at Pyt House was still lingering decades on; and I hope it does so still, and seeps into the veins of its present occupants.

I didn't in fact head straight away for Wardour, which lay in my ultimate direction. Eventually I'd go there and marvel at the climbing potential of its ruinous arêtes and corners. Youthful acquaintance with a place like that would inevitably make you into a climber. Instead, I made first for the grounds of Fonthill Abbey to find the lake Shipton described there as being wholly surrounded by thick vegetation until you reach the water's edge, where he and Jim would dive from overhanging branches into still green depths. Here again was perfect *Bevis* territory – New Formosa, The New Sea, The Forest:

> '. . . they went through the meadow, where the dew still lingered in the shade, on the way to the bathing place, they hung about the path picking clover-heads and sucking the petals, pulling them out and putting the lesser ends in their lips, looking at the white and pink bramble flowers, noting where the young nuts began to show, pulling down the woodbine, and doing everything but hasten on to their work of swimming. They stopped at the gate by the New Sea, over whose smooth surface slight breaths of mist were curling, and stood kicking the ground and stones as flighty horses paw.[19]

A forest track led down to a lovely pool perhaps 150 yards long and 80 wide, obviously deep. Huge trunks of cypress and sequoia reared up out of rhododendron thickets – Himalayan shrubs! – around its banks. Moorhens called with that strange metallic sound like a cold-chisel striking rock. I sat down by the water's edge on a little jutting sunny promontory and watched the small waterfowl jerk and dab across the glassy surface of this heart-of-woodland secluded lake. The intense quiet, punctuated only by natural sounds, had a timeless resonance. He had sat here, in this exact place. I knew this with absolute instinctive certainty. If I could have looked through the dimensions of time, I would have seen the boy plunging and gasping against the water's shock; had I turned to look behind me, I would have seen the man, wintry-haired and blue-eyed in the

---

[19] Richard Jefferies, *Bevis: The Story of a Boy* (Dent 1966), p.79.

scene of his boyhood, standing behind me with that distant look of his – standing here as he often did when visiting his old friend and former lover Pamela Freston in nearby Ansty. The heavy boughs of the sequoias reflected across the mirrored plane I surveyed. On the opposite bank were vague paths leading away, frond-like mysteries obscuring them. In a stilled moment my heart heard him whisper how he had loved this pool, this area: 'If a man adventures in daring company during adolescence, he will probably do so throughout his life.'

Heading home for Wales a day or two later, I called on his son Nick in Bristol, described where instinct and that Jefferies sense of natural attunement from his father's writing had led. Nick gave me the Shipton gaze, attentive and levelling, hearing intently all I had to say.

'Oh yes,' he responded, 'the hidden lake at Fonthill – that's where we scattered his ashes.'

3

The Lost Domain of
Lieutenant Tilman, MC and Bar

The childhood and adolescence of Eric Shipton, as we saw in the last chapter and will see more of in the next, are excitingly suggestive of what was to come in his later life. From scraps of documentation and recollection, and a little empathic witnessing of the physical landscapes that affected the development of his character, something of his way of encountering the world begins to come into focus. It is an attractive, enticing, bold and inquisitive one. If we were to adopt the same approach with Tilman, and look for how the childhood shaped the man, we would not find the task anything like so straightforward. As with feelings throughout his long span, or as with icebergs, the greater part lies concealed. The two existing biographies of Tilman that have been written – and there will surely be more – between them muster approximately fourteen pages to cover the years of his growing, up to the age of sixteen. If childhood is the lost domain, Tilman's seems destined to remain thus. Add in Peter Steele's five pages on Eric Shipton's life[1] up to the age of twenty-one and the total is less than twenty pages, shared between three writers, for the early lives of both subjects. Their beginnings, where clues to their puzzling adult characters would surely be found, are left markedly mysterious and vague.

James Boswell, incomparably the greatest of English biographers, is notoriously skimpy on the early years of Samuel Johnson. Even so, the monumental and definitive Birkbeck Hill/Powell edition

---

[1] In fairness to Peter Steele, his biography is subtitled 'Everest and Beyond', which is rather more than just a sales shibboleth in this case – the vast proportion of his book's emphasis lies here, where its account is both detailed and knowledgeable.

takes seventy-seven pages to cover these years. Richard Holmes's life of Shelley – the first in Holmes's impressive sequence of literary biographies – stretches itself to 234 pages in covering the same span with his subject. These figures leave me with the strong sense that there remain two prime opportunities here of which a rising generation of mountain writers might avail themselves. I wish them luck. There are accompanying lodes of high-grade information deposited at the Royal Geographical Society and in various American university library collections available for the telling in detail from start to finish of two of the most fascinating of twentieth-century lives. But that is something which is far beyond the present book's compass.

There is an enigma about the friendship between Shipton and Tilman. If you subscribe to Montaigne's view that 'friendship is kept alive by communication'[2] and have accepted a once general – and in some quarters still current, though let me assure you from personal knowledge that it is essentially mistaken – view of Tilman as a surly and uncommunicative misanthrope (and a misogynist to boot),[3] you might be led to wonder how on earth the relationship between himself and Shipton functioned at all, particularly in view of the intensity of the demands placed upon it in mountain-exploratory situations, where erstwhile friendships can become exceedingly irrational and volatile. In terms of Tilman's history, here was a man who, when he met the younger, less life-experienced Shipton, seems to have responded to him with the same recognition that Kent accorded to Lear: '. . . you have that in your countenance which I would fain call master.'[4] That immediately makes me want to look at what there was in the early moulding-years of Tilman that made him so susceptible, so ready to accept the gracefully-chaotic version of natural authority that Shipton manifestly possessed. My first instinct was to comb the early sections of the two Tilman biographies for such clues as they might offer. Here's J. R. L. Anderson on Tilman's parentage, from his 1980 book:

---

[2] Michel de Montaigne, 'On Friendship', in *Essays of Montaigne*, ed. E. J. Trechman (Oxford, 1927), p.184.
[3] As an index to how mistaken this is, it's worth considering the Tilman fan-club among notable feminists. Libby Purves, for example, edited a selection from his sailing books, and there are quotations from Tilman scattered throughout E. Annie Proulx's 2012 memoir *Bird Cloud*.
[4] *King Lear*, Act I, Scene iv, 29–30.

He married Adeline Rees, who came of a long line of Cumberland hill-farmers. Some of the family went to Wales, which brought her into the orbit of Liverpool and her future husband. Her family was hard-working and prosperous, providing at least one magistrate for Wales. After living for a time at Rock Ferry, Birkenhead, the Tilmans moved to Wallasey, first to Radnor Drive, and then to the big house called Seacroft in Grove Road, that was to be J. H. Tilman's home for the rest of his life.'[5]

Now, for purposes of comparison, Tim Madge's version of this background, in which we could expect to find substantial additional detail:

His wife, Adeline Rees, came from a long line of Cumberland hill-farmers; she considered, it is said, that she had married a little beneath her. After all, John Tilman was, albeit successful, still 'trade'. Mr and Mrs Tilman lived for a while in Birkenhead and then moved to Wallasey, first to Radnor Drive, then to a big house – Seacroft – in Grove Road where they lived for the rest of their lives.[6]

What's interesting here are the omissions from the apparent source, and the clues these might hold, which we might examine more closely. From the Anderson version, we learn that Mrs Tilman's family at some indeterminate past date had moved to Wales (later in his book Anderson confirms that Tilman 'had Welsh ancestry on his mother's side, and for a lover of mountains and the sea there could be no happier place').[7] We might anyway have deduced that Tilman's grandmother at least had been married to a Welshman, from that surname 'Rees'. We could probably speculate a little more and take the 'Adeline' – an anglicisation of Adelina, as in Adelina Patti (1843–1919), considered by Verdi to be the greatest soprano of her time – as a further sign of Welshness, the so-called 'Queen of Song' having made her home in the Swansea valley at Craig y Nos and spawned as many name sakes among nineteenth-century Welsh girlhood as Kylie Minogue was to do throughout particular strata of English society in our own time. It also explains the presence of

[5] J.R.L. Anderson, *High Mountains & Cold Seas* (Gollancz, 1980), p.25–6.
[6] Tim Madge, *The Last Hero: Bill Tilman* (Hodder & Stoughton, 1995), p.21.
[7] Anderson, *High Mountains*, p.232.

Tilman's mother in Liverpool – 'Lerpwl' to the Welsh, and the long-established unofficial capital of North Wales. We could go further and draw parallels between Madge's point about the former Miss Rees having married beneath her, and the way Shakespeare teases the Welsh obsession with genealogies through the figure of Owen Glendower in *Henry IV Part I*; though to do so might lay us open to the charge of mockery. So perhaps we had better just leave it at the clear establishment of descent from sheep-farming stock on his mother's side and a connection too with Wales, the hills of which are to be seen from every street end and open space in Liverpool and the Wirral.

From this we might – if we want to strain at the point a little – deduce a reason for Tilman's elder sister, another Adeline, to whom he was very close throughout his life, having bought in 1947 Bodowen on the Mawddach estuary, for herself and her brother to live there in sibling companionship. I could even postulate a genetic link between Tilman's phenomenal physical hardihood and that of his sheep-farming forebears – the Welsh sheep farmers I've known and worked with being the toughest and most resilient human beings I have ever encountered, putting most mere mountaineers to shame on the hill and able and willing socially to drink them under any convenient pub table. (I could elaborate on this trait in Tilman, in whose company during his later years the drinking of strong home-brewed beer began at twelve noon. For proof of the effect of this I need only look at the photographs I took of him in those pre-auto-focus days, not one of which is sharp.) I certainly think that the presence of the magistrate mentioned by Anderson and omitted by Madge may vouch for a family culture of the absolute rectitude that was one of the hallmarks of Tilman's character. And if we wish really to labour this, I could point to another of the great pleasures of our distinguished old Major's life.

This was the communal singing at the hotpot suppers of the Barmouth lifeboatmen – all of whom attended and sang magnificently at his 1978 memorial service in the beguiling and eccentric little Victorian church of Caerdeon, high above the Mawddach estuary and looking across to Cader Idris. Tilman attended Sunday service here whenever he was home at Bodowen and able to do so. The hotpot-supper singing was often quite bawdy, according to his niece Pam Davis, though how she would know puzzles me, since she would certainly not have been present at the renditions of 'Eskimo Nell',

'Dinah, Dinah, show us your leg', and the rest of the male repertoire (this vein always in English, of course, Wales being a respectable nation). I'm left perplexed as to why Madge should have seen fit to leave out material from his source which is at least suggestive, and points in interesting directions that are slightly less than certain and slightly more than empty surmise, when there is such a paucity of material about the boyhood. Two more useful hints to be pondered come from a letter home quoted by Madge with no comment other than a stiff one upon how to respond to the epistolary register of an Edwardian schoolboy:

> No excuse for mater not going to the Island if she can cross the channel, nor Adds [his elder sister Adeline] either. I don't think I will be able to manage the Dee party, the earliest [train] I will be able to get is the 1–15 which does not get in till 6–35.[8]

What is being talked about here is presumably an excursion to Hilbre ('the island'), off the north-western tip of the Wirral peninsula where the family lived, and a long-established place of resort to which you can walk at low tide, occasionally having to wade a shifting channel across the treacherous sands of the Dee estuary from West Kirby. It sounds from this letter to have been familiar ground, and is an exciting and enterprising place to reach, now a wardened nature reserve, and surprisingly wild[9] for somewhere so close to suburban living.

Suburban living, too, is an idea that we can draw from our biographers' scant supplied information. That progression of the Tilman family from Rock Ferry to Radnor Drive to the big house on Grove Road in Wallasey village had a rising trajectory. Rock Ferry is a jumble of crowded terraces and Madge is quite wrong to suggest that living here (he has it as the less specific and even more down-market Birkenhead) bespeaks success in trade. By no means does it do that, but success was not long in coming to the bustling and punctilious little dynamo (he was five feet four inches in height) that was John Hinkes Tilman, Liverpool boot-maker's son

---

[8] Madge, *Last Hero*, p.26.

[9] Not so surprising, perhaps, if you remember the reference in the fourteenth-century alliterative masterpiece *Sir Gawain and the Green Knight* to 'the wyldrenesse of Wyrale' (ed. Sir Israel Gollancz, Early English Text Society, London 1940, line 701).

and ultimately a prosperous sugar merchant. Radnor Drive, where Harold William, the Tilman family's youngest child, was born, was a move up in social terms – a pleasant enough packed street of semi-detached Edwardian villas with tiny gardens front and rear on the northern side of Wallasey near the infirmary. It leads down to the Egremont Promenade, bleakly exposed to the north-easterlies, a family-and-dog-walking type of place the long curve of which gives unimpeded views over the mouth of the Mersey to the continuous line of busy docks stretching north from Pier Head. Seacroft, the big house in Wallasey village with all the enormous expense of its maids and motor cars and garden parties and cooks, was a quantum social leap away from these two locations.

What we can say with absolute certainty is that something about the ambitious character of Tilman's father, the aspirations of his mother, the social mobility of the time, and Britain's contemporary trading activity can be read into the sequence of house moves. They bespeak a man who is doing exceedingly well in the sugar import business that – as mainstay of the last leg in the triangular trade between Africa, the West Indies and home – was both a source of lasting prosperity to Liverpool and an early foundation of the port's mercantile success, particularly during the time of slave-trafficking, for which, along with Bristol, Liverpool was one of Britain's two chief centres.

The occasional insecurities John Tilman is said to have revealed about 'losing everything' are those of a man who had risen from impoverished beginnings to a state of some opulence in a highly competitive environment. As to his younger son, a bright boy from Rock Ferry would not have been sent to Berkhamsted School, as Tilman was. He would have stayed instead at the good local grammar school in Wallasey, or at best crossed the river each day to attend the Bluecoat School in Liverpool or Merchant Taylors' at Crosby – both of them highly regarded educational establishments. John Tilman might have been 'in trade', but he was among the successful ones in the commercial powerhouse of early-twentieth-century Britain. You can be sure that his two sons would have been made aware of the attitudes necessary for success in life as he saw it, and also of the advantages they enjoyed which their self-made father had lacked – formal education in particular.

I wonder what else young Harold William imbibed in his father's presence, for the two of them seem always to have been on good,

Shipton and Tilman

close, respectful and even fondly jokey terms (Tilman in his school and wartime letters home enquires after his father as 'the Guv', and on one occasion around Armistice Day 1918 asks of his mother 'did the Guv get blotto?'). The necessity always to strive and never to show weakness? Fiscal prudence, in which matter father and son were both exemplary? How much of the romance of the great ships forever coming and going in the seaway on which his father's livelihood depended impressed itself on young Harold (as he was known in the family throughout his childhood)? Did the two of them ever walk hand in hand – for this was a warm, close family – down to the bottom of Radnor Drive with the father talking to his bright and favoured son of the ships and their cargoes and ports of origin – subjects on which a child's imagination seizes so eagerly and which transmute inevitably into the protean forms of adult life?

These biographical lacunae of the early years are susceptible, then, from the few surviving clues to a great deal of speculation that balance of probability would uphold. But still, there is that brick-wall dearth of detail about Harold Tilman's youthful *activity*. Did he scramble on the tough little red sandstone rocks of The Breck, for example, as Wallasey street urchins have done for generations and athletic rock-climbers more recently? Did the family ever find their way to those horizon-rimming westerly hills from which the mother had come? Where did they holiday, and was it ever with relatives there? What of the future explorer's natural curiosity, deriving from the physical presence of the Welsh hills and the fund of family recollection that Mrs Tilman must surely have shared at some time during her younger son's childhood, if she did not do so continually? There is something at the very least odd about the silence surrounding all this – a silence in which the future explorer's consciousness was shaped, and which he himself maintained about his own origins and early feelings in all explicit ways until the day he last sailed away 'Beyond the sunset, and the baths/Of all the western stars'.[10]

Rather than spend any longer chasing shadows or attempting to plump out the slimmest of hints, perhaps it's better to move on and consider Tilman's education, for just as there are clear distinctions

---

[10] From Tennyson's 'Ulysses' – a highly significant poem in relation to the lives of our two subjects, and one which yielded the title for Shipton's second volume of autobiography.

between the class origins[11] of Shipton and Tilman – the former from professional and colonial stock, the latter descended from cobblers and merchants – here again we find interesting contrasts. Shipton, before failing his Common Entrance, had been down for Harrow – distinctly in the first rank of English public schools, and this counted for a great deal in the society of his time. Tilman, after preparatory school in New Brighton and a year at the local Wallasey Grammar School, at the age of eleven was sent away to the boarding school in Berkhamsted already attended by his elder brother Kenneth. Harry Calvert, in his excellent and forensically acute account of the mountaineering career of Frank Smythe – also an alumnus of Berkhamsted – tersely remarks of his subject, in explaining the social difficulties he encountered with the mountaineering establishment of his time, that he 'remained a failed product of a second-rank school, who had attended no university, let alone the right one'.[12] With that shaft, he neatly skewers aspects of the future careers of both our subjects in this book.

We should be on our guard here, however, against assuming that 'second-rank' means 'second-rate'. It is a social distinction and not an academic one. Berkhamsted, though quite recently established in the great English public school scheme of things, was certainly not the latter, and the choice of it for their sons' education had no doubt been well-researched by the Tilmans. It proved a remarkably good and happy one (far more so than for the novelist Graham Greene, six years behind Tilman at the school where his father by then was headmaster. Greene recorded in his autobiography that he was bullied and unhappy there, and several times attempted suicide before being sent to London for psychoanalysis). The school buildings occupied – still occupy – an imposing, grim and workhouse-like building on the Chesham Road, 'part rosy Tudor, part hideous modern brick the colour of dolls'-house plaster hams – where the misery started'.[13] For all its unprepossessing appearance,

---

[11] The significance of these pre-Great War can scarcely be overstated, and is ever-present in the literature of the period. The culling of all classes of men in the 1914–18 carnage undoubtedly abated its effect, though the older remnants of the 'upper' and ruling class, spared combat through age but still powerful within the country's institutions, ensured that class-influence held sway for a few decades more.

[12] Harry Calvert, *Smythe's Mountains* (Gollancz, 1985) p.128.

[13] Graham Greene, *A Sort of Life* (Bodley Head, 1971), p.12.

its academic reputation, like the Tilman family's fortune, was rising fast. The headmaster since 1887 had been Thomas Charles Fry, a doctor of divinity, a Christian socialist in the Charles Kingsley mould and a strict disciplinarian, who had personally funded the construction of the school's remarkably beautiful chapel – a small gem of high Victorian ecclesiastical architecture. Dr Fry may have been a man of rigid principles, but under his headship, in the typically understated words of the *Dictionary of National Biography*, his school 'attained a recognised position among the public schools of the country'. He was a man of mordant wit and the best Christian principles; a supporter of the Workers' Educational Association; and an angler, to emphasise his philosophical and outdoor side.

There was something else highly significant in what he brought to the imaginative life of the school. Anderson, in *High Mountains & Cold Seas*, observes that it 'is curious that what was then a relatively small school should have produced three such outstanding climbers as H. W. Tilman, Frank Smythe and Raymond Greene'.[14] It becomes a little less curious when you learn that the good Dr Fry, among his many other interests, was also a keen alpinist and member of the Alpine Club. When Dr Fry moved on, after Tilman's first year at the school, to become Dean of Lincoln – a post he held until his death and in which he raised what was then the astronomical sum of £100,000 to preserve the ruinous fabric of that wonderful cathedral – he was succeeded as head by his second master and cousin-by-marriage Charles Henry Greene (himself married to his second cousin Marion Raymond Greene, who became mother to a numerous and distinguished progeny including Graham Greene, Hugh Carleton Greene of the BBC, and Raymond Greene of whom we will hear more in a later chapter).

Charles – and it is rather charming the way in which the schoolboy Tilman refers to him thus in his correspondence home – was also a mountaineer of sorts. In his succinct and witty memoir *Moments of Being* – a memoir which also, significantly, is extremely light on childhood, allotting to this and to family background rather less than a single page (is 'children should be seen and not heard' the ruling principle here, I wonder, that extends even to life-writing among this generation?) – Charles Greene's son Raymond records that 'My father loved mountains and walking in them, but he was

14 Anderson, *High Mountains*, p.30.

never a climber in the sense of frequenting places where a rope around the waist was a necessity. Perhaps he had in his youth the itch to climb; he certainly encouraged the itch in his children.'[15] We may not be able to pierce the obscurity of the past, but our crystal ball is beginning to offer interesting presentiments about Tilman's future. They are for the present no more than that, however. Perhaps the idea, the imagery, the symbolism of mountains was established at Berkhamsted – in designs for the stained glass of Fry's school chapel for example?

The young Tilman was an outstanding pupil at what was academically a very good school. He was consistently top of his form across a wide range of subjects that included algebra, divinity, history, geography and French. His conduct was beyond reproach and his sporting prowess was such that he was captain of fives, an excellent gymnast, and played in the school's First XI at soccer (an interesting contemporary choice at a time when rugby was the predominant public-school sport). He was also an enthusiastic participant in the Officers' Training Corps, and a good shot. As he progressed through the school he was attracted to science; at the age of fifteen he won a foundation scholarship, which exempted him from tuition fees – a distinction that would surely have gratified his father. In due course, in 1916, had the world progressed in its peaceful Edwardian way, he would no doubt have been accepted into one of the more academically distinguished Oxford or Cambridge colleges. Instead, on the 28 June 1914 on the Latin Bridge in Sarajevo, as the sixteen-year-old Harold William Tilman was packing his bags for the long summer vacation and looking forward to a few rounds of golf on the links at West Kirby with the set of clubs his father had given him as reward for his academic endeavours, the Archduke Franz Ferdinand and his wife Sophie, Duchess of Hohenberg, were shot dead by Gavrilo Princip, a young Serbian nationalist less than four years older than Tilman, and within five weeks the Great War had begun.

Perhaps at this point we need to change our perspective, and instead of looking into our subject's past and lamenting what we don't know, from that crucial year of 1914 look into the future and see what he became in that. What particularly recommends this tactic is how different it is to the one we've adopted with Shipton. The

---

[15] Raymond Greene, *Moments of Being* (Heinemann, 1974) p. 1.

child's relative freedom from family constraints in Shipton's case, and the circumstances of his early years, ultimately allowed him to express himself through a markedly romantic and nature-orientated individualism. Perhaps for Tilman the clue lies in the contrast. His early life was secure, contained within the bosom of a loving and stable family – conformist and conventional too, and the more rigorously so because of the lowliness of the father's beginnings. It's hard to imagine a sixteen-year-old Shipton trailing those golf clubs around some suburban links. What is certain is that Tilman was very quickly caught up in the patriotic and martial fervour that characterised those first months of what was to be so dreadful and protracted a war. The autumn term of 1914 at Berkhamsted was to be his last. In November he took a competitive examination to secure a cadetship at the Royal Military Academy in Woolwich. He came fifty-fifth out of 111 – a curiously undistinguished result for a boy who had hitherto been doing so well, though we don't know the circumstances of his decision, the range of subjects on which he was tested, or how much time he had given himself for preparation – and in January of 1915 began training for a regular army commission with the Royal Artillery.

Soldiering, through the values it was traditionally seen to inculcate and before a series of infamies in the second half of the twentieth century damaged its reputation, had long carried with it a sense, perhaps more rooted in rhetoric than real chivalry, of the subordination of individual ambition to public good. Wade Davis's *Into the Silence: The Great War, Mallory and the Conquest of Everest* has examined with a degree of thoroughness the way in which this ethos played its part in the Everest expeditions of the 1920s. At a tangent, to illustrate this alliance between the ethos of soldiering and the traditional one of mountaineering, I'd like to bring in a story about John Barry – former captain in the Royal Marine Commandos and a man for whom the old-fashioned adjective 'dashing' might almost have been invented.

John was one of the best all-round mountaineers of his generation, a fine rock-climber, an outstanding ice-climber and a sound presence on many Himalayan expeditions. One Christmas he gave me a copy of that grand old soldier A. P. Wavell's moving and unpredictable anthology of poems committed to memory: *Other Men's Flowers*. John's inscription reads 'So that you might know how a soldier thinks.' I've thought much about that over the years, not least in regard to John himself. One thing that for me stands out about him is the occasion when he was climbing Everest in 1993. He was part of a group that had a perfect pre-monsoon May day for the ascent – a rare opportunity. John, well-acclimatised and an immensely strong performer at altitude, would have made the summit with ease. Instead, with another climber in the party suffering badly from altitude sickness, he volunteered to turn round and shepherd the sick companion down off the mountain whilst the rest of the group pressed on for the top. You might think this the natural human response, and morally it is. Sixty years before, Jack Longland had shepherded his eight porters down from Camp Six at 27,400 feet in deteriorating weather. In Longland's day, the altruism and acceptance of responsibility was automatic, axiomatic. I've always taken John Barry's selfless action on his own potential summit day – and these chances seldom come again – as a prime example of 'how a soldier thinks', and also of how a true mountaineer like Longland thinks, in quickly evaluating a situation and making the right, humane and unselfish decision.

Which brings me back to Tilman, and a conversation I had about him with his feisty and sharply intelligent niece Pam Davis – herself a soldier's wife, with clear and fierce blue eyes under the scrutiny of which any imposter might quail – at Bodowen, five years after his disappearance at sea in 1977. It was a long and wide-ranging conversation to which Pam, prompted and abetted by her brigadier husband Derek – one of those upright, informed and insightful officers who are the greatest strength of the British army – provided a long series of the most vivid recollections. One of them was of meeting Tilman at Liverpool's Lime Street station in the early June of 1940 after the evacuation of the British army from the beaches of Dunkirk:

> You just knew that he would come home. There were men all around him getting off the train in rags and remnants of their uniforms and there he was, dapper, with his fore-and-aft forage cap neatly perched. He was absolutely punctilious, always saluted smartly, always patriotic, never any question of fighting against authority. Once he was talking about the possibility of being taken prisoner of war: 'I will never, never stay as a prisoner,' he told us. 'Don't expect me to survive if that happens. I shall have to try to escape.' It wasn't false

heroics from him. 'You might as well know the facts,' he'd say.

There was the time with his battery in the Western Desert where he went on ahead and said to the bombardier who accompanied him, 'Stay twenty paces behind and step exactly where I step.' That poor young fellow had absolutely no idea until the danger was past that they'd walked straight through a minefield. But you see, in all this what I'd want to emphasise above anything else is that he was a professional soldier. The first time I ever saw him he was in khaki. I'd gone down with my mother to the Seacombe ferry and there was a man coming up the slope with a bush hat – he got in the car and his elbow broke the mica window, clumsy bugger that he was . . .

It is surely not too far-fetched to see the effect of his time at Woolwich in all this. Tilman applied himself to his studies there whilst the slaughter at Loos and Ypres was taking place just the other side of the English Channel and the demand for subalterns to replace their depleting ranks was growing ever more urgent. It could doubtless be argued that in opting for the Royal Artillery rather than an infantry regiment his chances of surviving the war were exponentially increased, but you can also be quite sure from his conduct through the Great War and the one that followed it that this played no part whatsoever in his thinking. He learned the triangulation techniques appropriate to an artillery officer that would serve him so well in the future as mountain explorer and sailor. He was instructed in all the mysteries of riding and equine management, a team of six horses being the motive power for each field gun used on the Western Front. At the age of seventeen, in July 1915, he passed out from Woolwich and was commissioned as a second lieutenant in the Royal Field Artillery. For the next six months he fretted around at various supervisory tasks on the home front and then, on a Saturday evening in January, whilst he was on home leave, a telegram arrived at Seacroft ordering him to return immediately to his barracks in Preston. By Monday night, still a month short of his eighteenth birthday, he had embarked for Le Havre. For most of the next three years, his home address was somewhere on the Western Front.

The literature of the Great War, like that of the other seminal twentieth-century blow to the ameliorative psyche which was the

Holocaust,[16] has produced a literature of industrial proportions, and one which, in a researched and ersatz way, is on-going through popular novels such as *Birdsong* and the Pat Barker trilogy that prefigure holocaust fiction like *The Boy in the Striped Pyjamas* or *The Reader*. The authentic works of the major writers who drew from direct experience – Henri Barbusse, Erich Maria Remarque, Wilfred Owen, Siegfried Sassoon, Isaac Rosenberg, Ivor Gurney, Edmund Blunden, Robert Graves, Henry Williamson, David Jones and so many others – have assumed the authority and familiarity of classic texts. A mere catalogue of names, some of them still of horrifying force and resonance – the Somme, Ypres, Passchendaele, Mametz Wood, Pilkem Ridge – evokes the appalling, disastrous, terrifying events through which these men lived and most others died. In view of our familiarity with this material it feels supernumerary to recount in detail Tilman's war service, though I will return to this in terms of its affect, having given the briefest of outlines.

The sources for the history of engagement of the regiments, divisions and brigades in which Tilman served and fought are clear and precise. The *History of the Scarborough Pals' Battery* by Foord and Northern, the *War Diary of the 161st Brigade* – these are where the military historian or the biographer looks, amid an immense stock of official records and first-hand accounts of service from this most literary of wars. Among their bald calendars of battles and losses and awards for valour you must let the eye of imagination discern the young subaltern moving among the smoke and the 'monstrous anger of the guns./ . . . the stuttering rifles' rapid rattle.'[17]

'We lost our best sergeant the other day, up at the OP. A whizz-bang came through the window as he was looking out. It's always

---

[16] The dropping of the American atomic bombs on Hiroshima and Nagasaki is surely another, and has always been heavily endorsed by the 'might-is-right' school of thought, which argues that it saved Allied lives – an historically dubious point – and thus attempts to make of it a philosophically different case. Its operating at a slight remove from direct human agency also serves to excuse it in some quarters. It still seems to me to count as an atrocity of the utmost magnitude. Though Tilman might well have disagreed with me here, he having written at one point in his best sardonically tongue-in-cheek and misanthropic manner that 'there is a strong case for dropping bombs on civilians because so very few of them can be deemed truly inoffensive'. Swift couldn't have put it better. I asked in one of our conversations at Bodowen if this apparently outrageous observation had been 'A Modest Proposal'.

'Indeed it was,' he responded, 'and we'll be having fricasséed baby for lunch.'
[17] Wilfred Owen, 'Anthem for Doomed Youth'.

the way – the best fellows get done in – the rotters escape.' That
happened in the days just before his eighteenth birthday on St
Valentine's Day 1916 – the period of the Somme battles was no time
for the army to heed niceties of regulations about age. Six weeks
after his birthday he was wounded in the thigh by shrapnel from
a rifle grenade. In less than a fortnight he was out of hospital and
back at the front. One of his first tasks was to instil some discipline
into the work of the wagons bringing supplies and munitions to his
battery. It was needed. This from a letter home of 24 April 1916:

> I came down in place of a man gone on leave, and the first day
> three brass-hats came round. They had a whole heap to say – I
> had nuffin', and at the end of a gruelling half-hour I had the air
> of one who has been caught in the machinery. In consequence
> I have sworn death and destruction to the NCOs and other
> ranks abiding at the wagon lines.

Those 'NCOs and other ranks' for the most part would have
been his seniors by birth. Authority was being bred in him at a
rapid rate. He was present with his brigade throughout the Battle
of the Somme, crucially involved in the taking of the seemingly
impregnable fortress of Thiepval, and still there at the incessant
labour of observing the enemy movements and laying and firing
the field-guns in the vain hope that their continuous bombardment
would cut the rolls of barbed wire laid in front of the German lines[18]
when this defining battle of the Great War fizzled out in November
rain and mud where over a million men had fallen in the space
of four months of murderous mayhem, their machine-gunned and
shell-ravaged corpses left hanging from the unbreached wire. I don't

---

[18] The American literary critic Paul Fussell, in one of the most intelligent
retrospective accounts of the Great War and its literature, gives the following
succinct and tragically accurate assessment of this project to cut the German wire
by artillery – a project that actually added to the astronomical casualty lists by
creating bottlenecks around the few gaps created in the wire, on which the German
machine-gunners could then concentrate their fire after rising from their deep
dugouts, upon the lifting of the British artillery bombardments in observance of
the metronomically-asinine orders from Haig: 'British attempts to break through
the German line . . . failed, first, because of insufficient artillery preparation – for
years no-one had any idea how much artillery fire would be needed to destroy the
German barbed-wire and to reach the solid German deep dug-outs.' (Paul Fussell,
The Great War and Modern Memory, Oxford, 1975, p.10.)

for a moment doubt that the Royal Artillery's collective failure in the task allotted to them, and the everyday ensuing massacres, registered savagely in the eighteen-year-old Tilman's conscience. This was the formative experience against which his whole future life and its sanguine acceptance of risk must be measured.

By mid January, amid the winter snows of northern France, he watched as the infantrymen of the Manchester Regiment went over the top, advanced on and took the so-called Munich Trench held by a crack Bavarian unit. With a squad of telephonists and runners the young artillery subaltern followed the infantry to the captured position and was again wounded, seriously this time and once again in the thigh. Despite this he continued with the work of establishing communications back to his battery until they were functioning, at which point he collapsed from blood loss and was carried back by his men to safety, evacuated to a dressing station, picked out as one of the fortunate ones among the thousands of wounded for whom something could be done, and eventually repatriated to a temporary hospital in Somerville College, Oxford. Had the war not come along, he might have been attending dances here. Instead he was a wounded soldier writing letters home that reveal much of how his cast of mind was being shaped by adverse circumstance, as in this one of 27 January:

> I'll just explain why I'm not up, a sort of history of the case, you know, not too technical you know, although I'm getting a bit of a high flyer at medical terms. Soon after I got here they took the stitches out of the wound (pronounced properly please)[19] which had healed. But unfortunately there was a whacking great blood clot inside dying to get out, so of course the wound burst open again. Since when they've been busy getting the blood out, which is now nearly finished when I hope it will begin to heal.
>
> Apparently the Le Touquet people, not too cleverly, sewed it up so close tight that absolutely nothing could get out. I thought I would just tell you this by way of explanation.

You can imagine the amount of stitching 'the Le Touquet people' had to do, and hence understand the occasional errors they made.

---

[19] The vogue pronunciation was to rhyme with 'sound'.

His next letter home, written to his parents three days after his nineteenth birthday, is very revealing of a growing irony that has attached itself to his wholehearted commitment to the fight, and also of the elliptical humour, jejune here but to develop into a subtle and characteristic brand, that enlivens all his later writing:

> . . . a shadow is spreading itself over hospital life, the convalescent home scare spreads consternation everywhere (poetry). Hotels are to be taken over for convalescents, these are only allowed out between 1 p.m. and 6 p.m. with blue-bands so that theatres are inaccessible and drinks unobtainable. What a war! Old boy, what a war! After, say, six weeks in the rollicking home of innocent jollity and mirth, the unfortunate sufferer is released for a space of ten days, when he is again gathered to the fold for light duty. After perhaps a day or two of this restful and exhilarating life, the unhappy man is boarded and passed fit for General Service.

Thus the principle, and now the view of one who it closely concerned, regarding likely consequence:

> Events now move rapidly, two hours see him in France, three and he is in the forefront of the battle. Two alternatives now present themselves to the 'arassed 'ero – a Blighty[20] and the prospect of a repetition of what he has just gone through, or a bloody end sur le champs d'honneur! Choosing the lesser of two evils the afore-mentioned 'H.H.' stops a five.nine with his heaving breast, thus passing into a land where convalescent homes are not and light duty is unknown.
>
>   This little picture (in no way overdrawn) of what is impending, is more than sufficient to make the blind walk, the lame see, the incurables die without waiting, and people like meself get better on time.

Hardly a reassuring letter for his mother and father to receive, you might think. And very indicative of how the combatants had come to view the conflict. But there was some good news for proud parents to ponder. In making it to Oxford (and a women's college

---

[20] I.e. a hospital spell in Britain, such as Tilman was on when he wrote this letter.

at that), instead of a degree, for his part in the Munich Trench action he was awarded an immediate Military Cross by his Corps Commander. It was conferred on him in April, by which time he was back on his feet and the troublesome wound had all but healed. He himself was back in action by June at the Battle of Messines Ridge – a dominant natural feature to the south of Ypres held by the German army that was ultimately taken by General Plumer's tactic of having Royal Engineers sappers tunnel beneath and lay a million pounds of high-explosives along twenty-one adits. With artillery support after the detonation of the mines[21] on the morning of 7 June 1917, infantry took the ridge, 7,000 German prisoners were captured and two miles gained, before the assault once more ground to a halt.

So it went on: good men dying or being maimed all around him; the incessant threat of instant destruction, arduous physical labour in managing the horses and guns, the need for instant stock-taking and response in every developing situation. He was promoted full lieutenant in July, and awarded a bar to his Military Cross. He professed not to know why (the citation read 'for gallantry and devotion to duty in action' – the hackneyed words carry an extraordinary weight, the inexpressible defaulting inevitably to these conventional forms, when you consider the reality of the events to which they apply). He was continually involved in the thick of the fighting, and particularly in the third Ypres battle of August–September 1917, at Pilckem Ridge and in the dire defining landscape, all dead stark trees and waterlogged shell craters each with their floating quota of human and animal[22] corpses, of Poelcapelle.

---

[21] Not all of the mines, it should be noted – two failed to detonate at the time. One of these went off in July 1955, injuring no one but causing damage in the nearby town of Ploegsteert. Another still lies under Ploegsteert Wood, biding its time . . .

[22] Before Michael Morpurgo's children's novel *War Horse* (2006), and Rosalind Belben's moving adult novel *Our Horses in Egypt* (2008) so graphically evoked their suffering, we forgot too easily the battlefield horses of the Western Front and other theatres of war, pulling guns and wagons through the omnipresent mud, terrified by the sound of shelling, often maimed or eviscerated by shrapnel. Throughout his life Tilman's empathy for animals was profound, and surely sprang from these experiences. In the Western Desert in the Second World War he adopted a cat. And in the conversation with Pam Davis quoted from above she told of how, before he left on his last voyage, he had asked if she would have Toffee – a rough-haired, amiable, barrel-chested and short-legged terrier-sized dog of indeterminate breed of whom he was inordinately fond – out of kennels for Christmas.

The summer of 1917 was one throughout which even the sky seemed to be continually weeping, and it gave way to the heavier rains and deepening mud of autumn. He could have accepted a post offered him behind the lines as orderly officer to a brigadier. He stayed at the front. When parcels of delicacies and treats arrived from home, he shared them among his mess mates. He did move on, but not to an easier option. What he chose instead, or rather what chose him, was a faster-moving and yet-more dangerous version of what he had been engaged in for the last eighteen months. In November he left his brigade and followed his commanding officer Colonel Cotton, who had been promoted Brigadier-General, into the Royal Horse Artillery, Number 1 Battery of which was attached to the 1st Cavalry Division. Cotton – a cavalier eccentric, one of whose quirks on misty mornings was to be out in no-man's-land shooting partridges – had recommended him to this as a particularly promising young officer. The RHA was distinctly a more prestigious outfit than his previous Royal Field Artillery, more mobile, equipped with lighter guns, and used to being deployed rapidly in support of infantry advances. (I wonder if there was a subconscious mirroring between this change from siege-tactics to a lighter, faster-moving and ultimately more successful style of warfare, and the great dialectic Shipton and Tilman engaged in throughout their mountaineering careers in favour of lightweight expeditions and against the massive operations exemplified by Everest '33 and '53 – the latter, it might be noted, even took along rifles and mortars as part of its equipment.)

He made new friends. They were soon killed.[23] The year turned. The Germans were withdrawing units from the Russian front and were preparing to use them against the Allied forces in their last major throws of the dice. The Germans were briefly in the ascendancy, their infantry forcing the British soldiers back, and Tilman engaged in a sequence of swift-moving covering actions with the Horse Gunners to guard the tactical retreat. A letter home gives the flavour:

. . . as you see we're scrapping. At the present moment I have

---

[23] Not all of them – another officer under Cotton's command who survived a war in which he fought through every major campaign was Major Edward ('Teddy') Norton, who established the pre-war altitude record on Everest in 1924. After Brigadier General Bruce fell ill of malaria on the 1924 approach march Lieutenant Colonel Norton, as he then was, assumed command of the ill-destined expedition. His leadership and personal qualities garnered the highest praise.

not eat for 24 hrs and have neither washed nor shaved nor taken my boots off for days. Wouldn't have missed it for a lot. Today has been great fun, we have had the Boche in view most of the time. The weather is priceless. This is <u>war</u>.

War it was (as well as being good training for serious mountaineering), and the tide was definitely turning. The German army, even after replenishment by those divisions drawn back from the Russian front where the Russian internal conflict had rendered them supernumary, was exhausted and decimated. In March 1918 a major German offensive, 'Operation Michael', was ultimately contained at the First Battle of Bapaume, Tilman's battery playing its part here in covering the initial retreat. The Allied forces were massively augmented by the late entry of America into the fray. In early August the Battle of Amiens began, giving way later that month to the Second Battle of Bapaume. These two battles are generally taken as the point at which ultimate Allied victory began to seem assured. The elation and total commitment of Tilman's little note are rather more than simply the lift in spirits freed from the omnipresent clinging mud. The tactics were changing, the attritional nature of trench warfare giving place to endgame, to Haig and Foch's Grand Offensive, and on 11 November to the Armistice. The shaping experience of Tilman's life was over. Yet beyond doubt the ghosts of these actions travelled with him for the rest of his life.

The Great War had given him much, apart from the ever-present nightmare of it all – the buffeting of high explosives, the air filled with razor shards of steel, the fast bullets and the slow putrefaction of the dead. (Consider his celibacy without prurience and with respect, asking yourself how could anyone look to flesh for pleasure, having seen its ultimate fate in the mud all around. How anyone could bear with all the mincing and moping of biological sparring[24]

---

[24] When I was young and presumptuous and enjoying the brief, mutually amused friendship that grew between us in the last year of his life, I did ask Tilman about the lack of women:

'I've had my peccadilloes, but the trouble with women is, they get in the damned way,' was his response.

I didn't press. And nor, incidentally, do I take this as a sexist comment. A woman devoted to a wholly active life could say exactly the same thing, and would surely have met with his approval. Though he still wouldn't have wanted her around. Madge's speculation about the likelihood or otherwise of his use of prostitutes, incidentally, to my mind is as distasteful as it is inappropriate.

after so long and close an acquaintance with eschatology. And as to his legendary abruptness, what use posturing fools to a man like this?) He had experienced the intense comradeship and mutual recognition of soldiers in action; through urgent and arduous labour his young physique had grown immensely strong and resilient, and his mind had grown to match; he had endured the rigours of weather, the rough diet, the plain food cooked over spirit stoves and wood fires. He had twice won the Military Cross – the third-highest[25] British decoration for valour after the Victoria Cross and the Distinguished Service Order, and granted in recognition of 'an act or acts of exemplary gallantry during active operations against the enemy on land'; had been on the Western Front in the thick of the fighting at a time when a subaltern's average life expectancy, it has been calculated, was eleven days. When the war finally came to an end he was still several months short of his twenty-first birthday.

Almost sixty years later I was a rather indulged young conversational partner he had met on a mountain and invited thereafter regularly to his home to take part in a favourite game of matching eighteenth-century literary quotations. I was used also, I suspect, as a willing and attentive listener to the life ruminations of a man who knew his time was drawing to a close. After the death in September 1974 of his beloved sister Addy, with whom he shared his life at Bodowen, he had been left quite isolated and lonely. 'I feel I have lost my sheet anchor,' he wrote to his biographer and friend John Anderson.[26] I asked him once, as we drank his bitter, gritty eleven o'clock coffee in front of a winter fire at Bodowen, this hovering question:

'What about the Great War, Major Tilman?'

He looked at me very sharply, held my gaze, shook his head, in the heaviest silence turned away and in a lost intensity studied the smoke and flames in his hearth. After a time he looked up again, nodded as if I would understand, and without words offered me more coffee. His lips were pursed and his eyes were moist. He was not a man who showed his feelings.

I know of only a very few things that he wrote about the Great War. The most significant passage among these is from his great

---

[25] A military historian would rightly point out that there were two other gallantry awards at this level – the Military Medal and the Distinguished Service Cross.
[26] Anderson, *High Mountains*, p.330.

post-war Asian travel narrative *Two Mountains and a River*, and it runs like this:

> . . . after the first war, when one took stock, shame mingled with satisfaction at finding oneself still alive. One felt a bit like the Ancient Mariner; so many better men, a few of them friends, were dead:
>
> > *'And a thousand thousand slimy things*
> > *Lived on; and so did I.'*[27]

It is the strangest and saddest summary expression of survivor guilt, in which the living and the dead somehow have become transposed, and those who still breathe have taken on the dreadful glisten of all those mutilated, mud-drowned shell-hole corpses.

Impossible for us to understand, then, how the Great War registered, in the consciousness of this man who had known so little of boyhood or adolescence, throughout the six decades that remained to him. All we can do is admire the authority, the hardihood, the rigour and the discipline that were forged in those flames. And then move on, to consider how they availed him and his companions in what was to come.

---

[27] H. W. Tilman: *The Seven Mountain Travel Books* (Diadem Books, 1983), p.517. The lines in italics are of course from Coleridge.

4

Mountains-bound: Shipton's apprenticeship

An idyll lived through at the right time can inform the whole of your life. The two and a half years at a crucial stage of adolescence that Shipton spent in Bevis-land shaped his whole outlook on the world thenceforwards, leading him into the realisation at which he arrived in his mid twenties of what was a viable way to lead his life. He described it as coming to him almost as an epiphany during his journey back to India from the north side of Everest in 1933. In company with the geologist Lawrence Wager he had made his way across a strip of unexplored country and over a new pass into Sikkim. The discussions he had with Wager on this mountain trek were a significant determining influence. They consolidated a new emphasis in Shipton's mountain activity away from the climbing of peaks for their own sakes to an enthusiasm for more general modes of exploration – to a fascination with wider questions of geography, in which the attainment of summits was incidental rather than central. Twenty years later, this shift was to provide his detractors in the conquest-at-any-cost, Everest-obsessed faction of the interwar and post-Second World War British mountaineering establishment with all too easy a target. In the epiphanic moment of 1933, unaware of future political implication, his mind worked over the ground thus:·

Why not spend the rest of my life doing this sort of thing? There was no way of life that I liked more, the scope appeared to be unlimited, others had done it, vague plans had already begun to take shape, why not put some of them into practice? It was a disturbing idea, one that caused me much heart searching and many sleepless nights. The most obvious snag, of course, was lack of private means; but surely such a mundane consideration could not be decisive. In the first place I was convinced that expeditions could be run for a tithe of the cost generally considered necessary. Secondly, if one could produce useful or interesting results one would surely find support; and as experience grew, so too would the quality of the results . . . The fact that I had no training in any particular branch of science was a more serious obstacle. But might not this defect be remedied as one went along . . .?[1]

This then, some years along the path beyond schooldays, was the blueprint for a future life the confidence for a drawing of which was rooted in the rural wanderings, explorations and encounters of his Cranborne Chase years. In those youthful journeys, finding what lay beyond the brow of the next ridge or on the other side of the tangled wood was a simple matter of finding the paths that led in the desired direction, studying the topography, developing an instinct for the lie of the land and examining carefully its features and their interrelationship from every new angle that presented itself. To read a landscape is an art every bit as complex, multidimensioned and long in the learning as that required for the proper reading of a book. Bare literacy is the norm in both. It would be difficult to overstate how important this schooling was in the approach to his future in exploration. And better, wider, gentler country for his novitiate than Cranborne Chase, the chalk downs and Dorset border region would have been hard to find. Tilman in his brief and laconic journal entries[2] often mentions Shipton's instinctive sense for a route, and compares it with his own. One such, for 30 May 1934, at the time they were engaged in exploration of the Rishi gorge, runs: 'Shipton's route-memory invaluable as usual, self hopeless'. This gift – and it

---

[1] Eric Shipton, *Upon That Mountain* (Hodder & Stoughton, 1943), p.139. (Shipton, p.400)

[2] For the opportunity of seeing extracts from these, duly deciphered from ancient pencil-scrawl, I am indebted to the late Dr David Pluth. As a correspondent and keeper of journals, incidentally, despite his protestations of incompetence and negligence Shipton is extraordinarily vivid and diligent – and very much in the ascendant here over his habitual mountain companion, who reserved his writing genius strictly for those droll, ironic, cultured masterpieces of the literature of mountain travel.

is such, deriving from fortunate circumstance fully experienced – Shipton owed in some considerable degree to the roaming days with Jim Horsfall and others in the west Wiltshire countryside during the first half of the 1920s.

Nor was the route-finding the only interest that founded itself in the experiences of that time and lasted into his mature years. Like Cecil Shipton, Jim Horsfall was a keen ornithologist. As with most boys of his day, this chiefly found active and acquisitive expression in a pastime now highly illegal in Britain, and rightly so – that of egg-collecting. On one occasion by their favourite hidden lake at Fonthill, Jim spotted a hobby, hawking after dragonflies and eating them delicately on the wing. They followed this beautiful, rare, noisy little falcon and located its ramshackle nest – formerly that of a crow – near the top of one of the high trees. From a neighbouring lofty perch they kept careful watch to confirm the identification, and check that they were not confusing their bird with the more common kestrel; then, the falcon being away from the nest, Jim climbed up and stole the eggs. It was one of only four species lacking from his collection, which in itself is an incredible and an appalling thought. For some few things we can be grateful that time and mores change.

Though idylls can have an afterlife in their effect on an individual's outlook and imagination, the actual life-phases inevitably give way one to the next. As Shipton was approaching his seventeenth birthday in the summer of 1924, whilst the boys were away on their vacation, Dr Crawford's educational establishment moved from the bucolic delights of the countryside around Pyt House to a place more convenient for the metropolis, where parents of most of the boys lived. The new location was at Aston Clinton, just east of Aylesbury and under the Chilterns escarpment. This more straitened physical environment was accompanied by the introduction of new school rules, to match the new surroundings of housing estates, golf courses, main roads and suchlike horrors of civilisation. The boys were now required to sport top hat and tails every Sunday – in his journal Shipton mentions that an old tail-coat of his – presumably one and the same – dragged out of his wardrobe and taken as spare clothing for the Nanda Devi reconnaissance was eagerly seized upon by Angtharkay). On weekdays a boater, its band displaying the school colours, was de rigueur.

These restrictions on former personal freedoms were, however, balanced by a new sphere of activity gradually emerging during his vacations. In the summer of 1923,[3] when he had just turned sixteen, his enterprising and itinerant mother, her second widowhood having thoroughly confirmed her in an addiction to travel, took Eric and his sister Marge to the Pyrenees – then as now the last great unspoiled mountain-wilderness area of Europe. In Pau, they walked along the riverside promenade that looks out on to range upon range of dramatic sawtooth peaks, and then travelled south into the mountains, where sights like the Cirque de Gavarnie, the Breche de Roland and the strangely twisted molar shape of the twin-summited Pic du Midi d'Ossau fired his imagination. Back at Pyt House that autumn, his chosen reading from the school library for the darkening evenings was Edward Whymper's *Travels Amongst the Great Andes of the Equator*, published in 1891–2. Again, in many ways the choice was fortuitous and the text a shaping influence. *Travels* is a wiser, slower, less disputatious, more curious and wide-ranging work[4] than Whymper's celebrated – and highly dramatic and competitive – *Scrambles Amongst the Alps* of 1871, to which Shipton came at a slightly later date and which recounted, among other mountaineering achievements, events leading up to the first ascent of the Matterhorn and the disaster that befell the party on the descent. *Travels* also describes wilder, higher, less visited and populous country. And it fixed the notion of mountain travel as

[3] There are occasional inconsistencies in given dates and other facts between Shipton's two published volumes of autobiography. These are most frequent in the years up to his departure for Africa in 1928. The ones used here have been cross-checked with correspondence, journals, logbooks and other people's accounts and assessed against Shipton's own recollections. I suspect that this area of confusion may have been a contributory factor in Peter Steele's cursory treatment of the period in what is otherwise a thorough and judicious account of Shipton's life, and I sympathise! There is no element of criticism here – memory stretched over decades inevitably tends towards the soft focus. The recurrent charges of vagueness levelled against Shipton by some of his companions, which might be taken as an associated foible, are based, I think, in temperamental misunderstandings, and are unimportant.

[4] Harry Calvert, in his highly intelligent, forensically argued, amiable and invaluable account of Frank Smythe's climbing career, profoundly disagrees with this assessment, and summarises *Travels* thus: 'Is there anywhere in the annals of mountaineering, a flatter, duller, more frankly factual account of any major expedition?' (*Smythe's Mountains*, Gollancz, 1985, pp.205–6.) I take it Professor Calvert isn't seriously asking for a list in response – it would be lengthy! He and I must agree to disagree. I read *Travels* whilst still at school and remember being captivated by its oddity, its incongruities, and the journeys it describes.

opposed to summit obsession firmly in its young reader's mind, not
least through Whymper's fine and exact engravings. Between the
two books there resonates the same tension that was to complicate
and ultimately define Shipton's own progress in mountaineering:
mountain-travel or – as the jargon of his day had it and the
frequently-suspect values of our contemporary press still proclaim
– mountain 'conquest'.[5]

At this stage of Shipton's development, another fortuitous chance
occurred. For the spring, summer and autumn terms of 1924 a new
face appeared at Pyt House – that of a Norwegian boy, Gustav
Sommerfelt, who was at the school to improve his English. Shipton,
recognising a fellow oddity, his essential decency requiring him
to offer protection against the teasing Sommerfelt endured from
other pupils on account of his odd accent and inadequate means of
expression in English, befriended him and took him along on many
of his Wiltshire explorations with Jim Horsfall. In return, in the
summer of 1924, a year after his family Pyrenean adventure, he was
invited to join Sommerfelt in Norway for the month of August, to
be spent in part at the Sommerfelt family's chalet in the Hallingdal
forest, and also on a walking tour of the Jotunheimen mountains.
After his reading of Whymper's Andean book, the prospect excited
him immensely. The desolate subarctic mountains of Norway, worn
down by ice-sheets and glaciation, are perhaps not at their best in
the summer months. But there were compensations.

He was with a companion who was experienced in travel through
this terrain, and already expert in use of map and compass and the
planning of a route through complex mountain country. It rained,
of course – more or less incessantly, and the midges swarmed. But
that's what it does in Scandinavia from June to September, and the
obduracy that facing out these conditions breeds would be invaluable
in future years. It wasn't even as exciting as he had hoped, particularly

[5] Throughout the many years in which I wrote obituaries of mountaineers for
The Guardian newspaper I had a running battle with innumerable young newly
Oxbridge-graduated subeditors over their incessant importation of this concept,
with which the British Establishment and its pet educational institutions are
deeply imbued, into my copy. For the record, I think the idea that a mountain can
ever be 'conquered' is the most fatuous nonsense – you may conquer yourself and
your own weaknesses, yes, but a mountain? Never. Consider the recent histories
of Everest and K2 if you doubt this. As an acid test, any mountain-themed book
or article with 'conquest' in the title deserves to be studiously ignored – not even
post-modern irony can justify this uncomprehending nonsense.

after having seen the Pyrenees; and a monotonous diet of fish-balls and sweet, sticky, fudge-like cheese lingered long on the palate and in the imagination. The mountains, however, began to assert their spell over him. Two experiences in particular branded themselves into his memory. In one of them, he and Gustav had to cross in company with another party a steep and complex pass where for the first time he tied on to a rope. The most memorable day, though, still lay in wait. The trip had been so arduous that Gustav needed to rest for twenty-four hours. Fretting at the inactivity, Shipton headed off by himself on to a nearby glacier:

> It was the first I had seen at close quarters, and the impression made by the vast mass flowing down from the silence of a mysterious ice-world was all the stronger for my solitude. In fear and exultation I climbed up until I came to a line of gaping crevasses.[6]

There you have it, in that seemingly oxymoronic collocation! 'Fear and exultation' – once the young mountain-bound human being has experienced this potent and disturbing combination of emotions, he or she is lost to the mountain experience, and left craving it ever more.

The craving, on returning home, he satisfied at first through reading. Vulcanology particularly captured his imagination, and even gave his rather wan interest in Latin a boost when he came across (in English translation at first, helpfully) the description of Vesuvius erupting in the Everyman edition of *Letters of the Younger Pliny*. Reading, though, is no substitute for experience, and he was thirsting for that. Late in 1924, he and his sister were taken by their mother to the winter-sports resort of Adelboden and the mountain theme tentatively begun in the Pyrenees and Norway would now be taken up with vigour. That early winter of 1924–5 – as were many of the winters in the early 1920s – was virtually snowless,[7]

---

[6] Eric Shipton, *That Untravelled World* (Hodder & Stoughton, 1969), pp.28–9.
[7] I have a postcard photograph of the North Face of the Eiger taken at this time. The first and second ice fields are non-existent, the White Spider vestigial, and the hanging glaciers beneath the ridge-crest over the Mönch and Jungfrau very much smaller even than in our current age of obsession with global warming. I would, of course, not wish this to be taken as anything other than a point for consideration arising from available evidence, and certainly not as the assertion of a point of

the skiing therefore non-existent. And so he came to make his first three climbs: in the Swiss Alps, in winter; spending nights in alpine huts and starting out before dawn; following his guide up ice slopes where step-cutting was necessary and a slip would have been fatal; noting the fear in his more experienced companions' faces; identifying the lurking monsters of the Bernese Oberland close at hand and glimpsing in the distance Monte Rosa, the Matterhorn, the Weisshorn; wearing snow-goggles, just as Whymper and his guides were depicted as doing in the engravings for *Travels*; climbing a rock aiguille, the Tschingelochtighorn, and finding the experience of standing on the tiny ledges of a mountain rock face no more terrifying than scrambling up those crumbling arêtes of Purbeck limestone at Wardour Old Castle; being taken up another climb by two accomplished and confident French amateurs who had already climbed – to the delight of his impressionable imagination – the Matterhorn, scene of the 1865 tragedy to Whymper's party, about which he had now read in *Scrambles Amongst the Alps*.

The obsession with climbing, once it has taken hold, chafes for opportunity and will brook no denial. At Easter 1925 Shipton's indefatigable travelling mother, forsaking her own interests in Parisian museums and galleries, the stained glass of great French cathedrals and the architecture of chateaux along the Loire (none of which had inspired her son's devotion, though they had contributed osmotically to his cultural education and future propensity for informed argument), was with her teenage children at Menaggio on the Lago di Como. Eric, in his walking shoes, took off straight away for a snow-covered hill above the town, choosing as line of ascent a steepening gully that cut through vertical shaly strata. On the high-angled snow slope above these his smooth-soled shoes slipped and he fell cartwheeling down the gully, coming to rest on the edge of the cliffs. Prudence turned a blind eye to his antics and he climbed straight back up, maintaining adhesion this time, reached the top, and descended the other side of the mountain to reach his hotel, where he had to invent some no doubt mildly mendacious account to explain away his very evident bruises and abrasions. His sister Marge, writing to him years later, commented:

---

view on a subject about which I know nothing. Though the word 'phasal' does spring to mind, as well as a personal perception that the Gangotri glacier snout seems to be in much the same place as it was in 1934 when Shipton visited there, if the account given in *Nanda Devi* is to be believed – as why should it not be?

How I used to envy you being able to go off as you did and
the way you used to get what you wanted with not lies exactly
but half-truths . . . As you say, Mother never stopped us doing
anything we wanted to do, but she never encouraged us to do
anything either.

In the same letter she goes on to recall a strange little incident from
Christmas 1924, of the kind on which families tend both to set great
store and later to amplify considerably in the frequent retelling:

Do you remember when we were at Adelboden we met a
brother and sister about our ages? Their mother had been ill.
She came down one evening to the lounge and on seeing you
she went in to a sort of trance. She kept telling us that you
would write; that you would make a name for yourself; that
you would go where no man had been before – in fact, she
kept on repeating herself with regular monotony all evening.
Have you ever thought of her again?'

Shipton's own summing-up of his mother's attitude to his early
adventures is well worth quoting, to fill out Marge's comments:

I was reticent about my new-found enthusiasm, but she was
well aware of its intensity, and it was her firm principle never
to stand in the way of either of us in the fulfillment of any
reputable ambition. For this and a great deal besides, I am
deeply grateful. I was very fond of my mother; but though
we had a great deal in common, we were never very close.
This was largely due to her reticence which prevented intimate
discussion, an indulgence to which I have always been addicted.

How interesting, then, that exactly this same tension between
disclosure and reticence should have been replicated in the most
significant male friendship of his early adult life, which is the subject
of this book. But we shall be coming to that. For the moment, the
Easter holiday at Menaggio is far from over. Thirty miles away
to the north-east was Monte della Disgrazia, at 3,678 metres the
highest peak in the Bergeller Alps and first climbed by Melchior
Anderegg with Leslie Stephen and Thomas Kennedy in 1862. Mrs
Haly – no doubt grateful for peaceful time with her daughter free of

the company of a restless adolescent male – and the hotel manager in Menaggio between them arranged for a mountain-guide to meet the sixteen-year-old Shipton in Ardenno at the foot of the mountain. A train ran there from Menaggio, tickets were booked, and away he went, to be picked up in a horse and cart by a short, squat monoglot Italian called Giacomo Fierelli, at whose house in San Martino, a three-hour drive up-valley, he was kitted out with badly-fitting nailed boots and an ice axe. They snatched a few hours' sleep, and accompanied by a porter, set off in the habitual alpine candle-lantern-lit procession at 2 a.m. for the mountain. At 7.30 a.m. the trio reached a hut, where they ate bread and pungent cheese and the guide and porter stretched themselves out on the *matratzenlager* and went to sleep.

The incredulous Shipton, after fretting upon this turn of events for an hour or two, stamped impatiently off by himself into the morning sunlight and was promptly reduced to wading waist-deep in melting snow. Chastened, he returned to lunch of bread and cheese; to supper of bread-and-cheese soup; to more bread-and-cheese soup for a breakfast at 12.30 a.m. and beyond that the even more unappetising 2 a.m. start into wind and whirling snow, at which change in the weather his companions seemed not remotely concerned – in fact they appeared quite gleeful. After four and a half hours of plodding into an inscrutable dark, in the faint lustre of dawn with thick flurries of snow still swirling around them they reached the crest of a ridge, which he was assured, with much back-slapping and congratulations, was the summit, and from which with no more ado they raced down the farther side, the two Italians pulling him along on the rope to repeated exhortations about the deadly danger of avalanches. They arrived once more in San Martino, where they ate a hearty breakfast (of which bread-and-cheese soup was not a component), and enlisted the village priest to establish a fee for the supposed ascent, after payment of which, and celebratory drinking of wine, a merry and triumphant Giacomo conveyed Shipton back down-valley at breakneck speed to the station in Ardenno.

Shipton remained convinced for the rest of his life that Giacomo Fierelli, taking advantage of his youthful inexperience and the lack of visibility, had duped him by taking him to a false summit on the ridge 2,000 feet below Monte della Disgrazia's highest point. In the summer of 1965, with his younger son John, he went back to try to establish where it was that he had climbed to and descended from on that April day in the 1920s. It confirmed his view of Giacomo's duplicity. 'The average Alpine guide,' he was later wryly to note, 'has his limitations.'[8] Those limitations, he would discover in the summer of 1925, were not always the case, though for the first part of his planned summer activity that year he would not be putting them to the test. The reasons for this were twofold. Guideless climbing in the mid 1920s for a Briton (and particularly for a very young Briton) was not yet quite the done thing, though the situation was fast changing, through the activities of Frank Smythe and also of a brilliant group of young Cambridge climbers, Longland and Wyn Harris foremost among them, who – when not spending their Sunday evenings sitting at the feet[9] of Geoffrey Winthrop Young through the duration of his salons held at 5 Bene't Place in Cambridge – were beginning to perform prodigious feats of peak-bagging and ridge-traversing under G.W.Y.'s[10] direction in the Alps.

For a not-quite-eighteen-year-old in the early summer of 1925, however, it had not yet changed, and the cost of hiring a willing and competent guide, particularly for routes that might recommend themselves to the ambitions of a young climber of the day, was prohibitive. Shipton's allowance for the holiday was not lavish, even given the very favourable exchange rate for sterling against the French franc and other European currencies that prevailed throughout the 1920s (and which, along with the economical rates for travel by boat and rail, made that decade an outstanding one for the literature of travel in English,[11] lasting right up to the time when Britain went off the gold standard in September 1931). Limited means therefore necessitated the canvassing of other options. The one on which he decided was that old-fashioned one of the walking tour, for which his choice of location was dictated by three factors.

The first was one to which he alone was privy: he wished to see for himself the peaks of the Dauphine around La Berarde that

---

[8] Shipton, *Upon That Mountain*, p.29.

[9] Pedants might insist on a singular noun here, given that Young had lost a leg in the Great War.

[10] Winthrop Young is generally known by these initials in the climbing world, where he was an enormously influential figure long held in great affection and esteem. His *Mountain Craft* of 1920 – a highly discursive text – was the technical manual for generations, until superseded by J. E. Q. Barford's popular 1947 paperback *Climbing in Britain*. More on G. W. Y. later in this chapter.

[11] For a wide-ranging and judicious account of this phenomenon, see Paul Fussell's *Abroad: British Literary Travelling Between the Wars* (Oxford, 1980).

Whymper had described in fond and thrilling detail in *Scrambles*.
To circumvent any possible – and indeed likely – maternal anxiety
or perhaps even disapproval regarding solo mountain ventures
(why invoke parental wrath when a path of diplomacy, albeit
a slippery one, can be chosen?), a walking tour that began from
the house of an old friend of his mother's, Monsieur Chalus, in
Clermont-Ferrand could just coincidentally lead him, unbeknownst
to her, in that direction. In doing so it could take him through the
Massif Central and particularly the volcanic region of the upper
Auvergne, for entry into which Clermont-Ferrand, just to the north,
was ideally placed. Also, M. Chalus initially suggested that he was
able to provide a companion of Shipton's own age to accompany
him and thus overcome any objections against his going alone. In
the event, the potential young companion in some mysterious way
involving a girl disgraced himself, and hence was grounded for the
summer.

So Shipton – of necessity now, plans being too far advanced for
their cancellation – would undertake his journey alone, maternal
anxieties notwithstanding. And anyway, he argued, as the quick-
witted young usually will when the prospect of parental disapproval
looms, it would improve his French so his school work would
benefit. He was not quite eighteen, and he was venturing on a
journey on foot through what is still some of the strangest, wildest,
least populous country in France. John Murray's *Handbook for
Travellers in France* of 1854 warned about the Mézenc range to
which he was bound that 'There is scarcely any accommodation on
this route, which can hardly be performed in a day; and the people
are rude and forbidding.'

The situation in its essentials had changed very little in the seventy
years to Shipton's time, except that the savage losses suffered by
France in the Great War had further decimated the already sparse
population. The wind-blasted, gorge-riven landscape of black,
ringing, phonolithic rocks had a primitive, elemental feel to it.
South and east of Le Puy roads gave way to mule tracks, and open
country haunted only by shepherds carrying rifles, with ferocious
dogs guarding their flocks.

> . . . after a sharp ascent of twenty minutes, [we] reached
> the edge of the plateau. The view, looking back on my day's
> journey, was both wild and sad. Mount Mézenc and the peaks

beyond St Julien stood out in trenchant gloom against a cold glitter in the east; and the intervening field of hills had fallen together into one broad wash of shadow, except here and there the outline of a wooded sugar-loaf in black, here and there a white irregular patch to represent a cultivated farm; and here and there a blot where the Loire, the Gazeille, or the Laussonne wandered in a gorge.[12]

That's not Shipton, but Robert Louis Stevenson from his entrancing account of a journey through the Cevennes with a very small donkey called Modestine, published in 1879 and still high on the list of everybody's favourite travel books. It gives a good impression of the bizarre landscape around Le Monastier, Mézenc and Le Gerbier de Jonc. This is one of the great watersheds of Europe, the Loire and its tributaries draining down from the northern and western slopes to set out on its long course to meet the Atlantic at St-Nazaire, whilst just a few miles away to the east the Rhône flows south to filter into the Mediterranean through the impaludistic, mosquito-infested landscape of the Camargue, west of Marseille. Looking over the Rhône valley from these old volcanoes and the weird heights of Auvergne and the Cevennes, visible on clear days rising far away to the east there is a long, serrated shimmer of white – the Alps, from Mont Blanc to Mont Ventoux. What bliss and allure!

We don't know what route Shipton took on his three-week ramble round roughest France: 'This journey took place a very long time ago, and as I did not keep a diary most of the details of times and place-names and the exact sequence of events are forgotten.'[13] He has left us a few scattered certainties, a handful of tantalising clues, one or two amusing anecdotes and resonant observations. There was the six-egg omelette at a little auberge in a wild, unpopulated region. Whilst it was being prepared – by a startled girl who had initially offered a standard and to his starving young belly meagre two-egg version – he sat at the table and set to with the *pichet* of rough country wine habitually provided. By the time the omelette arrived the wine was gone and he had to hasten quickly away without eating it, in order to be very sick around the corner. After which he was too ashamed to come back for his food.

---

[12] Robert Louis Stevenson, *Travels with a Donkey* (1879) (Dent, 1925), pp.111–12.
[13] Shipton, *Upon That Mountain*, p.24.

He developed blisters, strained an Achilles tendon; his load made his shoulders ache continually; on one occasion he frightened himself by getting lost among a particularly remote and trackless group of hills, devoid of trees, its settlements all in ruins, their springs dried up and their populations gone. Looking for water in that desolate land, he encountered a shepherd, who gave him a drink from his flask and took him back to the sheep-fold and to the deep natural well he used, over which he had rigged a rough windlass.

The shepherd gave the young Shipton shelter that night in his stone house where the wind in the roof tiles made a sound like waves sighing on to the shore. He shared with him a thick peasant soup, and afterwards Shipton watched as he poured acorns out of a bag on to the table, minutely scrutinising them, discarding ones that were too small or had imperfections. He sorted them into piles of ten, and when he had ten such, he returned the hundred acorns to their bag. Next morning, the shepherd introduced himself, giving his name as Elzéard Bouffier. He dipped his bag of acorns in water and walked off carrying a long steel rod instead of his shepherd's crook. Shipton, watching from the parallel path along which lay the first part of his day's journey, idling in order to satisfy his curiosity, saw him take his sheep to a grazing place and leave them under the guard of his dog. Then, with great care, a little way off he set to and planted his hundred acorns.[14]

The journey certainly took Shipton as far as the Gorges du Tarn, which he descended in a punt with a young chance-acquaintance Greek met at another auberge. He lived comfortably on ten francs a day – not much more than five pence in current prices. When he returned to the house of M. Chalus – by a different route, after what cannot but have been an immense journey on foot – the inhabitants barely recognised the ragged and filthy vagabond on their doorstep,

---

[14] Consult Jean Giono for the meaning of this trope, which perfectly expresses an aspect of the unconscious influences on Shipton in his formative years. The source will also tell you much about the type of country, and its atmosphere during this period, through which Shipton's journey lay. When the story to which it alludes first appeared, that wonderfully obtuse periodical the *Reader's Digest*, taking it as literal truth instead of the resonant fable it is, contacted Giono and asked him for a piece on Elzéard Bouffier for its 'My most unforgettable character' series, which he duly provided. If any reader wishes to take my paragraph in the same way, I would be delighted, though I should point out that the 'real' story locates in that remarkable area, very similar in many ways to the one traversed by Shipton, called the Diois, within distant sight of Mont Ventoux.

and their first response on letting him in was to run a deep, hot bath.

'I had a delicious feeling of personal possession, such as I had already felt for my first Alpine peaks, and which comes from a true understanding of the country.'[15] In many ways this journey prefigures the pattern of Shipton's later explorations. There is the immense energy of the undertaking, the tirelessness. I remember a long day's walk years ago in the Welsh mountains with his elder son Nick, who is very much of the same physical type as his father. There was something about the tireless easy rhythm with which he covered the ground that was remarkable, and impressive. People who have trekked in the Himalayas with his younger son John give the same account; and I imagine the father to have been thus and more so. (Frank Smythe, in his *Kamet Conquered*, vouchsafes us a glimpse that confirms this to have been the case: 'Shipton, a born mountaineer, has acquired to perfection the art of climbing a snow-slope with the minimum of effort . . . [an] almost leisurely rhythm.')[16] There is also the willingness to endure hardship and live off the land as its inhabitants do. There is that intellectual absorption in the mysteries of topography – the desire to come at 'a true understanding of the country'. But there is something beyond all this, too. For the Australian Aboriginal, 'going walkabout' was a rite of passage. This French journey feels to have been that for Shipton as he approached his eighteenth birthday.

In a fascinating and fiercely intelligent book[17] on British travel writing in the twentieth century, the writer Mark Cocker makes the following apposite points:

Few human experiences – except perhaps dreams and hallucinogenic drugs – are better able to reveal the unconscious mind to the conscious than travel. During the journey the whole processes of repression and accommodation by which the domestic environment was rendered safe and stable have been completely jettisoned. In its place is an unending, unpredictable and random stream of new sensory experiences – a flow of disorientating images which, when chemically induced, is known significantly as a 'trip'. In these powerfully

[15] Shipton, *Upon that Mountain*, p.25.

[16] Frank Smythe, *Kamet Conquered* (Hodder & Stoughton, 1938), p.157.

[17] Mark Cocker, *Loneliness & Time* (Secker & Warburg, 1992).

numinous encounters, the traveller can find the moment and the symbols in which to explore previously unknown areas of the psyche. Travel is, in a sense, the greatest image-association game that a human can play.'[18]

Cocker continues by making the following point, which is extraordinarily relevant in the case of Shipton. Having stressed the way in which the literature of travel often dramatises 'a return to the innocence and paradise of childhood', he outlines the psychological effect: 'By loosening the mental restraints that secure our adult relationship to the world and, in parallel, by liberating the libido, travel often initiates a state of consciousness that is extremely similar to childhood. In journeys we discover all over again the newness of the world.'[19]

With the inspirational experience of three weeks' wild and exploratory walking behind him, Shipton left the hospitality and friendship of M. Chalus's household behind, took the train to Grenoble, where he bought maps and saw photographs of the magnificent snow peaks of the Dauphine, the names of which he knew from the best and least sensationalised part of Whymper's *Scrambles* – La Meije, Mont Pelvoux, Les Ecrins – and next morning in drenching rain he took the bus for the village at the heart of them. La Berarde at the time was a tiny settlement of a little chapel, an inn and a few houses in a clearing among the silver birches that lined both sides of the river Vénéon as it surged and rumbled along its gorge in a series of cataracts, carrying boulders down from the wild, rocky valleys of its birth. The other passengers on the bus, rain dinning on its roof, mocked him when he confessed that he was going there to climb. And as they did so the mountain conjurors went to work, swept aside the clouds, held a glittering white peak – the summit of Les Ecrins – high overhead in the revealed gap and joined it with another and yet another, bathing them in visionary sunlight.

At the inn in Les Etages, where the bus-driver stopped for refreshments, there occurred another of the significant encounters that distinguish Shipton's life. He asked about a guide and was directed to Elie Richard – a bow-legged little chap five feet in height with a beret at a jaunty angle and an ever-present cigarette in his mouth,

---

[18] Cocker, *Loneliness & Time*, p. 255.
[19] Ibid. p.257.

sitting at a table drinking wine. He could have been excused had he feared that here was another Giacomo Fierelli. But when he had introduced himself and explained what he wanted, his needs and those of Richard meshed perfectly. The early summer of 1925 in the Alps had been a bad one, little work available, none of the ascents possible that Richard needed to graduate from being a *guide de deuxième classe*. No, he wouldn't need much money – sixty francs a day (and what Shipton had saved by his frugal living in the Auvergne would cover that) – yes, they could climb every day, starting tomorrow with Pic Coolidge, which would go whatever the conditions; then for bigger and better things, staying in huts, carrying their own food. He would come to the inn at La Berarde with a spare ice axe at 1 a.m. and they would be away – no time to waste!

Around the communal supper table in the little Hotel Tairraz that evening Shipton met a party of Parisian climbers from the elite organisation of the time, the Groupe de Haute Montagne (GHM), among whom a confident nineteen-year-old Englishwoman, Nea Barnard, was holding court. Nea already had three Alpine seasons behind her. She was later to marry Jean Morin, a Parisian art-dealer[20] and one of the leading French alpinists of the day, lost on a secret mission for the Free French early in the Second World War. Their daughter Denise would become a distinguished mountaineer and sailor in her own right, and was to marry Charles Evans, the man originally appointed as deputy leader to Shipton for the 1953 Everest expedition, and himself leader of the impressive lightweight one that reached the summit[21] of Kanchenjunga in 1955. All this is years ahead. For the moment, Nea drew the shy young man into her charmed company; introduced him warmly round, as she would later introduce him to the leading British climbers of the day ('it was through her,' he was later to note, 'that I made nearly all my early contacts'); and having been apprised of his plans for the next

---

[20] To visit Nea at the spacious flat in Church Road, Tunbridge Wells, where she lived in her later years, was a breathtaking experience. Two walls of her drawing-room were lined entirely with oil paintings by Corot, the other two walls floor-to-ceiling with luminous watercolours by the nonsense poet Edward Lear – dozens of works by each artist. And Nea's own conversation was as rich and varied as the art on display.
[21] The summit team of Joe Brown and George Band stopped just short of the summit itself, having promised for religious reasons to leave it untrodden.

day and mindful of them, at an appropriate time she firmly ushered him off to his bed. In her fine memoir that treats mostly of women's climbing in the twentieth century and particularly ascents by *cordées féminines* in the Alps, Nea has the following recollection of the meeting: 'At La Bérarde I first met Eric Shipton. His mother had sent him to France to learn French, but he immediately gravitated to the mountains.'[22]

Here, then, was someone with whom he could be open about his real reason for being in France. Nea continues, and in passing gives an insight at an early stage into something of the near-irresistible appeal[23] he held throughout his life for women:

> Eric was still a schoolboy and his whole appearance and demeanour were shy and diffident. It would have been hard to see in this slight, fair-haired youth with enormous, rather anxious blue eyes, the splendid mountaineer and intrepid explorer of the future . . . I, with all the weight of my three seasons' experience, felt heavily responsible for this dreamy-eyed youth, two years my junior.'[24]

If the long trek through the Auvergne and the Cévennes had been one rite of passage – and one that had fortuitously left him very fit indeed, which was as well in view of what was to come – the next ten days were an initiation to another level entirely. Elie Richard and the spare ice axe duly arrived in the depths of the night and from that point on he was driven unremittingly by a competent, hard taskmaster. He was roused from deepest sleep of exhaustion each day to yet another 2 a.m. start and all the unpleasant precedent aspects of the high-mountain experience: intractable boots, aching limbs, sore and bleeding sun-and-wind-dried lips that every smile would crack wide open once again; monotonous food and musty, hard bread and the consciousness of his own morning clumsiness.

---

[22] Nea Morin, *A Woman's Reach* (Eyre & Spottiswoode, 1968), p.26.
[23] His son Nick, in a manner somewhere between amusement and slight embarrassment, once related an anecdote to me about taking a girlfriend out for an evening and on returning to her home finding his father, who had turned up unannounced and without prior acquaintance, in bed with her mother. I don't remember the names of those involved in this story, and nor, when I reminded him of it recently, does Nick. Alan Clark would no doubt have approved.
[24] Morin, *A Woman's Reach*, p.26.

It is through endurance of this harsh discipline that the ease and the relaxation, the rhythm and the mastery come. They finished their ten-day engagement with an ascent of Les Ecrins and an agreement to climb together in the summer of 1926 at the same tariff for a longer period. In a brief succession of days devoted to the most intense physical activity and acquisition of new skills, Elie Richard worked away at the shaping of his young apprentice, and the imprimatur of his fierce instruction remained upon his grateful pupil for the rest of his days.

His independent holiday – if such it was – over, he made his way to Paris to join his mother and sister. They returned together to London, and there he and Marge both fell ill with scarlet fever, contracted in Paris and left untreated for too long, as a result of which he developed complications which incapacitated him for months and ensured he was unable to return to school for the autumn term of 1925. Instead, once sufficiently recovered from what had been a serious bout of illness, he went off on a banana-boat to convalesce in Tenerife, on which island is the highest Spanish mountain, the 12,198-feet Pico del Teide – third-highest in the world in terms of its height above the ocean floor, a dormant volcano which had last erupted in 1909. Shipton climbed it, of course, and not only to look at the El Chinyero vent through which the eruption had taken place. His interest in vulcanology was still strong, and his inclination was tending towards the possibility of reading geology at Cambridge, to which end he was officially withdrawn from school and put to a London 'crammer' to prepare for the entrance examination. By various ruses he circumvented most of his deficiencies in Latin, but ended up ploughing the unseen paper, and so after the summer vacation of 1926 he had to set to and prepare all over again. The summer vacation, of course, proved compensation enough for any number of resits, but in the event only one would be necessary.

The tribulations of trying to gain admission to Cambridge over for this year, he set off once again for La Bérarde – carrying with him his own ice axe, a pair of hand-crafted boots properly nailed with the required clinkers and star muggers[25] from Robert Lawrie, and 120 feet of Beale's alpine line with the distinctive red

---

[25] Clinkers were the broad edge-nails in climbing boots, and star muggers the star-shaped hobnails studding the centre of the soles. The distinctive pattern of both is retained in rubber boot soles of today.

thread running right through the lay – to resume his client–guide relationship with Elie Richard, this time with his mother coming along to check up on his activities and the company he was keeping, though she seems not to have done any climbing. Perhaps he had simply given her a very good report of the Hotel Tairraz. The French franc was trading at 240 to the pound – one franc for every old penny! He could afford Elie Richard's services for a month, especially now that he had paid a very moderate fee to join the Club Alpin Francais, and could hence use their extensive network of huts without charge. This also meant that they could travel very light, needing only to carry food and essential equipment. Both Shipton and Richard were keen to climb and augment their experience. They pillaged that austere and little-visited mountain group for its every worthwhile extant route, achieving twenty summits in the short space of weeks and in that time encountering only a couple of other parties on the mountains. Richard chivvied and bullied and shouted and abused his young client like some manic Rumpelstiltskin seeking to ensure gold was spun from straw, high endeavour from slack human clay. The end result was the mountaineer that Eric Shipton became.

It was inevitable, though, that his pupil would outgrow the pedagogic relationship, and Elie Richard become supernumerary. The signs that the process was under way began to surface in earnest during this second season. On ground new to both of them – and Richard was committed to the exploratory approach to mountains, so this was most of the time – gradually a more equal responsibility for decision-making in matters like route-finding and potential risk began to emerge. Not only that, but Richard's own limitations were bound to be exposed by the relentless pace and energy with which they were both progressing up the ladders of difficulty and achievement. On at least one occasion, for the traverse of La Meije, he insisted on the hire of a second guide to accompany them. If this was not in itself an admission of inadequacy, it was certainly a check on the extent of his competence. Shipton was always very generous about the role Richard had played in his progress into mountaineering, but implicit in both accounts he later gave (in *Upon That Mountain* and *That Untravelled World*) of their relationship is the understanding that the gifted pupil necessarily outgrows his master. His summary comments on his erstwhile guide, meditated on over long gaps of years, are gracious, decent and grateful; but they quietly acknowledge that after this second frenetic season, the time had come for the pupil, in full awareness of what a teacher happily appropriate to the time had given him, to move on from both this instruction and the area in which it took place. After 1926, though the Dauphine and his erstwhile guide would retain a place in his affections, there was no reason for Shipton to retain Elie Richard's services again. Gilbert Peaker's succinct assessment of Richard and his influence is well worth quoting here:

> . . . an admirable little man . . . retained by diffidence rather than lack of ability in the second class of guides. He must have been a very good teacher, though of course he had a singularly apt pupil. I think his was the only instruction in icemanship that Eric ever received.[26]

It was not the last time that Shipton would climb with a guide – right at the close of his next Alpine season, that of 1927, in the more formidable company of the Zermatt-based Theophïle Theytaz, in exceptionally poor conditions he climbed the Z'mutt ridge of the Matterhorn, the north ridge of the Obergabelhorn and traversed the Zinal Rothorn (and you can be sure that he and Gilbert Peaker, with whom he was climbing, paid Theytaz a good deal more than sixty francs a day for his services). The focus, though, for that season had already shifted, and the fulcrum on which it tilted lay far closer to home.

Nea Barnard, by common consent one of the finest all-round female climbers of the inter-war period, was residing at Easter 1927 in the Wasdale Head Hotel in the English Lake District – one of the traditional homes of British rock-climbing, a place redolent of the great names of that sport: Siegfried Herford, Fred Botterill, Owen Glynne Jones, the Abraham brothers, Haskett Smith. The standards achieved from this base both on rock and on ice were beyond question far higher than had been reached in any other mountain area of Britain.[27] In joining Nea's party there, Shipton was committing himself to an acquaintance with the strenuous

---

[26] Gilbert Peaker, 'High Pastures' (*Alpine Journal*, 1944), p.252.
[27] For a discussion of the inhibiting influence of the G. W. Y. claque on climbing standards in Wales, see Chapter 7 of my *Snowdon: The Story of a Welsh Mountain* (Gomer Press, 2012).

intricacies of another of climbing's core skills. Yet again he struck gold in the matter of an instructor.

Gilbert Peaker (as a result of an early confusion, for the first ten years of their acquaintance Shipton always called him 'George') was an intriguing character, very active at a crucial phase of both British rock-climbing and guideless alpinism. Shipton in *That Untravelled World* gives his age as eight years more than his own, though club journal obituaries from 1984 indicate that he was only three years older. He was a marathon runner and mathematics lecturer, and was promiscuous and often solitary in his mountain activity. There was a photograph of him by Douglas Milner on Grey Slab on the Upper Cliff of Glyder Fawr in the old Cwm Idwal climbing guide, taken some time after this route was first recorded by Menlove Edwards in 1932. Peaker is a stocky, powerful figure dressed in tweed jacket and knickerbockers, dark hair cropped close, high cheekbones, deep-set eyes and the inevitable pipe – a perpetual dummy the sucking on which seems to have been essential to the psychological well-being of every man of the period – jutting from his mouth. A thick hemp rope is tied directly round his waist and trails down from him unpunctuated by any impedimenta of modern protection. It is the stance that impresses, though. The hands are below waist level, merely resting on the rock for balance; the heels are low, the body upright, the expression intensely concentrated. It's a textbook-technique study of its time, hopelessly outmoded now, impossibly static for the demands of modern rock-climbing, but eighty years ago, this was how it was done – balance-climbing, in the Winthrop Young tradition. In *Mountain Craft*, the technical bible of its day, Shipton could read all about it, though I don't think it much appealed to him, and there is no record that he climbed very much on British rock. Shipton and Peaker were in Wales together before Easter in 1928, staying at Helyg – by then a climbing club cottage, which had been described a few decades earlier by George Borrow as 'a wretched hovel'[28] and has not really much improved from that day to this, though instead of shivering from the ague as in Borrow's day its present short-term inhabitants merely have to endure an overall patina of grease and the perpetual reek of testosterone and rancid bacon fat. The two men enjoyed some good weather during their first week, and managed to ascend a few climbs

---

[28] George Borrow, *Wild Wales* (1862) (Collins, 1955), p.146.

on Glyder Fach and on Tryfan, including the Terrace Wall Variant – a steep and pretty route well supplied with Tryfan's characteristically sumptuous holds and graded Very Difficult, which Shipton led in his clinker-nailed boots. Peaker succeeded in climbing the Helyg Boulder Crack – a neat and strenuous little problem fifteen feet in length, a few yards from the front door of the cottage – but Shipton failed to master the required techniques either of precarious lay-backing or arcane hand-jamming. Perhaps he simply lacked a sufficient degree of interest.

The massed ranks of the Cambridge University Mountaineering Club arrived to intrude on his and Peaker's solitude, and brought with them a change of weather. During their visit the clouds loured in their habitual Welsh way, and a cold and constant wind along that bleak valley modulated from driving rain to wet snow and back again. Only the most elementary of climbs were done. On one of them Peaker, whilst leading, fell off from one of the easier continuation routes above the Idwal Slabs, but came to no harm as he'd neatly lassoed a spike at the top of the steep little wall he was attempting.

One benefit of the Helyg stay was that Shipton did meet two Cambridge undergraduates, Peter Lloyd and Charles Warren, with whom he would share later Himalayan adventures. Jack Longland and Lawrence Wager also called round at Helyg, to rake with their wit the new generation of Cambridge student mountaineers, in a flying visit from a G. W. Y. Easter party at Pen y Pass.[29]

---

[29] The Pen y Pass Easter parties, held at the Gorffwysfa Hotel at the top of the Llanberis Pass by the start to the Miners' Track up Snowdon, were an annual – and highly exclusive – British climbing institution for most of the early part of the twentieth century up to the outbreak of the Second World War. They were hosted by, and the brainchild of, Geoffrey Winthrop Young (1876–1958). Much of the class-based mythologising of early British climbing derived from this source, was deeply distorting, and continues, of course, with the ongoing delusional obsession that George Leigh Mallory – a Pen y Pass regular – reached the top of Everest in 1924. G. W. Y. himself was a more rounded and complex character than all this might suggest. His Establishment credentials were impeccable – father a baronet and charity commissioner, Winthrop Young himself educated at Marlborough and Trinity College, Cambridge, where his pleasant if facile poetry twice won the Chancellor's verse medal. There were more difficult passages to be negotiated in his life than this easy progress might suggest. He was quietly removed from his five-year spell of employment as assistant master at Eton, which he took up after Cambridge, for behaviour that in our time would have ensured his hounding

To backtrack to Shipton's first acquaintance with British rock during Nea Barnard's 1927 Easter party in Wasdale, the weather

---

by the tabloid press. Instead, the discretion of polite society ruled and influence rescued him. At the remarkably young age of twenty-eight he became an inspector of secondary schools. The outset of the Great War saw him, a peace protester, sent to command a Friends' Ambulance Unit set up by Cambridge Quakers in Belgium, his conduct there earning him mentions in dispatches and decorations including the Légion d'honneur for his courageous and humane actions at Ypres. After Belgium he joined his good friend the historian George Trevelyan as the unit was transferred to northern Italy. Here, at the Battle of Monte San Gabriele, he received wounds that led to the amputation of his left leg. His refusal to accept this as an end to his stellar pre-war alpine career is rightly admired, his adaptation as rock-climber and alpinist to the artificial limb an example to many, and the book, *Mountains with a Difference*, in which he records these climbs has a flickering wry humour and not a trace of self-pity about it. He married Eleanor ('Len') Slingsby at the end of the Great War, and the tradition of the Pen y Pass Easter parties, which had faltered during the time of carnage, was resurrected – and grew slightly more inclusive over time. Certainly the louche and bohemian figure of Young had by the early 1920s become a revered institution. Geoffrey and 'Len' Young were established in Cambridge at 5 Bene't Place, where the two held Sunday evening mountaineering and intellectual *salons*.

A new generation of university climbers were thus invited along to Pen y Pass. Jack Longland described the tenor of Pen y Pass Easter parties as 'a social and intellectual background which is quite foreign to what I know of climbing today'. The saga of Pen y Pass (and its predecessor as 'elite' centre, Penygwryd), as related by Winthrop Young and those later commentators who borrow heavily from him, conceals as much as it reveals and presents a received version of British climbing history that is in all essentials little more than an ignorant imperialism fixated on larger-than-life heroes and their mighty deeds. As an eighteen-year-old freshman at Cambridge in the mid 1920s, Jack Longland was sexually involved with both G. W. Y. and 'Len' Young – a fact on which he swore me to secrecy as long as he lived, and – typical, this, of the mischievous aspect to his character – commanded me to divulge as widely as possible after his death (which was in November 1993). Jack's wife Peggy had her own contribution to make about Geoffrey's eccentricities, asking if I remembered the cloak he wore in several well-known photographs, and going on to tell of how he would come into the women's bathhouse at Pen y Pass and with a flourish swing it aside to reveal himself naked underneath: 'We would merely giggle at this – there was nothing there to make a girl feel afraid on her wedding night.' Sir Arnold Lunn's summary and elliptical comment in his *DNB* notice for G. W. Y. tells of how 'Len' had 'an affectionate understanding of his endearing weaknesses'. Which neatly defines the Establishment's contemporary view of these issues. We shall hear more of G. W. Y. in the course of this book, and his influence on the generation of climbers with which it deals was by no means entirely perverse or retrograde.

(Source for much of the above is correspondence between Sir Jack Longland and myself throughout the 1980s, which will be deposited in the National Library of Wales, Aberystwyth, after my death.)

then was conversely fine and the company supportive. Only the rock proved unaccommodating: 'I was extremely frightened and not a little humiliated. The climbs that were dismissed by the initiated as easy, struck me as formidable.'[30] He does appear on this holiday to have climbed up to a grade of Severe (Frank Smythe in *Kamet Conquered* – his account of the successful 1931 expedition to that peak – has him comparing sections on the ascent of a 19,815-foot peak above the Banke Glacier as 'being equal in difficulty to a Cumberland Severe').[31] Though he never became a committed rock-climber, under Peaker's careful tutelage – again, a case of finding an excellent teacher who was not himself of the first rank but could sympathetically impart knowledge – he certainly acquired a degree of competence on rock that was more than adequate to his ambitions at the time, and could on occasion overcome pitches of some severity when the situation demanded, the crux of the west ridge of Mount Kenya being a case in point.

From Easter 1927 at Wasdale to his next attempt at Cambridge admission was a short span of weeks. In June he took the entrance papers again (and was lodged in Wager's rooms, where he was captivated by the mountaineering books and photographs). This time he passed, only to encounter a further problem. The master of his prospective college poured all his lofty Cambridge scorn on Shipton's intention to read geology – with potential future tutors like Wager and Odell, how well might he have done with that direction of study? – leaving him, after all his efforts to secure a place, in a mood of some despondency. He turned to what was now his habitual means of emotional sustenance and, intending to stay for two months, at the end of June he went off to the Alps with Gilbert Peaker. This time he had no initial intention of hiring a guide.

The two men spent the first three weeks on a long expedition hut-to-hut from the Graian Alps to the Gran Paradiso, ridge-traversing in fine weather, moving on every day across new horizons into new country. They were benighted on their first night out from Pralognan and spent it in a cowshed. Thereafter, by way of the Grande Casse, the Motte, the Sassière and the Pourri, good views of the great peaks of the Alps all along the way, they ended up by crossing the Col du

[30] Shipton, *Upon That Mountain*, p.39.
[31] Smythe, *Kamet Conquered*, p.193.

Géant and heading down to Montenvers, where by chance they met
Nea, who had been based there whilst attempting the first ascent of
the Aiguille du Roc – an ambition that was to be thwarted by bad
weather until the following year. Peaker needing a rest after their
arduous approach to Montenvers, Shipton joined forces with Nea
and two other climbers, Winifred Marples and Bill Hennessy, and
they set off with the intention of climbing the Aiguille du Peigne.
Nea tells the story:

> From the Montenvers we took the Plan de l'Aiguille path and
> then over moraine and up a steep little tongue of permanent
> snow to the foot of our peak. We had not gone far up the
> couloir between the Peigne and the Aiguille des Pèlerins when
> the weather, which had been menacing for some time, went to
> pieces and down we came in a torrent of water and stones. At
> the top of the tongue of *névé* Eric and I suggested to the others
> that they should wait while we ventured upon the snow slope
> to see if it was safe to glissade. Almost at once we came to ice
> underlying a thin layer of slushy snow and in a jiffy we were
> both on our backsides gathering speed rapidly; but we had
> kept hold of our axes and we both managed to stop ourselves
> in mid-slope. We were level with each other and about fifty
> feet apart with the rope stretching between us. The others had
> not waited as we advised, and to our horror we saw them
> come hurtling down out of control, having dropped their axes.
> In a flash Eric had the same idea – we would try to hook them
> up with our rope as they shot past us, but all we succeeded
> in doing was giving [Winifred] a black eye. Down they went
> with alarming speed straight onto the rocks below and it was
> a miracle neither of them was badly hurt.'[32]

It is worth remembering with regard to this incident that Shipton
was still – just – a teenager. The competence he displayed, and the
quick thinking, was exemplary, and he was climbing with a partner
herself closely associated with the leading alpinists of the day. In the
mountaineering community, word quickly gets round. A reputation
was being established.

The same bad weather that had driven Nea's party down from

---

[32] Nea Morin, *A Woman's Reach*, p.39.

the Peigne soon hastened Shipton and Peaker away from Chamonix by bus to the more familiar and clement environment of La Berarde. On 1 August, Shipton's twentieth birthday, they were descending the north face of Les Bans – a serious undertaking very seldom considered at the time – when he was hit a glancing blow on the head that knocked him out, though no lasting damage was done.

Peaker has a very interesting account of Shipton during this season and the one following (1928), which is well worth giving at length to illustrate how far his mountaineering had already advanced:

It is generally held that no amateur, however able, is as good as the best guides at feats of sheer endurance. I am inclined to think that Shipton comes near to being an exception to that rule – I doubt if any guide could have exceeded some of his days in the Himalaya. Even at the time when we were climbing together, although he had by no means reached his full strength, he was a very remarkable goer. I shall not easily forget the day when we started at midnight from the Chanrion hut with heavy sacks, descended into the Dranse valley, traversed the Grand Combin, and finished by sitting in the Emperor's chair at Bourg St Pierre before dinner. But I did once see him tired. This was at an earlier stage in the traverse from the Mischabel to Mont Blanc, of which the Combin day formed part. In the course of little over a week he had climbed the Nadelhorn, traversed the Dom, ascended the Weisshorn and Zinal Rothorn, gone up the Crestone Rey and round the Bétemps skyline over the Lyskamm to the Feliksjoch, traversed the Matterhorn by the Zmutt and the Italian ridges and the Dent Blanche by the Ferpècle and south ridges. On these expeditions [in 1928] he was accompanied either by [H. M.] Kelly, or by me, or by both of us. But whereas Kelly omitted the Monte Rosa – Lyskamm traverse and the Dent Blanche, and I the Zinal Rothorn, Shipton had no day off at all.'[33]

In the course of little over a week . . .! The scale of this activity, even today, would be considered staggering by any keen alpinist. This little history has a comical conclusion in which Peaker, in habitual male fashion, asserts that whilst his prodigy may have

---

[33] Peaker, 'High Pastures', (Alpine Journal, 1944), p.255.

been phenomenal in some ways, in other manly pursuits he was still green behind the ears:

> The Dent Blanche is a big mountain and its western or Ferpècle ridge is an excellent rock climb – long, continuous, and quite steep. In my recollection it is distinctly harder than the Zmutt arête, though that obviously depends on conditions. The great gendarme, where O. G. Jones and his guides met their fate, exerts a somewhat daunting influence over the lower slabs, nor is the approach up the glacier altogether simple. However, the various obstacles were surmounted and the summit reached well before mid-day. After a long sojourn on top we were hunted down the south ridge by a thunderstorm, turned off down the west face, and reached Bricolla before dinner time after an eventful but exhausting day. While dinner was being prepared we ordered a litre of wine. I had drunk a pint of wine and water and was gazing out at the wreathing clouds on the Dent Blanche, when a heavy thud caused me to look round. Eric was lying on the floor. A cursory examination showed that he was not ill, not dead, merely dead drunk – the combined effect of youth, fatigue, and an empty stomach.[34]

Shipton's recollection of the incident is one of waking to find a priest at his bedside pouring peppermint cordial down his throat. Kelly went home and Shipton and Peaker moved on to Chamonix, where they met Jack Longland and George Trevelyan[35] and joined forces for an attempt on the Rochefort Ridge, which stretches from the Dent du Géant almost to the first slopes of the Grandes Jorasses in an 'entrancing series of snow and ice-crests . . . Like a mile-long wave about to break, its tense white edge curled and twisted ahead, a foreground to stupendous views on either side as one followed it',[36] according to Dorothy Pilley. This beautiful snow

---

[34] Peaker, 'High Pastures', pp.255–6.
[35] Later Sir George Trevelyan (1906–96), 4th baronet, New Age philosopher, founder of the Wrekin Trust and a fine, patrician and distinctly 'left-field' old sage who added to the gaiety, and perhaps the depth, of nations throughout his long life.
[36] Dorothy Pilley, *Climbing Days* (2nd edition, Secker & Warburg, 1965), p.192. This is one of the classic texts of mountaineering literature. Much of the activity Pilley describes takes place in the company of her husband, the influential literary critic and theorist I. A. Richards.

arête high on Mont Blanc has a very loose section of rock-climbing to reach its high point in seasons with less than average snow. Such a year was 1928, and the relative absence of snow gave rise to a genteel little spat between Dorothy Pilley and Winifred Marples – previously encountered in the rather-too-speedy descent from the Aiguille du Peigne. Pilley had recommended the route, remembering a sublime traverse on good and plentiful snow in 1922. In 1928, Miss Marples quizzed her friend in these terms: 'Do you really like miles of dull, rotten rock?' Conditions of the year apart, more than half a century on from 1928 Jack Longland – acclaimed as the foremost British alpinist of his day – still recalled with a thrill of appreciation the ease, unflustered assurance and fluent speed of the novice alpinist Shipton's movement along that acute, fissile crest in rapidly worsening weather. The party was stormed off before the worst passage of loose and shattered rock leading to the ridge's high point, but not before karma had visited a compensatory mishap on Peaker to keep the record even after the drunken incident: 'I once fell through a cornice, and might have spent the rest of my life making an entirely unauthorised entry into Italy had not Eric Shipton immediately leapt down into France.'[37] This was the recommended procedure when one member of a party of two fell whilst moving together roped up along a sharp alpine crest (and the Rochefort Ridge is a perfect example of just that) – though it perhaps placed more faith in Beale's red-strand alpine hemp line than was wise.

Peaker, too, after their Mont Blanc adventure now had to return home for a new teaching term. Casting around for a partner, Shipton joined forces with Graham MacPhee, a Scottish doctor of notoriously difficult temperament, best known as second man to Colin Kirkus on Great Slab, the first of Kirkus's 1930s pioneering exploits on the finest of British cliffs, Clogwyn Du'r Arddu. MacPhee was eventually to die at the age of sixty-five after a fall whilst climbing alone on the Canary Islands in 1963. It is proof positive of Shipton's own congenial and tolerant character, that he could keep company like this in the intense sphere of contention, dispute and ruined friendships that is the Alps. After a mishap in a hail-filled *moulin*[38] on the Mer de Glace, when he was trapped by the feet for two hours and at one point seemed in danger of drowning,

---

[37] Peaker, 'High Pastures', p.251.
[38] A water-formed hole in the surface of a glacier.

he and MacPhee repaired to the Couvercle hut and climbed from there for the rest of Shipton's Alpine stay. The ascents they made together were on or in the vicinity of the Aiguille Verte, magnificent both as mountain and as viewpoint on the whole of the Chamonix ranges, the first ascent of which in 1865 is memorably described in Whymper's *Scrambles* in a passage remarkable for its expression of frank and simple pleasure in climbing rock: 'Charming rocks they were; granitic in texture, gritty, holding the nails well.'

Shipton's time in Europe was rapidly coming to an end. When he had decided against taking up the place at Cambridge in 1927, he had opted instead for a course in estate management at a London college – something that would provide for his immediate future and also, fortuitously, serve him well after the Everest leadership debacle of 1952–3.[39] The outcome of that decision, in the autumn of 1928, after what was to be his last Alpine season until 1965, when he climbed in the Alps again with his son John, was a passage on board ship for Mombasa. His farewells to mother and sister were said. His apprenticeship as a mountaineer was over. His reputation for competence and range of contacts had been firmly established Europe-wide. In a remarkably short time he had developed an expertise and gained broad experience in all the disciplines of climbing, and had proven himself among the outstanding British alpinists of his day (and one with clear predilections which augur interestingly for the future). Now, with characteristic originality and independence of mind, at the age of twenty-one he was lighting out for the territory. His real career in mountain exploration was about to begin.

---

[39] After leaving the Outward Bound school in Eskdale, he became for a time an agricultural labourer on an estate near Bridgnorth in Shropshire. My fellow *Guardian* county diarist Paul Evans – a Shropshire man – remembers his father telling him of how, at this time, Shipton would run up and down old, steep quarry inclines on Brown Clee and Titterstone Clee Hills to keep fit.

5

Into Africa

Tilman, on this occasion, went first, his future habitual leader following him only after an interval of nine years. Beyond the Armistice, he had pondered his future. The possibilities open to him were widely divergent. He was twenty-one on 14 February 1919. Seven weeks later he returned to Britain from where he had been stationed in post-Great War Rhineland, and the matter of how to spend the rest of his spared life became more pressing: 'To those who went to the War straight from school and survived it, the problem of what to do afterwards was peculiarly difficult. A loss of three or four years upset preconceived plans, and while the War was in progress little thought was devoted to such questions.'[1] His precocious excellence at Berkhamsted, allied to his native intelligence and distinguished war record, particularly latterly in a unit with a long and honourable tradition, would have ensured that acceptance by a good Oxford college was more or less a formality. Or he could have returned to Merseyside and put himself under his father's authority, working in the family's prospering sugar business. Though neither he nor his older brother Kenneth seemed attracted by that possibility, and there is a certain amount of testimony to the effect that John Tilman ruled with a fierce rigidity within the family home, and his work environment.

To rise in rank through continued service in the Royal Horse Artillery was another option. It was the first to be discarded. As early as December 1918 he was considering resigning his commission, and was probably well-advised to do so. Promotion within the RHA, with all its social cachet and bizarre ritual attire

[1] H. W. Tilman: *The Seven Mountain Travel Books* (Diadem Books, 1983), p.19.

and functions, might well have proven an expensive frustration in peacetime, however good a wartime officer he had been; and I doubt the ceremonial duties of the regiment would have been much to the taste of a man who notably displayed a fine sense of the absurd in his writings from the 1930s and later. Instead, in May of 1919, his commission had been duly resigned and Major Houblon, his commanding officer, was thanking him for his service and bidding him farewell in the following avuncular and distinctly fond terms: 'Well, old bird, be good and look after yourself, make tons of money, marry young, and live happily ever afterwards'.

Tilman implicitly rejected the more particular of these directives. What he did instead is succinctly conveyed in the stanza by the socialist poet, pacifist, and patient of W. H. R. Rivers at Craiglockhart, Max Plowman – one of the many surprises with which Tilman's writings face us[2] – that he used as epigraph to the first chapter of his first book, *Snow on the Equator*[3]:

> 'Young soldier, what will you be,
> When it's all over?'
> 'I shall get out and across the sea,
> Where land's cheap and a man can thrive.'

It was exactly this advice that he took, prompted by what he always

---

[2] He was deeply conservative in many ways and in certain habits of thought close to the Old High Tory persuasion. He turned down the opportunity to be published by the very reputable house of Gollancz in the 1930s, for example, on the grounds that he believed Victor Gollancz, who ran the Left Book Club, to be a Communist, which in fact he was until 1940 when he left the CPGB. Yet Tilman's sympathy with the political left was by no means wholly absent, as his respect for the fighting ability, bravery and commitment of the Italian communist partisans during the Second World War demonstrates. And thirty years later he frequently received me into his house in the friendliest manner, despite knowing that I was a card-carrying party member.

[3] G. Bell & Sons, 1937. Note that all references to Tilman's writings will not be to the rare and expensive first editions, but to the 1983 compendium volume that I edited for Diadem Books under the title *H. W. Tilman: The Seven Mountain Travel Books* (still currently available in 2012 under the Baton Wicks/Mountaineers imprints in the UK and USA/Canada). A companion volume for Shipton, *Eric Shipton: The Six Mountain Travel Books*, was published in 1985 under the same imprints, and is also still available, though references to Shipton's work in the present book are to individual publications, for reasons of personal convenience, my collection of these having been annotated over many years – apologies for any confusion arising!

liked to explain as having drawn in a lottery for ex-servicemen a square mile of what was then British East Africa (BEA). More properly it was a grant of land to ex-officers, and the element of chance came into play only in terms of the quality of land allotted. Tilman was lucky in this. He drew a plot near Kericho. It was half a degree south of the Equator, and within forty miles of a branch-line off the Kampala–Nairobi–Mombasa railway in one direction. Forty miles or so away to the west was Lake Victoria. His 'square mile of African bush of the most prodigious thickness' was at 7,000 feet above sea level and hence relatively temperate for equatorial Africa. Wood and water abounded; the clouds towered and tropical rains poured down each afternoon; a few lethal snakes slithered and hissed, though far fewer than you might find in the average human society. A group of eleven white male settlers, Tilman included, ex-soldiers all of them, was moving in to cultivate the area.

He had to get himself out there, of course, and this was no easy matter in 1919 when the whole of Europe and its colonies were milling around globally in the process of reordering themselves. Even through the good offices of his father's shipping contacts, the best passage he could secure to Mombasa, at a cost of £35, was in a steel deckhouse without cooling fans and shared with four other men, right by the poop of a passenger cargo vessel, with pens of live sheep on either side and the East Indian seamen's cookhouse directly below continually wafting aromatic smells aloft to set their appetites on edge. Of the heat as they sailed through the Red Sea in August he commented that 'even Shadrach, Meshach and Abednego might have remarked on it'. He sweated it out patiently, and read the early Victorian novelist Robert Surtees,[4] and Dr Johnson. The ship berthed in Mombasa in October and by the end of the month he was at the site of his farm-to-be, from which he wrote to his sister Adeline in America to describe the new life he had undertaken:

---

[4] Author of *Jorrocks' Jaunts and Jollities* of 1838, among other books. Surtees is a very funny and still readable writer who exercised a considerable influence on Tilman's own brand of humour, in which there are frequent references to, and elements redolent of, the Jorrocks/James Pigg hunting relationship from Surtees's best-known novel. In this context, his own coming friendship with Eric Shipton – distant, affable, complex at times in its dynamics – is a good example of life imitating art.

We live in tents, rise at crack of dawn, breakfast, and then harry a gang of 30 Lumbwa 'boys'[5] till it begins to rain about one o'clock. Lunch and then odd jobs between storms till 4.30. After tea the rain generally stops and we push off for a walk in the bush. At sundown we get into pyjamas, cardigans and coats, light a huge fire, bath, dinner, smoke, turn in. Of course, on my own place I shall have work and worry ad lib. There are only pigeons and partridges to shoot round here, but a few days' safari south is a great game country, including elephants.

Shades of George Orwell in that last phrase – 'a sahib has got to act like a sahib'[6] – and of course what he records of this activity is shocking to our wildlife-conservation-minded age. For an explanatory parallel you might look at the memoir *Out of Africa* by Karen Blixen.[7] The wanton slaughter particularly of lions – 'Oh you take this one, Denys – here's the rifle' – recorded there is extraordinarily distressing to a modern conservation sensibility, yet the book has remained popular. Perhaps its warm-hearted – where humans are concerned – evocation of a period of colonial history now entirely gone serves as explanation. Certainly *Out of Africa* is indispensable background reading for this African phase of Tilman's and Shipton's lives. As for Tilman himself, I'm inclined to the view that eventually he grew out of the British East African bloodlust culture of his time. Flaubert, in the second of his *Trois Contes* – his retelling of *La Légende Dorée*, the St Julien legend – describes the epiphanic moment when the young male consciousness realises life's sanctity and is finally consumed by guilt for his previous murderous actions; and Tilman, in *Snow on the Equator*, in his habitually laconic style, describes something of the same shift in awareness: 'Possibly the most urgent desire of the newcomer to a country of

---

[5] A racist and demeaning term to our modern ears, and the use here is purely historical. I did ask Tilman in 1977 how he felt about present-day Kenya, and his wry and distinctly ironic response was that "the boys' are getting a little unruly these days'. As his Himalayan record demonstrates, anyone less inherently racist than Tilman would be hard to imagine.

[6] George Orwell, 'Shooting an Elephant', in *The Collected Essays, Journalism and Letters of George Orwell Volume 1: An Age like This*, (Harmondsworth 1970), p.269.

[7] 'Isak Dinesen' was Blixen's pen name – an ornate and exotic Danish prose stylist whose other works include the wittily atmospheric *Seven Gothic Tales* and the exquisite moral/aesthetic fable *Babette's Feast*.

big game is to go out and kill something. Fortunately for most, this
unsporting blood-lust is soon satiated.'[8]

The actual moment of sudden repugnance and responsibility he
records thus:

> . . . an obvious bull [elephant] came to a stand right opposite us,
> broadside on, offering a perfect target. 'We do it wrong, being
> so majestical; to offer it the show of violence,' was certainly
> how we felt about it . . . I had with me a new heavy rifle which
> I was itching to try on something worthy of its weight. One
> shot between eye and ear dropped him stone dead, leaving us
> aghast at the suddenness of it and feeling like murderers with
> an 'outsize' corpse on our hands.'[9]

Another activity happened along to capture his imagination, that
was ultimately to displace this outgrown and demeaning one; but it
did so under the most unfortunate circumstances.

These came about in 1924, when Tilman had been farming in BEA
– or Kenya Colony as it had been known since 1920 – for five years.
In this time he had cleared land, built bridges (the early, makeshift
efforts were made of timber baulks lashed together with war-surplus
German barbed wire – the same material the Allied artillery tactics
had failed to cut, and on which the machine-gunned corpses piled
up through each new offensive: 'We found it just as intractable and
spiteful to handle here as it had been in France'),[10] erected houses,
put acres firstly under flax, which was financially disastrous for
many who had invested (as Tilman wisely did not) in the necessary
and complex processing machinery; and then, increasingly, under
coffee, on the sale of which his father could advise him (the two
formed a partnership to buy more suitable land and put it under
cultivation in the mid-1920s). He had soon acquired a reputation
as a loner and also as something of a misogynist. One woman,
Marjorie Sneyd, who married into the community in 1923, recalls
her husband Robin warning her that Tilman was 'very annoyed at
the prospect of having a woman in their midst'. She also remembers
that in the event he came to heel quite readily, turned up regularly

[8] Tilman, *Seven Mountain Travel Books*, p.30.
[9] Ibid. p. 35.
[10] Ibid. p. 22.

with the other men for tea at her house on Saturdays, reciprocated the pleasure by inviting her to tea at his bachelor mud hut with its bookshelves lined with Everyman Library volumes, and was godfather to her two sons when she and Robin began to breed, as married people in those days mostly did.

In 1924, however, a family tragedy disrupted these peaceful routines, resulting in Tilman's first trip back to England since 1919, and the first stirrings of a new interest that was to change the direction of his life. His elder brother Kenneth had finished the war in the newly-formed Royal Air Force, and stayed on in the service after cessation of hostilities. In March of 1924 he was observer in a Fairey IIID reconnaissance biplane – a type very recently commissioned into the Fleet Air Arm – during sea trials in the Mediterranean in which the Royal Navy's aircraft training-carrier, HMS *Argus* was involved along with the newly-commissioned aircraft carrier HMS *Hermes* and a flotilla of attendant destroyers. The *Argus*, like the equally design-problem-plagued *Hermes*, was a prototype vessel with a long history of developmental difficulties. It had been based on the hull of an unfinished Italian cruise-liner requisitioned whilst under construction at Clydebank. Both carriers employed catapult systems – huge, tensioned slingshots in essence, with the aircraft attached by means of a trailing hook. Off Majorca Kenneth Tilman's plane was launched thus from the *Argus*, veered off to the right out of control on leaving the deck, hit the sea and somersaulted, to come to a halt upside down and sinking. One of the accompanying destroyers was at the scene in minutes to pick up Kenneth and his pilot. The latter survived, but the former had been knocked unconscious in the accident and drowned. Artificial resuscitation was attempted, to no avail. He was buried at Puerto Pollensa, a cross made for his grave from the plane's propeller, and the family were duly informed. The letter to his widow, in a more-than-usually crass service attempt at sensitivity, told her that 'he only had a large bruise on his temple, but otherwise was quite normal to look upon'.

Tilman returned as quickly as he could – still a matter of several weeks by train and boat – to Wallasey to find his parents devastated by the loss; and there was more emotional trouble brewing. His sister Adeline had been courted by a staff officer and friend of his, Alec Reid Moir, and the two were married in the spring of 1918. After the Armistice the newly-wed couple had emigrated to America, where Alec pursued a business career and Adeline gave birth to two daughters – Joan, born in 1920, and the redoubtable Pam, Tilman's favourite niece, who followed in 1922. By the time Tilman arrived back in Wallasey in May of 1924, Adeline was already there, and whisked her younger brother away to the Lake District, ostensibly to take a break and spend a few days fell-walking, but in fact to confide in him about the failing state of her marriage.

It was in the course of this Lake District stay that Tilman and his sister made their first acquaintance with rock-climbing, having seen one of the little posters on which the man who was arguably the first Lakeland mountain guide,[11] J. E. B. Wright (later the founder of the Mountaineering Association) advertised his fixed tariffs for taking clients up various climbs. Intrigued, Tilman and Adeline retained Wright for a day and were instructed in the very moderate technicalities of Langdale's Middlefell Buttress before continuing up to Stickle Tarn and following the airy scramble of Jack's Rake across the face of Pavey Ark to reach the ridge at Thunacar Knott. They then honoured the mountaineering tradition of the time, which insisted on a walk over the tops after a rock-climb, by following this ridge over Harrison Stickle and Pike of Stickle all the way round to the Stake Pass and the rough descent into Langdale again – a first day on rock and hill the details of which he could relate with perfect recall even over a gap of fifty years that had included many far more difficult and protracted expeditions.

Having been introduced to mountains in his sister's company on the one hand, on the other, with neither of his parents showing any interest in attempting to save their daughter's marriage, he felt under a compulsion to try to talk his friend Alec, as he saw it, back to his senses. With that in mind, before May – a busy month! – was out, the surviving Tilman siblings crossed the Mersey to the Cunard passenger-liner terminal and embarked on the newly recommissioned Blue Riband-holder the RMS *Mauretania*, bound for New York on a marital rescue mission. The trip was not a success. The marriage and his friendship with Alec both foundered. Tilman took his leave of the warring couple regretfully and made his way back

---

[11] Millican Dalton (1867–1947), the self-styled 'Professor of Adventure' who lived in the Bowderstone caves in Borrowdale in the post-Great War period, has an equal claim to being this. See Matthew Entwhistle's warm and evocative *Millican Dalton: A Search for Adventure and Freedom* (Mountainmere Research, 2004).

to his African farm, and before the year was out, Adeline and her daughters were once more on board the *Mauretania* and returning to Liverpool for the last time from the USA. Two more pieces had fallen into place in the jigsaw of Tilman's future. The beloved elder sister companion and her young family with whom he was to spend the greater part of his life were now back on British shores. And from a brief few days of sad and intimate sisterly company in the Lake District was implanted the notion of mountains and climbing that was to become a presiding interest of his life, and lead on to some of its greatest achievements.

The implanted seed took several years to come to fruition, and we might stand back and leave it to germinate at this point, confident in the fact that nothing much happens in Tilman's African sojourn for the remainder of the 1920s. There was a visit from his father, enabled to travel by the presence at Seacroft of Adeline – now acting as housekeeper, occasional chauffeuse, bridge partner and generally supportive presence to her parents – and the young daughters upon whom their grandparents doted. John Tilman's visit to his son went surprisingly well, and led to a closer understanding and a new business relationship between them. There was, however, a growing pioneer-mentality in the younger Tilman that was becoming dissatisfied with the notion of the established and settled life of which his industriousness had left him increasingly assured.

His imagination provided a ready answer to this conundrum. The early days of bringing a native wilderness into cultivation had evolved into what for him was the much less congenial task of routinely attending to a coffee plantation. He knew that in this situation he was in danger of becoming what was known in the colonial slang as a 'hill-topper' – a man so used to domestic solitude that, from his deliberately chosen hilltop and approach-route-surveying residence, binoculars ever to hand, he has ample warning and opportunity 'to escape into the safety of the neighbouring bush' should undesired and undesirable human company with the intention of visiting be spotted. Tilman already had 2,000 acres of land near Sotik, on the plains away to the south and thirty miles farther from the rail head. He also had a new business involvement other than the one contracted with his father. An old Wirral friend, Richard Royston, had agreed to act as manager on the existing Kericho plantation, John Tilman having undertaken to guarantee his salary of £200 per annum in the unlikely event of profits failing to cover it. This arrangement, which left both Royston and Tilman *fils* free to travel or take holidays when the mood arose, made perfect sense – 'all that was needed between the two of us was the sort of understanding that John Jorrocks had with his huntsman James Pigg, to wit "that master and man should not both get drunk on the same day"'. And it ensured that Tilman was able to concentrate his energies on developing the new land – a task much more appealing to him than staying put and merely enjoying the fruits of past labours. In 1929, after ten years' hard labour at Kericho, he moved to a house he had built on the land at Sotik. We shall leave him there for the time being, and turn now to herald the arrival in Kenya Colony of the man we last heard of ascending the Aiguille Verte.

Eric Shipton, newly qualified in estate management, arrived in Mombasa in October 1928 aboard the British India Line's SS *Modasa* – a rather more comfortable means of travel than Tilman had enjoyed nine years earlier. Only a few short weeks had elapsed after his last momentous alpine season, and he was carrying with him all the impedimenta of ropes, nailed boots and ice axe used throughout those hectic and exhilarating months. He had seen mountains marked on the map in the area to which he was bound, and they had played a crucial part in his decision to go there and not to revert to the still-available possibility of reading law or classics at Cambridge, as the officious college master had advised the preceding summer.

The legal profession's loss – for Shipton would have made a persuasive barrister – was mountaineering's gain. It was also for a time that of Kenyan coffee-planting. He was apprenticed to a huge coffee estate, run by two partners, one of whom was Irish and – not uncommonly or unreasonably for an Irishman of the time – loathed the English. It was at Nyeri, north of Nairobi, about 160 miles east of Tilman's plantation in Kericho and only twenty or so miles away from Mount Kenya. In *Upon that Mountain* Shipton described the view that greeted him as he emerged from his bungalow on his first morning in Nyeri:

The whole northern horizon was filled with a gigantic cone of purple mist. The cone was capped by a band of cloud. Above this band, utterly detached from the Earth, appeared a pyramid of rock and ice, beautifully proportioned, hard and clear against the sky. The sun, not yet risen, had already touched the peak, throwing ridge and corrie into sharp relief, lighting here and there a sparkling gem of ice.[12]

It's that first vision of Les Ecrins from 1925 renewed and revisited. It's another phrase playing out in the theme of 'All experience is an arch wherethrough/ Gleams that untravelled world . . .' And the reality of it had now to be explored, with a confidence and technique his alpine seasons had given him. 'I was enchanted by this lovely mountain', he wrote, forty years later, 'and consumed by an aching desire to reach it.'[13]

Mount Kenya comprises a high and difficult coronet of rock peaks, the eroded remnants of an ancient volcano plug, that reaches an altitude of over 17,000 feet and is interspersed with and adorned by glaciers. In 1929 it was in every way remote and serious. The higher of its twin main peaks, Batian, had only had one ascent, by the Swiss guides César Ollier and Josef Brocherel with their client Sir Halford Mackinder on a large expedition in 1899. Numerous attempts to repeat their climb had all failed. Its marginally lower and adjacent twin Nelion was still unclimbed.

A competent companion was needed, and with the usual luck of the young Shipton, he was fortunate in that there was one to hand – and an exceptional one at that; of whom Jack Longland could write that 'he was the best climbing companion that I ever had'; with whom Longland, the most accomplished all-round climber in Britain during the latter half of the 1920s, 'formed a partnership in endeavour that I never quite found again'.[14] In Shipton's summer alpine season of 1928, climbing on the Rochefort Ridge with Longland and George Trevelyan, he had confided his African plans to them and they had told him to look up their old Cambridge chum and university mountaineering club companion Percy Wyn Harris, who had been newly posted to Kenya as a junior officer, an assistant district commissioner, in the Colonial Service.

When Jack Longland had arrived at Cambridge in 1924 Wyn, as he was invariably known, had been the CUMC secretary.

---

[12] Eric Shipton, *Upon that Mountain* (Hodder & Stoughton, 1943), p.46.
[13] Eric Shipton, *That Untravelled World* (Hodder & Stoughton, 1969), p.51.
[14] From Sir Percy Wyn Harris's obituary by Jack Longland (*Alpine Journal*, 1982, p.271.

Wyn's regular climbing partner was its president of the time, Van Noorden. Longland had duly trooped round to Wyn's rooms in Caius, knocked, and a sepulchral voice from somewhere above and behind the door bade him enter. He did so to find Wyn and Van Noorden playfully chimneying[15] along at ceiling level between the keeping room and the bedroom and was invited to join them, which he did, thus ensuring his acceptance. That these two were set to become the rising British alpine stars of their day was proven the following summer, when they made the second ascent of the Brouillard Ridge on Mont Blanc – a high, rotten and storm-plagued feature first climbed by Josef Brocherel in 1901, a couple of years after his Batian ascent, with a competent and forceful Italian client, Giovanni Battista Gugliermina, whose name is now scattered throughout the Alps in connection with many of the more difficult routes of his day.

On returning from the Alps, Van Noorden headed off to Wales intending to help Herbert Carr in the research for his climbing guide to Snowdon, which was to be published in 1926. On one of the smaller cliffs in Cwm Glas, Carr fell whilst seconding a difficult pitch. Van Noorden was dragged from his inadequate stance and belay and both of them plunged to the foot of the crag. Van Noorden was killed by the longer fall and greater velocity from having been pulled from his stance. Carr lay injured and unable to move for days, until eventually a search party of which Wyn was a member found him still alive by the body of Van Noorden. This tragic accident to Wyn's closest friend had happened barely three years before Shipton arrived in Kenya. But mountaineers become inured. Wyn was ready for an adventure, and once he and Shipton had made contact, a plan was formulated for Batian. Wyn had attempted this in 1928 only to be foiled by heavy snowfall and his companion's having gone down with paratyphoid at their high camp.

The plan immediately ran into difficulties in the form of a plague of locusts, which meant that anyone passing through Nairobi was conscripted, issued with locus-exterminating gear, and sent out into the wild to eradicate the pest. Wyn, as a colonial officer, found his freedom of movement curtailed, so Shipton arranged for his old

---

[15] A term from rock-climbing. In a parallel-sided cleft (a 'chimney') the back is placed against one wall, the feet on the other, pressure is exerted and the climber can move up, down or across as s/he desires.

friend from Norway, Gustav Sommerfelt, also now resident and working in Kenya, to join him on the venture. At the very last moment, on New Year's Eve, Wyn managed to slip the official leash and the three met up in Nairobi's Indian bazaar, hired a decrepit half-ton lorry and a nervous driver, loaded it with food for sixteen days, pots and machetes, tent and cooking equipment, and set off for Chogoria Mission, starting point for their mountain. The 160-mile journey was an eventful one. As darkness fell, imagined threats loomed ever more vividly into the driver's consciousness, and were dispelled by Sommerfelt's waving around pieces of a rifle he extricated from the truck bed. They arrived at a camp two miles beyond Chogoria at midnight, and celebrated the New Year with plum cake. At first light they were already busy rounding up porters, of whom they employed twenty-two[16] at a shilling a day, and at 9 a.m. the little caravan set off into the forest on an eighteen-mile trek with 4,000 feet of climbing to their first camp, at which they arrived just before nightfall.

Shipton was limping heavily as a result of breaking an ankle falling from a cliff into a tree a fortnight before he left for the trip – a small detail insufficient to deter him from going. Another day's march took them clear of the forest into a region of grassland dotted with bamboo groves and solitary giant trees. A comfortable if basic lap-board wooden shed, the Urumandi Hut, had been built here for the use of the few enterprising travellers who came to the region, and when Shipton and his party arrived there was a surprise awaiting them:

> . . . the hut was occupied by Miss Vivienne de Watteville . . . She was stopping here for several months engaged in writing a book about her travels. It seemed unkind to disturb her peace, but she welcomed us with charming hospitality, and gave us a dinner that would have done justice to any English home. We would certainly have been tempted to prolong our stay,

---

[16] Thus in Wyn Harris's account for the 1929 *Alpine Journal*. Shipton gives the number as fifteen. I have no idea whose figure is the accurate one. The more I read of Shipton, a frequent humorously self-effacing quality aside and a distinctly tongue-in-cheek playfulness on occasion too, the more I find myself inclined to trust his versions. He was an exceptionally acute observer, and in an odd way a master too of all the subtle arts of self-concealment. In this case, however, there is independent testimony to confirm Wyn's version. See also note 28 below.

had we been less impatient to reach the glaciers. Our hostess promised to pay us a visit while we were there.[17]

Ms De Watteville had only arrived at the hut, 'set snugly in a little dip sheltered by giant heath and a single green tree . . . wonderfully welcoming in the midst of that vast solitude',[18] just before Christmas Day, installing herself there intent on a two-month stay with a gramophone and a plentiful supply of Beethoven, for 'his ruggedness and gloom and sudden, tempestuous joy, above all his great-heartedness that would drive through to the summits with the irresistible energy of an Atlantic breaker: all this was the very soul of the mountain. Uplifted on the wings of his greatness, I felt that I could look out over the whole of life from the top of the peak.'[19] Fortunately, the climbers encountered no such elemental competition from orchestral tsunamis in their attempts.

Vivienne de Watteville, a great beauty and a witty conversationalist according to Karen Blixen, was the daughter of an English mother who had died of cancer when Vivienne was nine years old, and an aristocratic Swiss naturalist father who had been killed by a lion in 1924. She herself, having been unsuccessful in the attempt to save her father's life after the lion's attack, and despite suffering from the relapsing condition of spirillum fever, had resolutely continued the collecting trip for the natural history museum in Berne on which they were engaged, and had shot and stuffed all the specimens they had been seeking, including a white rhinoceros. She had brought with her to the Urumandi Hut a copy of *Walden* by Thoreau,[20] of whom she claimed to be a disciple, though what that simple-living and susceptible vegetarian philosopher would have made of her is apt matter for speculation. She loved to be naked outdoors ('few

---

[17] Shipton, *Upon That Mountain*, p.52. Curiously, all mention of this lady disappears between Shipton's first and second essays at autobiography.
[18] Vivienne de Watteville, *Speak to the Earth* (1935) (Harmondsworth, 1988), p.221 – a deliciously overwrought piece of writing, thoroughly recommendable, that abounds with glimpses into the stranger depths of that most intriguing of places, the human female psyche.
[19] De Watteville, *Speak to the Earth*, p.287.
[20] Henry David Thoreau (1817–62), American transcendentalist, finest of all writers on nature, friend of Ralph Waldo Emerson and author of *Walden, or Life in the Woods* (1854). The best introduction to Thoreau other than his own work is Robert D. Richardson's magisterial *Thoreau: A Life of the Mind* (University of California Press, 1986).

things are more delicious than to feel the sun and wind on one's body') and bathe in waterfalls ('one moment of icy spray and then the weight of white water dashed over my shoulders like ice or fire'), was an expert cook, could contrive the meanest rum punch in the colony, and perhaps as much as anyone was responsible for the thorough exploration of the surroundings of Mount Kenya. Little more than eighteen months later, in July of the following year, after innumerable proposals from him she would become the wife of Captain (later General) George Goschen, a grandson of one of the great liberal statesmen of Gladstone's era, with whom she lived firstly in Shropshire at Hopesay, where they are both buried, and then at Farnham, Surrey.

At the time Vivienne met Shipton, Sommerfelt and Wyn, she was twenty-eight, unmarried, a very free spirit who had given up hunting and now shot her specimens only with a camera. It's delicious to conjecture on what our diffident blue-eyed boy of twenty-one must have made of her, or she of him and his handsome Norse and suave diplomat friends. And to marvel yet again at the extraordinary good fortune that followed him around. Still, he had, if it's not too indelicate a phrase, bigger fish to fry. After their English dinner – her own Christmas dinner at Urumandi had consisted of plum cake and Heinz tinned spaghetti in tomato sauce, in that order apparently, so perhaps she was seeking to impress – with promises from Miss de Watteville that she would meet them higher on the mountain in a few days' time, as dawn broke the climbing party advanced towards its objective.

The ascent of Batian led by César Ollier and Josef Brocherel had been by way of the south-east face, but the pioneering instinct of Shipton and Harris was aroused, and after scrutinising the face Nelion presented to the Mackinder valley by which they were approaching, and concluding it was unclimbable, they decided on an attempt on Batian by the north-east face, which 'danced temptingly before us in the sun', in Wyn's words. It rebuffed them – twice. 'Our defeat on the north-east face had been complete and decisive', he noted in a crestfallen way. They were out of sorts, through the effect of altitude, and no doubt also that of entrancing late-night company. Of necessity they gave the mountain best on this occasion. (In fact, the route they had attempted, which was climbed eventually in 1944, is now regarded as one of the easier ways to the summit of Batian, though the route-finding is complex, weaving through difficult ground.) Instead, they decided to concentrate their efforts on the south-east face, and shifted their camp round to what was known as 'the Skating Lake'[21] – a small frozen tarn alongside the Lewis glacier at a point where there had once been another timber hut, smaller than that at Urumandi and now in ruins, storms having razed it to the ground.

> It had collapsed in a sheet of ice, out of which a coil of rope half-emerged, frozen stiff as a hawser. It was a pathetic wreck – like a ship in the Arctic – back broken and the ice strewn with splinters of doors and walls. On the floor (the only part left intact) was an incongruous pair of high-heeled brown shoes, bleached and sodden as orange peel.'[22]

Their first effort was by way of Batian's south ridge, and petered out at a formidable buttress, 'smooth like the prow of a ship' (an Arctic one, perhaps – the maritime theme seems to have been catching), that overhung the farther side of a notch at which they had arrived in a thinning mist: 'Again the verdict was distressingly simple.' The thought of possible failure, and this on a climb thirty years old and from the very dawn of African mountaineering – an inimical conclusion for young men – entered their minds. As compensation or exorcism of such pessimistic thoughts, there occurred one of the moments that are scattered throughout Shipton's mountain-narratives, and which have so much in common with traditional nature-mysticism:

> For us, in the midst of the scene, a part of it, it was profoundly impressive. First Point John appeared, we were nearly level with its summit, an island in a restless sea of soft pink and grey. Then, all about us were spires and wild buttresses, floating, moving; and above, infinitely high, the rocky dome of Batian.[23]

Everyone familiar with their mountains will recognise the

---

[21] In Ms de Watteville's book it appears as 'the Curling Pond'. They are one and the same place.

[22] De Watteville, *Speak to the Earth*, p.254.

[23] Shipton, *Upon That Mountain*, p.58.

disorientating nature of these conditions[24], their separating-out of
the individual from his or her temporal world, and their beautiful
sense of prefiguring what so often and so quickly follows on from
them:

> The level rays of the sun had broken through. We looked
> towards the east and saw there a great circle of rainbow
> colours, sharp and clear, framing our own dark silhouettes.
> It was the Spectre of the Brocken – the only one I have ever
> seen.[25] Mountains have many ways of rewarding us for our
> pilgrimage, and often bestow their richest treasures when least
> expected. For my part, all disappointment, all care for the
> future were drowned in the great joy of living that moment.
> We climbed slowly down the ridge and . . . back to camp.[26]

Morning saw them beneath the face again, determining on a new
line to attempt, with Shipton still possessed by the preceding night's
vision and gazing up 'in a dreamy bewilderment without the faintest
idea of how to start', whilst 'a fiery spark seemed to have kindled in
Wyn . . . and as soon as we had roped together he led off up rocks
with such energy and decision that he might have been an Alpine
guide climbing a familiar peak'.[27] A teasing and complex route
with stretches of quite technical rock-climbing opened up before
them, and after traversing into and out of a spectacular gully where
Tilman was later to suffer a potentially serious mishap and lose his
ice axe, it led them with unexpected ease at its very end not to their
intended objective but on to the hitherto virgin summit of Nelion.
A gleaming dome of ice was visible above the clouds to the south –
Kilimanjaro, Africa's highest mountain, 250 miles away. From far
below came a congratulatory bellow from Gustav Sommerfelt, who
had been watching through binoculars. They climbed down into the

---

[24] They were present on Everest in 1924 when Odell had his last glimpse of Mallory
and Irvine, and may explain his surely mistaken conclusion – around which Odell
himself created confusions – that the pair had been above the so-called 'Second
Step', an obstacle far beyond Mallory's technical capacities, or indeed his physical
ones at that stage.
[25] He did, of course, know Whymper's account of seeing one from the Matterhorn
during the first ascent.
[26] Shipton, *Upon That Mountain*, p.58.
[27] Ibid., p.59.

Gate of Mists – the gap between Nelion and Batian – cut steps in hard snow across the northern slope of the ridge beyond, and soon emerged on Batian's summit – the second party ever to reach that point, almost three decades after its first ascent. With Shipton going first to find the way and Wyn as senior partner protecting him from above on each pitch before descending himself, they retraced their steps over Nelion and down the face again to reach their camp. Two days later they did it all over again for the benefit of Sommerfelt, who accompanied them. On this occasion, the two leaders armed with prior knowledge, they found it all much more straightforward.

Below them, meanwhile, Vivienne de Watteville and three porters,[28] armed with plum cake and flasks of hot Bovril, were questing around on the glacier in a state of some anxiety looking for them. She had earlier heard voices but could not identify where they were coming from, until 'by chance I raised my eyes to the peak, and there, standing on the topmost summit, were three figures diminutive as ants'. The three figures descended, Vivienne watching:

> . . . through the glasses I could make out the climbers, the rope showing up very white and linking them together. To watch them climbing down, swinging from ledge to ledge of what seemed a perfectly sheer precipice of a thousand feet, held me in miserable suspense; and a sudden avalanche of rock glancing against the side with a hollow ring put my heart in my mouth.

For all that, now that she could see them close to she dashed back to the Skating Lake/Curling Pond (where she found that her porters had kindly erected her tent on the wooden floor of the old hut), lit the lanterns and put the kettle on before returning to greet the three climbers with the plum cake and flasks of Bovril as, perfectly synchronised with the setting sun in her account, they reached the ice. Back at the camp she 'seized the tins that bore the most inviting labels, and the saucepan of potatoes cooked by the faithful Hezekiah, and joined the climbers. Their tent was even smaller than

---

[28] According to Shipton in *Upon That Mountain*. Wyn Harris, in his account for the *Alpine Journal*, gives the number as eight. I suspect a running joke between these two – see note 16 above. The more interesting figures in mountaineering are seldom wholly serious – mortal danger has that effect. I wonder if 'The Affair of the Yeti's Footprint' (see Epilogue) is being prefigured here in an ongoing mutual tease.

mine; and shutting up every crack and crevice we successfully defied the cold, ate to our hunger, and I heard the story of the climb.' They deferred their planned retreat from the Skating Lake and spent the following day instead accompanying Ms de Watteville around the Lewis Glacier and its notable features. From one rocky gap below Point John they were rewarded with particularly good views of the mountain faces on this side of the peak, which she photographed. 'It is pleasant after a climb,' observed Shipton later, 'to have leisure to trace from afar the scenes of recent adventures. Above our gap to the west stood a rock peak, as slender and graceful as the spire of Salisbury Cathedral.'[29]

This was called Cleopatra's Needle by Vivienne de Watteville. Shipton later named it Midget Peak, and it will figure further in the present chapter. What's fascinating about that comparison to Salisbury spire (one that he used also of Shivling in the journal extract quoted in the prologue) is how, in the moment of his greatest mountaineering achievement so far, the parameters for comparison still default to the Wardour Vale and Bevis-land of his schooldays.

The little party wandered back, stopping for a Thermos of tea cached at the edge of the glacier beneath Point John and resting there for half an hour as the light faded before the last long uphill traverse across the glacier to the Skating Lake. It was at this point that Vivienne discovered that she had lost her sun hat.

It had been tucked into my belt most of the day and I had no clear recollection of when I had seen it last. It was the only sunproof hat I had, but even as the calamity fully dawned on me I went on doggedly saying that it did not matter. Had it contained all I had in the world, I was past forfeiting one step of that hard-won climb to retrieve it. But turning a deaf ear to my protests, one of the mountaineers quietly slipped off his coat and began scrambling down over the way we had toiled up. In that vista of grey broken scree and big boulders which all looked alike, nothing was more difficult than to retrace our route, and it was by great good fortune that after a time he actually found the wretched hat.[30]

29 Shipton, *Upon That Mountain*, pp.63–4.
30 De Watteville, *Speak to the Earth*, pp.265–6.

Ms de Watteville's great good fortune indeed, and if the obliging retriever was not the youngest, blue-eyed member of the party, I think I would eat my own hat.

The weather turned spectacularly that night, enforcing a retreat that was necessary anyway in order for Wyn to depart on home leave. Vivienne de Watteville now fades enigmatically from the picture after a night in a snow-filled tent at the Skating Lake. Shipton, Sommerfelt and Wyn were given a lift from Chogoria to Nairobi in a lorry by a Dutch missionary and the first two earned a king's ransom of £2.10s od for providing an account of their climb to the *East African Standard*, where it made front-page news under the banner headline 'New Conquest of the Twin Peaks of Mount Kenya' – journalistic jargon never seems to change, and the crassness of the presentation is said to have exasperated the mild, reserved and diplomatic Wyn.

In March, Shipton left Nyeri and went to Turbo in the Uasin Gishu region close to the Ugandan border to work with Sommerfelt. At first they shared a one-roomed bungalow, living on basic produce from the farm where they worked, saving most of their salaries of £15 each per month and buying an old station wagon to jaunt around in together and take out girls they met at dances, as young men will. Shipton caught malaria, though it was only of the benign tertiary kind. His mother sold her London house and family finances ran to buying a farm at Turbo (Mrs Haly installing herself there from time to time when not travelling) – a wise move with the Wall Street Crash of October 1929 imminent and her investments in jeopardy. Shipton befriended the local Nandi tribe, a pastoral people like the Masai, though without the latter's reputation for extreme sexual promiscuity. (In Tilman's words, the Masai 'have no morals as understood by us'. They were deemed to be responsible for the exceptionally high incidence of syphilis in the colony. Baron Bror von Blixen, Karen Blixen's husband, had contracted syphilis from liaisons with Masai women, and in turn infected his wife, who suffered from the debilitating symptoms of its secondary form for the rest of her life despite painful and distressing attempts at a cure, the earliest of which used mercury. The problem and source was as well known among Kenya's colonial population of the time as that of AIDS is in the present day. Shipton's youthful innocence and diffidence was a heaven-sent prophylactic, and gives a perspective on the very guarded and physically limited nature of the relationship with a widow[31] of his own age, Madge Anderson, that began during his time at Turbo. With the threat of having this dreadful disease passed on to them by a male population among whom the proportion of rakes appears to have been distinctly high, chastity or abstinence from heterosexual physical relationships seem to have been very attractive options for the women.)

In December of 1929 he took another trip to Mount Kenya with Pat Russell, a young lawyer from Eldoret and a friend of Wyn Harris's (the latter being based in nearby Kakamega). His intention was to probe at the north-western approaches to the mountain, but he was laid up at the Silverbeck Hotel in Nanyuki for a week with the malaria and left with only enough time for himself and Russell to repeat the route of January and make a first ascent of Point John. The ascents were written up – more briefly this time, and by one of the paper's local stringers – in the *East African Standard*, a copy of the paper found its way to Tilman's plantation at Sotik, a mutual acquaintance by the name of Melhuish who had himself attempted Mount Kenya heard of Tilman's interest and gave him Shipton's address. As people did in those civilised days, early in 1930 Tilman sent him a letter. It would have been brief, courteous, to the point: 'Dear Shipton . . .Yours, H. W. Tilman.' Shipton recalls that it told of having done some rock-climbing in the Lake District on his last trip home (six years before); and that it asked for advice on how to go about climbing in Kenya.

Tilman's recollection in old age was mildly confused: 'We must have met for the first time in the latter half of 1929. We were both growing coffee in Kenya, the farms 160 miles apart; and whether he wrote to me or vice versa I cannot remember; most probably the latter.' It would almost certainly have been the latter, given the salient facts that Shipton exactly recalls (an interesting point, this, which does argue that reliance can be placed even on his distant accounts). Tilman himself gives no contemporary account of the channels through which they came to meet – the two sentences

---

[31] Her husband Murray, described in those early Barbara Cartland days as 'tall, dark and handsome', had drunkenly driven his car, overladen with party-goers, into a river on his way back from a dance he and Madge had been attending and drowned. One of the several revellers who had been given a lift was thrown clear, and dived back down to drag Madge out of the submerged car by her hair before she suffered the same fate as her inebriate husband. She was twenty-two at the time she was widowed.

quoted above from his 1977 *Himalayan Journal* obituary of his old friend are the only record he leaves, and in his first book, *Snow on the Equator*, he dispenses with explanation altogether and launches out *in media res*:

> On the last day of February 1930, S. and I forgathered at Nairobi, whence we left by car for the mountain. S. who like myself was a coffee planter, had a farm north of the railway about 160 miles from mine. In the middle of it was a great tooth of granite, which soared up for about 200 feet – an eyesore to a planter, but to those of the Faith better than water in a thirsty land. S. had worked out several routes on it to which I was later introduced.'[32]

In the *Himalayan Journal* obituary he tells how, on his first visit to Turbo, he was introduced to these climbs on Mount Elgon, and comments that 'Young though he was, his climbing experience exceeded mine, for I had started late, and he was the better climber.' It's possible – and quite likely had Tilman been on a regular visit to Richard Royston in Kericho, which is much closer to Turbo than Sotik – that this first visit to Turbo followed on very quickly from the receipt of Tilman's letter and took place in January or February of 1930, for the latter further comments that 'we made plans, and in 1930, on two separate trips, we climbed Kilimanjaro [for the purpose of which they had foregathered in Nairobi on 28 February] and then made the traverse of Mount Kenya by the West ridge'.

What is plain is that Shipton thought very well of his new climbing companion, despite his experience being so limited that many would have deemed it inadequate for the projects that his mind was circling around, most notably an attempt on the west ridge of Batian. His assessment of Tilman from his first autobiography, written at a time when the friendship that developed between them had gone through a period of significant stress, is a very generous and revealing one that implicitly says a great deal about both men at the very outset of a defining decade of British greater-ranges mountaineering:

Early in 1930 I had a letter from H. W. Tilman, who had

---

[32] Tilman, *Seven Mountain Travel Books*, p.39.

been given my address by Melhuish. This turned out to be a most fortunate contact and we were destined to share many mountain ventures together. At that time Tilman had not done much climbing . . . But I have met few people so admirably adapted to it both physically and temperamentally. He was very strong and tough, he had a natural aptitude for moving about difficult country, I have never known him rattled, and he had a remarkable ability to put up with – even a liking for – unpleasant conditions. He said very little, too little I thought, but, like many quiet people, when he did speak he was generally worth listening to. As a companion the qualities I liked best were his tremendous sense of humour and his constant readiness to embark on any project. When I first met him he was a recluse, and to my way of thinking too antipathetic towards the softer forms of human pleasure, such as novel reading, cinemas, or any form of social intercourse. Most of our occasional quarrels arose, I think, from our disagreement on these matters.[33]

Leaving aside the insoluble question of whether or not they climbed together at this early juncture on Shipton's farm rocks, which seems to me probable if only for 'S.' – as Tilman invariably refers to him in his earliest writings – to establish how the newcomer performed before they embarked on any more serious ventures such as the west ridge of Mount Kenya which he already had in mind (and I hope he kept to himself the fact that he and Sommerfelt invited girls round to pyjama-parties on these same rocks, so as not to offend the older man's sensibilities), they were soon heading south through the great southern game reserve of Kenya and into Tanganyika Territory[34] for a putative ascent of Kilimanjaro. Today this dullest of high mountains – 'nothing but a long and, in the conditions we encountered, somewhat gruelling walk',[35] and elsewhere 'quite devoid of interest for the mountaineer'[36] in Shipton's view – is a magnet for charity challenge walks and the like, the participants relentlessly scrutinised for symptoms of HACE

---

[33] Shipton, *Upon That Mountain*, ibid. p. 67–8.

[34] Now Tanzania.

[35] Shipton, *That Untravelled World*, p. 60.

[36] Shipton, 'The First Traverse of the Twin Peaks of Mount Kenya', (*A.J.* 1930), p. 146

and HAPE, and anyone with a mild headache being dosed with Diamox[37] and ordered off the hill by the international division of the Health and Safety Executive. However, this oversized plum pudding of a hill does reach an altitude of 19,341 feet on Kibo, the highest of its three eminences, and at that altitude, for the unfit and the unacclimatised, problems can develop.

They did, in the form of what Tilman defines in a sally from a later book as 'mountaineer's foot – or the inability to put one in front of the other'. Leaving their porter and guide, Solomon, at Gillman Point, the first of several bumps around the summit crater rim – Kilimanjaro is another extinct volcano – they shuffled on through soft waist-deep snow and in mist towards an imperceptibly-highest point inconveniently placed on the farther rim of the crater and called the Kaiser Wilhelm Spitze (a *spitze* is a sharp point or peak, which this most assuredly is not). Tilman was being sick, perhaps through the name being unwelcome to a Great War veteran; both were dispirited and weary; and on what was probably the easiest mountain attempted throughout their partnership – and the first – they turned back ('. . . waist-deep in snow . . . We struggled over four summits when, seeing nothing higher, retraced our steps')[38] collected Solomon, who had turned 'the colour of a mottled and over-ripe Victoria plum' – a sign of anoxia, apparently – and scuttled down the mountain as fast as their relieved legs could carry them, neglecting as they went to don their snow-goggles and hence having to spend a very uncomfortable night at the draughty Hans Mayer caves to which they retreated suffering from snow-blindness, only human eyesight and not ultraviolet light being baffled by mist.

A day of rain and snow – by no means pleasant at around the

---

[37] Diamox (acetazolamide) is the altitude-climber's panacea of choice, and rather an unpleasant and contradictory one too, its diuretic effect being directly counter to the body's urgent need to stay hydrated at altitude. Also, it makes you feel peculiar and doesn't help that much with the effects of altitude. My view on it is much as that of the good old coward King Mark of Cornwall in Malory's *Morte d'Arthur*: 'And but we avoid lightly, there is but death.' The Sherpas put their trust in hot chillis, garlic and *charas* – a much more appealing and organic remedy. But all this is the province of doctors, and I should not be treading there or commenting on their drug-fixated ways. I was going to add that I hope this gets right up their noses, but I fear it would be misinterpreted. It all reminds me of the old quip originating from Raymond Greene (here in its feminist version): Q. What's the difference between God and a Bachelor of Medicine? A. God knows she's God – a Bachelor of Medicine just thinks she is.

[38] Shipton, 'The First Traverse', p.146.

16,000-foot contour – followed, and convinced them that steely determination to mount another attempt on the high point was of far less interest than retreat to Peter's Hut with its stove and door and walls and warmth. More rain as they waited there, and dramatic thunder and lightning, and inactivity which eventually so frustrated them that they set out on their fourth day since the summit-bid debacle for the rotten-tooth satellite spire of Mawenzi – distinctly a *spitze* though not called one – of which they succeeded in making the third ascent, after which never was more rapid a retreat witnessed from this ghastly sequence of mountain experiences. Even the journey back to Nairobi proved nightmarish, the direct roads being washed out by what were called 'the long rains', Tilman's car having to ford rivers pushed by gangs of workmen, and on another occasion finding itself grounded by the axles on a ridge between deep ruts of the road and having to be pulled out by a lorry. Shipton needed urgently to be back in Turbo, so was forced to take a morning train, whilst Tilman and car were loaded on to a flat-bed rail truck that evening and followed on behind. If ever there was an inauspicious start to a partnership and a decade of high achievement, this was it. For a time, then, they both went back to the Kenyan way of life – of which Shipton gives a fascinating and resonant summary in *Upon That Mountain* that probably defines its appeal for both himself and Tilman at this time:

> . . . it was a good life, full of interest and variety, and there was a great sense of freedom. Each day's work showed a concrete result in so much land cleared or ploughed, a drain dug, trees planted, a wall built – too few occupations in our modern world yield this satisfaction. One was always engaged in some experiment, thinking out new schemes, discussing them with neighbours, visiting other districts at weekends where friends were engaged in some totally different undertaking.[39]

That visionary appeal of the mountain, though, had taken root and was working ever more strongly on his imagination. 'I know no mountain in the Alps, with the possible exception of Mont Blanc,

---

[39] Shipton, *Upon That Mountain*, pp.66–7.

that presents such a superb complexity of ridges and faces as the twin peaks of Mount Kenya . . .'[40]

Barely four months after the Kilimanjaro adventure, in the late July of 1930, Shipton, Masede the tractor-driver from the Turbo farm, and Tilman were motoring in the latter's car to Nanyuki, in what the European settlers called the Happy Valley between their objective and the Aberdare Highlands to the west. They called in at the Silverbeck Hotel – a sprawling, high-chimneyed, quasi-Jacobean brick-and-half-timbered structure of which Shipton had fond memories ('. . . combined the friendly unpretentiousness of an English inn with a service that left little to be desired . . . miles ahead of anything I have ever met with in India'), run by an ex-British naval commander with the unfortunate name of Hook – perhaps this was why his promotion stopped at that rank? Tilman was not to be persuaded into availing himself of the hotel's creature comforts, so after arranging with the proprietor's brother Raymond – a notable white hunter – for pack ponies to take their equipment and supplies to a base camp in the Mackinder valley, they pressed on by car to the latter's farm. Within a couple of miles they were stranded in the mud, and had to walk the rest of the way and return next morning to rescue their possessions. By early afternoon they were on the march, and made camp before dark on luxuriant grasses at the verge of the forest, mysterious sounds echoing night-long to where they lay stretched out by a fire. Next morning as they ate breakfast a blast of trumpeting close at hand gave Shipton a fright: 'Tilman exhibited no more than a mild interest. Looking round I saw an elephant. We had no means of defending ourselves, but the beast appeared to share Tilman's nonchalance, and to my relief he turned and trundled off into the forest.' Farther along their route that day they passed rhinoceruses, and were constantly serenaded by honeybirds,[41] by the behaviour of which Shipton was entranced. On their second night out, perhaps a mile from the cliffs of Batian and at the head of the Mackinder Valley, they found a deep, square-entranced cave

---

[40] Shipton, *Upon That Mountain*, p.71.

[41] Also known as indicator birds and of the order *Piciformes*, these fascinating creatures guide not only humans but also, reputedly, honey badgers to wild beehives – a wonderful example of symbiosis. Their nesting behaviour is similar to that of the cuckoo, and, like the cuckoo, the female bird incubates the egg for an extra day inside her body to give it an additional advantage over the host nestlings.

in a low outcrop at an altitude of about 14,000 feet, with giant groundsel growing handily all around as fuel for their fire and a flat, swampy floor in which they dug channels to drain and over which they scattered grass and groundsel leaves.

Still known as Shipton's Cave (in fact there are two in the same outcrop), and popular with trekkers round the mountain, this was to be their base camp for the duration of their stay. The ponies and their attendants were sent back down to Raymond Hook's farm with orders to return in ten days' time, Masede settled into his role as base camp manager and Shipton and Tilman went off for a day on a training and acclimatisation expedition that took them up two granite needles close at hand, from which they had perfect views of Batian and Nelion's north faces. But these were not their objectives. Shipton had come to climb, if possible, the west ridge of the mountain, perhaps its most dramatic feature. Castellated and pinnacled, steep and blade-crested, it ran down from Mount Kenya's highest summit all the way to a difficult and ice-bound col dividing Batian from the massive satellite peak of Point Piggott.

Their reconnaissance gave Shipton reason to pause and ponder. This west ridge was palpably a serious proposition, unremittingly steep, much of it not visible, studded with fearsome-looking natural obstacles, to two of which they immediately gave the straightforward names by which they're still known of Petit Gendarme and Grand Gendarme. His companion for the undertaking – an exceptionally serious one – was a man the sum total of whose climbing experience when they had first met brief months before was the guided ascent with his sister of a moderately difficult English outcrop climb in Great Langdale followed by an easy scramble. He knew the plan was ludicrous. Even with the vastly more experienced Wyn Harris as an equal pioneering partner, he would still have felt tentative, nervous.

> The west ridge was obviously a formidable proposition; certainly not the place to take a novice for his first serious mountaineering exploit, and it was stupid of me even to think of doing so. I was aware of my responsibility, but for a while I fooled myself with the thought that we might at least 'have a look at it'.[42]

---

[42] Shipton, *That Untravelled World*, pp.62–3.

There is a complex psychology at work in a successful climbing partnership. As with a marriage, its basis is in trust. That this had grown remarkably quickly between Shipton and Tilman is obvious from the former's even being able to think of attempting such a problem with so entirely untrained a companion. Nor do I think there was anything of the *faute de mieux* about the position in which Shipton found himself. He wanted to climb what he saw as his splendid mountain's finest feature, yes – but he could have waited for the return of Wyn from his home leave. There was someone whose abilities were tried and tested, and whose experience was beyond question adequate, and there were no other climbers milling around eager to snatch the prize. So why did he embark on the biggest ascent of his mountain career so far with a novice? The backlash, had they come to grief, would have been savage. He would have been ostracised as surely as was the insane F.W. Giveen after the catastrophe that befell his party descending from Craig yr Ysfa[43]. Was it that in the solidity, the competence, the imperturbability of Tilman's character there was something of the fatherly security he had never known? Does that explain too the acceptance of the reserve, the unsociability, the refusals of intimate disclosure? Also, the taking of full responsibility for success or failure of a climbing venture with some people enables them to climb out of their skin, perform to the utmost level of their ability. Whatever the underlying reason for accepting the situation may have been, the fact is that they went ahead and succeeded in getting up the thing – one of the most significant ascents in pre-war British mountaineering, and accomplished by a young leader on his twenty-third birthday with a near-novice as backstop. I'm tempted to say 'Wow!' And then to adduce as further evidence a passage from Shipton's account that,

---

[43] 'Giveen of Wadham undoubtedly had a hole in his mind,' according to Raymond Greene. He abandoned two novice companions in the snow on their way back from an ascent in poor conditions of the long and difficult Great Gully of Craig yr Ysfa in November 1927. He himself with another novice member of the party repaired to the 'miserable hovel' of Helyg, cooked themselves a good meal, went to bed, and did not see fit to call out a rescue for their by now deceased companions until the next morning. Needless to say, all this sat ill with the mountaineering conscience of the day, especially after an inquest was opened, adjourned and not resumed. See Greene's *Moments of Being* (Heinemann, 1974) for more on this unedifying saga. Giveen ended up shooting himself after wounding a man in a mistaken-identity attempt at murdering Greene – all good ammunition for those who consider most climbers to be insane.

if it had been written by an adolescent son about his father, would scarcely cause the momentary raising of an eyebrow: 'How I hated Tilman in the early morning. Not only on that expedition, but through all the years we have been together.'[44]

That last phrase defines a friendship that, however undemonstrative and lacking in intimacy it may appear to have been, existed at a very profound level.

> He never slept like an ordinary person. Whatever time we agreed to awake, long before that time (how long I never knew) he would slide from his sleeping bag and start stirring his silly porridge over the Primus stove. I used gradually to become aware of this irritating noise and would bury my head in silent rage against the preposterous injustice of being woken half an hour too soon. When his filthy brew was ready he would say 'Show a leg', or some such imbecile remark. In moments of triumph on the top of a peak I have gone so far as to admit that our presence there was due in large measure to this quality of Tilman's, but in the dark hours before dawn such an admission has never touched the fringe of my consciousness.[45]

Humorous ironic distance of the writer notwithstanding, if this is not the perfect evocation of adolescent son railing impotently against the infuriating habits and routines of his father, then I do not know what is. And I find myself laughing at Shipton's projective insight, and the comic temerity of its expression, every time I read it. There is proof positive here of Shipton's habitual gift for sly comedy, in the expression of which is to be found one explanation for the bond between the two men.

Some detail – tedious though the minutiae of climbing ascents may be – is needed to give a sense of the actuality of their climb and the interplay of character along it. On 31 July they reconnoitred as far as the difficult col between the ridge and Point Piggott. It involved crossing a bergschrund and cutting steps in the high-angled ice of the Josef glacier before following a steep snow gully that led to the col. They repeated this the next day after a pre-dawn start from the cave (parties repeating the climb these days tend to bivouac at

44 Shipton, *Upon That Mountain*, p.74.
45 Ibid., p.74.

the col for the preceding night, which saves three or four hours of approach), their progress speeded by the steps they had already cut. Halfway up the gully they took a left-hand branch that missed out a difficult lower section of the ridge and led to directly beneath the Petit Gendarme, 'with the whole day before us. And what a day! Crisp, sparkling, intoxicating. I have never known more complete physical well-being. The western face of Batian caught the full light of the newly risen sun, and every lovely detail of ice fretwork and powerful granite column was hard and clear.'[46] It would be a shame to respond in jaded fashion to Shipton's characteristic rapture in response to his mountains. If you're tempted to do so, then you can always use Tilman's account, which brings widely differing descriptive virtues of the succinct variety into play, as a sober corrective: 'We were there by 8 a.m., and sat on its knife-edge for a breather with our legs dangling over the Tyndall glacier below.'[47] The previous day, both of them suffering from altitude headaches, they had debated climbing Point Piggott to get a clear view of the traverse round the Petit Gendarme, thus delaying their attempt on the ridge by a day to help them towards being more fully acclimatised; but they concluded that it would be a waste of the steps they had cut thus far, which might not last two more days, so they did not see what lay ahead. 'Had we done so,' wrote Shipton, 'I doubt we should have attempted it.'[48]

What followed from their second arrival at the difficult col is where Shipton's trust in his novice companion becomes quite breathtaking. Masterful alpine-trained route-finder that he is, he picks out a rising traverse line across the flank of the Petit Gendarme. It is on hard ice overlaid with a layer of crystalline snow at best two inches thick, and usually less. When the sun comes to shine directly on to the slope, as it will once it has climbed above Point Piggott, this layer will simply melt away. Speed is of the essence. Both Shipton and Tilman are wearing tricouni-nailed[49] boots. They

[46] Shipton, *Upon That Mountain*, p.75.
[47] Tilman, *Seven Mountain Travel Books*, pp.49–50.
[48] Shipton, 'The First Traverse', p.140.
[49] Technical nails with a serrated profile that were secured to the edges of the boot (best done when wet so that they rust into place according to the received wisdom). The late Tom Patey, doyen of Scottish winter climbers in the 1950s and 1960s, used to consider them the most effective footwear for mixed rock-and-ice climbing, particularly on his favoured Cairngorms granite, but these days the

rope up. Tilman's sole experience of ice-climbing before this trip has been wading through waist-deep snow on Kibo. Both of them carrying the standard long-shafted, straight-picked, non-technical ice axe of the era – and only one each – they set off on a diagonal traverse of the slope. It is at a steep angle, and beneath them it ends in a vertical drop of over a thousand feet to the Tyndall glacier. The thin hemp line tied round their waists is no protection for Shipton, and little more than a reassurance for Tilman. Ice-axe braking[50] on terrain like this is a nonsense. They kick their delicate toeholds into that crystal veneer and proceed steadily, cautiously across with the axe for balance, having to cut toe nicks in the hard underlying ice here and there where the thin overlay gives out. The traverse takes an eternity of nerve-racking, precise endeavour and brings them back to the crest of the ridge beneath the Grand Gendarme.

Shipton's eye for the route takes them across its left flank into a steep and mysterious gully, every section of it hidden from sight as they climb, and an impasse likely at any moment. Here and there they can move together, for speed. At one point they climb a crack leading to a small overhang. Tilman jams himself in beneath it and Shipton stands on his shoulder to overcome the problem and reach rotten rock above. This brings them out on the ridge above the Grand Gendarme, but any hope they might have of being beyond major difficulties is dashed by what lies ahead – a pitch that is still regarded as the crux of the climb. It's a 120-foot-high wall of red rock, overhanging at its base and near vertical above. On either side of the ledge at its foot are huge drops, the ground plunging away into the void. Shipton again climbs on to Tilman's shoulders and can just reach two good finger-edges. He convulses upwards, gets his feet high, straightens for a hold and works his way steadily on, one teetering balance-transfer without handholds on to a single nick for a boot-nail using up all his technical and nervous resources, for a fall from here would be fatal to both of them. The rope comes tight just as he reaches a cleft into which he can wedge himself below the top of the wall and from that position haul Tilman bodily over the first

---

ubiquitous choice would be front-point crampons, and tricouni-nailed boots are all but unobtainable.

[50] I.e., trying to arrest a fall down the slope by use of the ice axe – easier in theory than in practice, and virtually impossible in a situation like this. You might refer back here to the 1927 incident below the Aiguille de Peigne recounted in the previous chapter.

bulge. The lead was devoid of protection, the climb into unknown territory, of a good Very Severe standard, and accomplished in nailed boots. Put yourself in the situation, and be impressed.

It began to snow. The remainder of the ridge was sustained and uncertain but less challenging. The quality of its rock deteriorated. There was now no possibility of retreat, their commitment absolute, the rope not being nearly long enough to abseil down the red wall. At 4.20, with the mist that had obscured the onward view and added to their uncertainty still swirling all around, after a difficult ice-pitch they reached the cairn on top of Batian that Shipton and Wyn had built nineteen months before:

> There was no chance of getting down before dark, but I was much too happy to be bothered about that. Needless to say, much of the joy stemmed from sheer relief; for, since climbing the red step, failure to reach the summit would have placed us in an ugly situation, and the issue had remained in doubt till the last few minutes. Bill had been magnificent; he had shown no anxiety throughout the climb, and his stoicism no less than his innate skill in climbing and handling the rope made a vital contribution to our success.'[51]

They both ate a tin of meat essence in celebration and started what was now a familiar descent to Shipton over snowed-up rocks. In the gully below the summit of Nelion, Tilman slipped, came briefly on the rope and was held, but dropped his ice axe. Shipton began to vomit, his meat-essence having been bad. A cold east wind wuthered across the face to banish thoughts of a bivouac. 'The climb down the SE face in the uncertain moonlight will always remain in my memory as a combination of sublime impressions and grim reality.'[52] By the moon's fitful and distorting illumination they continued, Shipton experiencing, in the midst of another rapturous moment, the ghostly sense of a third member accompanying the party:[53] 'The

---

[51] Shipton, *That Untravelled World*, pp.66–7. It is interesting that Tilman was so skilful in handling a rope at this early stage – a result, perhaps, of his Woolwich training.

[52] Shipton, 'The First Traverse', p.143.

[53] A strange and noted mountain phenomenon, this, and surely psychogenic. T. S. Eliot refers to it in *The Waste Land*, and many climbers have reported it, sometimes after the deaths of companions on a peak, at other times with no such prompt.

most vivid impression that remains in my mind of this grim ordeal is how S., in the feeble state he was, not only climbed, but led the way unerringly and safeguarded his companion.'[54] Eventually they reached the Lewis glacier, and instead of persisting on over the col between Point Lenana and Point Thompson to reach their cave, exhausted after twenty-four hours of continual movement mostly over new and difficult ground, they diverted to the Skating Lake, built a fire from timbers of the ruined hut there, and shivered away the dark hours until the dawn, when, re-energised by the rest, they returned over the col and down the long valley to their cave. Masede greeted them and they lay in their sleeping bags gorging themselves on a ten-pound Cheddar cheese and a jar of pickled onions until sleep finally supervened: 'I still regard the traverse of the twin peaks of Mount Kenya as one of the most enjoyable climbs I have ever had – a perfect and wholly satisfying episode, shared with an ideal companion.'[55]

The remainder of their holiday afforded them a couple more first ascents – one of Point Piggott, from which they could belatedly look across to the west ridge and relive in relaxation and pleasure their epochal ascent. The other was of the Salisbury Cathedral-like spire that Shipton was to call Midget Peak after the nickname of his widowed and chaste young paramour in Turbo. Difficult and exposed, the line of ascent they chose gave them some excellent rock-climbing, and a near disaster in the descent during a heavy snowstorm that arrived whilst they were resting on the summit. Tilman was knocked unconscious in a fall from a difficult move leaving a now snow-covered ledge as they reversed the climb, and once he had recovered his senses the rest of the retreat was a very edgy and tenuous affair. At one point, his companion insensate below, Shipton had been climbing down a narrow gully with the whole weight of Tilman 120 feet beneath dangling from the rope tied round both their waists, until finally the unconscious man came

---

Peter Boardman and Nick Estcourt both experienced it on Everest in 1975, after the disappearance of Mick Burke, as did members of the 1970 Annapurna south face expedition around the time of Ian Clough's death. Tall tales for base-camp evenings! A more recent example occurred during Stephen Venables' 1988 solo ascent of Everest's Kangshung face, and is thrillingly recounted in his story of that climb (*Everest: Kangshung Face*, 1991).

[54] Tilman, *Seven Mountain Travel Books*, p.51.
[55] Shipton, *Upon That Mountain*, p.80.

to rest on a ledge out of sight of his leader, and the strain came off the rope, at which point he tied Tilman off and climbed down to a point from which he could communicate with his dazed companion, who by now was recovering consciousness. They survived, perhaps more through good luck than good practice on this occasion, and on the next day – their last on the mountain – whilst Tilman rested after his ordeal Shipton took Masede up to see a glacier. The only thing that seemed to interest Masede was how much Shipton and Tilman were being paid by the government for all this strange behaviour of theirs. Shipton protested innocence, but was not believed, and particularly not after they had stopped at Government House in Nairobi on their way back from the mountain – to collect their reward, in Masede's view. What intrigues me about this last anecdote is why Shipton tells it. Certainly, when we come round to his time as consul-general in Kashgar – one of the crucial listening-posts of empire, pivotal in the Great Game – and his later very hurried exit from the consular post in Kunming, allied to the extremely cautious or even paranoid behaviour he showed, and which was widely commented on at the time, during his 1952 expedition to Cho Oyu, right on the Chinese border, the question again comes up of what he is trying to tell us here.

Was Shipton a British spy, and recruited quite early if we take the possible inference from this anecdote? This, though, is for the future. For the present, we need to relate what happens in the dog days of our subjects' African sojourning.

6

The Widening Gyre

Shipton's trajectory in the aftermath of his Mount Kenya exploits soared ever more dramatically. His Alpine record in influential company, and particularly his week in January 1929 with Wyn Harris, came to the attention of Frank Smythe, the most famous British mountaineer of the day. Smythe, greatly respected by Shipton for his two outstanding ascents on the Brenva face of Mont Blanc in 1927 and 1928, was planning an expedition to a traditional object of British mountaineering interest, the peak of Kamet (25,447 feet) in the Garhwal Himalaya, 'that most Alpine of Himalayan districts'.[1] Not one of the seventy Himalayan peaks over a height of 25,000 feet had been climbed in 1930. Kamet had been attempted as early as 1855 by the Schlagintweit brothers, and reconnoitred more seriously by Tom Longstaff, General Bruce and A. L. Mumm in 1907, after the former's ascent of Trisul on the borders of Kumaon to the south-east – an ascent which held for many years the altitude record for a successful summit climb. Later attempts were made on Kamet by A. M. Slingsby of the Yorkshire Ramblers' Club in 1911, by C. F. Meade in 1912, and by Kellas and Morshead in 1920. In all there had been ten attempts and all had failed, but in doing so they had focused attention on, and added to the sum of knowledge about, the peak. Smythe hoped to capitalise on this, and also had in mind that the expedition might traverse from east to west the spectacular ranges at a slightly lesser altitude around Badrinath – Kamet being about fifteen miles as the alpine chough might fly from this settlement – and cross the watershed to the Gangotri glacier before descending this and making its way back to Ranikhet. Here, surely, is the ur-text of all

---

[1] Eric Shipton, *That Untravelled World* (Hodder & Stoughton, 1969), p.73.

Shipton's early Himalayan obsessions. At Easter 1931 he was once more on board a British India Line passenger cargo ship, the SS *Khandalla*, steaming through the Indian Ocean at a steady eight knots bound for Bombay.

His first experience of India was tinged with the usual Western ambivalence and recoil from the inequities and brutality of life in that beautiful and disturbing country. He watched the beggars from the grandeur of Bombay's Taj Mahal Hotel on Apollo Bunder; took the train across the Rajasthan Desert and on through Delhi, with its even greater disparities between wealth and poverty; helped marshal all the paraphernalia even of a relatively small and efficient expedition out of the teeming confusion of the capital and by train and lorry up from the hot plains of northern India and on to the hill-station of Ranikhet, where Shipton and Smythe arrived on 22 April, with fellow climbers, Sherpas and porters making their own way to join them there over the next three weeks. From Ranikhet to the Kamet base-camp was a further eighteen days' walk. If ever a plan were formulated for perfect acclimatisation, this was it.

The Kamet expedition has been well described elsewhere. I recommend in particular the accounts by Smythe and Greene. It was a model of its kind, extremely well run by Smythe, providing what Shipton called 'a gentle and wholly delightful initiation' to the Himalaya. The youngest of the team by seven years, he was lucky with his companions – particularly Raymond Greene, a languid medical man six feet four inches in length when stretched out in his specially made sleeping bag, who could relate tall and risqué stories endlessly and exercised his kindly ironies at everyone's expense. He was lucky with the provisioning, which blended the best delicacies Fortnum & Mason could supply, from chocolate almonds to tinned quails in caper sauce, with local produce served up in the mess tent by their accompanying Indian cook. Shipton himself was deputed to the role of supervising the scavenging for eggs and flour from the villages through which they passed – something he would turn to good future account. He was also appointed to what Smythe, in a rare moment of humour, called 'the food commissariat', in which crucial and difficult role he won nothing but praise: '. . . the work of rationing is more likely to evoke blame than praise, and the fact that it worked without a hitch on Kamet goes to prove how efficient were the arrangements of Shipton'.[2] The expedition luxuries also included a gramophone and records supplied by HMV, which included Kreisler playing the Brahms and Elgar violin concerti and Gracie Fields singing 'My Blue Heaven', with which Raymond Greene would always duet. There was a plentiful supply of brandy, too, in which to toast their success. He was lucky too with the timing of the expedition, the significance of which he describes as follows, giving a glimpse of his own self-image as he does so: 'Himalayan mountaineering was then barely beyond its infancy; it was in a state analogous to the early years of the Golden Age in the Alps, when the simple mountain explorer with no special ability was still free to pick the plums in a random harvest of delight.'[3]

Most of all, he was lucky in that he acclimatised well on a high but not excessively difficult mountain (though rather more difficult than some recent commentators, seeking to mock Smythe's popular-audience dramatisations, have sought to imply); he socialised easily with his fellow team members; he shared a tent with Smythe, reputedly an awkward and cantankerous personality, and the two 'yarned' together over their post-prandial pipes[4] amiably and endlessly, setting the world to rights as they did so; he impressed one and all with his climbing ability and mastery of rhythmical movement over rough, steep ground; and thus he enjoyed the whole experience, as many who go to the Himalayas do not. He was in the five-strong first summit party – over three days the expedition put a remarkably high proportion of its members and Sherpas on the summit of a mountain that, at 25,447 feet, was by far the highest yet attained.

His crowning good fortune was in the expedition's plan for the aftermath of their climb. Their sortie into the Badrinath ranges took them into some of the most intimately beautiful parts of the Himalaya. It's tempting here to quote Smythe at some length, despite the lushness of his prose, for the impression he gives of the wonderful richness of the landscape through which they passed:

> . . . the rain now was light and warm, like the rain of a spring day in a Devon combe. Lower down we entered what I can only

---

[2] Frank Smythe, *Kamet Conquered* (Hodder & Stoughton, 1938), p.298.
[3] Shipton, *That Untravelled World*, p.72.
[4] See note 58 below.

describe as an Eden of flowers. Growing among the rocks was the tiny stemless *Primula reptans*; the flowers of the commoner but beautiful *Primula denticulata* covered the hillside, and above the glacier were three varieties of androsace. Between clumps of creamy dwarf rhododendrons, the ground was purple with dwarf irises, and blue and yellow with pansies and fritillaries. As the track descended we came upon the most beautiful of all Himalayan flowers, the mecanopsis (blue poppy). Its petals are as blue as a glacial lake, and its stamens as golden as the sunset glow on the great peaks beneath which it grows.[5]

There is much more in this vein. If you've been brought up on James Elroy Flecker (or Ella Wheeler Wilcox, for that matter), you'll respond to it positively and uncritically. It seems to me an unfashionable but valid attempt to express what Simone Weil memorably calls 'the plenitude of being'. Shipton, having passed through this gorgeous landscape in what he later considered 'by far the most enjoyable part of the expedition',[6] found his own way of expressing 'plenitude of being' through a frenzy of peaks-and-passes-bagging. He climbed five of the latter, and traversed eleven of the former, each of them over 19,000 feet high. On the 21,400-foot Avalanche Peak, Smythe gives an unforgettable impression of keeping company with Shipton on a mountain: '. . .no one who climbs with Shipton can remain pessimistic, for he imparts an imperturbability and confidence into a day's work on a mountain that are in themselves a guarantee of success'.[7] The ascent of Avalanche Peak may have been a success. Its descent was almost a disaster for Smythe. As the pair of them and their Sherpa companion Nima Dorje glissaded in line down a slope of wet afternoon snow under a thin wind-crust, Smythe, lowest of the three, was engulfed in a small avalanche set off by the two above him and came very close to being buried by it in the bergschrund

---

[5] Smythe, *Kamet Conquered*, p.196. Interesting to note here that a limited edition of Smythe's 1949 book, *The Valley of Flowers*, came in a wooden presentation case that also enclosed tiny drawers of seeds gathered from the Bhuidhar valley ('the valley of flowers'). I'd be fascinated to know how many of these were germinated, and are still flowering. Imagine the bureaucratic and conservationist brouhaha these days!

[6] Shipton, *That Untravelled World*, p.74.

[7] Smythe, *Kamet Conquered*, p.226.

below the slope. He escaped from heavy snow that was clasped around him like setting concrete with no more than a broken rib, and thereafter the three proceeded down to camp prudently and, in Smythe's case, gingerly.

Shipton came back to Kenya in the autumn of 1931 from what had been a happy and immensely successful expedition. His stature as one of the finest young mountaineers of his day had been greatly enhanced; he now had a first-hand understanding of the demands of running a relatively small Himalayan expedition; and had also a curiosity about Himalayan topography and its absorbing problems that had been vastly stimulated by the gorgeous sublimities of the mountains of Garhwal. Kamet was another of the crucial strokes of good fortune in Shipton's career, and he had responded to it with his habitual energy and grace. In Kenya once again, he returned to picnicking with Madge Anderson, guiding her around the ballroom of the Eldoret Hotel, partnering her at doubles in tennis – always with her mother, of whom Shipton had grown exasperatedly fond, present as chaperone to ensure there was none of what was quaintly termed 'hanky-panky' (a chaste version of Elinor Glyn's 'it') – and attending to the seasonal duties of his farm at Turbo. But he also had some unfinished business in the form of the last, and the most mysterious, of the three mountain ranges in the central part of the Dark Continent to visit: 'Tilman and I had decided to go to Ruwenzori at the earliest opportunity.'[8]

Tilman had been occupied in diverse activities whilst Shipton had been on Kamet. These included a spell as assistant to a friend, Horace Dawson, who had been appointed vermin control officer and delegated the task of dissuading a large herd of elephants from occupying a farmed valley the location of which he coyly does not divulge. The dissuasion, of course, involved a degree of extermination, and makes for unpleasant reading, but the account Tilman provides also gives latitude for an absurdist grotesque humour, particularly in the matter of an elephant embryo, pickled in methylated spirits and sealed into an oil drum, that Dawson had been commissioned to acquire for 'some learned body in England engaged in research work'.[9] The rifles, however, had been cleaned,

[8] Eric Shipton, *Upon That Mountain* (Hodder & Stoughton, 1943), p.86.
[9] H. W. Tilman, *The Seven Mountain Travel Books* (Diadem Books, 1983), p.64. Tilman hints that during the elephant embryo's transmission back to England it

oiled and put away for the last time. He had endured and Shipton had danced away the gaieties of a colonial Christmas. With Shipton only brief weeks back from India, his well-worn and trusty ice-axe and Tilman's new model that replaced the one lost on Mount Kenya were loaded into the latter's car. Very early in January 1932 ('that month being specially picked because in most parts of East Africa it is the driest', Tilman records, before adding that 'The forethought went unrewarded'),[10] the two men drove the five hundred miles from Turbo to Fort Portal at the northern end of the Rwenzori[11] range – the 'Mountains of the Moon'.

This mysterious range of tectonic peaks reaching to a height of nearly 17,000 feet above the headwaters of the White Nile on the border between Uganda and the Democratic Republic of the Congo had long been a geographical mystery. The early explorers of an unsettled region had simply failed to see them through the dense and near-constant clouds. By the time of Shipton and Tilman's visit, all their higher summits had been reached either on the 1906 expedition led by the Duke of Abruzzi or on later explorations conducted by Captain (later Dr) Noel Humphreys.[12] This foreknowledge detracted not at all from the exotic and frustrating nature of the three weeks our two later explorers spent here. Rainforests are a bizarre environment wherever you find them, and the approach to the peaks lay entirely through this terrain. Shipton gives the flavour:

At an altitude of about 10,000 ft. one gets into very strange country; probably unique anywhere in the world. It is a fantastic tangle of rotting vegetation – giant groundsel, lobelia and giant heath – all thickly covered in moss. Moss is everywhere, one

---

blew up and derailed a wagon of the train on which it was being carried. This may or may not be true. The longer you spend with our two comedians, the more you suspect a leg-pull in every perhaps-innocent phrase. Though this particular story does remind me of the one about the Barnsley blue whale that destroyed the town's municipal incinerator in 1968 – an urban myth rooted in bizarre fact, for some of which I can vouch, having seen the same whale on a Manchester bomb site in 1954. But we digress (and in a manner of which Tilman would have approved).

[10] Tilman, *Seven Mountain Travel Books*, p.66.
[11] The older spelling of the name – since about 1980 the closer approximation to the native name of Rwenzori has been official.
[12] Who went as doctor on the 1936 Everest expedition.

wades feet deep in it and walks through tunnels of it. All the streams are hushed and not a sound is to be heard anywhere.[13]

Tilman's take on it is even more claustrophobic:

Overhead, tall trees wrapped about with a tangle of creepers formed a dense canopy which shut out the light; underfoot was a matted carpet of undergrowth – ferns, brambles, fallen bamboos, giant nettles (said to be capable of making even an elephant sit up), and dead trees – over which we sometimes crawled, sometimes crept beneath on all fours, and sometimes we had to cut a way through with the panga . . . Through a window in the living green wall of our prison we saw for a brief moment the ice peaks of Stanley and Speke, filling the head of the valley, before they vanished once more in wreathing cloud. ..but for one other occasion, this was the only time the peaks revealed themselves to us between dawn and sunset.[14]

Of that other occasion, Shipton gives a vivid picture:

. . . when we pitched the camp we had no idea where we were. At sunset that evening the mist cleared, and we looked straight down into the Congo. Never have I seen anything to rival that scene. A sheer precipice of broken glacier, from which angry clouds strove to detach themselves, was in the foreground. Beyond, like a hazy map beneath us, stretched the Congo, with the Semliki River coiling like a silver snake. To the south was the huge expanse of Lake Edward. But the whole was flooded in the deepest blue – a blue so vivid as to be reflected by everything around us, becoming more and more intense the farther one gazed over the Congo, until swallowed up in a blazing sunset. For the next twenty-four hours it snowed almost continually . . . we set out in the vain hope of finding our way about the glaciers, but spent a fruitless day getting mixed up in snow flurries and losing ourselves.[15]

---

[13] Eric Shipton, 'Mountains of the Moon' (*Alpine Journal*, 1932), p.90.
[14] Tilman, *Seven Mountain Travel Books*, p.77.
[15] Shipton, 'Mountains of the Moon', p.91.

They slept in rock shelters warmed by huge fires of giant groundsel, which made excellent fuel for all its slimy and rotting appearance. In this constantly wet environment the native Bakonju tribe who were acting as their porters had evolved a fascinating way of carrying fire with them, by wrapping smouldering embers within a tightly thatched cigar-shaped tube of straw eighteen inches long which they carried slung over their shoulders, ready to blow into life when needed. Tilman reports that the slow-burning fire could be carried thus for up to a month. Of the weather they endured in this supposedly-dry season, Shipton gives a revealing vignette from one of these rock-shelter camps:

> It was good, sitting in the evening before a fire, sheltered from the rain, to watch the clouds driven wildly about the craggy foothills of the range, clinging to gullies in enormous rock precipices; to listen to the roar of a thousand torrents . . . to see the flickering of lightning towards the high peaks.[16]

Somehow, in the course of their three-week stay, they managed to find and also make ascents (most of them the third, after Abruzzi and Humphreys; these things matter to those mountaineers who are preoccupied with counting) of the higher peaks – a remarkable achievement, given the conditions, and one which left its indelible stamp on both of them. In their accounts they put on a brave face about their experience. Both men place their emphasis on exquisite isolated details – 'cornices of a strangely beautiful feathery appearance'[17] – and the rare moments of clear weather, as here from near the summit of King Edward Peak:

> Shortly before reaching the summit, the whole range of high peaks cleared and we got a superb view of Mt Stanley. After having been surrounded by impenetrable fog for so many days, the effect of such a sudden and complete clearing is indescribably wonderful; the feeling it produces is of a great load being removed from one's mind.[18]

---

[16] Shipton, 'Mountains of the Moon', p.90.

[17] Tilman, *Seven Mountain Travel Books*, p.81.

[18] Shipton, 'Mountains of the Moon', pp.93–4.

Lost? Imprisoned? A load on the mind? The vocabulary here is revealing, for all the comparisons both make with days in the Lakeland fells and their familiar glimpses down through cloud into a welcoming valley at the end of the day: 'Ruwenzori, like our Lakeland, would lose a great deal of its beauty, mystery and charm were it deprived of its continuous cloud and damp. Nor did we go there for comfort or freedom of movement.'[19] Making a virtue of necessity seldom came much more rigorous than this. And even here, the implicit reminder is of that incessant Cumbrian rain that can fall for weeks with only the briefest of pauses. In the Rwenzori they endured these conditions without benefit of any kind of waterproof clothing. But what these three weeks did give them, apart from new and unique mountain country to explore, were more insights into each other's qualities: for Shipton, into the uncomplaining hardihood of Tilman's character; for Tilman, into Shipton's extraordinarily refined and acute instinct for mountain topography. Also, Rwenzori gave latitude for the two men to do that which they most enjoyed, as defined here by Tilman in telling of a day in the course of which they had climbed both Semper Peak (15,483 feet) and Edward Peak (15,986 feet):

From the col we would drop down to the unnamed valley between Mount Baker and Mount Stanley, on the south side of the Scott Elliott Pass, returning to the Bujuku valley and our camp over this last-named pass. It meant a long day, and was rather a shot in the dark, but in spite of the prudent adage, we preferred the unknown to the known . . .[20]

They had dismissed or left behind at a base-camp cave shelter within the vegetation zone all their porters, and gone up to the glaciers for these ascents carrying all their supplies and climbing and bivouac equipment, heavy and sodden through the incessant rain, while they themselves most of the time were soaked to the skin. Alexandra David-Neel's stories of Tibetan lamas left on glacier ice in clothes deliberately made wet, who dry them out through their own body heat, seem relevant here.[21] Let's leave the last word

---

[19] Shipton, *Upon That Mountain*, p.88.
[20] Tilman, *Seven Mountain Travel Books*, p.84.
[21] See *Magic and Mystery in Tibet* (1929). Alexandra David-Neel (1868–1969)

on the 'Mountains of the Moon' with Tilman, who knew about rain and mud and nightmare landscapes:

> Over all a clammy mist hangs like a pall, and a deep silence broods. Even the innumerable brooks and rivulets are hushed as they flow deep below ground level in a narrow trench of moss – moss that seems to breed wherever the mist touches, on tree, plant, earth or rock.
>
> Such was the nightmare landscape across which we toiled . . . and such is the nature of all the high valleys below the snow-line, giving to Ruwenzori a mystery and strange beauty that has not its likeness in any other land. A country that only the language of Lewis Carroll could paint, the natural habitat of Snarks and Jabberwoks and jub-jub birds.[22]

Within six months Shipton had gone from the summit of Kamet to these plumed snow-crests high above the equatorial rainforest. His next venture was to surpass either of these. Both men returned to their respective farms, and would not set out together on another mountain for over two years.

Tilman came back to Sotik determined to increase his climbing experience, and within a month was heading for Britain on home leave, both of his plantations now delegated to Richard Royston's care. He arrived back at Seacroft in Wallasey to the delight of his parents, sister and young nieces, and immediately arranged for a repetition of their last time together almost eight years before.

Firstly, though, thirsting for some rock-climbing, he went away to Snowdonia over Easter with a school friend, John Brogden, who was in general practice in Hartlepool. They came back from Wales after the weekend, picked up Adeline, who had arranged for her parents to child-mind, and also a family friend of Brogden's called Vera Brown, and set off for Coniston in the Lake District, where they put up at a hotel. The Sunday of their stay – it was the 10th

---

was one of the most interesting early travellers to Tibet, received on several occasions by the Dalai Lama during the time the country was forbidden to most Westerners. Her books have been influential in shaping Western perceptions of Tibet. It's fascinating to conjecture what she, Shipton and Tilman would have made of each other had they met – as could easily have happened, given the timing and extent of their travels.

[22] Tilman, *Seven Mountain Travel Books*, p.78.

of April – dawned dull, cold and windy. Adeline, who would never miss Sunday service, went to church. The other three set off along the Walna Scar path before branching over Little Arrow Moor for Goat Water, intending to climb on Dow Crag above. Brogden was the most experienced member of the party, and the route he chose was Jones's Route in Easter Gully. It was graded Very Difficult (climbing grades being relative, this is not exactly as it sounds in common parlance – a Very Difficult climb being at the upper end of quite straightforward, if that makes any sense at all to the uninformed reader. The grade itself would certainly not have been thought entirely out of the question for a reasonably fit and active beginner), and the route dated from the close of the previous century.[23]

However, so much of climbing on the great cliffs – and Dow Crag is one of these, characterful and wholly atmospheric, its compact sound rock a pleasure to handle – depends on psychology, and the individual's response to the crag environment. Easter Gully is an oppressively dark and steep place, scene of the two first ascents by Joe Roper[24] in 1919 and 1920, Great Central Route and the even more difficult Black Wall, which were certainly among the hardest mountain rock-climbs in Britain between the wars. Colin Kirkus fell from the easier pitch of the first, Menlove Edwards had to be top-roped off Black Wall, and they were the outstanding climbers active in Snowdonia during the 1930s. The route Brogden had chosen, though not in itself unduly technical, was high up in the gully and neatly bisected these two, sharing its first stance with the former and on its second pitch traversing out to the right into an exposed scoop in a steep facet wall of 'E' Buttress. Black Wall – an exceptionally steep climb for its day – came up the rock directly beneath this scoop. Over to the left, beyond the Severe fissure of Hopkinson's Crack, was the crux pitch of Great Central Route.

---

[23] It had first been climbed, thirty-four years to the day before Tilman's accident, by the great Lakeland pioneer Owen Glynne Jones, who was killed a year later on the Ferpècle Arête of the Dent Blanche (see preceding chapter).

[24] As well as being one of the meteoric talents in British climbing history, Joe Roper was a shipyard worker and an Independent Labour Party member and staunch trade unionist from Barrow-in-Furness who read economics at Ruskin College and went on to become a distinguished writer on colonial labour relations. His Penguin volume on *Labour Problems in West Africa* (1958) is still a standard work in its field.

This was impressive territory, which would necessarily have preyed on the mind of Vera Brown.

Brogden led the diagonal traverse across the scoop and reached the grass ledge above, where for some reason – perhaps because he wanted to look down and encourage Brown as she climbed – he failed to belay on a good, sound bollard in the wall behind. Tilman, again perhaps in order to encourage, the nature of the place being so daunting – had climbed up to the base of the scoop and taken a poor block belay mentioned in the climbing guide book to Dow Crag just to the right of its foot. According to Brown's later account, she had an attack of nerves, and simply fell off backwards. This pulled Tilman off his poor belay, and the two of them now hung on the rope directly over the verticality of Black Wall. Brogden, unbelayed, yelled down that he could no longer hold them, was catapulted from his ledge, and all three fell the best part of a hundred feet into the bed of Easter Gully, ending up just above its cave pitch. Brogden and Tilman were knocked unconscious, and Vera Brown was seriously injured.

When he came to his senses, Tilman crawled over to the other two, and then descended to the cave below to seek help, having heard voices beneath. No one being there, he climbed back up to Brown and Brogden, both of whom were still alive, the latter unconscious. He secured them and told Brown that he was going to seek help. He himself had cracked several vertebrae, though his spinal cord was intact. He then descended the gully again and, unable to stand, crawled for four hours and succeeded in reaching Coniston, 'a deed of wonderful endurance and heroism' according to the accident report in the journal of the Fell and Rock Climbing Club.[25] People at the hotel, seeing him enter thus covered in blood, thought at first he was an injured dog.

A rescue party including a doctor and several local quarrymen set off – Tilman had to be physically restrained from accompanying them – and reached the accident site with difficulty in the dusk. Brogden was dead. Vera Brown was lowered on a rope down the

---

[25] Senior representative body of Lake District climbing, and quite a liberal body for its day, particularly in its policy of admitting women, which none of the other senior clubs did at the time. Some of these latter held out until the 1990s, haemorrhaging members as they continued along in their Palaeolithic way. Though it might be noted in this context that the women-only clubs still don't admit males.

rock-pitches that Tilman had reversed with a broken back. It was entirely dark as they reached the foot of the crag and set off back to Torver with a corpse and a casualty:

> The conclusion to be drawn from this accident in the opinion of those on the spot was that Jones's route should never have been attempted by that party on a cold, wet and windy day – in fact, the girl, a complete novice, should never have been on that climb at all. It is also probable that the accident would not have been fatal had the leader been belayed himself or had Tilman's belay been an efficient one.[26]

Luck can run out, and when it does, the conclusions drawn often appear unequivocally harsh. In this case they were allayed by the clear fact that Tilman's heroic actions had saved Vera Brown's life – and by the shrill acclamations of this in the popular press (the headline in the *Daily Sketch* on 12 April ran: 'Heroic Journey by Injured Companion to Summon Help'). It is pointless to ponder whether the insouciance and skill shown by Shipton on their shared climbs had bolstered a confidence in Tilman that led to what the official view regarded as overreaching here. The official response would have been as censorious had grief befallen the two of them on their west ridge climb, when Tilman was the novice. Climbing has always been a sport predicated on the notion of safety hard-won from danger. Accidents as tragic as this have happened throughout its history. Sympathy here is rightly with Vera Brown for having been introduced to so perilous a situation by more experienced companions in whom she placed trust and confidence, and for the carnage resulting from their misjudgement and her moment of panic. That all three paid dearly for the error is perhaps the only conclusion that we, the wise and distant onlookers, should allow ourselves to draw.

What we can say further, though, is that Tilman's response to the serious personal injuries he sustained was as remarkable as anything we know about the man. The doctors, naturally, told him he would never climb again as they discharged him from hospital and sent him home to Seacroft to be nursed back to health by his mother and Adeline. There are those who submit to iatrogenic tyranny and accept the word of doctors as gospel; and there are those who do not.

---

[26] *The Fell and Rock Climbing Club Journal* (1932), p.206.

Tilman was avowedly of the latter, more independent persuasion. Less than four months after the accident he was travelling across France in a third-class railway carriage – not the most comfortable conveyance for someone with a recently broken back – bound for Grenoble, whence on the recommendation of Shipton, whose road to Ephesus this had been only seven years before, he took the bus up to La Berarde, booked into the Hotel Tairraz, and retained the services of a guide (not Elie Richard, sadly). Over the next ten days, a little fractious at times from the back pain that plagued him for the rest of his life, he climbed the Pain de Sucre, Les Ecrins, Les Bans, La Meije, Le Planet and La Grande Ruine. He tried out a pair of crampons in crossing the Col des Avalanches and was impressed.

After a stay that would have been demanding enough for someone who was thoroughly fit, he moved on to Chamonix – not quite the seething fleshpot then that it is now, but still unpleasant enough to an austere misanthropist – where he added a few more climbs to his collection, including the Col du Chardonnet, Col de la Fenêtre, and the Aiguilles du Tour and de l'M (both of which must have seemed easy and almost trivial after Mount Kenya). Towards the end of August, with a guide, he set out for Mont Mallet, the impressive shark's tooth of rock at the end of the Rochefort Ridge. The extent to which he was shadowing his Africa climbing companion's experience is notable here, and a further echo comes through in his having to retreat from the attempt – not in the face of a storm, but because the guide baulked at the prospect of crossing the bergschrund, so they didn't even make it to peak or ridge. The contrast with Shipton's ever-present enthusiasm, confidence and by no means negligible quota of skill must have been very marked. 'Fed up with the whole business,' Tilman noted in his diary. 'Decided to go home.'[27]

The decision in part was as a result of a letter from the former vermin control officer Horace Dawson, to whom he had sold half of his holding at Sotik and who was now busily reinventing himself as a gold prospector in the area around Kakamega near to Tilman's other estate at Kericho. Tilman joined him, staked out a few claims and worked for six months in the outdoors. He made no significant

<hr />

[27] Tilman's diaries are now in the exploration archive at the University of Wyoming. I am indebted to the late Dr David Pluth for various hints about and transcriptions from these.

money, but after selling the claims on at a profit, nor did he make a loss. He went back to stay with the Dawsons on his former holding at Sotik for a while, and took part in a point-to-point race at a local gymkhana (his riding was still well up to scratch from his Woolwich days), in which his pony collided at full pelt with one of a herd of oxen that had wandered on to the course and sent Tilman sailing over its head: 'I slid along on my face for several yards, "biting the dust" in a very literal fashion – bit it to such a purpose, in fact, that most of my teeth were unshipped.'[28]

He went to Nairobi to have his teeth repaired and replaced, and whilst his facial abrasions, which had been quite severe, were on the mend, he drove south over the Masai Plains and remedied his and Shipton's omission from March 1930 by returning to Kilimanjaro: 'As S. was not available, I had to go alone, and though solitary mountaineering is not in accordance with sound mountaineering practice, Kilimanjaro is, perhaps, a mountain where this vice can be indulged in with more safety than usual.'[29] With a forty-pound pack he made it to the Kaiser Wilhelm Spitze, close to which he bivouacked in the open, pleased that the effects of altitude were minimal.

After a further brief foray into gold-prospecting north of Lake Victoria on the Ugandan border, which also came to nothing, he reached a decision that he would give up on Africa and return home to Britain. He sold his car and most of his belongings, packed a small rucksack with rather less than most of us would consider the barest essentials, and on 14 September 1933 he took a train from Nairobi to Kampala in Uganda. Once there, though no cyclist, he bought a bicycle, 'an ordinary English make, costing £6 – I might have had a Japanese one for £2'. This has often been taken as a slightly Blimpish example of patriotism, and whilst there's no doubt that Tilman was passionately patriotic, in this instance it was no such thing. It was simply a way of guarding himself against the wily Ugandan-Asian bicycle-shop-owner's attempts to offload stock that had been rusting away on his premises since the start of the Great Depression. The bike he decided upon was a sit-up-and-beg heavy black Raleigh, its durability proven by the fact that forty years later it had still not rusted away, even in the Welsh rains, and he was riding it regularly down from Bodowen, his house on the Mawddach estuary, into

---

[28] Tilman, *Seven Mountain Travel Books*, p.99.
[29] Ibid., p.100.

Barmouth to collect his provisions from the local wholefood shop.

With a map torn out of the back of a magazine, and on a diet of eggs – often bad – and big, coarse, female baking bananas (the male ones are used for brewing beer) that he cooked in the ashes of his fire, enlivened occasionally by potatoes and paw-paws, he set off to ride from Kampala through Uganda, the Belgian Congo, French Equatorial Africa and French Cameroon to a west-coast port and a steamer for home. The journey of two months proved to be easy, and disappointing for a man whose boyhood dreams had centred around the stories of Rider Haggard[30] and H.M. Stanley. The white man's headlights now shone into all corners of the Dark Continent and it had all become rather too civilised and tame for Tilman's taste:

> My ship came up the river and I prepared to embark by buying myself a coat and a pair of trousers . . . Sailing day arrived, bringing with it for me the mingled feelings of most 'last days'. Countries, if lived and worked in long enough, have a queer way of making a man feel an affection for them, whether they have treated him well or ill. For fourteen years – a fifth of our allotted span – Africa had been my task-mistress, and now I was leaving her. If she had not given me the fortune I expected she had given me something better – memories, mountains, friends.[31]

The most significant of those friends, meanwhile – the one who, in that slightly pining phrase, 'was not available' (Tilman only ever gives away his fondness in these elliptical phrases, but it is that, and present, nonetheless) for the return trip to Kilimanjaro – had been sailing back to England in the luxury of a P&O liner from Calcutta at the time Tilman was wheeling his way across Africa. On the same date of 14 September, and exactly a year before the latter had set out from Nairobi for Kampala, a beige message form[32] of the Kenya and Uganda Telegraphs Service had been delivered to Shipton's

---

[30] Interesting to ponder what implanting effect novels like Haggard's *King Solomon's Mines*, Conan Doyle's *The Lost World*, or even H. G. Wells's strange novella *The Country of the Blind*, which actually uses a mountaineering expedition as framing device, had on Shipton's and Tilman's later attraction towards exploration.

[31] Tilman, *Seven Mountain Travel Books*, p.147.

[32] Definitely beige, though in *Upon That Mountain* Shipton describes it as 'a bit of pink paper'. I have it, velvety with age, on my desk as I write. I had better ask Dr Steele if colour-blindness is another possible manifestation of dyslexia . . .

farm in Turbo. It read: 'To E. E. Shipton, Turbo valley mount everest committee[33] invite you join expedition subject medical approval strictly confidential please reply goodenough.'

In a typical piece of fooling around, Shipton suggests in *Upon That Mountain* that an Irish friend staying with him at the time had immediately replied to the august personage of Royal Geographical Society President Admiral Sir William Goodenough in the terms 'Good-enough-Shipton', and that he had managed to intercept it in time. I have my doubts about this story, and by the time of *That Untravelled World* it had disappeared without trace (unlike the telegram itself, which he clearly treasured and had kept among his prized mementoes). What can be said with certainty is that in fact the telegram came as no surprise. Frank Smythe – thought difficult by most of his acquaintance yet with whom Shipton seems to have forged a surprisingly warm friendship on Kamet, had alerted him to the probability in a letter of 24 August:

My dear Eric,

Please regard the following as <u>strictly confidential</u> and do not tell a soul unless by the time this reaches you a public announcement has been made. The Tibetan Government have <u>invited</u> us to have another shot at Everest in 1933. It is in the hands of the Everest committee. They are meeting on September 1st . . . your name is naturally one of the first that occurs and you may be sure I will do everything I can. I only hope the Everest Committee will do the right thing and send out a <u>team</u> not a collection of individuals.

I think it can be regarded as certain you will receive an invitation though this is only my personal opinion . . . Wyn Harris is another obvious possibility . . . and so is Wager and Longland. I'm afraid Romilly [Holdsworth][34] has done in any

---

[33] The newly-re-formulated (as of 19 March, 1931) joint committee of the Royal Geographical Society and the Alpine Club that oversaw Everest expeditions and associated matters.

[34] Holdsworth, a classics master at Harrow and a double blue at Oxford for soccer and cricket (traditionally a good basis for inclusion on Everest expeditions, as in the case of the distinctly inexperienced Sandy Irvine in 1924 – though Irvine was a rowing blue and Holdsworth a boat-rocker, which no doubt explains all), had been a popular and efficient member of the Kamet team, and also its botanist, an association from which both Smythe and Shipton derived lifelong interests.

chance he might have had by some very ill judged remarks in public against the Alpine Club. As the President was there the fat was firmly in the fire . . .

Cheerio yrs,

Frank'

Smythe wrote to him again, in the same gossipy vein, on 21 September after his acceptance of the invitation had been received ('It's simply splendid that you are coming. There was of course never a doubt'), to tell him that he had been one of the six asked outright, and that other invitations were likely to go out to Wyn Harris, Longland and Wood-Johnson. He also outlined the strategy being promoted by the bespectacled and scholarly Hugh Ruttledge[35] – who was the committee's appointee as leader, and perhaps an unwise one – of establishing camps and doing everything as far as possible in advance to spare the climbers, who would be organised into assault pairs, and conserve their energy. Shipton's humorous concern in response was that the climbers might develop bed sores from all the lazing around they would have to do. Smythe asked Shipton if they might make a pair together, discussed Norton's[36] views of the slabs at 28,000 feet ('not nice at all and there isn't a belay anywhere'), canvassed the choice of route, which from the north col was one either of the ridge or the Great Couloir, Smythe's preference being for the former, as 'there is a better chance of a camping place at 28,000 on the arête than on the face which is beastly smooth and slabby', and ended with the following fond exhortation:

---

[35] Ruttledge was a retiree from the Indian civil service, and no mountaineer. His appointment in retrospect was seen by many as disastrous, though he went on to lead the expedition of 1936. Smythe's name was considered for the leadership, but – heresy of heresies in the age of the amateur! – he made his living from writing and lecturing on mountains, and also had a fine capacity for making people bristle. The Gentlemen were perfectly happy, however, to take him along as a Player.

[36] Lieutenant Colonel E. F. Norton, who had taken over as leader in 1924 after General Bruce fell ill. Norton had established an altitude record (given with wonderful precision as '28,126 feet', which Shipton would blithely argue was 'a manifest nonsense, such exactitude being impossible in these situations') which was not to be broken until the Swiss expedition of 1952, on which Tenzing and Raymond Lambert reached 28,200 feet or thereabouts on the south-east ridge, and convincingly in the ascent by Charles Evans and Tom Bourdillon of Everest's south summit on 26 May, 1953 – three days before Tenzing and Hillary made it to the summit. It was equalled several times in 1933, by Wyn Harris, Wager and Smythe – all of them without supplementary oxygen.

Now for God's sake take care of yourself. Don't go out and bust a leg or get mauled by a lion! At this moment I have a letter from your Mother. She has written to you to get you home. She is quite right. You will have to be outfitted properly. It is not like Kamet and there will be many things which really make your presence here essential. If the press try to interview you please do not breathe a word of what I have told you especially about the tentative scheme.

The same sensitivity regarding the press acquiring information about the expedition permeates the legal agreement that all invited members had to sign ('3: That from the date hereof until the expiration of three years after the date of the first publication of the official account of the expedition I will not publish or allow to be published any account of the expedition in any form written by me or hold any communication with the press or any press agency or publisher . . . without the previous sanction of the Committee in writing'). What lay behind this was undoubtedly the paranoia stemming from the entrepreneurial activities of Captain J. B. L. Noel after the expedition of 1924 – the so-called 'affair of the dancing lamas'[37] – when the Tibetan government had not only taken grave offence at Noel's bringing back lamas from Tibet to perform religious dances at public screenings of the expedition film, but also jibbed at representations in the film of Tibetans searching each other's hair for head lice and cracking them with their teeth – the British viewers of the film thought they were eating fleas, a misapprehension perpetuated in the recent Wade Davis book on Mallory. All this had led to refusals of permission for further expeditions to Everest in 1926 and 1931, and the one planned for 1933 was in consequence regarded as diplomatically very sensitive.

The expedition was a huge and lavish affair that set out in the spring of 1933 from Darjeeling. It made its way to Kalimpong, where

Kanchenjunga, which had been covered in thick cloud, suddenly poked his head out. It was a very remarkable sight. You know how high a mountain can look when the top is

---

[37] For a full account of this, and most other matters pertaining to Mount Everest, see Walt Unsworth's *Everest* – an authoritative, monumental and immensely readable history of the mountain (many editions).

just seen over the clouds – at that moment Kanchenjunga looked simply incredible – I think everyone regards the sudden appearance as a good omen – the porters and natives were very impressed.

From Kalimpong they cantered on ponies out of Sikkim and across the plains of Tibet:

The ponies were very fresh and we clattered off at full gallop. At short intervals for about a mile there were large crowds who cheered us with the result that our ponies panicked and charged faster and faster. How I stuck on I don't know. It would have been most undignified to have been thrown off with so many onlookers.[38]

For six weeks they made their way across the plains of Tibet. Much of the time Shipton marched or rode with Wyn Harris: 'We had long talks. I seem to get more and more fond of him. I think we are to be a climbing pair, at which I am more than glad as there is no-one I want to climb with more.' Describing the landscape to his mother a fortnight after leaving Kalimpong, he asks her to 'think of an <u>absolutely</u> flat plain without a stick of vegetation anywhere, in the middle of which rises a "town" consisting of a jumble of low square houses built of mud and yak-dung. We arrived here today in a snow-storm and it's been snowing hard ever since.'

In the same letter he tells of a little escapade before they had left Sikkim:

We stopped for a few days by a lake just the other side of the frontier at about 12,600 feet. It was a very pleasant spot with lots to do. We did a bit of rock-climbing . . . Jack [Longland], Wager, Wyn and I broke bounds and pushed a camp over to a very attractive peak called Chomonbar (about 17,500 feet). We had a good deal of difficulty getting to it . . . managed to climb the peak after a long and rather difficult climb. We made ourselves rather sick in the process. I was pleased to find that I was less affected by altitude than the others. Jack was rather

---

[38] Letter to Mrs Haly, 6 March 1933.

bad. It was a grand climb – though we were ticked off by Ruttledge yesterday for doing it.

After we had rejoined the others by the lake we crossed over into Tibet. You can imagine that I felt a great thrill in crossing the frontier. It was a beautiful day and a marvellous sight coming over the pass. The whole of the Kanchenjunga massif we saw that morning behind us and in front Chomolhari,[39] one of the most beautiful mountains in the world . . . Over the whole march to Everest we don't pass through really high mountain country, and we have had no close-up views of the big fellows.[40]'

The small advance party of which Shipton was a member had orders to wait for the others at Gantse:

Tom Brocklebank, Wyn and I found a delightful little side valley with the most glorious colouring – the like of which I haven't seen outside England. We put a light camp there and we three lived in wild luxury for two or three days, round a large log fire. It's the last vegetation we will be with for many months to come now. The day before yesterday Wager came up and we explored the head of our valley. It was a fine day and we had a really interesting time working out the topography of the surrounding country . . .

Yesterday we descended into the main valley to meet Ruttledge and the rest. R. looks very tired and worried. There are also two Army men who are to run the wireless from Base Camp. We are all much annoyed at having wireless with us. Yesterday Birnie, Wager and I went up into our little valley to spend the night. I shared a tent with Wager, of whom I am awfully fond. He is just about the soundest and most genuine person I know.[41]

A few days farther along their march through the harsh and beautiful desert country, Shipton and Wager

---

[39] Chomolhari (24,035 feet.), a mountain with a fascinating history and mythology, lies right on the Bhutanese border with Tibet, and was first climbed in 1937 by Freddie Spencer Chapman and Pasang Dawa Lama.
[40] Letter to Mrs Haly, 22 March, 1933.
[41] Ibid.

wandered up a hill and sat for a long time under the shelter of a rock contemplating a glorious view to the north. The colouring is amazing. Though not a scrap of vegetation is to be seen anywhere, the variety and vividness of the colouring is more striking than I have ever seen before. To the north as far as the eye can see (and many thousands of miles further) stretch the purple hills of Tibet – To the south is ranged the mighty mass of the Himalayas, the glaciers of which produce an astonishing contrast to the desert we are in.

These early responses of Shipton's to the vast landscapes that became his consuming passion, as well as the focus of his life's work, seem to express a sense of awe that is close neighbour to the essence of religious experience. They are elaborations, versions, of Hölderlin's[42] succinct formulation of the religious impulse: '. . . *immer/Ins Ungebundene gehet eine Sehnsucht.*' ('A longing always towards the Infinite.')

The expedition reached Rongbuk and made its way to the foot of the mountain up the East Rongbuk Glacier. 'The country is grim beyond words,' Shipton wrote to his mother, 'these mountains are utterly different from those around Kamet. They are much less startling in appearance, and one is never in danger from ice-avalanches – but everything is very harsh and cold. Your scarf as usual comes in very useful and I sleep in it every night.'[43]

They failed in their attempt, and the details of that failure are widely available. In the view of Jack Longland,[44] for once it was not merely down to the weather they experienced:

The crucial point was when the two soldiers, Boustead and Birnie, took it on themselves to say that conditions were too cold to establish Camp Five on May 20th. Wyn Harris, who was an infinitely more experienced mountaineer, thought this an absolute nonsense. I remember I was at Camp Four at the time and Wyn came down in a complete fury, saying 'The

---

[42] Friedrich Hölderlin (1770–1843) is one of the greatest of German lyric poets. Though in no sense a follower of any formal religion, his verse is pervaded by religious feeling and of the fragile, alienated and lonely nature of human existence – a good poet for mountaineers, then?

[43] Letter to Mrs Haly, 22 April, 1933.

[44] As expressed in a taped interview with the author in 1985.

fucking soldiery!' And he was right, because on the 20th for the next three days not only was the weather good but it was before the upper slabs were covered with new snow.

Shipton's marginally more emollient account is useful in augmenting this:

> . . . they were forced to retreat from 24,500 owing to the wind. Actually there was some difference of opinion about the wisdom of this decision, and a hot-tempered argument raged most of the succeeding night, by the end of which the subject under debate had become rather confused.[45]

It does seem, as Jack Longland states, to have been a crucial failure to grasp a rare opportunity on 20 May, which, had it been taken, might just have led on to success, with a strong team well acclimatised by then and established high on the mountain. The decision to retreat from 24,500 feet instead of pressing on and establishing Camp Five at 25,500 feet had been taken by the de facto deputy leader[46] of the expedition, Bill St John Birnie 'of Sam Browne's Cavalry and Adjutant to His Excellency the Governor of Bengal's Bodyguard' (also 'one of the best polo and squash racket players in the Indian Army, and an expert big-game shot'[47] – though unfortunately not a man with any great experience of mountaineering). This was the man of many parts – most of them inappropriate to the present context – who had seen fit to overrule the judgement and desire of Wyn Harris. One of the several curious aspects to this little military debacle is that the decision was taken by Captain Birnie despite his being junior in rank to his companion Major Boustead. Clearly Birnie was a forceful personality, if not a forceful mountaineer.

The outcome of this incident – apart from, as Longland says, costing them their one realistic chance of making the summit in the brief window of good weather – was that on the following day Hugh Ruttledge, lame and approaching fifty, limped up to Camp Four, to which the party meant to set up the next camp had retreated,

---

[45] Shipton, *Upon That Mountain*, p.114.
[46] Edward Shebbeare, the original choice for this role, had fallen ill.
[47] Smythe, *Kamet Conquered*, p.37.

and after a rigorous examination of all parties into what had taken place, even this diffident and mild-mannered ex-civil servant ended up by tearing strips off 'the fucking soldiery'.

Major Boustead had the good grace to apologise to his leader, whilst the scowling and heavy-jowled Captain Birnie flung out in the highest dudgeon, went off to sulk in his tent, and remained in ill humour for the rest of the expedition, in consequence of which he was not invited on another Everest attempt. (There is a fine group photograph in Raymond Greene's witty and gossiping memoir *Moments of Being* which shows the team members in Sikkim in the prelude to the expedition. Even here the facial expressions and body language tell you much – Jack Longland cringing away from Birnie,[48] whom he sits alongside; Ruttledge behind, stoop-shouldered with chin firmly aloft, Wyn Harris knit-browed and pugnacious at one end of the back row . . .)

For all that the expedition failed to achieve its objective, was factionalised, and went through periods of considerable disharmony, Shipton again came out of it with credit. In Raymond Greene's view, 'Frank Smythe and Eric Shipton . . . were not only very fit, but outstandingly the best climbers of us all.'[49] With Smythe he climbed without oxygen to a point two hours above Camp Six, which was at 27,400 feet, before he began to feel sick. A tin of the meat essence seems to have been the culprit again, and he had to descend, leaving Smythe to toil a little higher on his own before he too had to retreat. They accomplished these exceptional feats, it might be remembered, clad in half a dozen Shetland wool pullovers, flannel long johns the thought of which makes me want to scratch, an outer shell layer of cotton windproof fabric, woollen balaclava helmets and clinker-nailed heavy leather boots, felt-lined and with an asbestos intersole for insulation. They had no crampons, and their long-ashwood-shafted, straight-picked ice axes were unchanged since late Victorian times. With the latter, and a rock piton or two conjured up by Jack Longland – the kind of bounder who would surely shoot

---

[48] For all his sulks and the Cambridge faction's very apparent dislike of him, Bill Birnie seems to have been well-regarded by the determinedly non-factional Shipton – further proof of the latter's affable character. The two of them spent time together at Simla in the early years of the Second World War, and later in that conflict Birnie served as adjutant to Field-Marshall Wavell during Wavell's time as Commander-in-Chief in India.

[49] Raymond Greene, *Moments of Being* (Heinemann, 1974), p.158.

a fox!⁵⁰ – from his pocket, Smythe in particular accomplished some considerable feats of climbing short stretches of overhanging ice at altitude.

After Smythe's solo summit attempt had sensibly been abandoned, the entire party, in the face of bad weather, was soon withdrawn from the mountain, and a half-hearted resumption of their project a week later soon petered out in the face of more wind and snow on the incoming monsoon. In a letter to his mother dated 3 July 1933, Shipton gives a vivid impression of the immediate aftermath of the expedition, and his feelings about the mountain. They are far from boundlessly enthusiastic, even at this early stage of his Himalayan career:

> Before leaving Base Camp Brocklebank and I did a ripping expedition together. We went up an unexplored valley to the south and camped at 20,000 feet on a ridge. From there we traversed a fine peak of 22,500 feet back to Base Camp. It was a glorious show and a grand climb. We were lucky with the weather and had splendid views over unexplored ranges. I was surprised to find how much Everest had taken it out of me. All one's reserves seem to have gone, and one is in need of a long rest.
>
> We are now camped in a <u>green</u> valley and it is <u>raining</u> hard. What a wonderful joy it is to see green again and the rain is glorious. Life is full of joys after two-and-a-half months of the Rongbuk Glacier – one of the grimmest parts of the world. I'm just longing to see a tree again.
>
> All my love, Darling, from Eric.

This sortie with Brocklebank was not the end of the affair for Shipton. Habitually curious, with Wager he made his way to the Raphu La, the pass crossing the north-east ridge between the East Rongbuk and the Kangshung glaciers, and climbed the small peak high above it marked as 6,833 metres on the RGS Mount Everest Region map, which afforded them views across the vastness of the Kangshung Face to Lhotse and Lhotse Shar:

> I managed to get to the Raphu La and to look down into the

---

⁵⁰ A variation on the phrase by which Longland gleed over the Establishment response to his having placed a piton for protection during his epoch-making eponymous climb of 1928 on the west buttress of Clogwyn Du'r Arddu, in North Wales.

most gigantic cirque in the world, enclosed by Chomolonzo, Makalu, Lhotse and the great South Face of Everest. The most astonishing sight I have ever seen. The ice scenery is fantastic. The great ice wall of Everest, 10,000 feet high, with its mad array of ridges and flutings is a thing one can't believe in unless one has seen it, and from the Raphu La we had leisure to gaze at it from quite close, for many hours, and to watch the avalanches thunder continuously down its sides. Dawn, with masses of cloud filling the bottom of the cirque and covering all in the distance except the great head of Kanchenjunga, seventy miles off, with all the unimaginable colours that a dawn can produce, was an experience bound to last one a lifetime.[51]

In his first autobiography, he returns to this experience, describing its contrasting beauties succinctly: 'delicately fluted ridges of purest ice, a hundred peaks of exquisite form, deep, wooded valleys; what a contrast to the bare, unlovely slopes of rubble above the Rongbuk glacier!'[52]

A few days later, Ruttledge contacted the Mount Everest Committee to suggest withdrawing to the Kama valley in the hope of making another attempt on the mountain post-monsoon. Goodenough replied by cable to tell him there was no money available for that plan, and ordered the expedition to abandon Everest for this year and withdraw to Darjeeling. Freed from the drudgery, on the morning of 13 July Shipton left the main expedition and set off on horseback with Laurence Wager, the Sherpas Sonam and Pasang and ten porters to return by a route south of their approach, intent on crossing the Lashar Plain and forcing their way across a pass into northern Sikkim. Deep snow on the first day's march hindered their passage to Phuru, where 'the hospitality of the Dzongpen was so lavish and his "chang" so powerful that our 3 a.m. breakfast on the 14th was more than usually unpleasant'.[53]

---

[51] Letter to Mrs Haly (undated, early July 1933).

[52] Shipton, *Upon That Mountain*, p.131.

[53] Eric Shipton, 'The Lashar Plain' (*Alpine Journal*, 1934), p.129. The claim in Peter Steele's *Everest and Beyond* that Shipton and Wager spent 'two months on the Lashar Plain' is considerably at odds with the precise dating of this account, in which their sojourn here is given as lasting from 13-22 July; though the mistake is entirely understandable given the habitually enormous amount packed into the brief period of days.

Despite the hangovers, that day they climbed a 20,000-foot peak in the Nyönno Ri massif and glimpsed through gaps in the cloud the extensive and unsuspected ranges to the south-east. On the following day, pursuing their journey, they camped with a group of nomadic Sikkimese who were on a pilgrimage to Mount Kailash, and next morning the Britons moved on to visit the cliff-dwellings of Changmo. Here it snowed heavily in the night, and early on the 16th Pasang left with the horses to rejoin the main expedition, whilst Shipton, Wager and Sonam walked on with the porters to the foot of a valley leading up on to the Lashar Plain.

> Such views as we got, then and later, of the country to the south of the Lashar Plain gave an impression of an immense tangle of high peaks, many in the region of 24,000 feet. Attempts we made to fit any of it in with the country indicated on the map were in vain. Of course we had neither the time nor the opportunity to do much, but we could see that problems of great topographical interest are awaiting solution in the region . . .[54]

For the present, the allure of the peaks to the south proved too strong to resist. On the 19th, Shipton and a porter, Aila, made the second ascent of Lhonak Peak (21,460 feet), which had been climbed over several days by G. B. Gourlay and W. Eversden three years before. Wager, meanwhile, explored the col to its north, after which, more snow having fallen in the night, they abandoned plans to climb Kellas Peak and discretion allied to anxiety about the likelihood of avalanche conditions on the descent into Sikkim hurried them along on their journey:

> . . . we started to descend into Sikkim early on the morning of the 20th. The descent proved more than troublesome. We discarded some snow-covered rocks on the left in favour of an ice-fall; but here our way was barred by a huge crevasse system and we had to go back again. Our eventual success in reaching the Lhonak glacier by way of the rocks was due to a fine bit of route-finding by Aila.[55]

[54] Shipton, 'The Lashar Plain', p.130.
[55] Ibid. p.131.

This last note of confidence in and admiration for his Sherpa companions is one that will sound recurrently through the coming years. For now, the focus was shifting, and the company he was in reinforced the new direction of interest. In *Upon That Mountain* Shipton points out that 'Mountain climbing has its roots in mountain exploration, and in little-known ranges it is not unnatural that the mountaineer should tend to revert to the basis of his pursuit.'[56] His experience of the last four months on Everest, insulated from his surroundings by the large travelling community of which he was a part, fixated on a mere and pre-decided objective of summit attainment, had proved in some respects an alienating one. But this little coda to it of less than a fortnight spent in entirely congenial company[57] proved to be its best part.

Six years earlier Shipton had stayed in Wager's rooms whilst taking his Cambridge entrance papers, and had been captivated by the mountain books and photographs there. Now he was travelling in tandem with the man himself through unknown country, and the experience was of enormous significance. The conversations between the two of them had a profound and lasting effect on Shipton's future approach to mountains, and he gives a delightful vignette of their beginning and their consequent development and influence in the following passage:

> My chief interest was in climbing peaks. Wager, on the other hand, as a geologist, had a wider view. He had already tasted the joys of serious exploration in Greenland, and his main enthusiasm was for the country itself. Though I disputed the matter hotly at the time,[58] I gradually became converted to his

---

[56] Shipton, *Upon That Mountain*, p.138.

[57] Laurence Wager (1904–65), a close friend and contemporary of Jack Longland and Wyn Harris at Cambridge, was not only one of the outstanding mountaineers of his day, he was also from an early age a committed wanderer who by the time of Everest '33 had already been on two exploratory trips to Greenland, including one in 1932, the year in which Gino Watkins was lost. Wager's distinguished career as geologist took him to a chair in Oxford which he held from 1950 to his early death. On Everest in 1933 he and Wyn Harris equalled Norton's high point of 28,200 feet – or thereabouts! – before the row with 'the fucking soldiery' broke out. It was on this day that they found Mallory's ice axe (a relic Shipton managed to lose in London, albeit briefly, at a later date – or so he said! I suspect another wind-up in this story).

[58] So hotly, in fact, that Shipton tells of how Wager persuaded him to begin smoking a pipe, in order to shut him up from time to time. Though those of you

way of thinking. Something of my early feeling for mountains began to revive.[59]

The last sentence here is extraordinarily telling, is yet another example of that pronounced psychological predisposition to return to the grace state of innocent early wandering of which we saw much in earlier chapters. In Wager he had found yet another of his significant teachers; and as we reflect on that, we should consider too what a ready pupil Shipton always proved to be under sympathetic instruction – his interest so keen, his ego never getting in the way and clouding the issue. We might ponder too how fast was the shift away from fixation with reaching the top. There is in the simply stated precepts of this crucial passage a tacit admission that Wager had it right, and that under his wise guidance, Shipton was brought round to a mature and lasting mountain-exploratory perspective.

They crossed their difficult col into Sikkim and made their way down to reach Tangu in the Lachen valley on 22 July. Here they separated. Wager headed back north into Tibet, the country that held his heart-strings. Shipton was left to brood on his conviction that within 'a huge organisation' was no way to approach any mountain, and to reflect in habitually fair-minded fashion on the many friendships made or cemented in this grotesquely inflated enterprise, as he 'double-marched down the Lachen Valley to the comforts and worries of civilisation'.[60] These latter, he found on his return to London, had taken the form of a bloody and deeply divisive feud between the established forces of the Royal Geographical Society on the one hand and on the other the young mountaineering bloods of Cambridge with whom he had often associated, over the dithering nature of Hugh Ruttledge's leadership. The ten days he had spent in crossing the Lashar Plain and descending into Sikkim with Wager had not only confirmed a direction in life for which he had a natural predilection. They had also, fortuitously, spared him

---

with working memories and an attention to detail will recall that he and Smythe enjoyed 'yarning' over their post-prandial pipes on Kamet two years before, and may therefore suspect another of those strange, on-going Shiptonian gags on a par with the dyslexia, the Mount Kenya porters, or even the Yeti. As to the latter, well, as Robert Graves has it, 'I was coming to that.' (From 'Welsh Incident', in *Robert Graves: Collected Poems 1965*, Cassell, 1965, p.93.)

[59] Shipton, *Upon That Mountain*, p.139.
[60] Shipton, 'The Lashar Plain', p.131.

an inevitable necessity, had he been in London, of having to take sides, and of being drawn in to the controversy, with all the damage that would have entailed in the future.

As it was, his absence ensured that he retained the friendship of Hugh Ruttledge, who was to prove an influential future mentor and friend, especially in the public assessments he would make of his young protégé's achievements in a field dear to his own heart – that of mountain exploration. Shipton's luck, once more, had held.

7

Vagabonds and Rishis

In the autumn of 1933 Eric Shipton had disembarked in England to find himself feted by all factions of the British mountaineering establishment. The underlying reasons for this warmly affectionate response were as much to do with his energetic and gregarious character (not to mention quiet charisma, youthful innocence and those hypnotic blue eyes) and the growing substance of his climbing record in the Alps, Himalaya and Africa as with his endeavours on Everest, where the less personable Frank Smythe had performed even better. It's clear that Shipton throughout his life held to an original delight in natural and mountain environments. That prerogative of buffoons and inadequates which is the pursuit of fame played no part in his seeking these out – they were not an instrument for his ego but an agency of joy. From time to time, however, as an early (and necessarily quite low-key in a society where the cult of the amateur was still potent) example of the professional mountaineer,[1] invitations where a degree of celebrity was an inevitable concomitant would naturally come his way.

Everest in many ways was an unwelcome but irresistible distraction from his original exploratory impulse towards mountains, which latter had received such powerful validation from his forceful mentor-companion Lawrence Wager in the aftermath of the 1933 expedition. As the 1930s progressed, Shipton's own mountaineering value system became clearly defined. It was to prove quite at odds with public and Establishment obsessions and the latter's preferred modus operandi; and eventually it led to that defining moment

---

[1] Not in the sense of being paid directly for his participation in mountain expeditions, but from 1933 onwards it could justifiably be said that mountaineering was his profession.

in the divergent philosophies and practices of mountain activity: his removal from the leadership of the successful 1953 Everest expedition.

Back in England in the declining days of 1933, his African time, though he did not yet know it, had more or less come to an end. Within a few months he would write from Garhwal to his mother to apprise her of the situation there:

> More drought and hailstones in Kenya! Poor Philpotts' crop has been wiped out according to Tilman. I haven't heard anything from Hull. The original sum the Land Bank agreed to lend was £1500 but I decided to cut down expenditure and try to get through on £1000. That is why development is not being done on the lines outlined in the original proposal. Unless I get a lot of lecturing and writing to do at home I think I ought to go out and look at things, but I can't really formulate any definite plans yet.[2]

He wouldn't be going back to Turbo. His love-interest there was now dancing her nights away with another man, to whom she had become engaged (and who was heartily detested by Shipton). Kenyan farming generally was in difficulties. Tilman too, as we saw in the last chapter, had pulled out of active participation by 1934 though his remaining land holdings were not sold until ten years later. And Shipton himself had taken refuge in his mother's new residence at 100a Lexham Gardens, London W8. This long row of elegant white-painted six-storey grand terraced houses with their porticos and black wrought-iron railings, Kensington High Street three or four blocks to the north and private gardens with lawns and flowering cherry trees just around the corner, has fluctuated up and down property's exclusivity ladder over the eighty years since Shipton and his mother first lived there. In the 1960s it was run-down bed-sit land, battered Minis parked outside, exotically gorgeous young women with heavy eye make-up floating and fluttering their way along it like *Nymphalidae* on a breeze in the direction of Biba[3]. Today it is

---

[2] Letter to Mrs Haly, 3 July 1934.
[3] A female fashion store that started out on Kensington Church Street in the 1960s and later moved to Kensington High Street, about which the London

conspicuously wealthy, kerb-to-kerb Chelsea-tractor territory, a Range Rover at every doorstep.

In the 1930s it was a moderately respectable address in a good, if slightly decaying, area. As a London base it was within a few minutes' walk of the Royal Geographical Society on Kensington Gore, and hence mighty convenient for the young explorer. The social side of Shipton's character could also find expression here, and he and his mother, as his letters to her reveal, were emotionally close (protestations of distance in his second autobiography notwithstanding), and maintained a surprisingly warm and mutually dependent relationship down the years – one that was quite intimate enough for her more reserved character, and with propinquity and this new domesticity holding them together in their widely differing orbits. Her disapproval of all his potential girlfriends, and filling of the consequent emotional vacuum in the time-honoured fashion of mothers and sons, kept him free of sexual snares and entanglements for a time yet.

His adventurous spirit in the declining days of 1933 was in need of a new focus, a new project, and of one thing he was quite sure – that it would not be in the same style as the lavish venture in which he had been engaged for most of the year. A basic Hegelian concept comes into play here to ensure that what he did next would be the antithesis of that from which he was newly returned. In the crucial sequence of conversations held with Lawrence Wager in their crossing of the Lashar Plain it had not just been the over-numerous proximity of his fellow men against which he had railed in misanthropic Tilmanesque fashion: 'For my part I loathed the crowds and the fuss that were inseparable from a large expedition . . . The small town of tents that sprang up each evening, the noise and racket of each fresh start, the sight of a huge army invading the peaceful valleys', all of which was 'so far removed from the light, free spirit with which we were wont to approach our peaks'.[4] He had also been considering the psychological and financial aspects. Of the first, essentially, he considered that to be a small cog

---

women I knew in my twenties tended to talk in excited tones, or even – 'The horror! The horror!' – insist you accompany them there. Beached by the changing tides of fashion, it closed down in 1975. Those same London women, older and statelier now, tell me with a certain wan nostalgic gleam that it has re-opened recently in some new guise. We have been warned . . .

[4] Eric Shipton, *Upon That Mountain* (Hodder & Stoughton, 1943), p.134.

in a large machine was demotivating and dispiriting ('It is vitally important that no member of a party should at any time feel that he is superfluous, or that he is simply there in case someone else breaks down'). Of the second, after Everest, with farming in Kenya now in abeyance Shipton had his living to make, and without a private income – for his mother was financially incapable of subsidising him on any grand scale, new house notwithstanding – extravagant ventures were out of the question. Nor did he consider them desirable: 'I was convinced that expeditions could be run for a tithe of the cost generally considered necessary.'[5]

As London became his social focus from the time of planning for Kamet onwards, and as he withdrew emotionally and intellectually from his African interlude, so too did he make a new circle of friends. Among these again it is notable how strong was the mutual attraction between this modest, bright and quietly ardent young man and the significant figures in the field to which he was inexorably drawn. Whilst in London in the intervals between expeditions and farming in the early 1930s he had pursued an acquaintanceship with another old Africa hand, Noel Humphreys, whom he frequently visited in the Orange Street[6] garret where Humphreys had lived for four years – until qualifying as a doctor in 1931 at the age of forty-eight – on twenty-four shillings and sixpence a week whilst training in nearby Gower Street. Humphreys was a remarkable character who had been a Royal Flying Corps pilot in the Great War, in which he was shot down and interned. He had spent his time whilst in the prisoner of war camp studying botany,[7] his ultimate expertise in which led him to make seven expeditions to the Rwenzori during the 1920s. Here, then, was another mentor in the light-and-frugal expedition style from which Everest, through its pre-eminence and the brand-appeal – disgusting term! – that it had in Shipton's day

---

[5] Eric Shipton, *Upon That Mountain*, p.139.

[6] Orange Street is behind the National Gallery, running from Haymarket to the Charing Cross Road. Rents there these days are rather steeper than in Noel Humphreys' time.

[7] Projects like this, involving subjects non-threatening to the camp authorities, were quite common among British PoWs, and tolerated, in both world wars. John Buxton's classic 1950 monograph on the Redstart, published in Collins' *New Naturalist* series and written from notes and observations made in a Bavarian PoW camp after Buxton's capture in Norway in 1940, is an excellent example. Derek Niemann, one of the *Guardian*'s 'country diarists', has recently published a fascinating account of the phenomenon – *Birds in a Cage* (Short Books, 2012).

and still has for the less discerning 'adventurers' of our time, was
then and now mostly excluded.

The passion in Shipton for a new approach, the dislike that he
had for the grandiose scale and its human implications, and the
tradition with which he was becoming increasingly aligned all find
expression in an important passage from *Upon That Mountain*:

> Fantastic equipment was evolved, dynamite brought to blow
> away obstacles, aeroplanes used for dumping supplies on
> the mountain, all the delicacies known to culinary art were
> provided to sustain the exhausted climbers, whole populations
> were uprooted from their homes to carry this stuff up the
> glaciers – with the consequent risk of famine the following
> year due to the neglect of agriculture. Needless to say these
> tactics met with very little success, and not one of the peaks
> attacked with such ferocity was climbed. But the sad thing was
> that the lessons taught by the great pioneers of Himalayan
> exploration – Longstaff, Conway, Kellas, Godwin Austin,
> Freshfield, the Schlagintweits – who achieved so much by the
> simple but hardy application of their art, were forgotten or
> ignored.[8]

The name at the head of that list was soon to become the pre-
eminent influence on Shipton in what is now widely recognised to
have been his most important role – that of mountain traveller and
explorer. His proficiency within the core skills of mountain activity
remained throughout his career not an end in itself but suited to his
exploratory needs, rather than to the pursuit of difficulty for its own
sake. Which is not to say that he was remotely incompetent in any
aspect of mountain craft – he was simply not at the forefront of its
technical advances, nor even interested in being so. Tom Longstaff
(1875–1964) was himself arguably the most important Himalayan
explorer throughout the first three decades of the twentieth century.
Shipton had already been in his company briefly at La Bérarde in
1926, but had been too much in awe of this bristling little red-bearded
choleric man to talk with him. Which was a pity, because Longstaff,
capacity for ire aside, was a kindly and supportive character. He was
possessed of substantial private means – his father had subsidised

---

[8] Shipton, *Upon That Mountain,* p.137.

Captain Scott's first Antarctic expedition to the tune of £25,000, a fortune in those days. After Eton and Oxford, Longstaff had qualified in 1906 as a doctor but by this time was already committed to a life of exploration and never practised medicine. In 1905, with the Italian guides Alexis and Henri Brocherel, he had visited Garhwal with the intention of exploring around the highest peak in the British Empire, Nanda Devi, and had reached a depression at a height of 19,100 feet just behind Nanda Devi East in the ridges encircling the Nanda Devi basin which was known thereafter as Longstaff's Col. From here, he and his companions were the first to look down into the secret shrine that was to become a focus of mountain-exploration interest for decades to come.

On a second expedition in 1907, with a different party which included General Bruce, he made the first ascent of Trisul (23,360 feet) with the Brocherel brothers, climbing the final 6,000 feet in a single day and establishing a record for the highest summit achieved that was to last for twenty-three years. Even before Trisul, Longstaff had been active in Tibet and had made a daring attempt on Gurla Mandhata (25,243 feet), the fierce bulk of which lies on the other side of Lake Manasarowar from the holy mountain of Kailash in the south-west of Tibet, and which was finally climbed as late as 1985 by a Japanese/Chinese expedition. Longstaff's party were swept 3,000 feet down the western flank by an avalanche. After bivouacking without shelter above 20,000 feet, they retrieved their ice axes and carried on up the mountain, only relinquishing their attempt at difficult ground a thousand feet below the summit after spending another night in the open at 23,000 feet.[9] This was a man to be reckoned with, and in his advisory pep talk to younger members of the 1933 expedition at the RGS before departure, 'Tomstaff', as the young bloods familiarly called him (though not to his face, in view of the slightly lewd pun[10] involved), eyes flashing fire and finger pointing aloft, had left them with the ringing exhortation that 'The man who collapses above the

---

[9] For more on the adventurous season of 1905, see the account by his companion, Charles Sherring, a deputy commissioner in the Indian civil service, in his *Western Tibet and the British Borderland* (Edward Arnold, 1906)

[10] 'The same being a reference to Longstaff's legendary priapism' – this from Jack Longland, whose own name was subject to a neat variation from much the same behavioural reason. It always rather surprises me, given the company he kept, that Shipton's own sexual initiation was so late in arriving, though the domestic arrangements with his mother surely played a role here.

North Col is a scoundrel; a scoundrel, sir!' Here was a story that surely gained much in the retelling, and no doubt Shipton rehearsed it to himself frequently and with affectionate amusement as he strolled back to Lexham Gardens that night.

Tomfoolery aside, he did take something crucial from Longstaff. In the notice he wrote for him in the *DNB* Shipton observes of Longstaff's many ventures that

> all these expeditions he conducted with Spartan simplicity, unencumbered by elaborate equipment and living largely upon local produce. This was from choice, not necessity; for he was a keen exponent of light travel which not only gave him freedom of movement but enabled him more easily to establish contact with the local people and to achieve close harmony with his chosen environment.[11]

'Spartan simplicity'; 'close harmony with his chosen environment'; – a consistent theme is emerging here. First Wager and now Longstaff, had endorsed Shipton's philosophical and practical drift and exorcised for him the troublesome spirit of that vast Everest offensive. All he needed now was an objective and a companion; and perhaps a little money too, though his old school- and Africa friend Gustav Sommerfelt had arranged through family connections for him to do some lectures on the old milch cow Everest in Norway – a necessary skill to master if he was going to make a living from exploration – and they would bring in funds.

The objective, too, fell into place quite easily. At first he had designs on 'a thorough exploration of the much-discussed range which lies between the sacred shrines of Badrinath, Kedarnath and Gangotri'.[12] This region, home to some of the world's most spectacular and beautiful mountains, had been attracting a degree of attention in the early 1930s, as it still does to this day. Whilst Shipton had been on Everest in 1933, Marco Pallis, the Buddhist scholar and Liverpool mountaineer, led a trip here on which the leading Welsh rock-climber of the time, Colin Kirkus, and Charles Warren, who would be doctor to the Everest forays of 1935, 1936 and 1938, reached the summit of a mountain they called Central

---

[11] *Dictionary of National Biography 1961–1970* (Oxford, 1981), pp.675–6.
[12] *Alpine Journal*, 1935, p.59.

Satopanth Peak (almost certainly what is now known as Bhagirathi 2, opposite Shivling on the ridge between the Gangotri and its tributary Chaturangi glaciers). Longstaff, however, dissuaded Shipton from giving precedence to this plan and it became something in the nature of a coda to his final purpose, urged on him by Longstaff, which was to enter the Sanctuary and reach the foot of Nanda Devi: 'Such advice coming from such a quarter was too valuable to neglect, and though I confess I had some misgivings as to the feasibility of the proposition, I welcomed it with open arms.'[13]

What's mere feasibility between friends-in-adventure? His acquaintance through the Kamet expedition with Garhwal – loveliest of Himalayan regions in the view of many – reinforced the attraction of Longstaff's proposal. It was easily accessible either from Calcutta or Bombay and then by train and bus along to Ranikhet. No political problems were entailed in getting there, it being since the Nepalese War of 1815 a north Indian administrative region, from 1858 to 1947 under the British Raj (and now part of the north Indian state of Uttar Pradesh). Here, among sublime mountain scenery, lay what had come to be seen by 1934 as *the* fascinating and challenging contemporary problem in Himalayan topography. It was a lost world; a precipice-ringed paradise-valley to which not even the hardiest indigenous peoples had ventured; a physical reality to match the literary imaginings of H. G. Wells and Sir Arthur Conan Doyle. Though it was much talked about in exploration circles, nobody, by 1933, had succeeded in entering the Nanda Devi Sanctuary.[14]

This exquisite and complex interlocking-horseshoe-shaped sequence of alps[15] was hemmed in by a double barrier of high ridges comprising a matchless sequence of rock spires and ice arêtes with Nanda Devi – the goddess Nanda, at 25,645 feet the highest

---

[13] *Alpine Journal*, p.59.

[14] Designated a UNESCO World Heritage Site in 1988 (since 2004 one of the same body's biosphere reserves), and one to which entry for all who do not have privileged guidance through the labyrinths of Indian bureaucracy is now both forbidden and near-unobtainable – probably a repercussion from the 1965 placing of a nuclear-powered Chinese-missile-test monitoring device at 22,000 feet on the peak by the CIA in association with the Indian Army. The device was swept away by avalanche and attempts to recover it have been unsuccessful, hence raising fears of radio-active contamination in the Sanctuary. There are reports that some of the climbers involved in its placing died of radiation poisoning. See Howard Kohn, 'The Nanda Devi Caper', *Outside* magazine, May 1978.

[15] Used here in the Swiss sense of mountainside pastureland.

peak in the British Empire,[16] spreading her ample skirts and raising her stately profile (for this is less graceful spire than substantial damely presence) right into the centre of it, connected to the outer rim by a ridge abutting close to Longstaff's Col that ran from the subsidiary peak of Nanda Devi East (24,379 feet); and all this rising out of sweet grasslands where undisturbed flocks of bharal, the wild horned blue sheep of the Himalaya, grazed. Both Tom Longstaff and Hugh Ruttledge had looked down into it from their cols on more or less opposite sides of the rim in 1905 and 1932 respectively. During his time on Everest Shipton had listened to the donnish and self-effacing Ruttledge talk in unusually animated terms about the attraction and difficulty of this extraordinary geographical feature, which he had made no fewer than four attempts to enter from over the rim. Tilman, in his account of the ultimate ascent of the mountain at the Sanctuary's centre, quotes from Ruttledge's account in *The Times* in summing up of the difficulties faced by those seeking access:

> Nanda Devi imposes on her votaries an admission test as yet beyond their skill and endurance. Surrounded by a barrier ring, seventy miles long, on which stand twelve measured peaks over 21,000 feet, and which nowhere descends lower than 18,000 feet, except in the West, where the Rishi Ganga river, rising at the foot of Nanda Devi, and the sole drainage of 250 square miles of ice and snow, has carved for itself what must be one of the most terrific gorges in the world. Two ridges converging on the river form as it were the curtain to an inner sanctuary within which the great mountain soars up to 25,645 feet. So tremendous is the aspect of the gorge that Hindu mythology described it as the last earthly home of the Seven Rishis[17] –

---

[16] From 1820, when its height was first triangulated by the Survey of India at 25,479 feet, to 1845, when the height of Chomolungma – as it then was and still should be – was first assessed, Nanda Devi was thought to be the highest peak in the world. Fortunately, the Survey of India relieved it of this curse and bestowed it on the soon-to-be-named 'Mount Everest' instead.

[17] The Saptarsi (also the name for the constellation of the Plough, or the Great Bear) or the Seven Sages appear as early as the fifth century BCE in the Sanskrit epic text the Mahabharata, and also in early Vedic and Hindu texts. The tales of their antics and alliances are as highly imaginative, entertaining and sexually convoluted as those of the Homeric gods.

here if anywhere their meditations would be undisturbed.[18]

Here, then, was a gauntlet thrown down. Once back in Britain after Everest, it had been during an evening at the Royal Geographical Society – Shipton reasonably confident that a meat-essence-gluttony-occasioned retreat from close to 28,000 feet did not constitute a collapse and consequent damnation as a scoundrel – that he had taken up the theme of mountain exploration in Garhwal with Tom Longstaff. In consequence, he had been invited down in short order for a weekend at Longstaff's house by the river Test in Hampshire, despite the latter's impending departure for the Arctic. Ferdie Crawford, another member of the 1933 team, lived nearby and when he heard that Shipton was to visit he primed Longstaff's seven adolescent daughters – a terrifying thought! – about his piano-playing abilities, and the innate modesty that prevented him from ever demonstrating them.

Having negotiated this jape with embarrassment or disappointment as appropriate to the involved parties, Shipton listened as Longstaff diverted him from his main plan, based on the post-Kamet journeys, of investigating the Badrinath-Kedarnath watersheds, and recounted in full detail his own attempts in the first decade of the century to gain the Inner Sanctuary of Nanda Devi. He told of the idyllic route by which he had skirted past the middle section of the gorge above Joshimath, and of how his desire to force a passage through that upper gorge of the Seven Rishis into the Nanda Devi basin to which it led had been compromised by lack of food and time. He told of the location of his camp at its foot, and of how he was certain that, by keeping to the north bank of the river along that section, this was the key to the enterprise.

So Shipton, leaving the seven daughters musically frustrated ('howling at me like a set of scorched cats' according to the incorrigible Crawford), departed to make his plans and draw up budgets, which latter came in at an irreducible minimum of £150 per person – most certainly a tithe of the cost for each member of the Everest trip, but still rather more ready cash than a young man about town without gainful employment could easily lay his hands on in the pre-sponsorship days of the early 1930s; though there

---

[18] *H. W. Tilman: The Seven Mountain Travel Books* (Diadem Books, 1983), p.157. From an article first published in *The Times* on 22 August 1932.

were still the Norway lectures, with whatever they would bring in. Undeterred, he set about seeking a companion. His first choice was Noel Humphreys, who was both enormously enthusiastic about the project and also most probably unavailable, having just contracted to lead the 1934–5 Oxford University Ellesmere Land[19] expedition. At this point the Seven Rishis seem to have smiled on Shipton's schemings: 'In January '34 I had my best stroke of luck, in a letter from my old friend H. W. Tilman.'

It was two eventful years after the trip they had shared to the Rwenzori when the letter with a Wallasey postmark dropped through the door of 100a Lexham Gardens, telling him of the banana-fuelled bicycle ride across Africa, informing him that the writer was now kicking his heels at his parents' house on Merseyside, and asking whether he would be interested in a couple of weeks' rock-climbing in the Lake District. Tilman, than whom there was no one of more spartan simplicity or hardihood, was back in England and at a loose end. Shipton responded by return of post to his letter with a counter-proposal for seven months in the Himalaya and it was accepted without question:

> His return to England was most opportune, and I believe that the course of both our lives would have been profoundly changed if he had arrived a few months later. For, while he would probably not have gone to the Himalaya during the next five years, thus missing the experiences which laid the foundation of much of his subsequent career, I for my part owe the success of the Nanda Devi venture very largely to his support . . . For the plan I had devised, Bill was nearly the ideal partner . . .[20]

Tilman reinforces and adds to this in the obituary he wrote of Shipton for the *Himalayan Journal*:[21]

---

[19] Thus at the time, but now properly Ellesmere Island, this huge land mass, some of it mountainous, within the Inuit homeland of Nunavut is the northernmost island of the Canadian Arctic archipelago. It lies to the north-west of Baffin Bay, and is divided from Greenland by the Nares Strait. Interestingly, the last two exploratory voyages by Tilman in his own final boat *Baroque* (John Shipton, Eric's younger son, was a crew member on the first of them in 1975) had Ellesmere Island as their objective.
[20] Eric Shipton, *That Untravelled World* (Hodder & Stoughton, 1969), p.84.
[21] Vol. 35, 1977, p.337.

I eagerly accepted the chance of a combined effort in the Himalaya, the forcing of the Rishi gorge and the Nanda Devi basin. The large *bandobast* of an Everest expedition had inclined Eric to go to the other extreme. His wish for simplicity and economy found a fervent backer with the result that together with three Sherpas we spent five[22] happy, memorable months in the Himalaya at a cost of £140 each,[23] including fares out and back in a cargo vessel. That we starved ourselves and our followers is patently untrue, for one cannot work as hard and cover as much difficult ground as we did without sufficient food.

With the European composition of the party settled, and Tilman's possibly humorous suggestion of bicycling to India dismissed in those pre-Dervla Murphy[24] days, Shipton went off to Norway to master the art of lecturing and earn some money, leaving Tilman to do his share of expedition organisation. In this the Seven Rishis smiled upon him too, for through his father's shipping connections Tilman exceeded all prudent expectations in booking a passage on the SS *Mahsud* of the Brocklebank Line for themselves and their equipment at a cost of £30 each. This pleasant surprise was complemented by another in the matter of their requirement for three Sherpas, and this time the luck was not just their own.

Before Shipton had set off for his Norway lecture series, he had written to Willy Merkl, leader of the projected Deutsche Himalaya Expedition 1934, asking which Darjeeling porters he would be using for that year's attempt on Nanga Parbat, and if he might make use of those not required. Merkl replied promptly in a letter dated 14 March to say that 'Shebbeare [Ruttledge's deputy on Everest 1933] has arranged the matter of coolies for me', and to tell of those who would not be accompanying them to Nanga Parbat. Shebbeare therefore was asked to retain three Sherpas for Nanda Devi, and he duly delegated the matter to Karma Paul, who was known to

---

[22] The apparent disparity between this and Shipton's original proposal is explained by the month's voyage in either direction.

[23] Shipton notes in *Upon That Mountain* (p.141) that the negotiation of the cheap steamer fares 'put the project just about within our grasp, though even then Tilman had to advance some of my share against uncertain security'. The cost to both men ultimately came out at £143.10s.0d.

[24] See *Full Tilt* (John Murray, 1963) – Dervla Murphy's marvellous account of a solo bicycle ride to India from Ireland, one of the modern classics of travel writing.

Shipton from the Everest trip, on which he had served as translator – a role he had been fulfilling since 1922. The three men Karma Paul provided ('It was more by good luck than good management that Tilman and I had such a remarkably good trio')[25] were Ang Tharkay, Pasang Bhotia and Kusang, all of whom had been on Everest with Shipton, Ang Tharkay and Pasang having helped to establish Camp Six at 27,400 feet.

Capability at altitude aside, Ang Tharkay was beyond question the outstanding Sherpa of his era, and the Seven Rishis obviously held his fate and that of his companions dear too and preserved them from catastrophe, for the 1934 German Nanga Parbat expedition of which they might otherwise have been a part was one of the worst disasters in mountaineering history, in which ten lives were lost on the mountain along a complex and overextended chain of camps. Apart from the fatalities, many of the Sherpas involved suffered terribly from frostbite and the community of Sola Khumbu was affected for years thereafter. As were Ang Tharkay, Pasang and Kusang when news of the tragedy filtered through in the later stages of the Nanda Devi expedition.

The last weeks before departure were hectic. Surveying was going to be a crucial part of the project if they succeeded in effecting an entry to the Sanctuary, and so Tilman, brushing up on his own past expertise as an artillery officer, read widely round the subject whilst Shipton enlisted tutorial help through contacts at the Royal Geographical Society. Tilman also came down from Wallasey to London, where he and Shipton spent two days mastering the subtle arts of plane-tabling with an alidade[26] under the expert tutelage of Noel Humphreys in Richmond Park – an environment that was not entirely suitable preparation for what was to come:

> On entering the basin we commenced our plane-table survey, but found it very different work here from what our few lessons in Richmond Park had led us to expect. We found great difficulty in identifying peaks, particularly those on the rim, and in having enough in view to obtain a reliable resection.[27]

[25] Shipton, *Upon That Mountain*, p.150.
[26] The revolving optic fixed to a plane table, used in surveying.
[27] H. W. Tilman, 'Nanda Devi and the Sources of the Ganges' (*Himalayan Journal*, 1935), p.6.

Whilst the future expedition was foregathered in London, they went along to the bespoke bootmaker Robert Lawrie in a side street near Marble Arch to be fitted for their expedition footwear, carefully nailed according to Shipton's specifications with a combination of clinkers, tricounis and star-muggers. Before returning to Lexham Gardens, they sauntered along to Holborn where they ducked into an establishment that had all the appearance of being a miscellaneous junk shop but was in fact Clarkson's Secondhand Optical Stores, 'purveyors of Prismatic Binoculars to the Royal Geographical Society for the use of the Mount Everest Expedition'. Here they purchased for the princely sum of ten shillings an obsolete hypsometric aneroid barometer out of an aeroplane that would have cost them £14.10s.0d. had they bought one new from Steward's on the Strand: 'Our Sherpas conceived a great affection for it and called it "Shaitan", probably because we consulted it so frequently. It worked very well until we dropped it.'[28] What Mrs Haly thought of all this activity and her son's taciturn and monkish older friend is not on record, though perhaps his reserve and polite demeanour as well as the ever-present humorous glint in his eye might have appealed to her. Tilman went on from London to pay the obligatory visit to Tom Longstaff near Romsey (further delaying the latter's Arctic departure), Shipton excusing himself from going with him on the grounds of embarrassment over his musical ineptitude.

Over forty years later, by Tilman's fireside in his 'winter quarters' at Bodowen, midday past, his potent home brew flowing and the mischievous twinkle present that was seldom far from his eye, he told of what happened on his arrival at Longstaff's house:

> The housekeeper met me and said, 'the doctor's out on the river getting some fishing in before the close season', and she gave me directions, so I walked off along the banks of the Test – delightful chalk stream, d'you know it? Said to be very good fishing. Trout everywhere the size of small whales. I rounded a corner and there was Longstaff, his back to me, rod in hand, in the company of a very attractive young woman who was quite naked. I had no more than a glimpse, unfortunately, before she spotted me and, gathering up her clothes as she went, promptly disappeared into the bushes. Not his wife, of course,

---

[28] Tilman, *Seven Mountain Travel Books*, p.235.

and I believe he and Mrs Longstaff parted company not long thereafter. They had seven daughters, charming girls, musical apparently . . .

By the beginning of April, all their equipment and those supplies and items of clothing (Shipton's old school frock coat included) which they intended taking with them were assembled. Their plan was to live as far as possible simply and off the land, buying such basic supplies as were available along the way and taking with them only ten tins of pemmican (no meat essence on this trip),[29] some farmhouse Cheddar cheeses wrapped in cloth, and as luxuries tea and sugar, lentils and ghee. Their basic diet throughout the trip was intended to be that of the Sherpas, who lived off chapattis, rice and the roasted barley meal called tsampa, which can be eaten as a porridge (to both of these the Sherpas would add any available spices, vegetables or pulses), or mixed into tea to make a food-drink:

At first I found this simple fare very bleak, and sometimes, particularly at breakfast or when I was tired, even repulsive; though nothing would have induced me to say so in the face of Bill's stoicism. But soon I became accustomed to it, and before long ate my portion with ever-increasing relish.[30]

As you do in those environments where even daily cabbage curry, rice and dhal becomes equivalent to *Babette's Feast*.

In the first week of April, Shipton travelled up to Liverpool on the train:

I got the train with Humphreys with about five minutes to

---

[29] A history of poisoning by early tinned food would be an interesting topic. One book on the Franklin expedition of 1845 propounds the thesis that its members all died as a result of the lead solder used on the tins in which their food came, and even went so far as to exhume bodies buried on Beechey Island during the expedition's first winter and test them for lead poisoning. I have my doubts, insufficient comparative control results having been adduced, and found the prurient photographic coverage of the corpses in the media quite as distasteful as the later exploitation of Mallory's corpse after its discovery on Everest in May 1999. Amazing what you can get away with simply by labelling your project as 'research'.

[30] Shipton, *That Untravelled World*, p.85.

spare and shoved all my stuff in the [guard's] van as I could not even get a corner seat. At Oxford however I got a side to myself and slept. I attracted attention at Paddington running about with a largest-sized solar topi[31] on my head and an ice-axe in my hand – particularly as the topi had a label flapping in the breeze. It was nice of Humphreys to come and see me off. I very much hope he can get clear of Shackleton and join me. He is fearfully keen to come and would be an ideal man for the job, though Longstaff advised me to keep the party as small as possible.[32]

Arriving in the north, he crossed over the Mersey to the Tilman house in Wallasey village and another trial by adolescent daughters – this time Tilman's two nieces Joan and Pam, the latter of whom has the inevitable recollection of the distant and dapper young man with the alarmingly blue eyes. On 6 April, with Shipton dressed in a long black woollen overcoat and pale trousers with suede shoes, Tilman in polished brogues and a baggy tweed suit, both men wearing ties and identical trilby hats and looking cool as you please in best Bogart style, Mr Tilman's uniformed chauffeur brought the Humber Snipe landaulette round to the front gate. Mrs Tilman was installed in the front seat, Adeline and her daughters waved goodbye from the pavement and the car headed through the Kingsway Tunnel under the Mersey and deposited them on the Brocklebank wharf by the SS *Mahsud*, 'a pukka old cargo boat with iron decks which will get very hot in the Red Sea and Indian Ocean', on board which they underwent a further brief trial-by-press ('several local pressmen to badger us – things like the *Liverpool Echo*')[33] before the ship cast off and headed out along the North Wales coast, round Anglesey, and down through St George's Channel into the Atlantic.

Apart from the serious exploratory project, that these two were engaged in an act of deliberate and conscious subversion should not be doubted for a moment. Shipton on his return bearded the old lions of the Everest Committee in one of their dens when he stated in a paper read to them at the Alpine Club on 5 March 1935:

---

[31] I.e. a pith helmet.
[32] Letter to Mrs Haly from SS *Mahsud*, 14 April 1934.
[33] Ibid.

One of the principal objects I had in mind when I decided to go to the Himalaya last year was to prove to my own satisfaction at least: first, that the small self-contained party is in a position to obtain far better results from the mountaineering point of view than the big, unwieldy expedition which, for some obscure reason, since the war has been thought necessary for a Himalayan campaign; and second, that the prevalent opinion regarding the cost of Himalayan expeditions is vastly exaggerated.[34]

Confidence is not lacking here. It might be thought a wonder, having rubbished the prevalent philosophy thus, that he was ever invited on a 'big, unwieldy' Everest expedition again. It can certainly be argued that these words came back to haunt him years later in the matter of the 1953 leadership debacle (though there were compounding factors there in a perceived necessity to get the thing done military-style for reasons of national pride, and a new and particularly slippery generation of machiavels who had come to prominence in Everest politics, to whom Shipton by then seemed very much of the old guard). For the moment, though, he and Tilman had a month in which to occupy themselves in the cramped quarters – a cabin each above the engine room – of a cargo steamer, make their plans, brush up on their surveying techniques and keep themselves reasonably fit. Tilman had thought to provide a medicine ball on board, and the crew rigged up an awning to fill with water and act as bathing pool during their passage through the tropics:

Our activities are pretty well the same each day . . . Breakfast at 8.30 sharp. Hindustani[35] lesson from 10–12; Exercise in the form of skipping and medicine ball, 12–1, Lunch 1 o'clock sharp. Read, work and sleep in the afternoon. Tea 3.30. More medicine ball and skipping at 4.30. Supper at 5.30!![36]

The pool in the awning provided means for a first catastrophe, for soon after the boat left Aden Shipton succeeded in dislocating or breaking[37] a toe in leaping from it on to the deck. Fortunately a

[34] *Alpine Journal*, p.58.
[35] Now Hindi-Urdu.
[36] Letter to Mrs Haly from SS *Mahsud*, 14 April, 1934.
[37] In *Upon That Mountain* (p.142), and again in *Nanda Devi* (3rd edition, Hodder

competent purser was at hand to do whatever needs to be done with an errant or fractured digit, though for much of the next month and the start of their trek out of Gwaldam the expedition's leader, even when snow lay on the ground, eschewed conventional mountain footwear in favour of tennis shoes, one of which had the toecap cut off.

They docked in Calcutta on a Saturday morning, and immediately experienced a hitch in their plans when they realised that they had not remitted train-fares and an advance on pay for the three Sherpas Karma Paul had retained for them in Darjeeling ('the porters had not arrived as they wanted money to leave with their wives'). Somehow this was resolved this by wire, and they were left with a weekend to enjoy the hospitality of Calcutta: 'Tilman of course won't be drawn by any of it and we work on the understanding that I do all the social work.'[38] At seven o'clock on Monday morning they betook themselves to Calcutta's Sealdah station in the hope of finding their three companions-to-be, none of whom spoke more than a smattering of English – a situation which obtained throughout the five months they spent together. Nor, it should be added, did Shipton and Tilman have more than a few words of Urdu, for all their earnest study of *Hugo*[39] for two hours each day during the voyage.

Anyone acquainted with the chaotic human flux of a railway station in an Indian city will realise the impossibility of the task they had set themselves. There was not a human form recognisably Sherpa to be seen. They quizzed any official they could find and drew blanks until finally a ticket collector vouchsafed that he had seen three exotic figures, apparently speaking Chinese, alighting from the Darjeeling Mail. They rang their hotel and were informed that three rum-looking coves had rolled up in a taxi an hour before. Back to the hotel raced the expedition leadership, to find three small men with red teeth[40] and purple shirts, wearing billycock hats from

---

& Stoughton, 1934, p.64) Shipton states unequivocally that it was broken, though Peter Steele avers that it was dislocated and 'reduced by the purser' – this latter presumably a medical term. (see *Everest and Beyond*, p.55). Whatever the truth of the matter, it was still causing Shipton much pain several weeks later.

[38] Letter to Mrs Haly, 9 May 1934.

[39] Standard Urdu dictionary and grammar from the great French dictionary publishing house.

[40] From chewing betel.

under which escaped shining black pigtails, who greeted them with perfect equanimity and were ready in an instant to depart for the docks and get the expedition's luggage on shore and organised for transportation to Howrah Station. Further archetypally-Indian small tribulations were all eventually resolved through a sufficiency of calm on the part of the Sherpas. Baggage and personnel were conveyed out of Howrah station and along to Bareilly by the Bombay Mail, whence they were to change for Kathgodam at the end of the branch line up Nainital for the bus or lorry – whichever proved available though whether there is any distinction is often a moot point – to Ranikhet. It was a typical Indian journey, in other words, fraying to newly arrived European nerves but negotiated with their usual sangfroid by the three Sherpas. Two of whom (Ang Tharkay, who usefully spoke Hindi-Urdu, travelled with Tilman and Shipton, to keep his eye on these neurotic and disorganised Europeans one suspects) they failed to locate at Bareilly, and feared had travelled on towards Bombay.[41]

Inevitably, after much more flapping by our explorers, the supposedly missing duo were found installed on the waiting Kathgodam train at its platform, where they were sitting on the baggage and calmly eating oranges: '. . . neither of whom had ever travelled by rail, neither of whom even knew the name of their destination, had contrived to get out at the right station and into the right train'.[42] The note of surprise here is very telling. And I think is deliberately stitched in to his text to underline the degree to which he came very quickly to trust, admire and rely on his Sherpa companions through the coming months. That now offensive term 'coolies' from Willy Merkl's letter might have been a prevalent European attitude towards the men on whom western mountaineers relied for their set-piece assaults on the highest mountains,[43] but the dialectic in

---

[41] As mentioned in the introduction, to avoid the confusions that might have arisen particularly when quoting from 1930s texts, I have used the names current at the time rather than official modern versions – Mumbai, Kolkata, etc.

[42] Shipton, *Nanda Devi*, p.57.

[43] Merkl was one of those to die in the Nanga Parbat disaster of 1934. The muddled thinking of Nazism is nowhere better illustrated than in its philosophy of 'pure Aryanism' – these Sherpa 'coolies' being as much or more Aryan than the Nazi mountaineers they served. An interesting aside here is that when it was suggested after the Second World War that Paul Bauer, leader of German expeditions to Kanchenjunga in 1929 and 1931, and to Nanga Parbat in 1938 (he was also a member of the 1937 expedition to this peak), be deprived of his honorary

the revolutionary text and classic of mountain literature that is Shipton's *Nanda Devi* sets out with wry humour and a warm sense of comradeship and fellow humanity to prove just how mistaken and demeaning it was. In *Upon That Mountain* too, looking back on the 1934 expedition, Shipton's praise for his three Sherpa companions in particular and the Sherpas in general is lavish and unstinting.

A ramshackle lorry, 'amazingly cheap', hauled them up the forest ridges and hairpins of Kumaon from Kathgodam to Ranikhet, loveliest hill station of the Raj, where they arrived at 10 a.m. on 9 May and installed themselves in a roomy guest bungalow: 'It is marvellous here Mum. You <u>must</u> come <u>with me</u> one of these days and see it all. You could fit it in some time when you come out east, and I am sure this won't be the last year I will come here.'[44]

A dozen Dhotial porters were hired and sent off to meet up with the team of five in two days' time at the settlement of Baijnath, fifty miles away at the end of the motorable road beyond Almora. Supplies and equipment were sorted out; kit of light windproof oversuit and nailed boots was issued to all the expedition members; tents, cooking equipment and food were organised; a raid was made on the Ranikhet bazaar for more food; the contents of the Lexham Gardens box room were distributed among the Sherpas (Pasang looking particularly fine in an old dinner jacket and Kusang in dress trousers); money was obtained in coin from the local native bank – a time-consuming and perplexing business in which the Sherpas once again came to the rescue. Finally, at first light on the morning of 11 May, their transport was once more loaded up, a last-minute foray into the bazaar brought eggs, lemons, potatoes and cabbages on board, and the lorry creaked and jounced its way out of town to start the six-hour drive to Baijnath.

From the very outset of the exploratory journey, the three Sherpas established themselves in Shipton and Tilman's affections, each of them bringing different qualities to the venture. Ang Tharkay, aside from later proving himself to be an outstanding mountaineer – 'as a route-finder we had many occasions on which to bless him' – was

---

membership of the Alpine Club, it was Tilman – who had more reason than most to feel strongly on these issues – who wrote in to support Bauer and point out that he had willingly taken part in the de-Nazification programme. This seems to me a measure of Tilman's humanity. (I am indebted to Ed Douglas, who possesses a photocopy of Tilman's letter, for this information.)
[44] Letter to Mrs Haly, 9 May 1934.

the obvious leader and negotiator with those they met along the way. He was a hard and shrewd haggler, to whom they left most of the bargaining:

> [Ang Tharkay] was a most lovable person, modest, unselfish and completely sincere, with an infectious gaiety of spirit. He has been with me on all my subsequent journeys to the Himalayas, and to him I owe a large measure of their success and much of my enjoyment . . . Often, on the numerous occasions when I was irritable or quarrelsome, I was made to feel thoroughly ashamed of myself by the example of the Sherpas.[45]

Pasang was equally brilliant in his aptitude for movement on rock, and acted as Shipton's personal batman. He was the most devout of the three, intoning prayers constantly and building little *chortens* of loose stone wherever they rested along the way – in which pastime Kusang, the youngest, simplest and most industrious of them, would also engage. Kusang was also chapatti-maker and fire-maker, able to create a welcome furnace blaze wherever wood for fuel was to be found. All three were thoroughly good-humoured, and ready to laugh on the instant at their own or any of the Westerners' petty mishaps and misdemeanours.

The lorry deposited them at Baijnath at midday. Waiting for them there were the Dhotial porters, who were soon picking up eighty-pound loads supported by means of a head strap, and setting out on the first march of ten miles with 5,000 feet of ascent to Gwaldam. Shipton was suffering from diarrhoea and found the going very trying at first. After a couple of days he had recovered, and was limping along in a state considerably beyond mere happiness:

> . . . we marched in the cool of the morning and lazed in the shade of the oak and pine woods during the heat of the day; we became fit and gloriously alive. The weather was perfect, the country magnificent. Our way led over ridge after ridge of forest-clad hills; not the oppressive rain-forest of the Eastern Himalayas, but gentle wooded slopes interspersed with grassy glades, moss and bracken and splashing streams.

---

[45] Shipton, *Upon That Mountain*, pp.150–1.

The rhododendrons were in bloom, and many kinds of Alpine flowers. Above were the sparkling white peaks of Trisul and Nanda Ghunti. The soft music of running water, the murmur of a light breeze in the trees, the summer note of a cuckoo, these were the sounds we awoke to each morning.

In his Shipton biography, Peter Steele mentions 'the somewhat purple prose into which [Shipton] occasionally slips'[46] and suggests that he wrote thus under the influence of Frank Smythe's 'notoriously verbose' style. I would take issue with this criticism on several fronts. First, a certain regularity of forced epithets aside (and writers of every generation on occasion have been prone to this – study our contemporary so-called 'new nature writers'[47] if you wish to pick up on some particularly thudding and egregious examples. It is at root surely a simple function of writerly insecurity, of 'trying too hard'), I don't find Frank Smythe's writing nearly so bad as Steele suggests. Rather like W. H. Murray, for all his occasional excess and an accompanying tendency to dramatise events in line with audience expectation, Smythe is an intelligent and graphic mountain writer whose books I can still read with a great deal of pleasure. As to the 'somewhat purple prose' – and I think the passage quoted above is in the style criticised – an obvious point needs making on this. The mode of description is an attempt at expressing a mood that is essentially enraptured. It is a type of near-mystical perception that is scattered here and there throughout Shipton's mountain writing, and is closely akin to Wordsworth's representation of 'a time when meadow, grove, and stream,/The earth, and every common sight,/To me did seem/Apparelled in celestial light,/The glory and the freshness of a dream.'[48] As I suggested in earlier chapters, the influence of the later work of the important Wiltshire writer

---

[46] Steele, *Everest and Beyond*, p.56.

[47] There are, of course, some very fine current nature writers: Mark Cocker, Horatio Clare, Paul Evans, Miriam Darlington. The more personal and authentic the experience, the more natural and simple the prose seems to be the ruling principle here, whereas those whose projects are essentially assimilative from the work of others, in order to distinguish themselves write in a tortured and artificial self-approved style that would surely cause Thoreau and Edward Thomas, Henry Williamson and W.H. Hudson, Gilbert White and Richard Jefferies to writhe in their graves.

[48] William Wordsworth, 'Ode: Intimations of Immortality from Recollections of Early Childhood'.

Richard Jefferies is very evident throughout Shipton's books, and is a healthy and significant one that echoes and mirrors many of Shipton's own underlying perceptions. Rather than dismissing it in these cliché-ridden terms, it is perhaps better to view it in the role of an emotional alternative discourse to the literal, event-based chronological narrative. Its presence in *Nanda Devi*, far from being a demerit, is an essential aspect of a book that is perhaps the finest in all mountaineering literature, giving it a very rich and satisfying dimension that few other books in the genre achieve.

To move on – they marched for ten days, crossing the Pindar and Nandakini rivers, tributaries of the Alaknanda which along with the Bhagirathi is one of the main sources of the Ganges, and making for Joshimath by way of the Kuari pass. Each of the ridges they breasted rose to the east in the direction of Trisul and beyond that Nanda Devi. After the long journey by sea and land, this activity was perfect for fitness and acclimatisation:

> Fine weather, magnificent scenery, pleasant mannered natives, all provided a graceful introduction to the Himalaya; marches of comfortable length, the nights in the open under clear, star-lit skies, and the bathes in snow-fed streams, attuned mind and body to the work ahead.[49]

The recognisable spare tenor of Tilman's prose is clear in that extract, and the Spartan rigour too (Tilman was throughout his life a devotee of naked bathing in cold mountain water – a quirk which left Shipton and other witnesses on occasion rather flummoxed). There was also the allure of what lay ahead, of the ever-changing skyline. In *Nanda Devi* Shipton tells of how there 'rose before us . . . a distant and broken wall of dazzling whiteness'.[50] It's the same vision of a serrated shimmer of white that he saw to the east across the Rhône valley from the heights of the Auvergne only nine years before – the horizon as 'arch wherethrough/Gleams that untravelled world, whose margin fades/Forever and forever when I move.' Here he is in a letter to his mother dated 20 May 1934:

We crossed the Kuari Pass yesterday. It was very thrilling as

---

[49] Tilman, 'Nanda Devi', p.2.
[50] Shipton, *Nanda Devi*, p.75.

we saw a great deal of our objective, the Rishi Ganga, and it was interesting trying to work out the topographical features which will play so large a part in our enterprise of the next month or so. Besides, the view from the Kuari must be one of the most beautiful in the world . . . The next six weeks should be exceedingly interesting, as we hope to get into a region that no-one has ever succeeded in reaching before, and it should be most interesting work exploring it and trying to make a map of it – if we can get in. We won't go very high – just high enough to get views of the country and fix our plane-table stations.

A definite hint there of the teenage Shipton's facility in explaining away his adventures to an anxious parent?

By Shipton's account, on these first ten days of their march it rained, or snowed; was too cold or too hot; they were plagued by flies and chased naked by unfriendly bulls when attempting to bathe; and food was hard to come by so they had to break into their precious rations, sacrificing one of the farmhouse Cheddars that was threatening to ascend to the heavens. But then the disparity in enjoyment between the two men's accounts is explained by the fact that for Tilman it was his first time, his first experience of the Himalaya, and Shipton had been along this part of the trek before, on the approach to Kamet in 1931. Both of them were momentarily disturbed by the manner in which, at one camp, the three Sherpas held out their billycock hats to fill them with resinous smoke from the fire, and then donned them quickly, smoke and all; but their immediate anxiety about what they might pick up from their companions over the coming months proved unsubstantiated, and they never did discover the reason for what had looked suspiciously like anti-parasitic fumigation.

The landscape had a familiar redolence, woodpeckers drumming and cuckoos calling from among brakes of holly, copses of oak and stands of chestnut. As they crossed the Bireh Ganga, Shipton the would-be geographer studied where a landslip dam had temporarily blocked the river and then burst, causing immense destruction down-valley. They baked potatoes in the embers of fires; spent one night in a shepherds' encampment; walked through wild-flower meadows; had a perfect view of all the Garhwali peaks ranged in line between Kedarnath and Kamet from the top of the Kuari pass at seven o'clock on a radiant morning; and traversed a high route from there which afforded them a glimpse of Nanda Devi thirty miles away to the east and led them to the settlement of Joshimath, a straggling village of stone houses high above the gorge of the Alaknanda river at its confluence with the Dhauli Ganga, of which the river whose gorge they hoped to ascend was a tributary.

At Joshimath, they procured 400lb of food for the Dhotial porters who had agreed to accompany them onwards; ate sweetmeats until they felt sick – minute quantities sufficing to produce this effect, as anyone who's visited an Indian sweet shop in Rusholme or Edgbaston, let alone the stalls along Janpath in Delhi, will know; observed that 'the bazaar fraternity had the fine independent air assumed by the owners of seaside lodgings at the height of a good summer season' (which throws an interesting perspective on the holidays of young Eric); and were fortunate enough to buy at inflated price three floating eggs,[51] with which commodity and a great deal of ghee to mask the flavour Ang Tharkay made them an omelette. Farewell feast duly devoured, and the consciousness on them that the reasonably fine weather they were enjoying would inevitably come to an end with the approaching monsoon, which thought put a 'limit to our wanderings in a country of such loveliness, where the air and the rivers, the flowers and the trees filled one with the joy of living',[52] on the morning of 21 May, with Shipton's account using a final quotation from George Borrow's gypsy friend Jasper Petulengro to wish them along their journey ('Life is very sweet . . .'), the little caravan picked up its burdens again, and headed east out of Joshimath bound for the Rishi gorge.

For the next five weeks Shipton kept a detailed journal, its slanting script written in purple pencil, perfectly legible, 10/10 for spelling and grammar, in a small cloth-bound notebook secured with a black elastic strap. From it, here's how he describes their setting out:

> We had a hectic morning getting ready for departure. There was still a lot to be done. We sent off the photos and article to Moore [Joshimath had a post office, among other amenities of civilisation]. It was raining heavily most of the morning but cleared up when we started out about 10.30. It was a pretty

---

[51] The test for whether or not an egg was bad was to put it in a bowl of water – good ones sank.
[52] Shipton, *Nanda Devi*, p.85.

short march and we have come a good way beyond Tapoban.[53] One of the Dhotials was sent back to Ranikhet and so far the remaining eleven are handling all our stuff. We have decided to climb Lata Peak if the weather is fine in order to get a start with our plane-table, that being the only 'station' on our sheet. One of the tins of sugar has been forgotten and one of the men has been sent off to get some more. We have come with only the small Edgington tent for ourselves. It is very difficult to get into but otherwise seems OK.

It's fascinating to see how the bare records of the notebook are worked up into the descriptions – particularly elaborate and glowing along this first stage of the journey from Joshimath to the Rishi gorge – published in *Nanda Devi*. The penny-plain account of the next day's march to Surai Tota is well worth checking back against its published version to see the extent to which Shipton, in the book, is taking seriously, or in the view of some overseriously, his new role as writer. For the purposes of this account, though, in order to drive the narrative on an edited transcript from the terse prose of the notebook is perhaps the best guide to their progress into the Sanctuary:

May 22nd: It has been a very long day. We started at 5 and made quite good pace till we got to about half a mile beyond the second bridge. We noted that there did not seem to be much water coming down the Rishi. We started to climb up the slopes of Lata at 6.50 and at once got entangled in thick bush. This went on until shortly before eleven – we were traversing diagonally upwards most of the time. We got on to a line of crags which we tried to climb instead of turning, with the result that after an hour of rather dangerous climbing we reached the point at which we had started – or another slightly lower. We melted some snow for a drink and continued the struggle. We eventually reached the top at 2.30. It was a hell of a sweat.

With a Survey of India triangulation station to work from – the

---

[53] A generic name in Garhwal, meaning, I believe, beautiful meadow. It is the same word, though not the same place, as Tapovan, above the Gangotri glacier, visited in the prologue.

last one they were going to find – they started immediately on the preliminary work for one of the main purposes of their trip: the surveying, if it proved possible, of the Nanda Devi Sanctuary:

> It was fine all day and all the peaks around the Rishi were clear. We set up the plane table and identified all the visible points; found the compasses to be working well and drew three maps to what appeared interesting objects. We got a perfect view of N.D. The peaks to the north[54] appeared very sharp and complicated and we could not identify any. Soon after four we started the descent and had much better luck. So much so that we completed the descent to the Dhauli river in under two hours. I wore tennis shoes without socks all day and gave my toe one or two bangs. T. bathed and Pasang and I washed and drank I regret to say, but by Jove, it had been thirsty work. We completed the two miles to [Surai Tota] by 7.30 and then for the rewards of labour I am writing this by fire light and am more than ready for bed.

In *Nanda Devi* Shipton describes walking up-valley in the cool of the evening, his tired limbs in sympathy with the fading light, and arriving at their campsite in Surai Tota to a fine fire, a pot of dhal, gallons of tea and the company of his old and garrulous friend from Kamet, Kesar Singh, who lived hereabouts. Kesar not only entertained them; he also arranged for more supplies of flour, and what proved to be the dubious benefit of eight men from the village to come with them up the Rishi:

> May 23rd: It was very pleasant sleeping out last night but cold enough to make me get into both sleeping bags. Kesar was about early . . . very voluble as usual. We got away about 8 . . . made quite good time to Tolma, a pleasant little village, clean and picturesque. We halted there a bit and struck straight up into the forest, soon to discover that no-one knew the way . . . We eventually got to the edge of a great precipice overlooking a nullah at the top of which we assumed this place [i.e. Hyetui Kharak – a high grazing alp] must be. We followed the ridge more or less and got here about 2.30. Many pheasants and lots

---

[54] Most likely Hathi Parbat and Durpata.

of wild garlic. It is a grand spot – one of the best we have struck.
But our enjoyment of it was marred by an announcement that
our supplies would not be here until tomorrow night. Heated
words and complicated plans followed. However the porters
have just rolled up (8 p.m.) and things look a bit brighter. But
some of them say that there is far too much snow on the pass
ahead for them to cross! Tomorrow is the crux of this part of
the show and will probably be a strenuous day.

It was to prove far more strenuous even than he had imagined.
Next morning, after a brief attempt at extortion, the men from
Surai Tota put down their loads and left. The Dhotial porters, who
had been observing proceedings with interest, divided up the loads
among themselves, and with eighty pounds each on their backs they
followed behind Shipton and Tilman as the two less heavily laden
Europeans floundered on, flogging a path through melting snow at
times chest-deep, towards the Dharansi Pass at a height of 14,700
feet in the ridge between Lata Peak and Dunagiri that they hoped
would lead them to the high grazing alp of Duraishi and beyond
that Dibrughita:

> May 24th: . . . It has been a bad day, especially for our gallant
> Dhotials, who considering everything have done splendidly.
> We now seem to be on the right route and given weather and
> further good health and conduct on the part of the porters
> we should get over to Duraishi tomorrow. We got a glimpse
> of the traverse of the other side of the pass. It looks very bad
> though clear of snow. This certainly is the crux of this part of
> the show, and I hope to goodness we get over tomorrow. It
> has been fine all day again – long may it last. It is a wonderful
> evening. We are sleeping out again but will probably perish
> of cold. A very hazy but wonderful sunset, Dunagiri standing
> up like a dream. I am writing this by the light of a half moon
> which is rather difficult.

The sun rose directly over Dunagiri on the 25th to set them on
their way for the pass. 'The chap who first found the way must have
had some initiative,' Shipton comments wryly, as he tells of hacking
and flogging through deep soft snow, at other times chipping steps
in hard gully ice, towards their next objective of Duraishi. 'The

scenery and topography is fantastic and would certainly merit some of those Whymper "wood-cuts". A ridge opposite rises in a series of nine gigantic leaning slabby peaks.' Arriving at the corrie of Duraishi in the afternoon, Shipton and Tilman walked down to the edge of its high alp, from where they 'looked straight down into the Rishi'.

> It was a most fantastic sight; but then, 'fantastic' is the only way to describe the Rishi Ganga. The cliffs fell away almost sheer for 5,000 feet into the stream, which though by no means big thundered with a roar like Niagara. No wonder superstitions concerning the place abound – it was a ghostly feeling to look down into those inaccessible depths.

By the afternoon of the 26th they were within sight of the farthest point reached by Longstaff, and had crossed the grazing alp of Dibrughita that he had described to them as an idyll. Even for Tilman, least effusive of men, it was 'a horizontal oasis in a vertical desert'. Shipton more practically observes that 'rhubarb, garlic and wild flowers abound – but no water!' So they gathered some of the former for their supper and descended to the valley below: 'Lying on a bed of dead leaves with silver birches and pines overhead, a torrent rushing by and vague glimpses of icy peaks – what more delightful a resting place could the heart desire.' He wrote to his mother that night:

> I am writing in what must be one of the loveliest places God ever made. A forest of pines and silver birches, with lovely little meadows already full of every kind of Alpine flower and with clear streams running through them. All of this tucked away in the fastness of this incredible valley. 'Fantastic' is the only way I can describe the Rishi Ganga itself and it is a unique experience to be in it. A whole day's march takes us about a mile and a half . . . I wish Humphreys was here – he would have loved it and been more than useful as surveyor and botanist. Could you give him a ring and tell him how we are getting on?[55]

---

[55] Letter to Mrs Haly, 26 May 1934.

Shipton and Tilman on board the S.S. *Mahsud* at Liverpool docks, outward bound for Nanda Devi in 1934.

Tilman (on left)
the cadet, aged 15,
at Berkhamsted
School, 1914.

War games,
Berkhamsted
1914.

Lieutenant H. W. Tilman,
1917 (on right).

Shipton at the top of Batian, first ascent 1929.

Shipton on the summit of Lyskamm, 1928.

Looking up the Rishi Ganga,
the formidable pale buttress of Pisgah
obvious high up on the right.

Descending the difficult ice-fall from
the Sunderdhunga Col after the second
reconnaissance of the Nanda Devi
sanctuary, September 1934.

Eric Shipton climbing the dangerous slope leading to the North Col of Everest, 1935.

Everest from the north, 1936.

Pasang Bhotia, paralysed after a stroke, is helped down to Camp Four, Everest 1938.

Role reversal for the habitual leader and his loyal adjutant – the Everest party of 1938, with Shipton and Tilman at centre.

H.W. Tilman, Art Emmons and T. Graham Brown, Nanda Devi 1936.

Noel Odell, wearing a protective face mask, nearing the summit of Nanda Devi in 1936.

Michael Spender, Shaksgam 1937.

Shipton the joker,
Shaksgam 1937.

Penitentes on the Trango
Glacier, the Trango Tower
beyond – one of the iconic
photographs that inspired
so much post-war
Karakoram climbing.

Tilman at Bodowen in 1977, with Toffee (behind the wheel) and the Raleigh bicycle on which he crossed Africa.

Tilman at his typewriter – taken having drunk two pints of his potent home-brew.

Tilman at the age of 79, still seeking the margins of 'that untravelled world'.

'What rough beast, its hour come round at last..?' A 'Yeti' footprint, as improved by Shipton, Menlung glaciers 1951.

Beyond Dibrughita, they were moving into ever more difficult and serious terrain, and still had their Dhotial porters, heavily burdened, their imaginations demon-terrorised by what might dwell in the gorge to the foot of which they were bound, to look after and coax along to their desired base camp at Longstaff's old campsite near where the Rhamani and Rishi rivers joined:

May 27th. It has been a bad day. We set out expecting a short and rather easy day's march at about 7.15. Climbing diagonally upwards we reached the crest of the spur on which we had camped and then began a long series of gullys. Up and down, up and down – with always the worry that we would reach a 'cut-off', At last we got to a place where we could climb down. It was a difficult descent and took a long time. At one point I received a stone on the head, and the resulting wound, though slight, seemed to fairly spit blood. Then we got into a fearful tangle of scrub and at last hit the Rishi at this point. Now the question arises as to whether we should construct a bridge, cross the river and follow TGL's route or whether to risk this side. In any case we can't do base camp in one day. But the problem is an acute one.

Eight days of the most exhausting effort after leaving Joshimath, amid swirling flurries of snow, they arrived in the vicinity of Longstaff's base-camp of 1907 above the confluence of the Rhamani and Rishi rivers. Next morning they paid off their Dhotial porters, 'after which we had a most touching farewell – they seemed hardly able to drag themselves away. They were a wonderful lot and I regret having to part with them'. Now they could establish their own base-camp in the place occupied that night by the porters, under an overhanging wall of rock 200 yards up from the water's-meet, where they 'spent the day with details of accounts, stock-taking, eating, mending and the usual energetic off-day pastimes'.

Tomorrow we begin the serious work of finding this all-important way. We have got a splendid site for our base and I find the towering rock walls of either side intriguing. One snag is the lack of clean water. The Rishi is thick with glacier mud. Ang Tharkay observed when we were drinking tea made from it, 'the milk of Nanda Devi' . . . Tomorrow, if fine, should be a

most interesting day and give us an idea of our task. I am all
excited, and nervous in consequence.

They were a bare four miles from their objective of the Nanda
Devi Sanctuary, a formidable gorge between them and it, and five
hundredweight of supplies to relay between them along it and –
with luck – into the Sanctuary. The terrain itself had begun to exert
a psychological effect:

> I found myself to be very nervous and shaky on the steep grass
> slopes and slabs on which we had to climb. This was due to
> the fact that I was not yet used to the immense scale and the
> extraordinary steepness of the gorge and its surroundings.
> Tilman also suffered from the same complaint.

For all the nocturnal excitement he'd felt, come the dawn and
Shipton's habitual morning lassitude prevailed:

> May 30th. A long day! I don't know what time T. got up but I
> saw him about at 4.30. As usual I dragged my vile carcase out
> of my bag a good deal later and only after some protest from
> T. I always feel self-righteous on these occasions, however . . .

In *Nanda Devi* Shipton generalises around and elaborates upon
this little incident thus, and in doing so gives a good insight into
overt dynamic and silent seethe, as they appeared from his side
(the passage usefully counterpoints and augments that on the same
subject from *Upon That Mountain* quoted in the previous chapter
and relating to his feelings before the West Ridge climb on Mount
Kenya, and the tensions in the climbing relationship between the
two men):

> Whatever may have been my enthusiasm or impatience to
> be up and doing on the night before, the hour for getting up
> always finds me with no other ambition in the world than to
> be permitted to lie where I am and sleep, sleep, sleep. Not so
> Tilman. I have never met anyone with such a complete disregard
> for the sublime comforts of the early morning bed. However
> monstrously early we might decide, the night before, to get up,
> he was at least half an hour before the time. He was generally

very good about it, and used to sit placidly smoking his pipe over
the fire with no more than a few mild suggestions that it might
be a good idea to think about starting. Nevertheless I always
boiled (so far as my sleepy state allowed) with indignation,
and thought of many crushing arguments (never uttered) why
I should be allowed to sleep. Unfortunately it was easier to be
a passive obstacle than an active force, and I generally got the
better of the silent dispute. But on the morning of May 30th,
Tilman's efforts resulted in our leaving camp at 5.20 a.m., that
is to say, only twenty minutes late.[56]

Twelve hours later they were back at base camp, and in jubilant
mood: 'It is a great piece of luck finding a way so soon – far more
than I had hoped for. I think the route will do as it stands, too. We
are both rather tired as we kept up fairly high pressure.' In the paper
he read to the Alpine Club the following spring Shipton gives the
clearest impression of the ground they had to traverse on this first
day's reconnaissance of the upper gorge:

At first the task looked completely hopeless, but 1,200 feet above
the river we found a downward-sloping ledge along which we
could make our way. Our luck held in an extraordinary way.
Above and below the cliffs were impregnable and, had this
traverse failed, I think we should have had to admit defeat; but
by a remarkable freak of chance the slender ledge continued
unbroken. The complete lack of any alternative too enabled
us to avoid waste of time and, as may well be imagined, our
excitement grew as we progressed. Over and over again the
terrace we were on would peter out in some deep cleft, and
further advance would seem impossible, but on each occasion
there would be a kindly fault in the rock enabling us to climb
over to the continuation of the terrace beyond. Some of the
sections were very 'thin'[57] and had to be roped before they
were passable with loads.

The line of narrow terraces they were following was continually
slanting down, however, towards the river, and the prospect

[56] Shipton, *Nanda Devi*, p.112.
[57] I.e. with only small hand- and footholds to rely on.

of having to follow that icy torrent for the last section into the Sanctuary was not a pleasant one. Also, a huge rock buttress was looming on the opposite side, seeming to occlude any possibility along that bank – even assuming they could reach it:

> The chain of terraces, each dipping in an easterly direction, led us in a downward sloping traverse to the edge of the river some two miles further up the canyon [from their base-camp under the overhanging rock]. The last section of this traverse was very sensational though not difficult. The ledge, less than a foot wide, actually overhung the river about 300 feet below. The passage along it was exhilarating, while it was difficult not to believe that a kindly Providence had placed it there to wind up that long chain of improbabilities.[58]

It had led them down to a rock shelter by the river, where they dumped their loads and retreated back to the base camp. The journal takes up the story next morning:

> May 31st: We got up late-ish (7 a.m.) and spent the morning sorting things to go up. At 11.40 we started upon our first load-shifting relay. T. and I carried 30lbs each, Kusang and Ang Tharkay 60lbs each. Pasang taking another day off.[59] The first part was trying, through the rhododendrons, but higher up going was good and we got to the ridge which we will now call Camp One at 2.20. The descent was a delightful romp. It will be a long and tedious business getting through but we are lucky to have started so early. The Sherpas are enjoying some of our butter beans at the moment.'

> 'June 1st, intermediate Camp One: We got off at 7.30 carrying some 225lbs in all and were up here by 9.50. Pasang stayed up here while the rest of us romped down and ate masses of beans. Only 130lbs remained to be carried up so after a lie out in the sun we had a quick and easy safari up, to find that Pasang had found a good campsite a little above where we had left the loads. As I was writing the above it was discovered that the tea had been left behind. After some talk,

[58] Shipton, *Nanda Devi*, p.64.
[59] With a severe stomach upset.

T. and I tossed up as to who should go and fetch it. T. lost and
went off. He had the better of the bargain in the end as I took
Kusang and Ang Tharkay down to the bad slabs[60] with their
loads and tried to do some roping up. It was a difficult job and
I have decided to haul the ropes up the cliffs. While there we
had a short snow-storm then it cleared up again. Afterwards I
went right down the first traverse to see if there was a way of
avoiding the slabs. I went a long way down and got into the
gully beyond but found difficult climbing there and decided to
give it up. A long plod back to find T. had returned some time
ago. A nice evening and a nice camp, with a good view into the
Basin, which looks very complicated. I remarked on Pasang's
coat looking like that of the Dzongpen, which started a great
joke of which I could not grasp the point.

'June 2nd: We got away at 7.30. We spent about an hour
getting the loads up the slabs, and from there down to the next
gully was so difficult for the Sherpas that they decided to leave
behind their boots. While resting on the ridge beyond T's sack
rolled over the edge. It fetched up a couple of hundred feet
below but was cut to bits. Result we lost a third of our cheese,
nearly all the lentils, some 5 lbs of rice and some candles. This
will mean that the party will be some two days short of food
which is a bore.'

The lentils were a particular loss – in a note to his mother written
at Dibrughita he describes their diet: 'So far our diet is proving
a success – our staple food is lentils, which cook quickly, but we
have such luxuries as black treacle, jaggery, cheese and "Munch"
biscuits.'

The journal continues with the account of their progress
up-gorge, at one of the more spectacular sections of which they had
now arrived:

We made slow progress from there and later in the day found
the going very difficult with loads. However we got over OK
and found a slightly easier way down the last bit to the river.
This consisted of a very sensational traverse along a ledge a
foot or so wide overhanging a sheer drop to the river.

---

[60] On the approach to the long, descending terrace.

The terrace had obviously imprinted itself on his imagination.

They returned to their interim camp, and after sorting more loads were away on the morning of 3 June by eight o'clock:

> We made very good time over the slabs and beyond but when we got to the rhododendrons it began to snow in earnest and I feared that we would not get over the *mauvais pas*.[61] So I exhorted the party to a further turn of speed to which it responded well. But when we got to the bad bit the ground was covered in a few inches of snow. It was a bad business getting across. Pasang and Ang Tharkay went ahead but we roped Kusang up as he had the worst load. There were no belays and it was a thoroughly dangerous business. Beyond, however, things were better and it was a question only of plodding. The final sensational traverse went without difficulty and we arrived under a great rock shelter wet and cold. We collected a lot of wet wood and had a job to get a fire going. However we did so eventually and dried ourselves and our spirits.

Shipton, however, was anxious to drive on with the task, and the following episode gives a clear idea of the hardihood of him and his team:

> At about 3.30 the snow showed signs of stopping and I decided to cross the river [to the south bank]. I made a serious error, I think, in doing so, but we could see an excellent site beyond – lots of wood and clean water and the one we were in was miserable. Also, I had my mind set on the river route. We took our loads down to the water's edge and I led across with a rope around my waist. The water was far higher than it had been the other day and I had a lot of difficulty. T. followed and we then returned for our second loads. The water was up to our waists. After our second crossing I signalled for Ang Tharkay and Pasang, who started holding hands. At one point I thought that A. was sunk. He went in almost to his neck. They were badly shaken when they got over and said they would not return. It was freezing cold and our teeth were chattering. A

---

[61] Which, according to Tilman, 'remained to the end a nightmare which no amount of familiarity could dispel'.

quick decision had to be made and I suppose I made the wrong one. I went back to get a load of bedding. Hanging on to the rope I made the crossing OK with a box of matches between my teeth. We quickly made a fire and T. went off to get the second load of bedding and bring Kusang across. T. had a bad time and after he had got over the worst bit he fell down under the weight of his waterlogged load. The current is frightfully strong. T. and I were thoroughly chilled after our five crossings and poor T.'s legs were badly battered. Kusang was still singing! I noticed though that he stopped singing during the passage of the *mauvais pas* earlier in the day. We spent the next few hours eating and drying ourselves before turning in.

In all, despite the jubilation of that first day, it took a week of unremitting and dangerous labour, crossing and recrossing the turbulent river ('I shall be glad to finish with these aquatic sports', Shipton confided to his journal), linking together sequences of improbable ledges ('our route appeared to rely for its practicability upon the slender chance of a rock-fault'), rounding huge buttresses of vertical rock and continually toing and froing along each newly explored section as they relayed loads. One catastrophe that befell them was the loss of Tilman's pipe in one of the five river crossings they had to make: 'He is a confirmed pipe-smoker, and I think that the prospect of a month without one was gloomy to say the least.' Fortunately Shipton had the pipe Wager had reputedly insisted on his smoking the previous year on the Lashar Plain, so 'Tilman was able to get a smoke at the expense of an increased flow of argumentative conversation.'

The crucial day was 4 June. Morale restored by the warmth of their previous evening's fire and the good night's rest they had enjoyed in consequence, they began by cutting down three birch trees to make a precarious bridge back to the northern bank. At the end of the spectacular line of terraces, high up in the gorge on Longstaff's recommended north side, they had come to an apparent impasse. Shipton, Pasang and Kusang now tried their luck in the bed of the gorge itself, where their luck finally ran out. Tilman and Ang Tharkay had meanwhile crossed to the southern shore and climbed some way up to one side of the huge and seemingly impassable buttress that dominated that bank and had looked so hopeless throughout their approach along the northern bank. Their defeated companions after only a short distance and a lot of time had extricated themselves from the river option, and retreated to the rock shelter, from which they watched as the two high above on the southern bank started traversing horizontally out on to the face of the buttress, 'like ants on a gigantic wall'.

They disappeared from view, came in sight again attempting to ascend by what looked a wholly improbable line up a gully that seemed to run into overhanging rock, and then were lost again in the vastness. Rain started to fall and the light was failing. Shipton and his two Sherpas hunkered down in their camp and lit a fire to await the return of the southern party. They spotted them racing down in the gloaming, and as they neared the camp Ang Tharkay shouted the good news. Beyond the traverse of the buttress the way lay clear right through into the Sanctuary itself.

Another day was spent in ferrying the remaining loads across the rickety bridge ('our first business this morning was to get ourselves and all our loads over the "bridge". This was a perilous job and froze our feet most painfully, as most of the so-called bridge is under water. However, we all got across without loss of life or serious hurt to limb'). These then had to be carried up the hillside and around the buttress, which they had named Pisgah as being the place from which they could see into the Promised Land. On 6 June they finally reached a campsite at 13,000 feet, the highest point of the gorge route and beyond the confines of the Rishi Ganga in the Sanctuary itself: 'Even at that distance above the river I fancied that I could hear it grumbling at our escape.'[62]

For Shipton in his journal too, the note recorded is not the one of elation at treading the so-long-desired terrain that might be anticipated: 'So here we are at last in the Basin, and the first bit of our object accomplished. All being well we ought to see quite a bit of it. We have decided to concentrate first on the north side.' These words, written on their first night in this wildly beautiful and desperately inaccessible place, sound flat and tired. After all the labour, all the danger, the soakings and disappointments, the continual uncertainty as to whether what they were attempting would actually prove to be possible, to summon up an appropriate excitement in response to the moment of arrival was beyond their immediate powers. Much later, when Shipton reflected on what

---

[62] Tilman, 'Nanda Devi', p.5.

they had achieved and where they were, the 'emotion recollected in tranquillity' came flooding through, in the crucial passage already touched upon in the first chapter and worth giving in full at this critical juncture:

> We were now actually in the inner sanctuary of the Nanda Devi Basin, and at each step I experienced that subtle thrill which anyone of imagination must feel when treading hitherto unexplored country. Each corner held some thrilling secret to be revealed for the trouble of looking. My most blissful dream as a child was to be in some such valley, free to wander where I liked, and discover for myself some hitherto unrevealed glory of Nature. Now the reality was no less wonderful than that half-forgotten dream; and of how many fantasies can that be said, in this age of disillusionment?[63]

The transition from Wardour Vale to Nanda Devi Sanctuary here seems no more than a continuum in the individual consciousness, instead of the rigorous physical trial, the harsh and tenuous rite of passage these five men had endured. You could be led into thinking by these frequent harkings-back in Shipton's writing that the whole exploratory impulse is an attempt to recapture the freshness and glory of an enraptured childhood state. Perhaps in some measure the exploratory *is* a regressive instinct; one that social rhetoric suggests is properly put aside and eschewed by the stable and mature personality; one in some way allied to the physical curiosity that may have driven the many sexual relationships of Shipton's later life. Perhaps there is explanation here too for the lushness of the celebratory passages scattered throughout *Nanda Devi* in particular, but present even as late as his last book, *That Untravelled World*. One thing beyond any doubt is that after the enormity of effort, the magnitude of the achievement that first passage of the Rishi gorge and arrival in the Nanda Devi Sanctuary entailed and represented, these first human beings to enter into one of the world's most sublime natural shrines would not be allowing the time there to go to waste.

---

[63] Shipton, *Nanda Devi*, p.131.

8

Proud Head of the Goddess Bowed?

In mountaineering, there is little psychological fixity in the state of achievement. Once you have arrived at a summit or the top of a rock-climb all effort expended in getting there is dust, or worse than that the vapourings of popular acclaim. It remains only to go down. In consequence, the sport has its own acknowledged version of post-coital melancholy, exactly phrased by Tilman: '. . . a feeling of sadness that the mountain had succumbed, that the proud head of the goddess was bowed'.[1] Participants in climbing are driven to endless re-enactment in pursuit of fleeting moments of fulfilment in coition with their objectives – treading the peaks a more apposite form of words than mere surface meaning suggests.[2] Thereafter, ever-more-difficult is one channel to follow; always-the-new (or the unknown, which is the same thing in mountain terms) another.

For our five protagonists newly arrived in the Nanda Devi basin, there was no such quandary. The three Sherpas could express their practical appreciation of the place, marvel at the excellent yak-grazing, and wonder how they might get their animals up there. The two Europeans had work to do now, and very little time in which to complete it, given that the monsoon was expected before the end of June and their route of retreat back down the gorge, with its multiple river-crossings and swollen tributary streams, would then become a very different and potentially far more dangerous

---

[1] H. W. Tilman: The Seven Mountain Travel Books (Diadem Books, 1983), p.248.
[2] 'Treading' is also the correct term for avian copulation. If we consider the Nanda Devi Sanctuary in this context, the ambiguities multiply – a few brief decades of use by the worldwide mountaineering community, and this hallowed place was well and truly fucked. Small wonder the Indian authorities now stringently control access – and reason to be thankful for Shipton's and Tilman's testimonies as to its former state.

proposition. At most, they had three weeks' worth of supplies and opportunity to complete their intended work of surveying the basin and preparing a map of its uncharted territory:

> The main object of the expedition was mountain exploration rather than mountain climbing, and our time in the basin was taken up by a fairly detailed examination of each of the side valleys coming down from the outer ramparts. This in itself was a most fascinating task and we would have given much to have been able to extend the time limit imposed on us by the scanty supplies of food which, unaided, we were able to carry with us into the basin.[3]

Their first evening gave them one of the moments of glory, recorded as follows by Shipton in his notebook:[4]

> Towards sunset the clouds cleared over the Basin and we got a most heavenly view; first of N[anda D[evi] and then of a fine array of peaks to the north of it. It was one of those views which makes life up here totally worth while. Soft clouds twisting themselves about the incredible peak of N.D. and floating about the basin. Making the peaks look wonderfully high and remote. The sunlight gradually departing bright in all its splendour for one glorious moment on the upper face of N.D. and then suddenly went – leaving all a ghostly white . . . The Sherpas and P[asang] in particular were in <u>very</u> high spirits when the peaks came out.

Not that the mood of euphoria lasted long. The morning saw them contemplating a crossing of the broad river flowing out of the basin and into the gorge close by their newly established base-camp in the Sanctuary. They decided to take it at this point rather than walking upstream and crossing the two feeder streams from the north and south sectors of the basin separately:

> The river at that point looked fairly mild and so we descended to it. It proved to be anything but mild and we had another

---

[3] *Alpine Journal*, 1934, p.65.
[4] This refers to the 'First Rishi Ganga Expedition: May 21–July 2, 1934' notebook, from which I have quoted at length throughout this chapter.

bloody

Tharkay]

However,

It needs saying in defence of Ang Tharkay that his diminutive stature
meant that where for the others the water would be waist deep,
for him it was at chest height – icy, swift, taking his breath away,
battering him with rocks carried along in the current, glacier-white.
Since he figures large in our story, Shipton's assessment of him from
his final book is well worth giving at this point:

> Angtarkay[5] had distinguished himself on Everest in 1933, by
> weathering the three-day storm at Camp 5, which left most of us
> weak and dispirited, and then volunteering to carry on to Camp
> 6. He was five feet tall, small even for a Sherpa, lightly built and
> with pronounced knock-knees. He had a diffident manner and
> a flashing smile. Both his diminutive stature and his retiring
> demeanour belied the remarkable force of his personality, which
> was manifest in any crisis or adversity. Though then illiterate,
> he was intelligent, balanced and capable of shrewd appraisal
> of men and situations. Indeed, he was a shining example of my
> contention (based, no doubt on personal prejudice) that literacy
> is not a prerequisite of wisdom. He was to be my companion
> on seven more expeditions, and he acquired an international
> reputation which in no way spoiled him.[6]

To return to the river crossing, Shipton describes in the notebook
how they went to visit the junction of the two streams, looking for
a safer possibility and in a state of ultimately-justified anxiety about
how difficult their exit might prove with the glacier-melt and rain
that would arrive on the monsoon:

> We crossed slopes of thick juniper and reached a flat strip of
> grassland just above the junction of the streams. We could
> now see right up the North valley, which is very open indeed
> and <u>looks</u> most accessible. The snout of the main glacier is

---

[5] The accepted version of the name now is Ang Tharkay, and is given thus
throughout the text.
[6] Eric Shipton, *That Untravelled World* (Hodder & Stoughton, 1969), p.88.

– according to T[ilman]'s estimate – a mile and a half up. It looks a big affair. I got a great thrill looking up into the hitherto unknown.

The South valley is much narrower – we couldn't see far up the floor but there was no evidence of a glacier for a long way up. The first slopes on the S. side of it look very easy. The North river looks to me much the bigger of the two (T. thinks otherwise). On the hillside opposite we saw a herd of about six buck grazing a long way above us. We found a great quantity of onions at that spot – not the wild garlic we had found before. The blokes are going back for the rest of the stuff tomorrow.[7] We hope to get a bit of plane-tabling done.

The manner here in which he calls the Sherpas 'the blokes' resonates with his comments in *That Untravelled World* that on the Rishi Ganga trip he was for the first time 'able to treat these people as friends rather than as hired porters and servants', with whom to share 'food and tent-space . . . plans and problems.' These passages from the notebook are interesting also for the implicit shifts of balance they reveal of the authority in the relationship between Shipton and Tilman. That this starts to become discernible after Tilman and Ang Tharkay had been the ones to find the crucial and most imposing last link in the passage of the Rishi gorge by their improbable-looking solution to the traverse of the Pisgah buttress is surely significant. On their Mount Kenya ascents, Shipton as senior climbing partner would not have deferred nor perhaps even consulted Tilman on choice of route. Now he records his opinion on distance – a field in which Tilman's expertise as a former gunnery officer must have been obvious. And he gives too the older man's opinion on the size of the north river, even though it differs from his own. There is a growing mutual trust and reliance here, a recognition of pooled perceptions and shared responsibility. The initial marriage of convenience manifest on those African climbs where some might suppose an element of *faute de mieux* had been present – Tilman a steadfast and sanguine novice who, being immediately available, enabled Shipton to accomplish his dreams and ambitions in those mountains – is modulating into a more equal and inter-dependent

---

[7] This had been cached at the last camp before the basin, after the great rock buttress they called Pisgah.

partnership now, as well it needed to given how extraordinary a venture they had embarked upon. They started very quickly on their surveying task, beginning the task on the morning of 7 June.

> While the Sherpas went off to fetch the remaining loads we climbed 2,000 feet up the ridge above us with the Plane-table. We could see a lot but couldn't identify anything in the basin. After resecting our position from false points we were driven down by rain. We went up again in the afternoon and washed out all our morning's work – resected our position again but are not too confident of the result. We returned soon after seven – a most unsuccessful day. We had a scare on returning to find the porters hadn't got back. However they rolled up at 7.40 tired after a long day and having found the river crossings very bad. These rivers are a serious problem.

So they went on for the next several days; gaining expertise in the use of the plane table; slowly identifying peaks around the rim as they came into view; admiring the north face of Nanda Devi – 'one of the most gigantic bits of mountain architecture I have ever seen'; ferrying loads across the river to their camp and on towards the north glacier; experiencing violent squalls of snow and becoming 'frightfully cold waiting for the peaks to clear'; making rapid progress up 'an extraordinary broad strip of grass between the side of the valley and the lateral moraine'; and eventually pitching camp in a lateral valley directly opposite the formidable cirque formed by the north faces of the two Nanda Devi peaks: 'The middle portion is fantastically steep. The whole is far too steep for hanging glaciers, and the sound of avalanches is rare. The weather has been lovely . . . a wonderful day of beauty and interest.'

In the evening, wandering up a ridge above their camp, Shipton came across a single bharal,[8] grazing fifty yards away and quite

---

[8] The beautiful horned blue sheep found extensively throughout the Himalaya. They will feature as a food source during the journeys described in the next chapter. For an excellent and exciting account of Himalayan large fauna – Yetis not included, the author being a scientist and not a crypto-zoologist – see George Schaller, *Stones of Silence* (Andre Deutsch, 1980). Schaller was Peter Matthiessen's companion in the journey to the monastery of Shey Gompa beneath the Crystal Mountain described in Matthiessen's classic philosophical travel book *The Snow Leopard* (Chatto & Windus, 1979). Schaller's book gives a fascinating alternative

unafraid. At sundown, not bothering with a tent, he and Tilman slid into their sleeping bags ready for an alpine start. (The dispensing with a tent had its rationale: '. . . we found it so much pleasanter to sleep in the open, even at our higher camps. It seemed somehow to provide a continuity between rest and action, to deepen the sense of harmony between ourselves and our surroundings, which even the thin canvas walls of a tent can destroy.'[9] Implicitly, we are back with Shipton the mystic here, seeking oneness with nature.) They were away at 3.45 as it was starting to get light, making fast time over the glacier and beyond on excellent snow. At 6.20 they reached the base of the steep ice-slope leading up to a col on the crest of the surrounding ridge of the basin.

> We chose the left-hand side by some rocks as being the lesser of two evils. There was a very thin layer of snow covering the ice. Being still very early and cold one could go up without cutting many steps. We had decided that we could get down another way. The going became more and more thin until at last we got on to some rocks and clambered on to the ridge above and some way to the north of the col. Difficult climbing. It was blowing hard when we reached the crest and we took shelter behind a rock and had some grub. T. was feeling the height a good deal. The barometer read 20,300 feet but increased steadily as we sat there – lag, I suppose.[10] The view on the other side was a most amazing tangle of peaks of which we could make neither head nor tail. Nanda Kot to the south was obvious, and from that we could trace Longstaff's 1905 valleys, more or less.

After puzzling at the topography laid out in front of them for half an hour, they set off again along the steep and fissile crest to reach a final very narrow and corniced snow-ridge. They traversed across steep ice on the opposite side to the cornice and climbed cautiously to the top.

---

view of their shared journey – another story of Himalayan exploratory friendship between temperamental opposites.
[9] Eric Shipton, *Upon That Mountain* (Hodder & Stoughton, 1943), p.158.
[10] This was the Holborn aneroid (see previous chapter), or 'Shaitan' as the Sherpas called it – obviously more suited to the low life of London than the demands of altitude.

The aneroid read 20,900 feet but it was probably more. The summit was formed by a curious cut-off in the ridge – a great pyramid of ice. The wind was too cold to allow a prolonged stay on top. We turned the cut-off by descending a ridge to the north-east over some nasty snow-covered ice.

Eventually, after much step-cutting and traversing over some fearsome ground they reached a wide gully of perfect snow down which they plunged to reach without further difficulty the glacier and their camp.

T. was still feeling the effects of altitude badly, but I was feeling quite fit. I lay down for a rest and suddenly began a violent shivering fit and passed the remainder of the day and that night in a fevered delirium of which I have but a vague memory. The next morning I had recovered slightly but spent the day in my flea-bag in a weak state. T. spent two or three hours in the afternoon plane-tabling. I spent a reasonably good night and waited until the porters rolled up about 11 this morning [13 June] and came down with them. T. put in some good work with the plane table. I felt better tonight but am very weak.

They all spent the night curled up in the Sherpas' tent listening to the rain and hail, Shipton still too feeble to move in the morning and their time and supplies slipping away. The following night was even worse.

June 15th. We had a bad night. It started by being confoundedly hot and we could not get to sleep. I had indigestion. It started to rain and continued all night excepting that later it condescended to turn to snow. We were sleeping as usual with the tent spread over us instead of erected in the usual way. In spite of our discomforts I think that for the purpose of sort of bivouac camps such as we are using a wide waterproof sheet serves better than one of these very light tents. If one builds a sort of wall a foot high round one and puts everything inside and covers all over with the sheet one should be far more snug than in one of these light tents. Anyway up to 20,000 feet in the damper districts of the Himalayas. Of course in cold, dry districts a light tent is OK. I finally got off to sleep after midnight. It was a fitful slumber and I woke at 6 a.m. The snow had stopped falling but lay thick about us.

Not only was their time in the basin fast diminishing, so too were the supplies needed to sustain them there, and the weather signs were not good. They now had a fortnight at most before the onset of the monsoon, signs of the imminence of which were already apparent, that would render their route down the gorge impassable; and one of the party had fallen sick. Yet they persevered.

We sorted ourselves out, or rather T. did. The sun made efforts to come out, and after some scraps of biscuits and butter we decided to go and have a look at the col. We started at 8.30. The snow on the lower part of the glacier was very soft and we waded in up to our knees. Higher up it got better. Parts were very good. It was mostly flogging along until we were a few hundred feet from the col when our way was barred by a crevasse which stretched a long way across. At the left-hand end one could get up by cutting steps in ice over a traverse. T. hacked a wide pathway in the ice and I was narrowly missed by some falling stones. After that I took over the lead again and flogged up to the final slope where more steps had to be cut in ice. We saw a lot to the East from the col. I should say that it would be quite unjustifiable to take loaded porters over. One could get down no doubt but there must have been some 2,000 feet of very steep snow-covered rocks with a few very avalanchey gullys, which risk from above would be very great. We got to the top about 12.30. We made it just over 20,000 feet allowing for our machine's present state of uncertainty.

A cold wind springing up, they raced down as fast as the soft snow would allow and the Sherpas had tea ready for them, after swallowing which they hurried on back to the main basin camp, ate *satu* and pemmican, and at six o'clock, the rain falling again, crawled into the small tent. 'Hope it doesn't leak too much!' wrote Shipton, before he retired to bed. The party had decided to look next at the main north valley and its glacier,[11] which stretched up on their left hand from the subsidiary one of the initial exploration.

---

[11] This became known as the 'Great North Glacier'.

'T. suggested the valley coming down from Changabang and Kalanka be called Changalanka. Doubt if the RGS will accept this!' When they arrived there, Tilman was in no fit state to press the humorous point.

> June 16th. It has not been a good day's work, though we must be some three miles up the valley. We started late (8.30) and after going an hour or so T. was taken ill in the same way I was. A swelling below the groin and a shivering fit. We halted for nearly two hours. I fixed our position and then decided to change the sheet on the plane-table as we were getting too far north for the old one. T.'s load was divided among the Sherpas and we went on at 11.15; T. nobly struggling with us in spite of a lot of pain and sickness . . . We camped I should say rather more than half way up the valley at about 2.20. There are a lot of side valleys on the west side – only two of them of any consequence. However the others will require mapping.

The head of the valley curved round to a col that represented their only remaining chance of exit on the whole north side of the basin, and it was guarded by a difficult ice fall. Shipton was still in a weakened state, though recovering. As for Tilman, 'poor T. is flat out at the moment and likely to be *hors de combat* for a day or two'. And as for the weather, 'this dismal rain-snow is here again and we have to sleep out in it. It makes things rather bloodsome.'

Ang Tharkay and Kusang went down for bundles of firewood; Tilman was very weak and out of action; Shipton struggled on with plane-tabling, changing the paper proving difficult, then he and Pasang explored all about and found another remarkable grassy passage, this time between two moraines beautifully contrasting in their colours. At the west corner of the glacier they came across a large lake, 'beautiful and weird', lapping against a wall of glaciated rock and immensely deep. Beyond it at the west corner of the glacier, through the falling snow he thought he could make out a way to circumvent the difficult ice fall tumbling from the col, and returned to the camp where Tilman was resting just as the two wood-bearers arrived from down-valley: 'T. seems better, but is still very weak of course. So now we have a pukka fire, which is much more comfortable.'

In the notebook he went on to describe the surroundings:

There is quite a variety of birds here, which is strange, as the country is utterly desolate. There are several odd features of this glacier, but its chief is the vileness of what ought to be good sound snow. *Penitentes*[12] and small tables abound. At one spot I saw a huge stream enter an ice face and come out of the same face in exactly the opposite direction, only a few yards away. The effect was most curious.

The weather continued dire: 'It rained and snowed all last night and we got very miserable. We could not make an early move as everything was deep in snow.' On the morning of the 18th, the infinitely resilient Tilman rose and climbed with them up the valley past the lake and on over difficult rocks carrying equipment for a light camp, which they pitched at 18,500 feet, from which point Ang Tharkay and Kusang descended.

Snow falling heavily again and I don't know what will happen. We have two and possibly three days' food with us. I hope we can do some good in the time. We are having a spell of vile weather. I don't know if it is the monsoon or not. We got very cold this afternoon, but are quite comfortable now. It is about 10 to 6. A reasonable outlook, and we will soon have to be fighting our way down the Rishi with scanty provisions.

Before Shipton would give in and sound the retreat, he was determined to drive on through the small potential stock of days still at their disposal. They threaded their way through a maze of crevasses and ice-walls to a long ice-plateau which took them easily to that last potential col of passage on this side. What lay beyond, barring their way to the Bagini glacier, more than made up for the relative ease of approach:

I have rarely looked down such a long and sheer drop. It looks as if one could drop a stone on to the moraine-covered glacier at 16,000 feet. Our col must have been at least 20,500 feet.

---

[12] Pillars of ice occurring in groups on the surface of a glacier, with an ethereal appearance as of white, cowled monks. 'Tables' are formed by melting around an ice core initially protected from the sun by a capstone. The heroes of the Alpine Golden Age would toast their great deeds in glasses of Bouvier or Mummery's Blood around the same.

Of course there was no route down. We saw Dunagiri well. It looks quite impossible from this side. Indeed now I can't think from where one would stand much chance of getting up it.

From their col a peak of about 23,000 feet rose from the rim. Shipton decided to attempt it with Pasang whilst Tilman rested in a sheltered spot out of the fierce wind that was blowing. The condition of the snow was very bad for the two climbers:

After labouring on until 11 o'clock I chucked it regretfully. We found the glacier in vile condition coming down, but we got to camp about 1.30. One small mishap marred the descent. We were preparing to glissade down a steep slope of a crevasse only about 20 feet high. Pasang went off unexpectedly and pulled me off. I am annoyed about it as it was a bad bit of mountaineering.

In *Nanda* Devi Shipton adds ten feet to the height of the slope and notes that both Tilman and himself were pulled down after Pasang, though the landing was in soft snow and the fall, which was caused by pure carelessness, had no serious consequence.

Another attempt on the peak on the 20th took Shipton and Pasang a little higher, wading through knee-deep snow, climbing an ice chimney, and finally sounding the retreat again when they came to knee-deep snow lying on a slope of ice. 'It taught me not to underestimate these peaks,' he confided ruefully to his notebook. 'Nothing could have looked much simpler than ours, but ice and snow defeated us.' They trailed back to their high camp, packed up and moved on downwards, plane-tabling as they went. Food was running short now, the jaggery they were carrying ruined by the near-incessant rain, and they were more than a little alarmed by the sudden rapid increase of melting in the glacial ice and consequent effect on the size of the stream below. They spent a last night in their third camp in what they now called the 'Great North Valley', enjoying a fire from what remained of the bundles of wood the Sherpas had brought up, and retreated to the Glacier Junction camp:

We will have to look slippy and I think we can only afford to spend three more days before the downward journey. I think we ought to leave the Glacier Snout on 25th morning in case we are held up by rivers which I think we are sure to be . . . It is very pleasant to be down to grass and flowers again.

On the 22nd, they moved camp into a lateral valley numbered 5 on their survey. It was here in the evening, and in improving weather ironically, that they witnessed the 'wonderland' vision of Trisul and Nanda Devi given in Chapter One. By the morning its effect had well and truly passed:

> Pity one can't keep hold of one's romantic view of life through the night and during the morning. Life seems so very hateful when one is faced with the necessity of getting up into a cold and cheerless morning. All one's little hurts assume enormous proportions. Our lips are about twice their normal size, our fingers feel as though they have been through a mangle, and there seems no greater folly in the world than the exploration of nature's fortresses.

At least there was the consolation of his companion not being quite so chipper as usual, though this small mercy escapes mention. Shipton frantically worked away at filling in gaps in the plane-table survey for the north side of the basin. Tilman, who had been badly affected by altitude above 20,000 feet and was still struggling with the after-effects of the fever bout, had developed a carbuncle on the top of his foot to add to his miseries, the wearing of a boot agonising now. Shipton thought they should stay at their present height for an extra day, shortage of food notwithstanding, to rest it (throughout the notebook entries, where any frustration or irritation could easily have been expressed, his empathy both for Pasang initially and now for Tilman during their illnesses is very marked in contrast to the general state of anxiety and the desolate place, and it comes across most warmly – you sense this man was a good friend to have in any situation).

A day later, on the 24th, the monsoon broke. In heavy rain they began their retreat:

> I decided that the party might as well start on to homeward journey and get as far as it could. I never hoped to get as far as we did. Owing to my state of undecidedness we did not get

started until after 8. We took two hours to get to the snout of the glacier owing to the porters finding a large supply of onions. The first river looked a pretty hopeless proposition, however we decided to try it. Taking off, or rolling up my trousers for these river crossings, I experienced almost exactly the same feelings as I used to suffer when taking down my trousers for a beating at school.

Having entered the Sanctuary wonderland in the childlike euphoria of a Pyt House and Bevis-land mood, Shipton was now forcing himself away from it with memories of the sadistically abusive Gifford of his preparatory school uppermost in his mind. It's an odd reflection to come at this juncture, obscurely revealing somehow of his need for a safe and untrodden paradise-place, the leaving of which subconsciously was proving exceedingly painful.

We got down to where the river was divided into two parts. The first went easily but the second was a brute. We tried over and over again in various places but the water was too deep and the current far too vicious for us to stand a chance. We were just going to give it up as hopeless when Pasang suggested a spot. To me it looked suicidal, however I linked hands with him and we sallied forth with sinking hearts (at least mine was sinking). After a bit of a tussle we got across; one staying standing firm and giving support to the other while moving and *vice versa*. I am pleased to say we co-operated well. Pasang was wild with delight and wrung my hand.

He tells in *Nanda Devi* of how 'the rushing water made me giddy, and we knew that the least mistake would put us in a false position, from which there would be no hope of recovery. When the water reached my waist I knew that I had reached my limit, and any increase of pressure must sweep me off my feet. Pasang was splendid; never did he relax his concentration on himself or me for a fraction of a second.'[13] A rope was fixed and the others brought across. The sun even deigned to come out and dry them off as they cooked a meal, after which they hastened on to the other river, which was very high. The Sherpas found a level stretch by which to cross. Ang

[13] Eric Shipton, *Nanda Devi* (3rd edition, Hodder & Stoughton, 1939), p.163.

Tharkay and Kusang wanted to camp for the night and do so in the morning when the meltwater would be so much less, but the sahibs and Pasang voted to press on: 'There was nothing to it when the river bed was flat.'

Now they were beyond the two main river obstacles in the basin, and had found a large quantity of rhubarb to supplement their supplies. Tilman even added to that through the discovery of a nest with three pigeon-sized eggs in it, 'grey-blue with red spidery streaks'.[14] And so, well if oddly fed, they plunged back down into the Rishi Ganga.

The Sherpas were very anxious to get a move on and announced their intention of getting across the *mauvais pas* on the traverse before they camped. It is very amusing to see how well they go when their faces are turned towards the flesh-pots of Joshimath, as their loads are pretty heavy. They urged us on when we had barely finished our meal . . . T. lanced his foot this morning and extracted a lot of pus. It appears to be a bit better now but still pretty painful I should imagine.

They sat late that night in camp beyond the *mauvais pas*, making and eating *satu* cakes with their rhubarb, and by the time they turned in the rain had come on hard again:

T. and I had separate little rock-shelters. Mine leaked a good deal but was quite comfortable and I slept like a log. It was grand before dozing off to look out from my minute shelter, hearing the rain beating down and seeing the vaguely moonlit vapours twisting themselves about the weird, gaunt crags of

---

[14] As the oologists among you will be aware, this description, though it appears precise to a lay person, is hopelessly vague for purposes of identification. Nonetheless, through the good offices of my friend Mark Cocker, it was run past Pamela Rasmussen, the foremost authority on blue-eyed and red-legged shags and author of the two-volume Ripley guide to *Birds of South Asia*, and Douglas Russell, curator of the bird group in the Department of Zoology at the Natural History Museum. Their very tentative suggestion was that the eggs *may* have been those of a Variegated or a Streaked Laughing-thrush. Which information I'm sure Shipton and Tilman would have enjoyed and had fun with. I've long noticed strong similarities, incidentally, between the ornithological and the mountaineering tribes – check out Mark Cocker's *Birders: Tales of a Tribe* (Jonathan Cape, 2001) to see what I mean. Much of it is set in the Himalaya.

the Rishi Ganga . . . We have reason to congratulate ourselves that we have completed the exploration of the Northern section [of the Basin] just in time, though if we have time I want to explore the bit between the Basin and the Rhamani glacier. The river is exceedingly high now and above the rocks we were manoeuvering over when we made that last bridge.

The manner in which he progressively works up this notebook entry is interesting. As with Lawrence's story of Lady Chatterley, there are three extant versions, comparisons between which are instructive. Each will no doubt have its devotees. The latest of the three takes, from *Upon That Mountain*, is a good example of Shipton working towards his grand style:

> The gorge was even more impressive in foul weather than in fair. Particularly I remember one night of heavy storm. I was snugly wedged in a little recess between two boulders listening comfortably to the hiss of the rain outside, and to the thunder which, echoing along miles of crag, maintained an almost unbroken roll. Lightning flickered continuously upon the grim precipices and upon cloud banners entwined about buttress and corrie. The sense of fantasy was heightened by the semi-consciousness of a fitful sleep. At one moment it seemed that I was perched on an eagle's nest above an infernal cauldron of infinite depth, at another that I was floating with the mist, myself a part of an unearthly tempest.'[15]

Finally here's the second version, from *Nanda Devi*, which seems to me the most comprehensive and accomplished:

> I passed the night in a tiny recess between two boulders, and throughout the first half of it a thunderstorm raged above the gorge. The boulders provided inadequate shelter from the heavy rain which accompanied the storm, and I got very wet. The scene, however, was one not easily to be forgotten. Lightning flashes played continuously upon the grim precipices about me, while the fleecy rain clouds, entwining themselves about ridge and gully, accentuated their already stupendous

---

Shipton, *Upon That Mountain*, pp.158–9.

size. Echoes of the thunder and hissing rain provided fitting accompaniment.'[16]

Interesting how, in the latest of these versions (the high-romantic middle version given here), he forgets how wet he became. Perhaps the experience was like childbirth the way my female friends recount it – the discomfort and misery receding as the years pass, and memory retaining only the pleasurable and moving aspects.

At 3.30 on the 27th, 'four hours from our last camp and not rushing it particularly', they arrived back at their base-camp close to the junction of the Rishi and the Rhamani rivers. 'The route went well.' In two short days of descent they had covered ground that had taken nine days to find their way up at the beginning of the month.

> I found a blue poppy . . . we got a fair amount of a new green variety of rhubarb. When we were negotiating the slabs it came on to rain and has continued ever since with the result that I found the long descent to here rather unpleasant in tennis shoes. We found that the growth of trees and shrubs has increased enormously in the four weeks we have been away . . . We find that the biscuits we left have mysteriously disappeared. They must have been bunged in with the main lot going up. Most annoying, as we shall be short of food unless we get through quickly. A lot depends on how we get on tomorrow.

Though they seemed to have reached safety again, the rain and the melting snow had intruded yet another formidable problem between them and the reaching of Joshimath. They still had the Rhamani river, thundering down from its huge glacier, to cross; and the sound of it that night within the confines of the gorges would have been disturbance to any dreams.

That same evening Shipton and Pasang made a three-hour reconnaissance up-river along the Rhamani:

> We crossed the Rishi over the big rocks, passed Longstaff's old camp and traversed under overhanging cliffs to a fair-sized shore. We found that the Rhamani had swollen enormously.

---

[16] Shipton, *Nanda Devi*, p.166.

It is now a huge affair coming down in gigantic leaps and bounds through a most wonderful gorge. There was no hope of crossing it there and we were forced up and up to a great height before we could reach it again. At length we did so and decided that we could get across by wading. That would land us on a high traverse which is probably the one the Bagani Pass party[17] traversed in '07. Well, it is this route or the Trisuli nullah[18] way and I am in favour of the former. So tomorrow we attempt the crossing, and if successful commit ourselves to terrific days of coasting. I hope to heaven it goes. The Rhamani is a grand river and I would like to follow it up one day.[19]

They left the Rishi base camp on the 28th, leaving there the plane table, rope and food against their intended return post-monsoon, crossed the Rishi by the rock-bridge and made their way up alongside the Rhamani: 'I was carrying the suitcase,' Shipton notes bizarrely, 'which gave me some trouble as it swayed about.' The fording of the Rhamani proved almost anticlimactic, and soon they were a thousand feet up the ridge on the farther side enjoying magnificent views in clear weather down into the Rishi Ganga. The weather soon closed in again, the terrain began once more to assert itself, and they climbed in and out of deep and flooding gullies, not quite sure where they were heading. Even a wet night in a spacious cave struggling with a smoky and recalcitrant fire failed to douse their spirits and the following day, themselves and all they carried soaked through, toiling over wet rocks and slippery grass, through undergrowth bright with red potentilla and forget-me-nots, in pouring rain they reached Dibrughita. 'It is a great relief to be within reach of food, though it may take another three days to reach Surai Tota.' Moving on, Shipton discovered he had lost one of the several Shetland sweaters they each carried on the way up. He trailed back

---

[17] Now known as the Bagini pass (6,128 metres), this high pass between Dunagiri and Changabang, outside the wall of the inner sanctuary to the north-west, is the one by which Longstaff and Bruce descended to Shipton and Tilman's Rishi base camp in 1907. Nowadays it is a popular trekking route, being as close as you can still get to the Nanda Devi Sanctuary.

[18] I.e. the river flowing down from the Trisuli glacier. This would have been a long detour!

[19] He did in fact reach and explore the Rhamani glacier at its head during the Osmaston survey trip into the Sanctuary, post-Everest in 1936.

down to look for it but couldn't even find the route by which he had come so he gave up and followed after the others, catching them up on the pass before Duraishi.

> My legs felt very weak as I descended on the other side. We found that some shepherds had come up from Lata with their flocks. They supplied us with some most excellent goat's milk which went very well with satu. They are the first human beings we have seen besides ourselves for over a month. They are a very young lot and not very striking specimens of manhood. [They] seem to have been here about two weeks, which must be rather earlier than usual . . . we are running very low with our food and I hope we can get down to Tolma tomorrow – rather a long day, I should say.

At the end of that long day's march to Tolma, taken at breathless speed, all that they could buy in the way of food was some *atta*[20] and a few underripe apricots. 'They must be frightfully poor,' Shipton commented to his notebook. In the evening they watched a pedlar exchanging buttons, matches and Jew's-harps for unthreshed barley; 'a long process and a precarious existence but amusing to watch'.

> They were a nice crowd and one or two of the women were very fine and nice-looking. We came back to spend a miserable night being eaten alive by midges. It was also hot, although we are still at 8,000 feet. This morning we have had difficulty in procuring food and are breakfasting off baked wheat grains. The flies are awful here; heaven help us in Joshimath!

Empty-bellied and weary, they trailed off lethargically, their loads feeling heavier than ever. 'At Tapoban we hoped to find some food. We were disappointed and had to come on empty.' But now they were on the last lap leading to the creature-comforts of Joshimath.

> Tilman and I set off in front at a frantic speed, each thinking of HOT TEA, SUGAR, + MILK. We raced on through heavy rain and reached [Joshimath] soon after 3 o'clock. We procured

---

[20] A coarse brown flour made from durum wheat.

some sweetmeats which nearly made us sick, collected our mail and came up here. What joy and luxury to be under a roof with plenty to eat and drink! So ends a most successful expedition to the Nanda Devi basin. It is a week ago since we left Glacier Junction Camp – a very strenuous eight days and we have been lucky to get through so fast and so avoiding <u>real</u> hunger.

Judging by the frequency of references to the inadequacy of their provisions over the last two weeks, the hunger had been real and nagging enough. Now they could rest, eat, read and reread the mail that had piled up for them at Joshimath, and make plans for their next move. Their achievement in entering the Nanda Devi Sanctuary, the hardihood they had all shown there in contending with illness, dire conditions and short rations had been somewhere on the scale between stoical and heroic. Among their waiting correspondence at Joshimath had been letters from the Meteorological Department in Calcutta telling them that the monsoon might be expected to be established in the United Provinces – of which Garhwal was then a part – before mid July. Weather-forecasters then and now! As Tilman wryly observes, 'ever since the 24th June we had experienced enough rain to make plane-tabling impossible and travel uncomfortable.' It hadn't deterred them, which was as well, for plenty more was to come. But at least they could now take a deserved break from it and gather their resources before the next stage of their adventures that summer. 'We congratulated ourselves on having quitted the basin and now sentenced ourselves to a week's rest, plenty of milk, and whatever luxuries we could buy, for Shipton indicted us both on a charge of "insufficient energy in the basin". There was no prosecutor, but we accepted the sentence cheerfully.'[21] Nonetheless, from a stance of wholehearted admiration, I think we might enter pleas in mitigation on their behalf.

The 'First Rishi Ganga Expedition, May 21–July 2' journal ends on their arrival in Joshimath with that word 'hunger'. It covers little more than a quarter of their Garhwali journeyings in the summer and early autumn of 1934. I've given substantial extracts from it in this chapter not only because it is unpublished material by one

---

[21] H. W. Tilman, 'Nanda Devi and the Source of the Ganges' (*Himalayan Journal* 1935), p.9.

of our two major British mountain writers (and often relating to the other), and therefore is of intrinsic value and interest; but also because of the frankness and freshness, and the vibrant sense of being there in the situation with them as Shipton reflects on each day's events.

In a very long letter written to his mother from Joshimath the day after they arrived, before proceeding to a reflective gloss on their achievement, Shipton gives a good insight into Mrs Haly's character, and the nature of their relationship:

My own Darling Mum,

We got back here yesterday after being just over six weeks away. I found a huge pile of letters from you which gave me a delicious hour. I was thrilled about your visits to Vienna and B[uda] P[est], and frightfully pleased, as I know how you must have felt after all the time you have spent in England. How sudden it all seemed. You seemed to arrange it all over night! I should love to have been with you. Central Europe has always seemed to be <u>the</u> romantic spot of the world.

He continues by relating the ascent of the Rishi Ganga, complete with small explanatory diagrams, and of how 'our Everest "Tigers" worked splendidly', before giving her perhaps the best of the several accounts of his feelings on first entry into the Sanctuary:

It was a most wonderful feeling to be in that basin for the first time in history, and to have so large an area of country to explore. It was obvious, if we were going to produce a useful map, that we could not cover the whole area in the time, so we decided to concentrate on the section north of Nanda Devi and return for the exploration of the south section after the monsoon. We found conditions a lot easier than we might have expected, and travel was relatively easy. We found huge pastures covered with beautiful flowers, and three lakes. There was a tremendous variety of birds and any amount of game – most of which can never have seen a man, and stared at us incredulously. I was glad we had not got guns – it would have been a crime to shoot them. It was perhaps the most wonderful three weeks of my life, and I shall never forget a moment of it . . . We got back down in eight forced marches with heavy loads . . . T., poor thing, had a carbuncle on his foot but came along gallantly, carrying all his share. We ate most of your 'pine kernels' on the last day and found them a wonderful food. But we were not badly off as we found quite a lot of edible plants *en route*. So at last we arrived here yesterday in pouring rain. Today I am so stiff I can hardly move. We spent the morning washing and bandaging up our various ailments, and eating, eating, eating! Tea with sugar and milk is the greatest joy, I think – anyway, lashings of fresh milk – even if it has to be boiled . . . As to our plans, one thing is certain – we must go back to complete the exploration of the Basin, but it is no use doing that till the monsoon slackens. I think we won't start up the Rishi Ganga until August 10, and as I hope to do it in a more leisurely way I don't expect to reach Ranikhet until the beginning of October. Meanwhile we have a month to fill in. Longstaff was keen on my going to explore the Kosa glacier district, but I fancy that is getting too much of the monsoon and I think we will have to go further north nearer Tibet. I think we will go from here to Mana, and try and discover the true watershed of the main sources of the Ganges. That was my great scheme before Longstaff urged Nanda Devi. But I think we might have time to dabble at it now if the weather lets us.[22]

The sense here of the ardent explorer making up his itinerary as he goes along and not wishing to waste any of the precious time available is thrilling. Though there is no available source (apart from a sequence of letters to Mrs Haly) that is comparable to the Nanda Devi journal in its rapt immediacy for the mountain travelling undertaken after Shipton's party left Joshimath that summer, both men quickly wrote up their experiences on returning to England in accounts for the *Alpine, Himalayan* and *Geographical* journals. Shipton refined his for publication successively in *Nanda Devi, Upon That Mountain* and – much later, towards the end of his life – in *That Untravelled World*. These accounts are fascinating as material for study of the genesis of each man's writing style, of which they are the earliest published examples. Through the contrasting styles, the differences of character between the two men also become apparent,

---

[22] Letter to Mrs Haly from Joshimath, 3 July 1934.

and thus add a dimension to the history of their strange version of friendship – a growing friendship apparently devoid of intimacy that yet managed to sustain itself through stressful situations of the most intense intimacy.

No doubt a factor here which serves to foreground the contrasts in experience, character and expression is paradoxically that of a shared middle-class English culture, with its reliable set forms of communication – as also of discretion and silence. Of course there will be schism and dissent, but when it comes, perhaps because of the very lack of intimacy, and the mediation through a shared culture, it is handled for the most part with a graceful forbearance, Shipton's amiable impishness and sly mockery absorbed by Tilman's benign and fatherly tolerance, and the rancour occasioned by Tilman's occasional gaffes in dropping rucksacks and the like (this, remember, was the 'clumsy bugger' in Pam Davis's words who broke the mica window of the car with his elbow) *almost* never finding expression in open conflict. What you see operative between them is also very close to the distinction between an energetic Romantic individualism – the Shipton mode – and a stately and disciplined Augustan[23] outlook that finds apt expression in the carefully structured, stoical and at times markedly misanthropic antithetical periods of Tilman's classical prose-style.

It would be fair to claim that these Garhwali explorations are among the best documented as well as the most significant events in the history of adventure travel. The scheme outlined in the letter to Mrs Haly above was for a double crossing of the Badrinath–Kedarnath watershed. It was a first in both directions, full of adventures and occasional misadventures ('Tilman made the discovery that glissading on steep ice was too rapid, even in these fast-moving times, and we reverted to slow but safe step-cutting').[24] Even before they set out, they met one of the most interesting characters in all their joint journeyings, in his descriptions of whom Shipton's own geniality and affection for humanity is strongly to the fore, as here, from a note to his mother, describing 'Professor Ram Serikh Singh, known to all in the district as "The Master"':

---

[23] Post-Augustan, perhaps, with Marcus Aurelius a clearer antecedent.
[24] Shipton, *Nanda Devi*, p.192.

Last night we were entertained until very late by an old philosopher who has lived up here for many years and has travelled enormously. He speaks English quite well and is tremendously learned. He is mentally very Europeanised, doesn't like the modern Hindu, and has a tremendous admiration for the teaching of Christ. Of course he was frightfully interesting about the history and mythology of this place [i.e. Badrinath] and also very interested in the geography of these glaciers. They are very keen that we should find a pass over to Kedarnath across the range. Mythological stories say that one used to be known to the old High Priests at the temple but that it has now been lost. Later if we have time I should like to do a small journey with the old man. He has a very vivid personality.[25]

Writing to his mother from Badrinath three weeks later on 3 August, after their first crossing of the watershed, he tells her of the initial response to the Rishi Ganga exploration and describes their most recent journey:

I found a wire from Humphreys dated 12th July: 'My expedition starting. Best luck yours.' So they are off after all – a bit late, I should say. I have just got a most kind and generous cable from Hugh Ruttledge as follows: 'Hearty congratulations on splendid exploration.' Isn't it nice of him to go to the trouble and expense? Our 'Monsoon Interlude' has met with quite a large measure of success. As I told you we were to try and cross the great Ganges watershed and explore as much of it as we could. We started up the Bhagat Kharak Glacier where Meade is supposed to have seen a possible route in 1913, but we drew a complete blank. The cirque at the head of the glacier is a colossal affair, and doesn't drop below 20,000 feet anywhere. There was only one place which looked at all practicable, but the route to it for miles is in danger of being swept by ice avalanches, so we left it severely alone. It did not take much exploring, that part, and then we crossed three passes to the north and so connected up with the part we were in in 1931. The passes were all between 18,000 and 20,000 feet high. We

---

also climbed a couple of peaks. The weather was bad, but it never stopped us. We were lucky in that on the whole, as it was generally clear enough for us to fix our position fairly accurately. It was rather heavy work at first lugging all our food about, but after we got north into the Arwa Glacier system we could leave dumps of food and fuel against our return. We had just enough by then to cross the watershed by the passes we visited in 1931, and make long and rapid marches down to the Gangotri Glacier whose snout we reached on July 27th at a place called Gaumukh, which is the true source of the Ganges. So at last the range has been crossed completely and the headwaters connected up.

What comes across in this brief note is how the keynote to this crossing and the return one that followed was a quality common to both men – an intense curiosity about natural landforms, whether they be mountains, valleys, rivers, volcanoes or glaciers. This curiosity acts both as a bond between them and as a stimulus, a fund of energy continually to be drawn upon and used as a basis and point of reference in their explorations. Time and again in their books, both writers make summary comments on this: 'It was enthralling to disentangle the geography of the region . . . for me, the basic reason for mountaineering'; 'a desire to leave the route and wander off into the labyrinth of unmapped ranges that stretch away on every side'; 'to follow any river throughout its course is fascinating to me'. Or perhaps clearest of all, from this phase of the 1935 journeyings: 'Tilman and I climbed a peak of about 21,500ft. It was an interesting ridge-climb, but the pleasure we expected, and in fact received, from it was secondary to getting the hang of the Arwa glaciers on to which we were about to descend.'[26]

The watershed-crossings phase of the summer's adventures ended with their most arduous experience of the whole exploratory season. It began after they had negotiated a glacier that dropped in a series of stupendous ice falls from beyond the col[27] at the head of the Satopanth glacier, to the south of Chaukhamba (23,419 feet

---

[26] Shipton, *Nanda Devi*, p.193.
[27] The second crossing of this col did not take place until 1998, when John Shipton, Eric's younger son, was in the party.

– itself a focal point at the head of the Gangotri glacier). Having coped successfully with all the technicalities the glaciers and high cols could throw at them[28] – the descent of the ice fall alone took two days of effort in pouring rain – they found that those of the gorge beneath were to prove even more gruelling: 'The pass itself was very difficult and led us into an uninhabited and unexplored valley of fearfully dense jungle. The weather became very bad indeed and we did not see the sun from one week end to the next.'[29] They had thought, seeing it from the glacier, that the gorge would lead them with no great difficulty and within a couple of days down to the pilgrim route to Kedarnath. Soon after beginning its descent they ran into dense undergrowth with boulders underfoot; the rain still poured down in torrents, and on the evening of 11 August at an altitude of 11,500 feet they found themselves looking down a thousand-foot cliff. Above it a river disappeared below ground to jet out from the face of the cliff in a huge waterfall. Either they had to find a way down to its base; or soaked to the skin and with sodden loads they had to make their way back over the glaciers, cols and difficult ice falls by the route they had come to Mana in the Saraswati valley above the Hindu shrine at Badrinath. Alternatively, they canvassed crossing a lower pass to the south-east of their known route that would lead them over to the south of Nil Kanta – Frank Smythe's 'Queen of Garhwal' and one of the most beautiful of Himalayan peaks – and along the Khirao Ganga down to the temple at Hanuman, the next bridging point on the Alaknanda south of Badrinath.

Their supplies were desperately low. The *satu* and *atta* they were carrying had become saturated with the rain and were mouldy. Though they talked on late into the night, this was a choice that was no choice. Somehow the five of them, rock-climbing at times, roping down steep sections to link together descending terraces, contrived with their wet loads to reach the bottom on the morning of the 12th. Here's Tilman's account:

---

[28] Both Shipton and Tilman record how crucial the Sherpas, and Ang Tharkay in particular, were to the success of this section of the crossing. Tilman: 'But now, the Sherpas seemed to catch fire and would not hear of retreat. Whether it was the pure zeal of the explorer, the challenge of a difficult climbing problem, or the Badrinath goat meat that inspired them, I do not know; but we both feel the crossing of this pass was due to them.' (*Himalayan Journal* 1935, p.16.)
[29] Letter to Mrs Haly from Ukhimath Temple, 20 August 1934.

In the morning, after some delay, we found a way down
the cliff, lowering the loads and coming down ourselves *en
rappelle*, the rope being anchored rather hazardously to a
juniper root; but the going continued indescribably bad and
by two o'clock we had travelled only three-quarters of a mile.
For the next two hours we enjoyed rather easier conditions,
pushing through a forest of beautiful blue flowers on eight-
foot stems, until we emerged in pine forest close to the river
we expected and feared.[30]

They also encountered some good fortune in the form of an
edible and plentiful tree-fungus and a spring of good water, and at
10,500 feet they reached the upper limit of the bamboo, the shoots
of which together with forest mushrooms provided them with a
meagre source of nourishment. With darkness falling, they made
camp below a gorge spanned by what appeared to be a natural
bridge, beyond which Pasang thought he could make out a path.
Tilman sets the scene:

What a camp that was! The fragrant smell of the great pines,
the soft carpet of pine needles beneath us, the mushrooms and
bamboo shoots[31] off which we dined, the blazing fire round
which we lay and dried our sodden clothes; and as if this
were not enough to make us happy, was not the dreaded river
safely bridged? And was there not a path to lead us from the
wilderness? It was raining cheerfully in the morning, as it had
been doing off and on since we left the glacier, and we made
a leisurely start, struggling up through the forest till on a level
with the supposed bridge.[32]

The supposition was unfounded. There was no bridge. It had been
an optical illusion. In crestfallen mood, they quested up and down,
returned to the campsite, which now felt less idyllic and more a place
of captivity, and eventually found two flat-topped boulders with a

[30] Tilman, 'Nanda Devi', p.17.
[31] 'With a modicum of ghee added after the water had been drained off, these were
served and eaten as one would eat asparagus. Indeed Tilman's imaginative palate
detected some slight resemblance to that delicacy.' (Shipton, *Nanda Devi*, p. 240.)
Tilman the restaurant critic – how delicious a conceit is that!)
[32] Tilman, 'Nanda Devi', p.18.

span of twenty feet between them which they thought they could bridge. Ang Tharkay cut down two straight pines with his kukri for the morning, darkness fell, and round the fire a sense of foreboding was gathering. The nearest settlement shown on the map was called Gaundar and seemed to be eight miles away. But the map was old, remote villages could become abandoned, their rate of progress was desperately slow, a river had to be crossed in the morning, and for such food as the land supplied there was competition – the forest was full of bear tracks, bamboo shoots their favoured food, and the Sherpas continually shouted and sang to make sure the bears were aware of their presence and kept well away rather than being stumbled upon by surprise when they could be dangerous.

On the morning of the 13th, Ang Tharkay's kukri was once more in use cutting down two more trunks. As they shot them down a steep gully above the bridge site, a boulder Shipton estimated at two hundredweight was dislodged and hit Pasang, badly bruising his left arm and crushing a bone in his foot. Thenceforwards he was unable to carry a load, and was barely able to hobble for the rest of this section of the trip, his load divided between the other four members of the party. They, meanwhile, had managed to get one of the poles insecurely lodged on the far bank and braced with an even more precarious diagonal pole.

> On this flimsy structure Tilman, with a rope fastened to his waist, started to balance across the raging torrent. We stood watching him with bated breath as, inch by inch, he crept along the swaying poles. It was obvious that he *must* not either slip or upset the balance of the poles, whilst the further he went the more difficult was his task owing to the thinning of the tree-trunks towards the top and the consequently greater sag of the poles. But at length, with what looked like a cross between a leap and a fall, he landed on the other side.[33]

Once the bridge across the *nullah* had been reinforced and the party was across, the going became ever more difficult. The bamboo shoots dwindled and the mushrooms ran out:

> The side of the valley was exceedingly steep and we had to

---

[33] Shipton, *Nanda Devi*, pp.237–8.

hang on to the undergrowth to prevent ourselves from sliding down, while we hacked our way through the dense thorn-scrub. At times it took us as much as an hour to cover 25 yards, and we were hard put to it to go more than a mile a day. We used to halt each evening at 5.30. This gave us just time before dark to build a bamboo shelter under which we could protect a fire from the pouring rain, and so cook a meal of bamboo shoot and tea. Dead bamboo, however sodden it might be, makes most excellent kindling, and without it and a fair supply of paraffin we should have had to have foregone the luxury of a fire.[34]

Shipton comments in a letter to his mother on how they owed everything on this stage of the journey to the Sherpas 'wood-craft'. By the 17th, there was no more bamboo to be found, and they had omitted to pick and carry any with them. But they found signs of human passage in a shelter cave, were treated to some uncertain glimmerings of the sun, and ate half a cupful each of mouldering *satu* – the last food they were carrying. They covered scarcely three quarters of a mile before midday. Then deliverance! – suddenly they emerged from forest and brush into rough grazing land. Beyond it, on the far bank of the river, was cultivated land. The map had not lied. Gaundar, a tiny settlement of four houses, was still extant. Shipton records that Tilman responded with the same perfect equanimity he might have shown on a late descent into a Lakeland dale by commenting that they would be down in time for tea.[35]

'The old patriarch who met us was surprised almost out of his wits; almost, but not quite, for he retained sufficient grasp of himself to raise the price of *atta* to several times its current price; but we were too thankful to haggle.'[36] It had taken them nine days to cover the six crow-miles from the col above the ice falls and reach the

---

[34] Eric Shipton, 'Nanda Devi and the Ganges Watershed' (*Geographical Journal*, April 1935), p.317.

[35] This habit of reductive irony as means to emotional control was surely a result of – a way of coping with – his Great War experiences. It became a distinctive cast of mind, and we shall be coming to the most famous expression of it later in this chapter.

[36] *Himalayan Journal* 1935, ibid. p.19.

Madmaheswar valley. The inhabitants of Gaundar sold them, at the inflated price, all the food they could spare. It amounted to a few handfuls of *atta* and a cucumber. They also offered them shelter from the storm in a barn recently the quarters of the village goats. Two days later, in the still pouring rain, they reached the temple at Ukhimath lower down the valley, where the priests, intensely interested to hear of their travels, treated them with great kindness and hospitality and lodged them in the guest room, whilst a doctor tended to Pasang's foot. The increasingly disreputable (in terms of his dress) Tilman was even lent a pair of trousers by the secretary to wear for their dining and socialising: 'We seem to have caused no small sensation here and their hospitality is embarrassing in its lavishness, but I won't say it's not welcome after being wet for so long.'[37]

A mere six days' march from Ukhimath – on not quite such short commons, food being more plentiful hereabouts – took them along a good bridleway over a pass to the Alaknanda river crossing at Chamoli, where the postmaster advanced them some money and the local magistrate gave them a yoga lesson. With the rain now showing signs of abating, they moved on to Joshimath, where they hoped a few days' rest would allow Pasang's injured foot to mend sufficiently to allow him to carry a load again. The usual riches of correspondence awaited them, from which, among other matters, Shipton discovered that he was an uncle and his mother now a grandmother.

> My own Darling Mum,
>
> My very heartiest congratulations on your first grandchild. I couldn't bear to go off up the Rishi without knowing the news so yesterday I sent a wire to the hospital and got a reply just now: 'Mother and daughter doing splendidly'. I feel so excited about it that I wish I had someone to celebrate with.[38]

The implied reflexive comment on Tilman here is a very telling glimpse into the nature of their relationship. He carries on to mention a little plaintively that Wyn Harris now has a son, and asks his mother to write to 'Mrs Wyn', and he tells her also that he was

---

[37] Letter to Mrs Haly from Ukhimath Temple, of 20 August.
[38] Letter to Mrs Haly from Joshimath, 29n August 1934.

'most interested and surprised to hear about Wager's engagement. I do hope she is nice. I have a very deep friendship for old Waggers.'

Now began hasty preparations for a late return to the Nanda Devi Sanctuary and their unfinished survey work. Ang Tharkay was sent off to Mana to collect porters pre-arranged with Alum Singh, who had accompanied C. F. Meade on his Garhwali travels in 1912. The four left in Joshimath bought and packed food, and on 30 August the whole caravan was heading back for the Rishi Ganga. At Duraishi the shepherds were already preparing to leave for the winter. The hemp climbing rope left at the Rishi base camp had rotted in the perpetual damp and could be snapped like cotton. Thirteen of the Mana men came with them up the gorge itself, proving themselves safe on rock and indifferent to being alternately saturated and frozen:

> . . . before very long I came to have considerable respect for them as cragsmen, while their ever-ready wit and carefree laughter will remain as one of my pleasantest memories. They and the Sherpas came to be the very best of friends and I think there was a measure of genuine regret when the Mana men had to take their departure.[39]

Elsewhere Shipton tells of how they 'move just like cats on difficult ground, though they are tremendously impressed with the route'. The parting took place on 8 September, the Mana men having accompanied them all the way into the Sanctuary, where their first thought was to work out how they might get their herds up to graze. 'They had enjoyed the trip, but, shepherds as they were, they were sad to see such quantities of grass growing to no better purpose than to feed a few bharal.'[40]

Shipton and Tilman immediately set about exploring and surveying the southern branch of the basin, without the nervous strain imposed previously by those river crossings to the northern side:

> We are now in the southern section of the basin. The mountain structure here must be unique, and Nanda Devi itself is an

---

[39] *A.J.* 1935, p.72.
[40] *H.J.* 1935, p.21.

incredible sight. There seems to be even more game this side than in the northern section. I wish the weather would clear up. The fine weather is long overdue. Time is short and we are anxious to begin the exploration of this section. It will have to be rather a rough affair, and we won't have much time for plane-tabling.[41]

With the coming of the cold season imminent, they were anxious not to have to make a fourth passage of the Rishi gorge, and hence had to consider the two possible exits over the southern rim of the basin – the cols reached from the outside by Longstaff in 1905 and Ruttledge in 1932: 'We reconnnoitred the former col, which appeared to be practicable though difficult if one were carrying heavy loads, and, as the southern route would land us nearer home, decided to try it first.'

Tilman's perspective differs considerably on this:

. . . we saw enough of what we called 'Longstaff's Col' to decide us to leave it alone. It looked over 19,000 feet, and near the top, where it was very steep, we suspected ice. By now our boots were past their best, two of the Sherpas had no ice-axes, and we should be heavily laden.[42]

Turning their attention to Ruttledge's Col, they were diverted by the peak then known as East Trisul (now called Maiktoli Peak, 22,320 feet), which appeared from the Sanctuary side to present no technical problems. They placed a high camp at 20,000 feet. Tilman suffered severely from altitude sickness on the way up to it, and volunteered to return to the lower camp with Pasang to make more room in the tent for Shipton, Ang Tharkay and Kusang.

A more pleasant site . . . would be difficult to find, for it was situated in a meadow of short grass, sheltered by the moraine and huge boulders, with a clear stream running past the tents. It was at about 16,000 feet, but the nights were now fine enough to allow us to sleep out again. What a 'bedroom' it was! As dawn banished sleep, the opening eyes rested full upon the

[41] Note to Mrs Haly from Nanda Devi Sanctuary, 8 September, 1934.
[42] Tilman, 'Nanda Devi', p.22.

majestic outline of the 'Blessed Goddess' and watched the rosy light steal gently down her east-turned face.[43]

Apart from falling in love with a goddess, Tilman carried on plane-tabling in the southern sector of the basin, whilst on 12 September Shipton, with Ang Tharkay and Kusang, made the first ascent of Maiktoli Peak in dreadful snow conditions and 'a severe wind which was almost up to Everest standards'. There was a far more serious future objective to hand, however, and on 15 September from a camp at its base Shipton and Tilman set out to take a look at a subsidiary ridge that swept down from the intimidating south ridge of Nanda Devi in a great arc across the south face of both the mountain's peaks. Tilman's assessment of the possibility it offered was sanguine:

Having seen all sides of the mountain we concluded that this offers the only possible route. Yet from below this had appeared hopeless; we were surprised at the ease of the lower part: an experience which bears out the mountain 'proverb' – 'Rub your nose in a place before saying whether it will "go" or not!' At about 20,500 feet we turned back, having taken many photographs . . .[44]

Shipton's summing up of their reconnaissance of the route is serious and considered, and brings his growing sense of a necessary ethical approach to mountaineering into his consideration of the problems an attempt on Nanda Devi by this route might pose.

We were surprised to find that the rocks, sloping in our favour, were a good deal easier than they had appeared from a distance, so much so that before turning back we had reached an altitude which we calculated to be 20,500 feet, and I had come to the unexpected conclusion that the ridge was probably climbable. The general standard is certainly high and there would be no relief. Prolonged siege tactics would be too dangerous to be justifiable, since this method would involve too many porters and, if caught in bad weather high up, a party would be in a

43 Tilman, 'Nanda Devi', p.23.
44 Ibid.

very serious plight. Therefore I think that only a party of men
of proved capacity for quick acclimatisation and who have
had previous experience of mountaineering at 25,000 feet or
over should try the climb. I hope, too, that when the mountain
is attempted it will be tackled by a small party – in the spirit
of a sporting venture. Such a party will have the better chance
of getting up and are less likely to break their necks. We were
not equipped to make any serious attempt to go high and our
party by now was in poor condition.[45]

This is a very significant passage in many ways, and was taken as
such when it was read out in what was then British mountaineering's
main centre of power, in front of the activity's most influential
figures. In its weighing up of what he perceives as necessary for
success, there is a certain amount of special pleading, and a few
exclusion clauses, that suggest he was setting some considerable
store by the possibility of this peak for himself. I wonder at what
Tilman's response, when it appeared, would have been to the curt
laying down of rules about the necessity for quick acclimatisation
and experience at more than 25,000 feet. It is tantamount to a
dismissal of the notion that Tilman might have any claims on being
a member of anything but a support party in an attempted ascent.
Endorsement of the lightweight style they were establishing together
this summer notwithstanding, a bar is being laid down here. For
Shipton, Nanda Devi is a possibility. For Tilman, Shipton puts it
beyond the realms of reason. Yet judged by the available facts –
by that reality which in mountaineering decisions is an inevitable
and proper mode of accounting – Shipton was right. Tilman could
wax as sentimentally amorous as he liked about the goddess, but
the younger man was convinced that he alone was worthy of her
favours, and he had the evidence to support that view. How other
it would prove to be!

Two days after this quick foray on to the likely line of ascent, on 17
September the party began to make its way up towards Ruttledge's
Sunderdhunga Col. Before climbing the last slopes to the col they
made a huge cairn in which they stowed all the things which would,
by their discarding, lighten their loads. At the col, out came the plane
table and their last resections were made around the Sanctuary. The

[45] *A.J.* 1935, p.74.

ground plunged away beneath them to the south; beyond the snowy foreground the little Sunderdhunga river slipped out of a lake of vivid turquoise to disappear under the coverlet of cloud that spread away unbroken over the whole of the Gangetic plain. Their experiences on the watershed crossings now served them well as they stood in rags and cracked, nail-less boots and looked down six thousand feet of ice fall and precipice to the Sunderdhunga valley.

It took two days of patient and unremitting toil before they had worked out a complex route down to the summer grazing land of Maiktoli beneath. The outcome of each probing passage down was in doubt time and again until the last moment. On occasion, ice bollards had to be hacked out, from which they roped down, cutting off any possibility of retreat and committing themselves entirely to going on. The lethargic Holborn aneroid, anxious to regain the lower altitudes it preferred to record, escaped from the rucksack in which it was being carried and bounced away down the cliffs to come to its perpetual rest in the upper reaches of Maiktoli. So too did a tin of ghee, spattering its contents over the rocks, and the Sherpas swooped to cram it in their mouths or rub it into their boots and their hair: 'I made free use of the language with which Elie Richard used to curse me in those early Dauphine days.' Thus spruced or oiled, Ang Tharkay found the key that unlocked the last difficulty of the descent. It led to a shepherds' hut by the glacier, and a track leading down: 'That night we watched a vision of beauty beyond all possible description. There can be few cirques in the world grander and more awe-inspiring than the one we were in, and mists threading themselves about the glaciers and an almost full moon gave it an unearthly loveliness.'[46]

What was left was 'a struggle to find an exit from the grim gorge in the upper Sunderdhunga valley, into which we had blundered in a heavy mist; our last encounter with a swollen mountain torrent; an enormous feast of wild raspberries and Himalayan blackberries lower down the valley; the generous hospitality of the first villagers we met, and the sweetness of their honey.[47] Shipton wrote to his mother of the 'peaceful marches through gentle forest-clad hills – widely spaced oaks, open meadows teeming with pheasants and partridges. Long days of blissful peace – from the opening of eyes

---

[46] Letter to Mrs Haly from Ranikhet, 28 September 1934.
[47] Shipton, *Upon That Mountain*, p.169.

to see the smoke of the dawn fire mounting lazily into the trees, and the great ice-crests hanging in the upper air, to the blazing evening fire.' They were working their way across to and down the Pindar valley. On 27 September at Sameswar, they climbed on to a bus heading back south-east to Ranikhet, where 'four . . . long and interesting letters' from his mother were awaiting him, as well as one from Gustav Sommerfelt asking him to be godfather to the first child his wife was then expecting, and 'two very generous letters from Hugh Ruttledge who appears to be very excited about our first Basin effort.' What had been and to my mind still is the most radical and successful enterprise in the annals of mountain exploration was finally at an end: 'So another experience adds its quota to the store of memories, which, whatever happens in the future, must brighten life, even into very old age.'[48]

The sense throughout this correspondence with his mother, of a writer in the making, flexing his descriptive powers, trying things out to a trusted audience of one, is palpable. As is the fond closeness between them.

A few days later, on the station platform at Bareilly, after five months of intense mutual reliance, the party split up and its members went their separate ways: the three Sherpas back to their little township of Bhotia Busti above Darjeeling; Tilman to Calcutta and the Brocklebank boat; and Shipton back for the first time in many years to the Nilgiri Hills of Kerala, where his sister and brother-in-law and their new baby daughter lived, before moving on south to the Ceylon of his childhood, 'to recapture some of the enchantment of that lovely island which had sustained me in the first bleak years at school.'[49] Strange how his mind hovered around the abusive experiences at the Gifford academy during the most ambitious and exciting journeyings so far, or perhaps even of his life. He finally embarked for home in Colombo early in November on a cargo steamer, the SS *Makalla*.[50] This ageing vessel within a day of weighing anchor had developed engine problems, and crawled

---

[48] Letter to Mrs Haly from Ranikhet, 28 September 1934.
[49] Shipton, *That Untravelled World*, p.93.
[50] Another battered old Brocklebank boat, with its distinctive blue-banded single smokestack, sister ship to the SS *Mahsud* on which they'd sailed out from Liverpool seven months before. The SS *Makalla* now lies at fifty-five fathoms in the Moray Firth off Helmsdale, having been sunk by Heinkel bombers on 24 August 1940, and is a favoured location for diving.

across the Indian Ocean to Port Said at a speed of three knots. Without Tilman's loquacity to occupy him, Shipton for six weeks was forced into the unenviable and arduous occupation of writing the book for which his correspondence and journal gave such a fine basis: 'I doubt if in other circumstances I would have had the drive to persist beyond the first chapter. As with all my subsequent books, I resolved that this should be my last.'

There is an object lesson here in never taking the eternally playful Shipton entirely at his word. That this was to be his best book – which is not to dismiss the others, *That Untravelled World* in particular having all the flavour and complexity of a fine old cask-strength malt – was surely due to this intensely sociable man's shipboard confinement and isolation, allied to a subsequent lack of inexpert editorial interference. The sociable opportunities were restored once he arrived back at Lexham Gardens a week before Christmas 1934, and by then London had already been alerted to the magnitude of what he and Tilman, Ang Tharkay, Pasang and Kusang had achieved. On the correspondence page of the *Thunderer* itself in its weighty heyday, no less a personage than Hugh Ruttledge had written in the following terms:

To the Editor of *The Times*.

Sir, – Just over two years ago – to be exact, on August 22, 1932 – you were good enough to publish an account of the nine attempts which have been made to explore that great peak, Nanda Devi, the Goddess Mother of the Kumaun Himalaya, and the highest mountain situated entirely within British territory. The grim 70-mile ring of high mountains which surrounds Nanda Devi, with its 'inner sanctuary' and its only portal, the terrific gorge of the Rishiganga river, has kept the secret of the Seven Rishis so faithfully that until this year no human foot has trodden even the base of the main peak.

In April this year Mr E. E. Shipton, who was Mr Smythe's companion in the second assault on Mount Everest in 1933, set out with Mr Tilman to reconnoitre and, if possible, force the defences. The little expedition was organised with a complete lack of publicity or ostentation, yet letters which I have been privileged to receive from Mr Shipton convey the news that it has been magnificently successful.

Mr Shipton sent to Darjeeling for three of the Sherpas who

have done such splendid work on Everest; he kept them in reserve for the hardest work, and recruited locally in Kumaun the few men needed to carry his equipment and stores within striking distance. By deliberately 'living on the country' he was able to reduce numbers to a minimum; this is the secret of successful exploration in the Himalaya.

The chosen line of approach was the Rishiganga gorge, up which Dr T. G. Longstaff made his desperate attempt in 1907. In June the little party of two Englishmen and three Sherpas forced their way across the tremendous precipices of the gorge along traverses which were connected by the smallest and most fragile of links, and emerged triumphantly at the source of the river. They explored the northern glacier basin of Nanda Devi and hurriedly retreated by the way they had come, lest the first burst of the monsoon should cut them off. They spent July and a part of August in a difficult and incredibly laborious examination of the Bhagat Kharak and Arwa glacier systems and in finding their way up the Satopanth glacier and across the Badrinath–Kedarnath watershed. The weather was bad; at one period eight miles of progress cost them eight days of toil in pouring rain among thick jungle.

Then, the main strength of the monsoon being exhausted, they returned up the Rishiganga, mapped the southern basin of Nanda Devi, climbed a considerable distance up the peak itself, discovered what is probably, at the proper season, a practicable way to the top, and finally, in September, escaped over the very difficult Sonadunga [*sic*] col, the descent of which on its southern side was a masterpiece of icecraft.

I have given only the barest details of what I unhesitatingly declare to be one of the finest exploits of mountain exploration ever performed. For the full story we must wait till Mr Shipton's return home next month. Then we shall receive a lesson in organisation, handling of men, travel on small resources, courage, and the highest mountaineering ability. And I know that Mr Shipton will be the first to acknowledge the help which Himalayan mountaineers expect, and never fail to receive, from that prince of good fellows, the Sherpa porter.

I am, Sir, your obedient servant,

Hugh Ruttledge,

Gometra Island, Argyllshire.

Not a bad testimonial, on the whole, to receive from your former boss – and interesting, too, in the way that it endorses a style and values that essentially undermine those of the project of the previous year in which they had both been involved. It rather corroborates the widely held view among his contemporaries that Ruttledge was a man of decency and principle who was twice thrust as compromise candidate into a role for which he was quite unsuited.

On his return to England, Shipton quickly set about arranging the follow-up to the Garhwal adventure, the success of which had earned him the Royal Geographical Society's Gill Memorial Award – one of the lesser of the society's prestigious annual prizes, carrying with it a financial grant of £52 which enabled him to pay off all his small debts from the expedition. More importantly, through the RGS connection he was given to understand that the possibility of financial backing for future exploratory projects was open to him. Chief among these, obviously, was a return trip to Nanda Devi with the line leading on to the south ridge and an ascent by that as their objective. Events, however, were to move on rather quickly before even the 'back of an envelope', which was all Tilman and Shipton deemed strictly necessary for the planning of an expedition, could be filled with their scribble.

The catalyst was an evening meeting of the Royal Geographical Society on 4 February 1935 in the grand old lecture theatre at Kensington Gore – chosen as venue in recognition of the importance of what had been achieved, and the likely large audience in consequence – at which Shipton read his succinct paper published in the *Geographical Journal* for April 1935, 'Nanda Devi and the Ganges Watershed'. Its reception was as close to rapturous as gentlemanly would allow. It was noted particularly, in those penurious times, how the expenditure of the entire expedition, including food, fares to India and payment for their Sherpas and porters, amounted to only £143.10s.0d. each for Shipton and Tilman. These two were not only decent and enterprising young chaps, they came at a bargain price. All the distinguished old buffers present were reminded of when they too were insouciant, energetic, hard up and fleet of foot. And they were all there – Longstaff and Strutt, Schuster and Meade, Ruttledge and Norton and many others besides.

Before they huffed and bustled off to their clubs or Soho or to catch the late trains back to Godalming, Winchester or Saffron Walden, there was an intense discussion. Tilman spoke, modestly and to the point, concerned as ever to pass the credit back to his superior officer or leader:

> I have never previously faced an audience, and I beg to be excused more than a word or two. Really, there is nothing for me to add to what the lecturer has said. He has made clear every aspect except, of course, what he himself did. I should like to say that these small successes of ours were not quite fortuitous but mainly the result of very careful planning on the part of the leader. He expressed appreciation of the work of the Sherpas, but it must be remembered that these men will only give of their best under such leadership as we enjoyed. He also observed that we climbed on the shoulders of our predecessors, so I venture to hope that means will be found to build upon our work in the near future.[51]

Rather close to overt begging, this last, and I'm not sure how it would have gone down had the debate not quickly moved on and Tom Longstaff chipped in to praise the project at length, explain the background, and exult in its following of his own style of self-sufficiency and economy; Brigadier Norton, the real hero of the 1924 Everest expedition and a man held in near-universal esteem, stood up to say a few words about his fellow old soldier and former comrade in the Royal Horse Artillery that would have been well-received in this company: 'I had the privilege of working with [Tilman] nearly twenty years ago during the Great War. From what I knew of him then I am not at all surprised to hear that he was so able a seconder of so fine a leader.'

Damned fine adjutant, what! In an odd way, this last was the death thrust to their hopes of an immediate Nanda Devi return. How that might have worked anyway, so soon after the first reconnaissance and with Tilman lacking that 'proved capacity for quick acclimatisation' and 'previous experience of mountaineering at 25,000 feet' considered essential by Shipton, is open to question. Tilman had seemed time and again to reach a ceiling at around 20,000 feet. Another 5,000 feet or more is a huge addition at those heights. But it wasn't going to happen, and they would never go back to the Sanctuary or set foot on Nanda Devi together again. The

---

[51] *G.J.* April 1935, p.320.

great and the good and the merely influential of the mountaineering establishment at that February meeting had pricked up their ears at all those ringing endorsements of 'so fine a leader', and within the space of a very few weeks a project far dearer to those hardened, powerful and disputatious hearts than that of merely the highest mountain in the British Empire was once again under discussion. The highest mountain of them all had suddenly become available for two years running, the Tibetan Government quixotically granting permission for expeditions in 1935 and 1936. It was already the beginning of March, the Mount Everest Committee had £1,400 left in its kitty, and Shipton, for all his radicalism and exploratory bent, had 'previous' where this mountain was concerned:

> Having once taken a share in the attempts to climb the mountain, it was hard to stand aside . . . Any one year might yield the right conditions for an unhampered climb up that last, 1,000 foot pyramid of rock upon which so much eager speculation had been lavished. It was like a gambler's throw, in which a year of wide opportunity in untrodden fields was staked against the chance of a week of fine weather and snow-free rock.[52]

Shipton could even argue that he was extending his small-party/limited-budget philosophy to what was deemed the greatest prize of them all, and that if he could prove it effective in this context, the debate would be concluded and won: '. . . my dislike of massive mountaineering expeditions had become something of an obsession, and I was anxious for the opportunity to demonstrate that, for one-tenth of the former cost and with a fraction of the bother and disruption of the local countryside, a party could be placed on the North Col, adequately equipped to make a strong attempt on the summit.'[53] He was the obvious if not the only candidate who could be expected to lead a hastily assembled expedition in 1935 with the specific brief of finding out whether monsoon snow on the north side was sufficiently consolidated in July and August, to test likely candidates for the 1936 expedition that could now be planned, and to follow up and further the exploratory work of

[52] Shipton, *Upon That Mountain*, pp.172–3.
[53] Shipton, *That Untravelled World*, p.95.

the 1921 reconnaissance expedition to the mountain. The Mount
Everest Committee, scarcely needing the prompt supplied to them
by Ruttledge, duly appointed Shipton leader of a reconnaissance
expedition[54] (an attempt on the summit itself was specifically
forbidden in the contract) to head out within the month. He was
allotted almost all of the balance at their disposal, and he buckled
down to the task of planning.

His first consideration, the Sherpas being more or less self-selecting
if available, was to assemble the team of British mountaineers to
be taken. A natural first choice, difficulties with acclimatisation
notwithstanding, was his companion of 1934, who, true to his
belief that the definition of an expedition was a party with too many
members, proved not a little reluctant to forgo reacquaintance with
his beloved goddess of the majestic outline and averted face: 'At first
Tilman did not like the idea of abandoning our plans – I think the
idea of travelling with a large party oppressed him – but after a little
discussion he waived his objections.'[55] Shipton talked him round by
explaining that the structure of the trip would give them freedom
to wander through the valleys and over the peaks around Everest
for several months, and would also enable them to reinforce the
paradigm of the light party living off the land that they both held
most dear. His unsociable friend having been converted, he began to
recruit the remaining four members of the team.

There were two Cambridge medics, Charles Warren and Edmund
Wigram, and a Cambridge mathematician turned Marlborough
schoolmaster in Edwin Kempson. There was also an expert New
Zealand ice-climber in 'Dan' Bryant, a character who could on
occasion match even Tilman for taciturnity, though he was also a
gifted raconteur and proved to be an extremely popular member.

---

[54] A recent addition to the vast literature of Everest, Tony Astill's *The Forgotten
Adventure – Mount Everest: The Reconnaissance 1935* (privately published, 2005)
– a finely produced and well-researched volume that was deserved winner of the
Mountaineering History Award at the Banff Mountain Book Festival in 2006 –
recounts this important and underrated trip in great detail. Unsworth's dismissal
of the 1935 trip as of no consequence in his history of Everest seems to me lofty
and incorrect. Quite apart from its wealth of exploratory ascents around Everest,
Spender's survey work was of the first importance, the reports on weather and
snow conditions valuable, and the impressions of individual climbers' reactions
to altitude useful. In other words, it achieved everything it set out to do, which is
generally taken as a definition of success.
[55] Shipton, *Upon That Mountain*, p.172.

He had recently been taking a course at the London School of Economics and had spent a season of guideless climbing in the Alps before heading back to the Antipodes.[56] A seventh member was suddenly thrust upon them, and Shipton gives the curious tale of this in *That Untravelled World*:

> Lawrence Wager was then organising an expedition to Greenland, and I spent a weekend with him discussing food, equipment and other matters. Talking of the composition of his party, he told me that he had come to the conclusion that it was a great advantage to include one member so universally disliked that the others, with a common object for their spleen, would be drawn together in close comradeship. Though an expedient employed by most successful dictators, I was astonished to hear it proposed in this context, particularly by someone as temperate and warm-hearted as Wager. He went on to tell me that he had found the perfect subject for his experiment in Michael Spender, a brilliant surveyor and an excellent traveller, but a man whose overbearing conceit had made him most unpopular on each of his several expeditions. Happily he did not seem to notice, let alone resent the fact.[57]

Nor did the perennially decent Shipton ever relate any conclusions drawn from the experience of hearing very soon after his weekend with Wager that the surveyor delegated to the expedition by the RGS was to be none other than Michael Spender. No doubt Wager wore his habitual wry smile, and to postulate that he had played any part in the imposition is no more than conjecture – though his close friend Jack Longland was still snorting with amusement about the joke half a century later.

In a sense the 'experiment' backfired, because the effortlessly affable Shipton soon became a close friend of his near neighbour in Kensington – there is surely a lesson about the universal human

---

[56] Bryant's inclusion on the 1935 expedition – apparently the chance result of his dropping off whilst at the LSE an application form at the RGS for inclusion on an Everest expedition – through the genial and competent impression he made led directly to Ed Hillary and George Lowe's inclusion on the 1951 and 1953 Everest expeditions. So another success of the 1935 expedition was in determining the summit party of 1953 (see below).

[57] Shipton, *That Untravelled World*, p.95.

tendency towards calumny to be learned from this, which is to judge from your own direct experience and never from hearsay, the human capacity for malice and mendacity being so infinite (though neither Longland nor Wager was remotely thus – they were just humorous mischief-makers):

> It was easy to see how he [Spender] had made himself dis-liked, for he had an arrogant manner and a provocative way of expressing wildly unorthodox views, which effectively disguised the fact that he himself did not necessarily hold them. He was sensitive and honest enough to be well aware of his faults and sometimes revealed surprising humility.[58]

You can see from this why Shipton was much loved, but you might also deduce from its easy-going tolerance and non-judgemental tone why the doubts eventually began to be voiced about his capacity for 'leadership' in ventures of supposed national importance. 'They say he lacked the killer instinct,' that fine and distinguished old mountaineer Charles Evans once told me, before adding, after a perfectly-weighted pause, 'Not a bad thing to lack, in my view.'

The contract having been signed, a joint passport was duly posted from the British Residency in Gangtok for collection at Thangu, through which the team would pass. It stipulated that the climbers

> must not (a) roam about, at their will, in any part of Tibetan territory, up or down, other than that specified above ['the snowy mountain of Cha-ma-lung'], (b) offend the suscep-tibilities of the Tibetan by disturbing and killing birds or other wild animals inhabiting various sacred places and (c) beat or maltreat the people in any way. Responsibility must be accepted by all concerned without any shirking. Given under our seal on the 27th day of the 3rd month of the Wood-Pig Year. Black square seal of the cabinet ministers of Tibet.

Tilman, the expedition's quartermaster, as ever was the first to set sail, leaving Liverpool on 13 April aboard a Brocklebank ship,

---

[58] Shipton, *That Untravelled World*, p.96.

the SS *Matra*[59] – a lightly-laden cargo steamer of 7,911 tons that rolled in the calmest sea, gave a memorably miserable crossing of the Bay of Biscay, and had among its crew officers from previous Brocklebank ships on which Tilman had sailed. He occupied his time with chess, deck tennis, the usual frantic onslaughts on the medicine ball (on Good Friday it was lost overboard), and making brief entries in his terse journal-cum-commonplace-book:

> Tuesday 23rd April: 'Once in a saintly passion I cried in desperate grief,/Oh Lord my soul is black with guile, of sinners I am chief?/Then stooped my Guardian Angel & whispered from behind,/'Vanity my little man, you're nothing of the kind'.
> Tuesday 30th April: 'B[ugger]' – a Term of endearment used by sailors. Johnson.

He arrived in India on 10 May. By midday on the 12th – very swift progress, the last stage by bus at a cost of thirty rupees for the fifty-two steep miles from the Darjeeling Mail's terminus at Siliguri rather than the narrow-gauge trains of the Himalayan Railway – he was in Darjeeling, settling into the Planters' Club, busying himself about their logistical needs and awaiting the arrival eight days later of most of the other team members: 'How much nicer to be surrounded by these hill people than Bingalis. What faces some of them have – one can't help liking them.'

Shipton had travelled down to the south of France with his mother, and having picked up Kempson they joined Warren and Wigram, who had sailed from London on the P&O's SS *Strathwind*, at Marseilles (a photograph presumably taken by his mother shows the four dapper young gentlemen scrambling on the sea cliffs of the island of Chateau d'If in the bay at Marseilles – Kempson looks to have the most rock awareness among them). The whole party finally assembled in Darjeeling on 21 May ('Eric, Spender and Mrs Haly. Got busy packing') and set up camp at the Planters' Club. Spender, adopting the photo-realism tone of his younger

---

[59] As a token of the darker times coming that would end the 1930s mountain idyll, it's worth recording that the SS *Matra* was one of the early casualties of the Second World War, sunk by German mines in full view of Ramsgate in the Thames Estuary in 1939. The old, slow fleet of Brocklebank cargo-steamers that had been so crucial a factor in Shipton and Tilman's early explorations was decimated in this conflict.

brother Humphrey, described Darjeeling in habitually peremptory tones as follows: '. . . altogether like an English watering place in the rain. Stupid bored Europeans walking about. Natives cadging. A few poor cinemas. The whole false. Stayed at the Planters' Club amongst a few grousing old Colonels.' Probably fair comment, though it gives you an inkling of why, in some quarters, Spender was so heartily disliked, the mountaineer's ego often being a delicate affair.

Tilman had already been in contact with Karma Paul and together they had arranged for fourteen Sherpas to join the expedition, but on his arrival, Shipton concluded that they were perhaps still a couple short, so another row of young optimists was assembled. Each of them was hoping to win a prestigious position accompanying the sahibs on their otherwise incomprehensible quest for the lion of solid gold believed to grace the top of Chomolungma. They filed past in front of Shipton as he sat with Tilman and W. J. Kydd, the Darjeeling secretary to the Himalayan Club, around a table outside the Planters' Club. One of the score or so in the procession was a teenage lodger of Ang Tharkay's with no papers or experience as a porter, a new (and newly-pregnant) wife, a fine physique and a winning smile. The latter won him the job[60] and it was to prove a prescient choice on Shipton's part: '. . . there was one Tibetan lad of nineteen, a newcomer chosen largely because of his attractive grin. His name was Tensing Norkay – or Tensing Bhotia as he was generally called.'[61]

The caravan, much smaller than the one of two years before, fewer pack animals being needed, the Fortnum & Mason's hampers previously considered an essential stimulant to appetite at altitude having been dispensed with as undesirable as well as outside the £200-per-man budget, trailed out of Darjeeling on 24 May at a leisurely pace along the Tista valley into Sikkim and thence across

---

[60] This caused a certain amount of friction among the Sherpa community of Darjeeling, Tenzing having slipped in ahead of several certified and experienced older men. The fact that he was a Bhotia (a native of Tibet, rather than of Sola Khumbu, the Sherpa homeland – though in fact all Sherpas are of Tibetan extraction, and the point at issue was really one of how recently) probably exacerbated this. For an extended, highly intelligent and informed discussion of this and other matters relating to the Sherpas, the essential text is Ed Douglas's pithily written and diligently researched *Tenzing: Hero of Everest* (National Geographic, 2003).
[61] Shipton, *That Untravelled World*, p.97.

the Kongra La into Tibet, Tilman waxing almost loquacious in his journal:

Friday, 24th. 17 mules arrived, 8 [of] which took 34 maunds. 6 loads went by coolie to Testa bridge. Lot of photographing. Lunch at Plivas. Started 2.30, three men & 3 rucksacks in an Austin but only got to the garage where we were told the cars were overloaded. Finally settled on 3 cars at Rs60 instead of 67.8. Warren and I in last car left at 3.15. arrived Bridge @ 5.30, trouble with battery. Met [Karma] Paul and 6 coolie loads on car. Halfway up found B(ryant) and S(hipton) with big end gone. Arrived Himalayan Hotel but no sign of Paul. Had some tea and started to look for Paul in bazaar. Back to pub and set off again in dark . . . Went up to Pundit Jhong's House, Tibetan official – Pretty wife – invited in. No Paul. Car won't go with lights on – used hand torch – met mules 8 p.m. just arriving – back at pub 8.15, found Paul. Not clear what he's been doing. Dinner and a tough social evening – helped out by signing autographs and looking at photos. Bed at 11 – heavy rain. S[hipton] to escort a girl home 10m away – poor mutt. Incense – green spiral – for mosquitoes. Pray heaven the loads are under cover. Kalimpong.[62]

And again:

Sunday, 26th. Mules got away at 9–10 & we had a long slippery descent to Resi chu & up 2,000 ft to Rhenok where we had tea & bananas. Down again to Rangi chu, cantilever bridge. A long plug up 2,000ft to here Pakhyong at 9 p.m. All very tired, 2 mules not in. No chowkidar. difficult to get food. Big veg. soup. misty day – slight rain. Nobody very helpful, except K[empson] & S[hipton]. chupatties not very popular.

In his brief stay in London between return from Colombo and beginning the journey to Calcutta, Shipton had been working with Dr S. S. Zilva of the Lister Institute of Preventive Medicine on its project to define the role of vitamins in the nutritional deficiency

---

[62] For these transcripts from the University of Wyoming archive, I am indebted to Tony Astill.

diseases that were widespread in Europe and elsewhere. He and Dr Zilva had devised a diet to provide 4,000 calories a day based quite closely on what the 1934 team had eaten – cheese, sugar, dried milk, dhal, flour, ghee, biscuits and pemmican supplemented by vitamins, iron and what local produce in the way of vegetables, eggs, goat or mutton, garlic and chillies that they could acquire along the way. So quails' eggs and foie gras were out – 'they lose all their charm when eaten as a mangled mess out of a battered tin on which someone has probably cut his finger'[63] – and in their place were *aloo paratha*, mutton curry and cabbage *subzhi*.

> While we were on the march we lived largely off the country. Mutton was easy to procure, though at first the sheep were rather thin. We cooked the meat in pressure cookers and the result was a great success . . . We could generally get potatoes and onions . . . Eggs were plentiful in the villages.

They had Tilman with them, who added in his own 'small good thing' to the dietary arrangements – his ability to bake a fine loaf in a makeshift oven, apparently using *atta* and the yeast the Lister Institute had prescribed to ward off vitamin B deficiency problems. They all ate heartily throughout (apart from when altitude sickness affected them), thus endorsing a fundamental precept in the Longstaff/Shipton/Tilman ethos of travelling simply and using what food was available locally – though Shipton admitted he might have gone too far in coercing people unused to basic food into making so drastic a dietary change. The implications of their policy could potentially have brought them into conflict with the Tibetan authorities, who had observed the effect in the past of expeditions on the grand scale and were concerned that the introduction of a cash economy into remote regions was likely to have a deleterious influence on the local people; Shipton himself was sensitive around the issue and in his subsequent paper to the RGS he elaborates with considerable diplomacy around the point:

> Now as in 1933 we were received with the greatest possible courtesy and hospitality by the Tibetans. The head man of Sar gave us free use of his house. He held several banquets

---

[63] Shipton, *Upon That Mountain*, p.175.

at which we were fed lavishly and entertained by music and dancing. Our host was a great connoisseur of *chang*[64] and it was no penance to drink with him. The evenings occasionally became somewhat boisterous.[65]

In a letter to his mother of 26 June, Shipton glosses around this last point:

We had a good evening last night. We were invited to supper at the house of the local Dzong Pen [village head man] and did us very well. The evening opened with the usual and rather tedious shower of compliments from both sides accompanied by Tibetan tea (with butter and salt); then supper, followed by *chang*, and some very good local brandy and much dancing and singing. The evening was a very beautiful one, the colouring surpassed even that of the usual Tibetan sundown. This and the *chang* inspired a speech, which I believe really impressed our host. One felt at least that one was sincere in what one was saying. Anyway in his reply he said he was convinced that we must have been Buddhist monks.

To return to his representation to the Royal Geographical Society on the effect of passing expeditions on Tibetan communities, and the soundings he had taken among these, Shipton continues:

Several times this year I took the opportunity of asking these head men the reason for their objecting to Europeans entering their country. In each case they replied that they believed that money and Western civilisation could do nothing for them but promote unhappiness. I feel sure that the British Government would wish that this point of view should be respected.[66]

The same points were pursued in the correspondence columns of *The Times*, where representatives of a younger and more radical generation than that represented on the Mount Everest Committee

---

[64] The potent Tibetan beer.
[65] The veiled reference here is to an argument between Ang Tharkay and the only son of the headman, in which the two came to blows and reparation had to be made. For more detail, see Douglas, *Tenzing*, p.70.
[66] (*G.J.*, 1936), p.100.

expressed their views. The likes of Marco Pallis and Michael Spender were vociferous here, and the latter's contribution, besides giving a very good impression of the man's character and intelligence, is particularly cogent:

> The part of Tibet traversed by the Mount Everest expeditions is by Tibetan standards and in comparison with the northern deserts fairly fertile. But actually only just enough barley is grown or can be grown to pay taxes and to carry the population through the winter and spring. The flocks of sheep and yaks are just as large as the grazing will permit. When an Everest expedition comes with 300 animals and a horde of hungry porters, reserves of food are broken into and sold: while grass which should have fed Tibetan ponies goes into the stomachs of the visiting yaks. It is true that good silver, British Indian rupees, are given in exchange. But, as a headman remarked to us in 1935 just after receiving Rs. 200, what good will that silver do? It cannot buy more corn where there is no surplus, nor will it fertilise the pastures. But it will certainly cause the neighbouring headman to be jealous, and enduring quarrels may be started. Where the balance between production and consumption is already precarious and where there are no reserves to draw upon the effect of a large expedition is materially disastrous.[67]

Since their chief purpose officially was to study snow conditions during the monsoon, and since their contract with the Mount Everest Committee expressly forbade them from making a bid for the summit, they felt under no pressure of time and so Shipton took the opportunity to investigate the country to the south of the Lashar Plain with 'its impression of an immense tangle of high peaks' that had been such an enticement to Wager and himself.

> . . . we explored the very beautiful ranges of Nyönno Ri and

---

[67] Quoted by Tilman along with more from the correspondence in *Everest 1938* (Tilman, ibid. p.434). This title did not appear until 1948, but it makes clear that the dialectic was ongoing in the five years before the successful (and huge) quasi-militaristic enterprise of 1953 – when the expedition equipment even included mortars and bombs so that a *feu de joie* could be fired off when *conquest* was assured.

Ama Drime which had been so attractive to Wager and myself in 1933. The party was split up into three, and in this way we managed to cover much ground in a short time. There is a great deal of interesting work to be done in this district if the sanction of the Tibetan authorities can be obtained.[68]

In fact, as he well knew, their passport expressly ruled out any such errant projects and the party was soon whipped in. Tilman:

> June 21st. Spender arrived in the morning better. Arranged food for 2 parties of 3 and A[ng Tharkay] to cross Nyönno Ri & make for Kharta. Packed up remainder of loads. Any tin in any sack as we wanted to get done. Presented 3 bottles of Cod oil to Sar and threw away a lot of yeast. As we were having our last meal, Paul came to say the Headman had received a verbal message from Tingri to the effect that we were to follow the usual route to Everest. A letter of protest has gone off to some other official. Felt very ill all night – mainly I think as a result of eating too much. Sar.
>   June 26th. Negotiations failed & accordingly at 10 we all went round by the road. 25 donkeys & half-bred Yaks. Through Phuru (chang & eggs) & over a little pass & at 4 p.m. we reached Tranak. Pleasant spot by a lake. Masses of eggs & milk. Rain in the night – loads all wet.[69]

In unguarded terms in a letter to his mother, Shipton comments on how 'it is a great nuisance having one's leg tied by their silly medievalism. One has to be frightfully careful though in view of The Expedition next year'. Tibetan officialdom prevailed, however, and sent the expedition directly on its way to Everest.

The method Shipton had devised of maximising the party's potential for exploration by dividing it into three light teams capable of covering terrain at great speed was an effective one and – time spent on the central purpose of checking mid-monsoon Everest aside – enabled the phenomenal amount of pioneering work on lesser peaks and surrounding high passes that the 1935 reconnaissance achieved: 'Spender had been putting in some splendid work, and,

---

[68] Ibid.
[69] Astill transcript (University of Wyoming).

by starting at 2 a.m. every day, had covered an enormous amount of country with his photo-theodolite.'[70]

From the Nyönno Ri the party could see that weather conditions on Everest itself were perfect, and several mountaineering historians, ignoring the fact that Shipton was hide-bound by the agreement signed with his paymasters and mandated by the Tibetan government, have suggested that he should have attempted pulling off a coup. He had, of course, already been warned once by the Tibetans for straying beyond agreed boundaries, and had he done so, it would have been to risk another 'affair of the dancing lamas', which would not have gone down well with the Mount Everest Committee given that permission for a full-scale expedition in 1936 had been given and could as easily have been withdrawn. Even Walt Unsworth, in a generally well-reasoned and balanced account,[71] asserts that 'Shipton missed his one great opportunity of proving the viability of a small expedition on Everest.'

This seems to me a very dubious argument, which doesn't take into account the unproven (and in the event weak) nature of the 1935 team, and the dishonour, whatever the outcome and especially in the event of the likely unfavourable one, that would attach to Shipton as a man prepared on a whim to break a signed contractual agreement. Shipton acted perfectly correctly and with due sense of his wider responsibilities to the patrons as leader in the situation. He also did better by proceeding slowly and acclimatising his team on the lower peaks, and anyway was experiencing for the first time difficulties with the Sherpas, who were behaving erratically this year (Ang Tharkay's thumping of the Sar headman's son being a case in point), and proving intransigent on occasion around demarcation disputes over load-carrying – the start of the ascent of the Sherpas into a quasi-unionised aristocracy of mountain porters.

They arrived at Rongbuk on 4 July ('Everest greeted us with the grandest view I have ever had of her – only her head showing, frowning down on us from an impossible height above the clouds. In her mantle of monsoon snow she looks ten times as beautiful but also ten times as formidable'), and obtained the customary audience with the old abbot at the monastery. At Rongbuk also, an intriguing new possibility was tentatively reported to them: 'There are strange

[70] Letter to Mrs Haly from Sar, 25 June 1935.
[71] *Everest*, pp.196–7.

rumours of a messenger from the Government of Nepal, who is reported to be chasing me. I am vaguely hoping that it may be an invitation to cross the Nepal frontier, which would be very exciting indeed.'[72]

The supposed messenger duly turned up, having been waiting for them in the environs of Rongbuk all along. He was another Sherpa, a former lama, who had arrived there a few days before, having heard they were on the way. Sen Tenzing, 'The Foreign Sportsman' as he was known thereafter from his dapper habits of dress, was duly signed up and became a regular, energetic and popular member of the Shipton retinue thereafter, chanting them along their way with his outlandish stories of the Yeti and other such mountain marvels, and his incessant basso profundo prayers, he and Pasang duetting at times in their supplications to the deities.

Two days later they set off south along the glacier from Rongbuk, carrying food and equipment for a month. 'There is one good thing about this time of year and that is one does escape from that filthy wind.'[73] The glacial rivers were swollen and the crossings slowed them down. Over some of them rope bridges had to be constructed, and loads carefully ferried across. The monsoon had now begun and there was a great deal of fresh snow on the upper parts of the mountain. Branching off up the East Rongbuk glacier, they reached Camp Three on 8 July, within sight of which and only a few hundred yards away they came across the body of Maurice Wilson.[74] Warren

---

[72] Letter to Mrs Haly from Rongbuk, 5 July 1935.

[73] Ibid.

[74] Maurice Wilson (1898–1934) was the son of a wealthy Yorkshire mill-owner. He had risen to the rank of captain in the Great War. An exact contemporary of Tilman's, he won the Military Cross at the Battle of Passchendaele in 1917. Thereafter he had been severely wounded – he never fully recovered the use of his left arm – and spent some years drifting around America and New Zealand before a visionary experience in 1932 convinced him to fly to Everest and make an attempt to climb the mountain for religious and philosophical reasons. Despite many official manoeuvres to prevent him, in 1933 he succeeded in flying solo in a second-hand Gipsy Moth from England to India, where his plane, which he had intended to crash-land high on the mountain, was impounded. The following March he made it to Rongbuk in company with three Sherpas whose conduct towards him seems not to have been beyond reproach, and attempted the mountain. There are those who believe, as with Mallory, that he reached the summit, though in Wilson's case this is even more wildly improbable. One slightly bizarre note in this admirable saga is a story which circulated widely at gossip level to the effect that when Wilson's tent and remains were found, there were women's shoes (perhaps herein some parallel explanation for those found by

worried that the already delicate equilibrium with the Sherpas might be further upset by encountering the corpse, whilst Tilman noted of them laconically, 'Blokes seemed quite unmoved by W's body. One took his boots.' They wrapped Wilson's remains in those of his tent and buried both in a nearby crevasse. Kempson read to them from the diary they had found by the body. Afterwards they consolidated the food dump and intermediate camp at 21,250 feet before setting to work the following day on reaching variously the Lakhpa La or the Chang La (North Col). Here's Tilman's account of the situation from his journal:

July 10th. Four of the blokes [i.e. Sherpas] pleaded sick & refused to move. Rest very sticky & we did not start till 10.30 with 7 loads of food. It started to snow soon after starting which was some relief from blazing heat. The snow on the col was pretty good & we got to somewhere near Camp IV. I was cooked and K[empson] nearly & the blokes refused to go any further & left loads where they stood. All came down in bad tempers & very cold and wet. Back at 4, some tea & soup. Difficult to know what to do what with bad weather & the temper of the Sherpas. Talk of sending them down. Snow haranguing them? 6 p.m. still snowing.

July 12th. The North Col party left at 9.30. Jingmay and Nima (our 2 porters) left for Base at 10, so W[igram] & I are left sitting here to do what we like or can – attractive enough if I felt capable of moving but I don't. At 11 we started with 2 light loads of food & tent – crossed the glacier to a rock rib & dumped the loads a few hundred feet up, preparatory to a high camp . . . Started back at 1.30 having watched the N. Col

---

Vivienne de Watteville at the Skating Lake?) in the former and Wilson himself was wearing women's undergarments. This seemingly imperishable rumour has made him an unlikely hero of the transvestite interest. Heaven knows what the modern breed of mountain photographers would have made of it, or to what organs their 'exclusives' would have been sold, had it been true. However, when I recorded an interview with Charles Warren at his Essex home in 1986, Warren brought the subject up and was at pains to point out that he had seen none of these items, and that a purported 'sex diary' that featured in the story had also escaped his attention (this presumably not being the one from which Kempson had read to them in Tilman's account). He attributed the story to Shipton's sometimes mischievous sense of humour, which on this occasion was perhaps not in the best of taste. The echo of Vivienne de Watteville's story is interesting, however.

party reach the top [i.e. of the col]. Both felt incredibly weak coming back & reached camp dead beat at 4 p.m. Moved up into porters' tent on rocks. Camp 3A, 21,000 Eat food but no appetite – pemmy revolting.

'July 14th. Windy night. Started 7 a.m., very cold. The snow soon disappointed us by turning to great crust & soft below – Step kicking the whole way. Reached the col 8 a.m. . . . No view – all thick. Both very tired coming down – sitting glissade most of the way. Very done up on reaching tent. Decided to stay another night for the other peak. Very unpleasant. Nothing to smoke or read and nothing pleasant to eat if we felt like eating – which you don't. Damn all high climbing.[75]

Shipton, meanwhile, with more energy and rather better spirits was probing tentatively at the crucial approaches to the Chang La: '. . . we examined the slopes beneath the North Col with extreme care. Kempson had had wide experience of winter mountaineering in the Alps, and by now I had seen a good deal of Himalayan snow conditions. *We could find nothing wrong with the slopes.*' (My italics, to further emphasise a sentence that is loaded with significance.)

After three days of hard work, in which altitude problems were affecting Tilman and Bryant in particular, they had established a camp at the foot of the north-east ridge right on the crest of the North Col, stocked it with food for fifteen days, and had it manned by Shipton, Kempson and Warren with nine Sherpas. Here at 23,000 feet they intended to spend a few days acclimatising before taking a light camp up to about 26,000 feet to find out about snow conditions at that height. The weather, however, intervened, and they were penned in their tents for four days. When it cleared, there was so much soft, fresh snow that they decided to retreat, leaving food and tents in place for a further attempt.

'. . . the slopes below did not seem to have altered materially since we made our cautious ascent. We descended in two parties: Kempson and I were in front with five Sherpas, while Warren was somewhere behind with the other four. We had not gone far before we were brought up sharp at the brink of

---

a sudden cut-off which stretched for several hundred yards in either direction. This indicated that an enormous avalanche had recently broken away along the line of our ascending tracks: in fact, the whole face of the slope had peeled off to a depth of six feet. This was an alarming discovery . . .[76]

Brooding on the incident, Shipton accorded it major significance. It decided him immediately to abandon the stores and tents and have nothing more to do with the North Col during the monsoon; and it caused him ultimately to conclude that the period of possibility in which Everest might be climbed was the 'exceedingly short interval between the end of winter and early spring gales, and the arrival of the monsoon' – a reasonable verdict, given the equipment available at the time. He added that in 1933 there had been no such interval. All in all, the 'grim and joyless'[77] business of Everest had proven itself thus once again. The parlous conditions had even restricted one of Shipton's main aims on this trip:

Tomorrow we start up the Central Rongbuk Glacier, on a stunt for which I am allowing two weeks. The main idea is to get into and explore the Western Cwm of Everest. Judging from what we have seen from a distance it must be a pretty amazing place – but more about it when we have been there. We have also instructions to look for a new way of tackling Everest in this direction [i.e. from the northern side], though I could have told them that there was no such way before leaving England.'[78]

They were soon back down again, and in a letter to his mother Shipton sounded off about the tribulations of leadership (his terseness and irritability on this expedition show through quite clearly in this correspondence, Warren and Kempson coming in for sharp criticism):

I seem to get very little time to myself on our so-called 'off days', what with accounts to be done; complaints about tents;

---

[76] *A.J.* 1936, ibid, p.5.
[77] The telling phrase is Shipton's, from *That Untravelled World.*
[78] Letter to Mrs Haly from Rongbuk, 2 August 1935.

re. provisioning; someone has smashed his boots; someone else sees a snag in the plans; etc. etc.

There were consolations in coming down off the mountain that sweetened his tetchy mood:

> By Jove, it is good to see a few wild flowers and green vegetation after a month in the snow. The first flower which greets one as one descends is that most heavenly of all flowers to my mind, the Blue Poppy. Perhaps it owes some of its loveliness to the fact that it springs upon one in such unexpected place: the complete barrenness of a stony hillside, or the recess of a cave under a waterfall. This valley is pretty devoid of softness, but its poor patches of short grass seem heavenly at the moment.[79]

He filled in more detail about their exploratory activities and some of the political background to the planned expedition for 1936 in a second letter to his mother from Rongbuk, in which his customary mellowness begins to find voice again.

Rongbuk, 15th August, 1935

My Darling Mum,

We just got back here after quite a successful trip. I just got two letters from you (P. Said and Marseilles). I am terribly sorry to hear you were not well on the trip. I do hope you get over it soon. English food generally puts one right though. How odd sitting next to Mr Coffey and meeting Mrs G. Bruce. Yes, I knew he [i.e. Geoffrey Bruce] was offered the leadership (we were all very against it), also Norton. I think they both turned it down because they thought Hugh [Ruttledge] ought to be made to carry on . . .

I split the party into three for our last trip. I sent Tilman and Wigram up the main glacier to try and cross a gap we call the Lho La into the Western Cwm. They failed to get over but did some very good work in the neighbourhood. Spender recovered himself and followed up with Warren and completed the survey of the main glacier. I went west with Bryant and our light mountain theodolite to do some

---

[79] Letter to Mrs Haly from Rongbuk, 2 August 1935.

survey in that direction. We climbed several good peaks, which delighted Bryant. He has recovered at last, at any rate he was all right at the comparatively moderate altitudes at which we were working. He was very pleased with his new lease of life and he proved to be a very nice companion. We camped for two nights in a filthy wind on the main watershed. However we were rewarded in the end by some fine views into the Western Cwm and into some gloriously beautiful country in unexplored Nepal. I very much hope one day to get a grant and permission to take an expedition and explore it. It would offer several years' work. In spite of the wind we got a theodolite station on the watershed and I hope have got some useful data for mapping the mysterious Western Cwm which Hinks[80] is so keen on . . .

As in 1933, with the retreat sounded from the mountain the fun could begin. The extent of their ensuing fun was neatly summed up by Ruttledge and Longstaff at the RGS meeting on 2 December 1935, when the former asked 'if all of us have realised, when listening to Mr Shipton quietly describing his adventures, exactly what has been done in 1935, because the achievement he has been describing so quietly is one of the most remarkable in Himalayan annals. Quite casually at the end of his paper he said that twenty-six peaks of over 20,000 feet had been climbed . . .'[81] Tom Longstaff took up the same point: 'I do not think he has made it evident that during the expedition last summer about as many peaks of over 20,000 feet were climbed in the Himalaya as have been climbed since the days of Adam, as I remember the list.'[82] Thus the fun they had – the climbers out in Tibet, and their mentors drooling over the statistics when they arrived back in Britain.

In the six weeks beyond putting Everest out of mind, the sheer volume of their activity was astounding. Spender had surveyed indefatigably; Tilman had roamed over passes; the Western Cwm, eventual key to the ascent, had been photographed and the curiosity of Mallory, who had given the feature its Welsh name back in

---

[80] Arthur Hinks was secretary of the Royal Geographical Society from 1915 to 1945, and reputedly difficult, though Shipton seems to have charmed him and held his loyalty.

[81] *G.J.* 1936, p.107.

[82] Ibid. p.111.

1921, had been reinvoked; the 23,000-foot summits of Kharta Changri, Kellas' Rock Peak and Khartaphu had been climbed as well as a couple of dozen lesser ones in the course of the expedition. Shipton had had 'a delicious time' of it and the old boys had again been impressed. But there was sadness too, and the difficult side of leadership to be faced – something which had made the correspondence with his mother so uncharacteristically terse:

> . . . it was of some use to the Committee to test out various men during this preliminary expedition. In the choice of a team for such a project as climbing Mount Everest there is no room for sentiment or favouritism, and it is exceedingly unfortunate for us that the two best men that I have ever travelled with, Tilman and Bryant, were unable to acclimatise sufficiently well to come with the 1936 expedition.[83]

If this was a man entirely devoid of the killer instinct, then heaven preserve us from martinets – the growing authority here is surely firm enough for anyone. As to the responses from his discards, 'Though they were both bitterly disappointed, neither questioned my inevitable decision. Tilman's attitude may be judged from the fact that, later, he subscribed towards the funds of the 1936 expedition in which he was to take no part, although he had other plans of his own.'[84]

Shipton would much rather have stayed out in the Himalayas travelling and exploring; observing the strange psychology of H. W. Tilman, who would doubtless also have stayed on if asked, the crowds having departed, and gadded about as lightly and effectively as he had done in the closing stages of the Great War half his lifetime before; living with the Sherpas (their favourites had remained uncharacteristically grumpy and fractious right to the end of the 1935 trip – clearly there was something wrong, perhaps to do with the objectives being continually thwarted by Tibetan officialdom and Shipton's anxiety not to cause difficulties back home in his new role as leader of an official expedition – though the new Tenzing recruits both shone); and seeking answers to some very modern questions about conditions at altitude during the winter months.

---

[83] *A.J.* 1936, p.2.
[84] Shipton, *Upon That Mountain*, p.182.

But the expedition of 1936 was looming, preparations had to be made, and he had given his word that he would return and help.

In the event, it was scarcely worthwhile his doing so. The leadership question that had been left in an unsatisfactory state since 1933 was resolved unsatisfactorily, in the habitual manner of the knot of vipers that far too often made up the Himalayan Committee down the years. The decent and ineffectual Hugh Ruttledge, as we learned in the aside from Shipton's letter to his mother, was compromised into firstly resigning his leadership and later into having it messily confirmed. At his heels there snapped the ambitious and possibly a little devious figure of Frank Smythe, whose position the law professor Harry Calvert in his fine climbing biography defined as followed:

> . . . it was tacitly accepted by all that he would be the unofficial climbing leader on the mountain and his word was most influential in the selection of members of the expedition but there was no question of *de jure* recognition of his *de facto* position. Quite apart from anything else, Graham Brown was now on the Committee of the Alpine Club.[85]

For all the habitual politicking, an interesting and compatible team was assembled, including – surprisingly, given Shipton's dissatisfaction with two of them – Kempson, Wigram and Warren from the 1935 reconnaissance. There were a couple of new faces in Oliver and Gavin, who had been on a selection meet at Zermatt with Frank Smythe that summer (one of the two great British rock-climbers of the 1930s, Colin Kirkus, was on the same meet, but was not selected, most probably because he was still suffering from the serious head injuries he had sustained in the fall on Ben Nevis at Easter 1934 in which Maurice Linnell was killed); and a soundly eccentric choice as expedition doctor – despite its already having Wigram and Warren – of Noel Humphreys, making this perhaps the best-qualified medical team ever sent to Everest. The 'fucking soldiery' – to quote Wyn Harris again, who was included, new baby notwithstanding – was notable by its absence (though a Lieutenant John Hunt was considered, chiefly because of his sterling efforts

---

[85] Harry Calvert, *Smythe's Mountains* (Gollancz, 1985), p.139. Graham Brown, of course, was Frank Smythe's lifelong deadly foe from the time of their Brenva face ascents onwards.

on Saltoro Kangri – 'Peak 36' – a 25,400-foot mountain in the sub-Karakoram, and then rejected on medical grounds). When it came down to the expedition itself, however, there was and is very little to say. In *Upon That Mountain*, Shipton sums it up thus: 'The 1936 Everest expedition was a bitter disappointment.'[86] In *That Untravelled World* he is marginally more expansive, adding the following heartfelt paragraph:

> I had hoped that the achievements of the 1935 expedition, which were generously applauded, would convince the 'Establishment' of the virtues of a light and mobile party. In this I was sadly disappointed, and when it became clear that the 1936 attempt was to be launched on the same massive scale as before, I considered resigning my place in it. Having tasted the joys of simplicity and freedom in two long seasons of unrestricted travel, I felt so out of sympathy with the enterprise that I certainly should have had the strength of mind, the integrity, to refrain from joining it.[87]

The 1936 attempt started in a mood that was at once optimistic and tainted with faintly amusing mayhem of what was fast becoming quite a traditional kind:

Base Camp, April 24th

My Darling Mum,

We finished our slow and sedate journey and arrived here in glorious weather the day before yesterday. What a difference from 1933! No wind or snow – only blazing sun to greet us – it is almost too good to be true. After such a soft time in Tibet too everyone is pretty fair. The mountain is in perfect condition – would that we were up there now. It is too much to expect that this sort of thing will hold up for a month that will be needed to get us in a position to make an attempt. One comforting thought is that it is probably far too cold at night up there now, and any wind would be pretty impossible to cope with. Smidge[88] is up at Camp One with Jim Gavin fixing

[86] Shipton, *Upon That Mountain*, p.183.
[87] Shipton, *That Untravelled World*, p.99.
[88] I.e. W.R. Smyth-Windham, the wireless officer.

up the wireless station; so in a few days we should be getting
word from Calcutta telling us why we are being treated so well
now by the weather and when we are to expect the monsoon. I
suppose one must wait to base any plan on that. Also we hope
to hear the result of the Boat Race.[89]

What his mother heard, by contrast, was the result of a little fracas
involving the Sherpas:

Shekar Dzong . . . provided us with rather unwelcome entertainment. The night before we left Hugh's servant, Namgui,
attacked the Dzong Pen and was supported by Rinzing (who
carried to Camp Six in 1933 and was with me last year). They
both appear to have been drunk and between them they made
a pretty good mess of the Dzong Pen's face. Namgui is a native
of Shekar and must have realised what would come to him[90]
for in the morning he did a bunk and was seen no more. I put in
a plea that Rinzing should be let off with a fine of thirty rupees
as he had only been supporting a friend, and surprisingly the
Dzong Pen allowed it.

Shipton gives some interesting summary comments on the Sherpas,
and on his own vague future plans, as conclusion to the episode:

The best of these lads are always getting themselves into
trouble. Last year Ang Tharkay beat up the son of our host at
Sar and created a situation which was all the more difficult to
get round as A. was so obviously in the right. The Sherpas are
on good form now and seem to be very happy. A grand lot of
toughs came over from Sola Khumbu to meet us at Shekar and
it should be possible to select a fine team for work above the
North Col. My great ambition now is to go to Sola Khumbu.
What a time one would have there! I have looked down on it
from the peaks to the west of Everest which we climbed last
year. It looks the most heavenly spot.

---

[89] For non-Anglophiles, the annual race between two eights from Oxford and
Cambridge along the Thames between Putney and Mortlake, held on the last
Saturday of March or the first of April – an institution, in other words, of a
particular kind.
[90] I.e. a public flogging – Tibet truly was medieval at this time.

'I am getting very impatient now to get on with the job', is how he ends this letter.

Writing three weeks later from Camp Three, he relates how

I have been very busy sorting out the loads for the high camps, issuing equipment, and making the final selections for my teams for camps five, six and seven. I have got a grand lot and if we fail to get up it won't be their fault. We start up from the North Col with 35 of them! The extra camp involves a terrific extra organisation.[91]

The problem on Everest in 1936 was that the monsoon came very early, and though they had managed to establish Camp Four on the North Col by the beginning of May, the mountain itself was in highly dangerous condition and they had to retreat. Frustrated and exasperated by inactivity (and also by dynamics within the team – see below), after several days Shipton and Wyn Harris, his old mountain partner from Kenya days, were climbing up the same slope that had avalanched during the night in 1935 when this happened:

We climbed quickly over a lovely hard surface in which one sharp kick produced a perfect foothold. About halfway up to the Col we started traversing to the left. Wyn anchored himself firmly on the lower lip of a crevasse while I led across the slope. I had almost reached the end of the rope and Wyn was starting to follow when there was a rending sound . . . a short way above me, and the whole surface of the slope I was standing on started to move slowly down towards the brink of an ice-cliff a couple of hundred feet below . . .[92]

Wyn, a fine and instinctive mountaineer, had seen what was happening and reacted instantly, leaping back into the crevasse and managing to set up an ice-axe belay in time to hold Shipton on the rope. After that experience, in the face of continuing vile weather the whole huge dismal failure of an expedition cut and ran. In the manner of 1933, Shipton, Kempson, Warren and Wigram left

---

[91] Undated (16 May 1936?) letter to Mrs Haly.
[92] Shipton, *Upon That Mountain*, p.183.

the main party on 1 July and crossed the Kongra La into Sikkim, where they camped by the shores of Gordamah Lake. All the party made it to the impressively guarded col above, from which Shipton and Kempson made the first ascent of Gordamah Peak (22,200 feet) by the very steep west ridge, which gave them an enjoyable climb on snow and ice that were in perfect condition, and from the summit provided enticing views across to the looming flanks of Kanchenjunga.

Back in Kalimpong in mid July, a strong and interesting letter back home written on 15 July produced some revealing perspectives on this year's failure.

My Darlingest Mum,

By now at least you will have gathered why you have had no letter from me. It really has been the most frightful show having all our mails pinched as it has led to all sorts of trouble. Morris and Warren have both lost jobs through it, and a terrible lot of troubles and misunderstandings have arisen as a result of it, as you can imagine. But the thing I am most furious about is that you were caused all that anxiety by the scare notices in the paper. They were absolutely uncalled for and simply put in to serve the purpose of the confounded newspaper. Except perhaps once, we were always in perfect safety and took no risks. That once too was the stupidest affair, and would never have happened on a show which was even a reasonable size. Everyone was feeling very much on edge at the time and saying things they should not have done. The less experienced people were saying we were being defeatist in not tackling the North Col under the conditions. So Wyn and I decided to go up – entirely against our better judgement – with the inevitable and obvious result. I must say Hugh should have taken a stronger line – but then, he never will do so. (Please don't repeat this.) I am now more strongly convinced than ever of the utter hopelessness of these huge expeditions. I am going to make a very strong protest against all this when I get home. If the old men still won't listen – they can count me out for any future show.

The letter went on to outline his immediate plans:

I think I will stay here ten days before I go to Simla to lecture and try and get my interview with the Viceroy (to try and get him interested in a show I was planning for next year in Kashmir). I asked Humphreys to send you a wire. I hope you got it. It told you that I was going to Kenya for six weeks. Now however I am not quite certain. Major Osmaston of the Survey of India has been ordered to go and survey Nanda Devi and there is a suggestion I should go with him as a guide. I shall know in a few days whether the suggestion is official or not. I am keen to go as it will give me an opportunity to continue our explorations there and I would learn a lot about survey (a course in which I am going to take next winter at home). The only snag is that I will not be able to do my book on Kenya next winter – but I suppose that can wait.

This is the man for whom *Nanda Devi* was going to be his last book! Sadly, the Kenya account never appeared, but his mention of it leaves us in no doubt that he was now a professional traveller and writer.

There was other consolation in the year's travels for Shipton, for all the failure of the climbing ambitions and the debacle that was Everest. After years of flirtations and non-serious involvements which provided no outlet for the expression of physical affection and were often conducted under the censorious eye of his mother (who seems perhaps understandably to have been wholly inimical to the notion of sex), at Kalimpong early in March, and later at Gangtok further along the journey out, he struck up a friendship with a woman seven years older than himself and mother to a young daughter. Pamela Freston at the time was separated from an Indian civil service officer husband she would finally divorce two years later. When the expedition camped on the lawn of the British Residency at Gangtok, Mrs Freston was already installed as guest in a bedroom there, the window to which was conveniently provided with an adjacent drainpipe. The sexually inexperienced[93]

---

[93] Although he later made up for lost time, it does seem that Shipton's attachments to women up to this point, as in the case of 'Madge' Anderson, had been physically unconsummated, and some of them were distinctly odd. Charles Warren related one anecdote to me about Shipton having accompanied the artist Bip Pares (another older woman), whose pen-and-ink sketches charmingly illustrated most of his books and for whom he harboured a strong romantic attachment, on her

Shipton protested his misgivings about beginning an affair, to which Mrs Freston responded, 'Don't be so stupid, Eric – it's as easy as falling off a log' – rather an odd image in context. Eric was duly initiated into drainpipe ascents and the physical delights, and the relationship flourished (at least in the form of a correspondence over many years when intimacy was not possible, which was fondly preserved in a small blue crammed suitcase by her daughter Mrs Celia St John Armitage).

Shipton's itinerary for 1936 was by no means over with the Everest debacle, but while he was gainlessly employed on that overcrowded and overrated pile, the Everest discards were elsewhere engaged and the goddess and the Seven Rishis were smiling upon them. Her first sign of favour came in the form of a communication from across the Atlantic. It was from four young Harvard mountaineers who had formed the notion that they might succeed where the cream of Bavarian storm-troopers had failed and often died, and make the first ever ascent of an 8,000-metre peak – the objective in their case being that which Shipton had recently viewed from the summit of Gordamah Peak, the world's third-highest mountain Kanchenjunga. These four – Farnie Loomis, Charlie Houston, Ad Carter and Art Emmons – blithely unaware of the permissions needed for travel in Sikkim to the mountain, and perhaps also not quite understanding the scale of the undertaking they were setting for themselves, started planning an expedition, and sent Loomis to London to purchase equipment and liaise – perhaps not entirely a fortunate choice – with cantankerous and self-regarding old T. Graham Brown, who was personally known to Houston.

Another man who was acquainted with the four from his years of teaching at Harvard was Noel Odell, Cambridge geologist and

---

honeymoon. Charles suggested the husband 'was not overly pleased with this situation, despite reserving conjugal rights to himself alone'. I suspect a degree of confusion in this story, since Ms Pares was married twice, and even produced an illustrated book about her second honeymoon (called *Himalayan Honeymoon*), in the course of which she met with the 1938 Everest expedition of which Shipton and Warren were members. David Cox used to tell a similar story against himself in which he was invited on the honeymoon of Beridge Mallory (one of Ruth and George Leigh Mallory's two daughters), in order to climb with her in the Alps. 'She never got up early enough – in fact she was seldom to be seen out of bed at all – very uxorious pair,' he vouchsafed, so perhaps this strange behaviour was par for the 1930s sporting early-marital course – 'No, darling, of course I don't mind if you invite your climbing partner . . .' Though somehow I doubt it.

venerable Everester, last man to sight Mallory and Irvine in 1924, and a discard or reject from Everest '36 because of his presumption in pleading business interest over God, King and Country as a reason for not being able to go when invited in '33. To this team of six, ostensibly for Kanchenjunga, were added Peter Lloyd, a forceful and powerful alpinist from the late 1920s Cambridge University Mountaineering Club generations who developed into one of British mountaineering's most entertaining and straight-talking elder statesmen – and H. W. Tilman. 'Loomis liked them all, and they seemed to like each other! So it began. What cheek! We tempered this by naming ours the British-American Himalayan Expedition.'[94]

Houston later added. 'It's hard to believe how naïve and presumptuous we were ... Four American college kids ... inviting the best British climbers to join us on a major climb in the Himalayas.'[95] Kids they may have been, but they turned out to be a remarkably amiable, malleable and energetic lot who flourished under the gruff austerities of the leader they ultimately chose by secret ballot. It's a very good sign when a team sets out with no designated leader, and allows one to emerge by amicable consensus. It also needs saying about these young men that they were by no means inexperienced. Art Emmons had lost his toes from frostbite in the 1932 ascent of Minya Konka, a 24,790-foot peak in eastern Tibet, next highest to Kamet in achieved summits though of little technical difficulty by the original route. Charlie Houston had climbed extensively in the Alps with his father, Oscar, who also hoped to be a member of the climbing party (when Odell told him on the boat to Bombay that his health and fitness were inadequate to the demands even of reaching the Sanctuary, it caused a breach between the two which never healed).

In Alaska in 1935 Charlie had made the first ascent of the 17,400-foot Mount Foraker with Graham Brown, and friendship rather than controversy had come of it, which was a strong recommendation given the bad blood over Brenva that had festered unresolved

---

[94] From Houston's warm-hearted and vivid introduction to the very useful 1999/2000 The Mountaineers/Baton Wicks volume *Nanda Devi: Exploration and Ascent* (hereafter referred to as *E&A*) which reprinted the texts of Shipton's *Nanda Devi* (1936) and Tilman's *The Ascent of Nanda Devi* (1937), along with typically helpful maps, appendices and annotation selected by Ken Wilson.

[95] The quotation is from Bernadette McDonald's lively and fluent biography of Houston, *Brotherhood of the Rope* (The Mountaineers/Baton Wicks, 2007), p.43.

between Brown and Frank Smythe, each of whom through long, destructive years slunk around the climbing salons of Europe seeking to enlist supporters to their factions. Ad Carter was a member of Bradford Washburn's Alaskan survey, whilst Farnie Loomis was the son of the tycoon Alfred Lee Loomis and a distinguished Alaskan climber in his own right. For 'frat boys', these were a notably high-powered collection.

Their soon-to-be leader Tilman, being at a loose end in Wallasey, caught the Brocklebank boat to India in April with the expedition's baggage and provisions, intending on arrival in Calcutta to head up into Sikkim, 300 miles to the north, and there arrange for porters and supplies. On landing, he was told that permission for Kanchenjunga had been refused. They had suspected from the outset that this might be the case, particularly given the lateness of their application in February and the appearance it gave of seeking to 'bounce' the Indian government into acquiescence, and so had fixed on a reserve objective. In his introduction to *Nanda Devi: Exploration and Ascent*, Houston states that Loomis had asked around for alternatives in the case of refusal to go to Kanchenjunga and either Shipton or Tilman had suggested Nanda Devi. He adds that 'it is embarrassing to admit that we didn't appreciate what an extraordinarily generous offer this was. Only later did we learn that among their many adventures they had been the first to find a way through the Rishi Ganga in 1934 and certainly planned to return and make the climb.'[96] Given the timing and the fact that Loomis was in London, it is far more likely that this offer – essentially made in bad faith – came from Shipton, on the assumption that Loomis knew of their prior interest, and therefore would have done the gentlemanly thing (as Shipton was doing in offering the option) and politely declined – the proper response of any English gentleman in the circumstances: 'Oh no, old chap – couldn't possibly – perfectly aware that one's yours!'

But of course Loomis wasn't perfectly aware, nor were any of the other Harvard boys, and hence Shipton – if he was responsible for this ethical cock-up – was hoist on his own gentlemanly petard. It is also far more likely that the offer came from Shipton because, whatever his feelings – and he had been very strongly for going to Nanda Devi and not Everest in 1935 – it was not an option

---

[96] *E&A*, ibid. p.8.

that Tilman could have promoted, given his adjutant loyalty to Shipton and the fact that in 1934 he had been invited on Shipton's expedition. It was surely because of these factors that his preference all along had been for Kanchenjunga. But now he too found himself on the spot, responsible for what would happen, and unable to refuse, though it placed him in a compromising position.

Just how compromising he was shortly to find out, and it is notable that Tilman, 'who, as you know, is not normally very communicative',[97] in this instance was abnormally uncommunicative even by his standards of extreme reticence. He made one enigmatic and I suspect rather hurt statement to explain a situation that must have looked highly embarrassing to all informed contemporary observers, and that appears to have been the direct result of simple transatlantic misunderstanding (the failures of our supposed common language being a theme on which Tilman does enlarge in *The Ascent of Nanda Devi*, and with strong underlying reasons). The statement is brief, to the point, and unequivocal; and the more I look at it, the more plain its subtext becomes. It is a clear and terse refutation of any suggestion that he had gone behind Shipton's back in suggesting the mountain, and it could not be more forthright in pointing out that the latter had agreed the plan: '. . . for this objective, we had the goodwill of all who had had anything to do with the mountain'.[98]

So Shipton knew, and had approved, and now we can press on with the story. The juggernaut having gathered speed and the expedition soon to be converging on whichever objective was chosen, from Calcutta Tilman communicated the new, though anticipated, situation to the other members and – somewhat to the relief of the older and wiser head of Odell[99] – after brief discussion the alternative objective that had been offered was fixed upon: they were now going to Nanda Devi. So he arranged for the baggage to be sent by rail the 800 miles west to Kathgodam, and made his way to Darjeeling.

There is a postscript to this confused little episode, and emotionally

[97] Shipton, in letter to Charles Houston, August 1954.
[98] Tilman, ibid. p.166.
[99] Seven years older than Tilman, Odell was next in seniority to Graham Brown, who was eight years older again. This Anglo-American expedition was a remarkable blend of old world ancients and new world youth, yet it worked far better than might have been predicted.

it is a very revealing one. Thirty years ago, when I first considered writing about Shipton and Tilman, and was working with the publisher Ken Wilson on a project dear to both our hearts which was to see into print the compendium volumes of their books,[100] I had some correspondence with a young American mountaineer and scholar, Dr David Pluth, who had been researching in the newly acquired Tilman archive at the University of Wyoming in Laramie and knew both of my interest in the subject and, from correspondence in the archive, of my friendship with him. David wrote to me on 23 August 1981 and told of seeing among these papers a telegram (buff, of course, not pink) addressed to Tilman c/o The Planters' Club in Darjeeling, of which he had made a transcription on which at that moment he could not lay his hands, having just moved to Calgary and his papers being in disorder.

If I were to run this story past Harry Calvert, who wrote the excellent Smythe biography, I'm sure his magnificently professorial legal eyebrows would already be well raised by this point and he'd murmur some wry comment about 'the man from Laramie'. This is not reliable evidence. It is hearsay. It is at third hand. And I agree. All the same, David Pluth – a very fine photographer and geographer, a man of integrity, who died on assignment in Rwanda in 2009 – is not someone whose word I would remotely have doubted. He was a man of great principle who comes as close as possible to the ideal of an unimpeachable witness. His recollection of the content of the telegram was quite clear – it was hardly difficult to remember – and it intrigued him. He stated that it read thus: 'Tilman. Bugger you. Shipton.' Hardly the master's blessing on the venture! And my sense is that a certain concealed rancour on both sides, though it

---

[100] I was acting as editor for Ken's publishing company Diadem – later absorbed by Hodder – at the time, and turned up for work one morning with a recently published and very good Secker & Warburg/Octopus Franz Kafka compendium volume, which we thumbed through excitedly over coffee, and on which our subsequent Tilman and Shipton collections were based. I insisted on Tilman being published first, arguing for a greater consistency in his writing, and the wider appeal to sailors and military historians as well as to the mountaineering and mountain exploration interest making him more commercially viable. I think Ken would have preferred Shipton to go first, and his judgement may well have been the more sound, but for once he gave in gracefully. We had some heroic shouting matches in the time of our co-operation, but for the record, I think Ken's role in publishing mountaineering and outdoor titles over the last forty years has been momentous and unparalleled.

appears never to have been directly addressed, brought about an even greater distance ultimately between two men who could never have been termed the most intimate of friends.

To return to Tilman in Darjeeling, offending telegram safely stowed away among his papers on the first leg of its eventual journey to Wyoming (perhaps this explains the curious E. Annie Proulx/ Tilman connection mentioned in Chapter Three?), having recruited what leftovers were to be found in the Sherpa community, which had been drained by Everest and two other large expeditions in 1936, he went off trekking to try them out. In one of them – Pasang Kikuli, whose behaviour during the 1934 Nanga Parbat tragedy had been exemplary, and who was to die on the American K2 expedition in 1939 in an heroic attempt to rescue the American climber Dudley Wolfe – he was very fortunate, for this was one of the great pre-war Sherpas. Kitar too was a fine Sherpa with extensive experience at altitude, though he was to become ill and die on the expedition. The others were mostly superannuated Everest veterans, worn out in the service of that idol. Tilman being Tilman, the trek he chose was distinctly rigorous. He intended to attempt a crossing of the Zemu Gap, a pass that in reality was no such thing though a traverse of it had been rumoured, on a ridge leading east from Kanchenjunga to Simvu, which he hoped would give access to the lengthy Zemu glacier system.

On the way he made a cursory attempt on Pan Dim, a 22,000-foot peak above the Prek Chu valley, from which they retreated after running into a zone of dangerous stone fall. As to the Zemu Gap, it was guarded by an impressive sequence of ice falls that were capped by a 100-foot overhanging ice head-wall. True to his philosophy of rubbing his nose against an obstacle before deciding against it, he climbed to the base of the latter and decided to turn back, thus involving himself and Pasang in a very risky and precarious retreat. For all the failures, he was obviously in perky and audacious mood, and determined to prove his doubters of 1935 wrong in their assessment of him. He was also, very sensibly, giving himself time to acclimatise before a climb that, if successful, would reach an altitude he had never previously achieved. These early diversions and preparations were by no means gratuitous.

Turning now to the main objective, he and his two good Sherpas (the superannuated Everester quartet were left to follow on at their leisure) set out post-haste from Sikkim for Kathgodam and

Ranikhet, at which latter they picked up Farnie Loomis, the first of the arrivals, who had come on from London. Tilman, prepared to be unimpressed, was unimpressed. 'Loomis is not a fast walker and takes up a good deal of road,' he confided to his diary. They warmed to each other as the days went by. From Ranikhet Tilman wired the Rawal of Badrinath, who had befriended Shipton and himself in 1934, asking if he might arrange for fifteen men from Mana to meet them in Joshimath on 6 June. He also by telegram ordered rice, *atta* and tsampa to be waiting at Joshimath, and by the 16th, Tilman, Loomis, Pasang, Kitar and the men of Mana had conveyed 900lb of food and supplies through the Rishi gorge and cached it beyond Pisgah on the edge of the Sanctuary itself – a logistical tour de force which contributed enormously to the expedition's eventual success. It didn't come without cost. Near the *mauvais pas* Tilman was hit by a rock, took a twenty-foot fall, and came very close to bouncing down a further 1,400 feet into the river. He survived, somewhat flayed and with a sprained shoulder, thumb and cracked rib, though the descent back to Joshimath was purgatorial. A couple of days spent in the hot springs on the pilgrim route to Badrinath performed wonders of restoration, as did his determination to keep moving and walk it off, by double-marches back to the Forestry Service Bungalow in Ranikhet where the whole team[101] was to assemble. Charlie Houston relates what happened:

> Our first test came when Tilman approached the mound of supplies which we had, with great difficulty, cleared through customs in Calcutta. With few words (none were needed) he began 'bagging and scrapping', a euphemism we would become more familiar with as time passed. Cowed by this taciturn stranger, Loomis and Emmons could only voice pitiful pleas. About half the pile, mostly our favourite foods, had been set aside. Then Tilman repeated the process with the equipment which we had so carefully selected. My protests were futile.[102]

Over sixty years on, he could look back more philosophically on the process, though at the time its lesson registered painfully:

---

[101] Ad Carter, through a misunderstanding, didn't join them until they had reached base camp in the Sanctuary – showing remarkable initiative in doing so.
[102] *E&A*, ibid. p.9.

Somehow this early neo-confrontation did much to foster our togetherness; at least it showed us something about Tilman. He was careless of creature comforts, scornful of processed foods and seemed to believe bamboo shoots and barley an adequate diet. The Brits didn't know what to make of us Yanks and had some difficulty understanding our form of the language we were supposed to share. True to form, Tilman said nothing, but looked wary. Our celebration of the Fourth of July was viewed with tolerant amusement.[103]

Six days later they set out together on the – for Tilman at least – familiar march to Joshimath, with the monsoon by now well under way and Odell striding along the ridge above Gwaldam among the deodars waving his umbrella and exclaiming 'Gad! It's good to be back!' By 21 July they were beyond Joshimath on their way towards the Rishi Ganga, with the men of Mana and thirty-seven additional porters. The latter baulked at the first crossing of the Rhamani in spate so plans were hastily revised, the unwilling porters paid off, the projected time scale for the expedition curtailed from sixty to forty days, another rigorous session of 'bagging and scrapping' took place at the Rhamani/Rishi junction camp, and the much-reduced party set to ferrying loads up the gorge to a base camp within the Sanctuary which they had established, stocked with three weeks' fuel and four weeks' food, and occupied by 7 August.

Almost immediately, two disasters hit them. Pasang Kikuli developed snow-blindness. The other Sherpas too, whose carrying abilities beyond base camp had not proved to be of the first order, all went down with dysentery (Kitar, who had accompanied the late-arrival Emmons in along the Badrinath pilgrim route, had contracted a particularly virulent strain along that notoriously dirty journey and was to die of it three weeks later). In addition the main bulk of their tea-supply was lost[104] at Camp One – a grave blow to the morale of the British contingent.

---

[103] *E&A*, p.9.

[104] 'A full tin of tea, left on the platform outside one of the tents, had for some unexplained reason gone over the edge. The only witnesses to this tragedy were Graham Brown and Houston, who were working on another platform and suddenly noticed it rolling down the slope; and it was the more serious because, but for an ounce, this was all the tea we had left.' Tilman, *Seven Mountain Travel Books*, p.228.

There were positive factors at work as well, however: 'Personally I was astonished at the speed with which those who had not been high before did acclimatise, and how comparatively mild their symptoms were.'[105] So tea-less but acclimatised – perhaps the Americans were just the oxygen needed by the notoriously low-ceilinged Tilman, sharpening the intake of his breath – the sahibs set to carrying and establishing their own line of camps up the mountain.

> To this point we hadn't really had a leader because things just seemed to work themselves out. Looking back it's clear that Tilman, saying nothing, guided our progress. In the process he became more amiable, his barbs less sharp, even smiling now and then. One memorable evening, lubricated by a celebratory bottle of Apricot Brandy, he had even talked about his travels: our stories about Alaska dwindled to dust, and we listened spell-bound . . . That night by a secret ballot we chose Tilman as leader and asked him to name a summit team. He did, and next day in promising weather, the party moved Odell and me up to a microscopic ledge and left us at dusk to scratch out a tent 'platform' at 23,400 feet.[106]

The dawn came bright and still and Houston and Odell climbed steadily through soft snow and up steep, sound quartzite towards a summit that it became clear they would not make that day, though time alone, and not technical difficulties in the climbing, weighed against them; so they returned to the tent convinced that, in settled weather and with the trail broken, another day would mean the summit was theirs. They celebrated with a shared tin of corned beef. Odell, as senior, ate first and passed the tin back to Charlie. They had not noticed a puncture in the bottom of the can. Within minutes of Charlie eating it, rivers were bursting forth from both ends of his anatomy and he was wishing he could die. After a night spent crawling continually in and out of the tent over the prone and lengthy form of Odell, next morning Charlie was spent. Odell yelled down through the still air to the others that 'Charlie is ill', and the supposedly shared language failed them again. The listeners six hours away beneath registered 'Odell's familiar yodel, like a donkey

---

[105] H.W. Tilman, *Seven Mountain Travel Books*, p.227.
[106] Ibid. p.11.

braying',[107] as conveying the news that 'Charlie is killed' (correct American register in this situation demanding that Odell should have said 'Charlie is sick'), and started the long climb towards them, thinking they would be bringing down a corpse. Only Tilman had the foresight to take with him his kit. When they arrived at the platform, having been unable to make further contact on the way up, Odell's voice was heard saying 'Hullo, you blokes, have some tea.'[108]

Tilman commented that another such experience as this 'would almost reconcile one to the carrying of a small wireless set'; Charlie insisted on going straight down, ill (i.e. 'sick') though he was, to make room and hence not prejudice their chance of success, and the only person available and equipped to take his place was Tilman. He and Odell moved the tent a little higher to a better site at 24,000 feet, and at 6 a.m on the 29th, the two fit veterans[109] of the team set out through soft snow up to their knees for the top, with a hot sun rising in the sky to add to their miseries:

. . . hopes of the summit grew faint , but there was no help beyond plugging on and seeing how far we could get; this we did, taking our time and resting frequently. Towards 1 p.m. we were surprised to find ourselves approaching the final wall and, once this was reached, we felt the deed was done. There was a difficult bit of rock which Odell led and which I thought horribly unsafe, then we were landed fairly on the steep glacis with the summit only a couple of hundred feet above us.[110]

So far the goddess had been smiling, but she had a final heart-in-your-mouth moment to taunt them with:

. . . there was a sudden hiss and, quicker than thought, a slab of snow about thirty yards long slid off the corridor and disappeared down the gully, peeling off the snow where our steps had been kicked as it went. At its lower end the avalanche

[107] The phrase is from Tilman's paper read before the Alpine Club, 7 December 1936, (published as 'The Ascent of Nanda Devi' in *Alpine Journal*, 1937, p.23.
[108] Ibid. Generously, a last surviving ounce of tea had been allotted as incentive to the intended summit party.
[109] Graham Brown was suffering very badly from altitude sickness, had turned blue, and his behaviour had become increasingly erratic and paranoid.
[110] *A.J.* 1937, ibid. p.24.

broke away to a depth of a foot all round my axe, which was well driven in and which I was holding; the break at its upper limit extended to a depth of three or four feet.[111]

They climbed on, reaching the broad ridge forming the summit at 3 p.m. It was hot, 20 degrees. Both men slipped out of their Grenfell jackets, Odell displaying to the goddess the oddities of his wardrobe:

> . . . a hideous yellow sweater, a relic of the War, which weighed more than the five Shetland woollies carried by us all. At the highest camp he produced a hat which none of us had ever seen before and which, I suppose, had some attributes peculiarly fitting it for wear at 24,000 feet.[112]

They spent three quarters of an hour on the mountaintop, during which time occurred the moment which has become a part of the folklore of mountaineering – a line as famous in its own way, and significantly more playful, considered and intelligent, than Mallory's 'Because it is there': 'I believe we so far forgot ourselves as to shake hands upon it.'[113]

The element of self-mockery here is obvious. It is a wholly characteristic Tilman comment, that familiar operative principle of reductive irony used to check the expression of emotions for which words would inevitably seem insufficient, refuge taken in an odd and satirical version of litotes therefore. Look behind it and you see the shadowy horrors of the battlefield. It plays with the sense of the unsayable, gives distance, and in this case a means of encompassing the resounding ambivalence that asserts itself in the aftermath to all significant ascents.[114]

---

[111] Tilman, ibid. pp.247–8.
[112] Ibid. p.231.
[113] Ibid. p.248.
[114] Menlove Edwards, the leading rock-climber of the 1930s and one of the most interesting and tragic figures in the history of the sport, reviewed *The Ascent of Nanda Devi* in the *Mountaineering Journal* for June 1937 and in the course of a very favourable notice made the following comments – interesting and psychologically acute from the man who was certainly the finest-ever writer on the sport of rock-climbing: 'We can see Mr Tilman well from his book, and he looks there a formidable man, a campaigner who loves campaigning and has no use for perplexities, and an expert at direct living. One likes that in him and certainly admires him, on the cliffs of the goddess or crossing the Sahara

The two climbers descended, cautiously and with difficulty, pausing at one point 'to watch a bird, a snow pigeon, cross our ridge and fly swiftly across the grey cliffs . . . like the spirit of Nanda Devi herself, forsaking the fastness which was no longer her own.'[115] At base camp they were greeted with the melancholy sight of Kitar's new grave. He had died the previous day, and the other Sherpas had already raised a cairn over his corpse and surrounded it with a ring of stones. The mountain was in too dangerous a condition for further summit bids to be countenanced, and the whole team anyway felt that the success had been a joint achievement, every member playing his part – a sentiment that Tilman defined at the end of his expedition book with a sonorous and altruistic dignity that encapsulates something essential to the mountain ethos of the 1930s:

Where each man pulled his weight each must share the credit; for, though it is natural for each man to have his own aspirations, it is in mountaineering more than in most things, that we try to believe.

The game is more than the players of the game,
And the ship is more than the crew.[116]

---

on bicycle, and making himself at home. There is fine feeling of a sort too. You can see the man out in the open air watching the sky – "still snowing and blowing in gusts when we turned out, but there were breaks in the flying scud and a brighter patch of light in the murky sky assured us . . ." That is Tilman at his best. Meanwhile the action itself goes on through its conclusions, the whole length of the ascent: what has happened has happened. Out of his own sphere he is less formidable of course. All feelings are referred down to a single plane of expression, almost of non-expression, and when other planes are attempted they do not come out so well. "A curious gamut of feelings . . ." over the Houston incident. "Thoughts beyond the reaches of our souls" at the top; and a good deal of Kipling. Though it is always horrid to quote bits like that. None of the other individuals are brought out as characters; Odell perhaps, but not justice to the others, I think – the Americans and so on. More feeling for Pasang and the Mana men. The obviously tangled skein of personal relationships is hardly referred to at all, except as a possible block to progress, to be dealt with by frequent changes of company. But there you are, a classic of early twentieth century mountaineering.'

There is much here that can be used to give a perspective on the relationship between Shipton and Tilman, and the developments that were soon to take place within that.

[115] Ibid.
[116] Ibid. p.267.

The expedition may now have been on the point of dispersal, but in the strange way that climbing challenges have, a problem that had faced him down two years before now began working on Tilman's imagination. He recruited Charlie Houston and Pasang Kikuli, and the other members having left to work their way back down to Joshimath and Ranikhet, on 2 September the fire was put out, the ashes scattered, hearth covered over and these three trekked once more up the east glacier making for Longstaff's Col, from which he and Shipton had turned back two years before. Their crossing, in mist and unsafe snow, proved exciting enough: 'We were all very tired and made a sorry job of the descent, getting into trouble in a long ice runnel which was like a watercourse full of ice.' Eventually they gave up on their plan to locate and cross a further col – Traill's Pass, first used as long ago as 1830, and quite invisible and impossible to locate within the clouds. Instead they headed straight down into the Milam valley, making for Martoli, last settlement before Tibet. Charlie Houston recalled 'being frightened to death . . . We were exhausted before we finally found a small place level enough to camp well after dark. Bill was his magnificent indomitable surly self.' On the way to Martoli they were separated for a day on either side of a serious river, Tilman reaching the village first, where he was fed and pampered and interrogated about his relationship with the goddess whose mountain he had just climbed. Eventually, on 12 September, they reached Ranikhet, and Charlie caught the bus down-valley next day heading for the train at Kathgodam, a flight from Delhi to London, the boat back to America, and a new term at medical school.

Tilman stayed on in the Forest Service bungalow to wait for the others, pay porters, and wind up the expedition. Peter Lloyd recounted to him how, on his way down the Rishi, he had met Shipton on his way up into the Sanctuary with Ang Tharkay, Sen Tenzing and the small Indian Survey team led by Major Osmaston to which they were attached as guides, and told him of the success on the peak. Shipton was later to pick up some of the Mana men as porters, and one of them 'entertained us in the evenings by voluble descriptions of their adventures in the Rishi gorge during the monsoon. I was amused to find that these men had nicknamed Tilman "Balu Sahib" (*Balu* meaning a bear) owing to the speed with which he moves over steep forested ground.'[117]

---

[117] Eric Shipton, 'More Explorations Round Nanda Devi' (*G.J.* August 1937),

The arrival of Shipton and his Sherpas in the Sanctuary days after Tilman had left it in the opposite direction is a poignant moment in the history of mountain exploration. The ascent of the great peak was a remarkable feat, unexpectedly accomplished against the odds his altitude record laid down, by his co-conspirator in the radical mountaineering project of the day, and it was done in a style of which Shipton himself could not but have entirely approved. Indeed, when he presented the results of his further explorations around Nanda Devi – the reason for his hurrying into the Sanctuary when he met Lloyd – in the form of a paper given at the RGS on 22 February, 1937, Shipton was magnificently generous in his response:

> In my opinion the climbing of Nanda Devi is perhaps the finest mountaineering achievement which has yet been performed in the Himalaya; it is the first of the really difficult Himalayan giants to be conquered.[118] His expedition was a model of what an expedition should be: their party consisted exclusively of mountaineers; they avoided the great mistake which to my mind nearly all the major Himalayan expeditions since the war have made, and did not handicap themselves with a vast bulk of stores and superfluous personnel; each man was prepared to carry loads up to any height, and indeed all were called upon to do so during the most arduous part of the climb; above all, they avoided newspaper publicity. I was delighted to hear that Tilman had been one of those to reach the summit. He had done more than his share of the donkey work, having earlier in the year ascended the Rishi Nala and dumped provisions in the basin, and then returned all the way to Ranikhet to organise the transport of the party . . .[119]

Thus the public face, and I do not believe that Shipton is being remotely disingenuous here. It is well worth noting that his book, *Nanda Devi*, which appeared in the autumn of 1936, is dedicated 'To H. W. Tilman'. This was an act and sign of friendship, and there is no sense in which a charge of betrayal can be levelled against

---

p.105. I suspect the beginnings of the running Yeti gag between the two men in this (see Epilogue).
[118] Tut!
[119] *G.J.* 1937, ibid., p.98.

Tilman for having climbed the peak without him. Shipton was surely the one who presented it to the Americans as alternative to Kanchenjunga, and Tilman's own presence in the summit party owed far more to chance than design. It simply worked out that way for him, by good fortune. By the time of the delivery of the paper quoted above, Shipton had, I think, come to terms with the making of what he knew to have been a wrong decision to go to Everest, and the consequence of that in loss of a summit he had coveted. I believe he approved highly of the style of the Anglo-American expedition – which was, after all, his own but filtered this time through Tilman's sole and not their joint agency. He also knew – and this may have caused him a pang – of the warm fellowship and mutual trust that had grown within that group of which the ever-gracious and wise Charlie Houston could write movingly over sixty years on, in his old age: 'In describing our experience and my love for our party I have barely mentioned the two books [Shipton's *Nanda Devi* and Tilman's *The Ascent of Nanda Devi*]. Of course we did not see them until a year after our trip, and only then began to appreciate how warmly Tilman felt towards us.'[120] Elsewhere he notes how 'We had lived and worked together unbelievably well.'[121] So they had, and inevitably Shipton was excluded from this sense. He shared something with Houston, though, and it was more than the experience of being inopportunely poisoned by tinned meat. He shared the sense of lost opportunity.

After the debacle of '53 Everest – the expedition of which Shipton had been appointed leader and from which he was ousted by the shadiest politicking, thus tarnishing its success in the eyes of those who were privy to these machinations – Houston wrote to Shipton at the Outward Bound Mountain School in Eskdale where he was then director. Houston had not only known the disappointment of Nanda Devi as a young man. In maturer years he had seen what became 'his' mountain in much the same way that Nanda Devi was Shipton's – K2, in the exploration of which he played an outstanding role, and to which he led expeditions in 1938 and 1953 – climbed by the Italians Lacedelli and Compagnone in 1954. So he wrote to Shipton to tell of his feelings about the latter and explain that through them he knew how he must now be feeling about Everest.

---

[120] *E&A*, ibid. pp.13–4.
[121] Ibid. p.13.

A part of the latter's response, from a letter dated August 1954, runs thus:

> I was very touched by your thought of writing to me. I understand so very well how you felt when you heard about K2, and I know that the wound is going to hurt for some little time yet. The ache feels like the corrosion of one's innermost self. To you I can now confess that I experienced it when Bill Tilman climbed Nanda Devi as well as last year, though in the latter case the sad fact that Everest had succumbed to a mass assault rather than to a small unpublicised expedition acted as a counter-irritant to the purely personal hurt. K2 was certainly yours by right, and I have no doubt at all that you would have got to the top last year but for your damnable luck with the weather. I feel equally convinced that Everest could have been climbed last year by a small, lightly equipped party . . .

Note the singling out of Tilman, when both Tilman and Odell had made the summit. This – disappointment? – had been held in for the best part of two decades, and here seems to have found (small matter of a possible telegram to the Planters' Club aside) its sole discreet and significant expression. Though I wonder how Shipton had felt being back in the Sanctuary, seeing that magnificent peak above him, knowing that a man significantly his junior in terms of mountaineering accomplishment had scooped the greatest prize of the decade – *his* mountain. I wonder in what ways it ultimately fed back into their relationship after this year.

What is clear is that Shipton's innate decency on reflection quickly won through, and he was concerned with sincerity to congratulate his friend and join in the chorus of praise. To Pamela Freston – his lover, and no doubt his consolation in this bitter time – he wrote that 'I confess I wished I had been with them instead of wasting my time on that ridiculous Everest business.'[122] Indeed, his time after the 1936 Everest attempt, on the Osmaston survey with his favourite Sherpas, Osmaston himself and the formidably competent Indian

---

[122] This letter is dated 8 September, 1936, so it must have been an immediate response to receiving the news from Peter Lloyd in their chance Rishi gorge meeting.

surveyor Fazal Elahi[123] had proved far more enjoyable than either Ruttledge expedition, served to hone his surveying skills and gave him close and friendly contacts within the Indian Survey through Major Osmaston and Captain Crone that were soon to prove very useful indeed.

This second trip to the Sanctuary and its environs also provided him with one of the loveliest 'Bevis-land' moments in his writing, in which it is noticeable how much more controlled and precise the quality of his observation has become. It took place after he had descended with his Sherpas from the Bagini glacier that flows north from between Dunagiri (which he attempted to climb with Ang Tharkay, reaching a point on the south-west ridge a thousand feet below the top) and Changabang – country that was to figure large in the ambitions of mountaineers four decades on:

> Next morning below the snout of the glacier we found a blaze of autumn colours. The bare, almost feathery branches of the birch woods contrasted with the brilliant green of rhododendron and juniper, and the whole valley was interlaced with vivid patches of red, flame and copper. The glades were filled with long, wavy grass the colour of ripe corn in the morning sunlight. In place of the raging torrents of muddy water which issue from Himalayan glaciers throughout the summer we found sparkling crystal streams. The air too had a sparkle of frost which enhanced the beauty of the autumn tints. Early in the day we reached the village of Dunagiri where we found all the population busily engaged in reaping their crops and storing the grain for the winter. The houses were decorated with huge yellow marrows and cucumbers. The whole valley seemed steeped in sunshine and the rich colourful ripeness of autumn hues.[124]

These are also, of course, the illuminated perceptions of a man newly in love. At least he now had the intimate confidante that Tilman could never be. And days of sweetness too, for before returning to Britain he met up with Pamela Freston, and together with Ang Tharkay and Sen Tenzing they trekked up to the Kurumtoli

---

[123] Sometimes rendered as Fazal Ali.
[124] Shipton, 'More Explorations', p.103.

glacier that had been visited by Longstaff in 1907, to finish some of the Osmaston survey work. Mrs Freston kept a journal of the trip, and years later – the letter is dated 30 April 1973 – Shipton wrote to her where she then lived at Ansty in Wardour Vale (also a special place to her no doubt), asking in a letter that she annotated as 'very special' if she remembered those days by the Kurumtoli glacier. 'Yes, yes, oh yes!' she had written, Molly Bloom-like, breathless and panting in the margin. 'The voices of the Sherpas drifting up from below, and an eagle circled high overhead.'

I'm tempted to think that this memory between them was worth more than any summit – even one inhabited by a goddess. Shipton's long-time editor at Hodder & Stoughton, the estimable Margaret Body, when I told her about the letter and its marginal note, gave me a sidelong, amused, *matronising* look and responded thus: 'Well, I suppose that's better than commenting on the state of the ceiling decorations.'

Is this to say men are the more romantic sex, after all? In which case Dr Longstaff's warning to those gathered at the evening meeting of the Royal Geographical Society on 22 February 1937, after hearing Shipton lecture on his activities during the Osmaston trip may have been timely. He told of the pile of footwear at the mouth of the Rishi nullah that had belonged to the many suitors of the goddess Nanda, bride of Shiva. They had been eaten by a great serpent a hundred yards long for daring to come near the bride and her bridal veil.

As all the religious seers from Aeschylus and Blake to Professor Dawkins have known, those gods and monsters dwell in the breast of man. That Planters' Club telegram seems to me a joke – and it undoubtedly was a joke – of a very Freudian kind. By its agency our heroes and erstwhile friends had passed beyond innocence and the place of warning. Perhaps it was of their fate that the myth foretold? To be eaten by serpents, though whether from without or within remained to be seen . . .

9

On the Darkening Green[1]

Tilman's father died on 5 September 1936. At the time Tilman himself was in Martoli, on his way down from the first crossing of Longstaff's Col. His sister Adeline wrote to tell him not to hurry home, and that all was taken care of, though when he would have received this letter is debatable. By the new air mail service[2] he might conceivably have had it during his time in Ranikhet, but this seems unlikely. First reports of the Nanda Devi climb did not reach Britain until 9 September, eleven days after the successful ascent. The story was then headline news. The absent son arrived back at the family home in Wallasey late in October to find himself both financially provided for and in the public eye – neither of which facts was of overwhelming interest to him. The second was an irritant to a man profoundly shy throughout his life; the first was useful in that it would enable him to lead the life he chose, without any of the money worries that beset his friend Shipton, causing him to fret over means of earning a living and the question of how he would support a wife when eventually he decided to marry. Tilman being wholly disinclined to this state of human bliss,[3] he

---

[1] Cf. William Blake, *Songs of Innocence*, VII, 'The Echoing Green'.
[2] Imperial Airways had been running an airmail service between Croydon and Delhi since 1929.
[3] Charlie Houston records that when he, his father and Tilman were the first Westerners to trek through the Sherpa homeland of Sola Khumbu in the autumn of 1950 they had with them a close friend of the Houstons, the experienced and competent mountaineer Betsy Cowles, a wealthy and distinctly feminine forty-eight-year-old divorcee and Vassar graduate from Colorado Springs who insisted on carrying lipstick in her backpack and wearing colour-coordinated clothing. 'For four days Tilman sulked, walking ahead or behind us, eating separately, shunning all of us. But then his allegedly misogynist barriers crumbled, and he and Betsy became friends. Walking together they were quite sweet, if such a word

could therefore consider himself even better provided for financially.

His family had found the loss of John Hinkes Tilman easier to bear through the pride they felt in his son's achievement on Nanda Devi. Mrs Tilman didn't long survive her husband, dying the following April, by which time, having corrected the galleys for his book on *The Ascent of Nanda Devi* that came out in May of 1937 from Cambridge University Press, as well as those for his African book *Snow on the Equator*, which was to follow in the autumn of that year, Tilman was already on his way back to India.

Shipton, meanwhile, had dawdled back from Garhwal with Sen Tenzing – an interesting alliance between the inveterate practical jokers. Before leaving the district he took the results of his further exploratory work around Nanda Devi to the branch office of the Survey of India to which Major Osmaston was attached in the Raj hill station of Dehra Dun. Whilst he was doing this, Ang Tharkay squired Pamela Freston to Agra and with her visited the Taj Mahal. The four of them met up again in Bombay, the Sherpas returning thence to Darjeeling after seeing Shipton and Mrs Freston on to the boat for home. The voyage gave Shipton ample opportunity to ponder his next objective. So far, almost every trip had had the effect of suggesting a further exploratory expedition, branching out from and furthering the potential of its own itinerary. 'I had hoped that Tilman and I might soon be able to break away from the influence of this strong attraction and chance our arm in the mountain ranges of Alaska, or in the southern Andes, or in the Sierra de Merida of Venezuela, or in the southern mountains of New Guinea.'[4]

The perspective here is one that obtained just prior to the Everest 1936 trip. In that year two things intruded into the concept of an ever more widely radiating version of the travels of 1934 with the same trusted companion. The first of them was a crucial conversation,

---

could ever apply to Tilman, and later exchanged letters, even rare visits, leading me to ask Betsy what the future might hold. She laughed it off but the platonic affair lasted until she died.' Tilman's first mention of her presence is a little more brusque. 'Hitherto I had not regarded a woman as an indispensable part of the equipage of a Himalayan journey, but one lives and learns.' At the Banff Mountain Festival in 2005, where we were both presenting (Charlie died in 2009 at the age of ninety-six), in the bar afterwards, discussing Tilman and this his sole known romance, Charlie confided in fond and amused tones, 'I guess Tilman was pretty struck by Betsy.' He also mentioned that they had so far approached intimacy as to groom each other for fleas and lice – Tilman being infested and Betsy not.
4 Eric Shipton, *Upon That Mountain* (Hodder & Stoughton, 1943), p.193.

the most exciting thing to have come out of those dispiriting weeks and months around Everest in 1936, with the expedition's transport officer, John Morris[5], on the way down from their base camp to Rongbuk. Discussion of exploratory projects had been a recurrent theme within the party. Shipton and Noel Humphreys had talked of those southern mountains of New Guinea, whilst Morris had enthused about the coming fiftieth anniversary of Francis Younghusband's momentous 1887 journey from Beijing to India through the Karakoram by way of the Aghil and Mustagh passes.[6] He asked Shipton if he had ever considered travelling and exploring along the crucial section of Younghusband's route between Hunza and Leh, starting up the valley of the mysterious Shaksgam river and crossing over the Karakoram range by way of the Kurdopin and Hispar passes, between the Hispar and Biafo glaciers and in the vicinity of Martin Conway's quasi-mythical Snow Lake,[7] which by a process of slow inflationary accretion over more than four decades had grown in the collective mountaineering imagination into the supposed mother-lode of all Karakoram ice streams. In the same way that his conversations and travels with Lawrence Wager after the trip three years before had seized upon Shipton's imagination, so too, and profoundly, did this idea, which was to preoccupy him for the next twenty years until supplanted by the lower, but more distant and remote, terrain at the southern tip of the Americas.

The 1936 Everest team having dispersed in July, Shipton returned to Glen Rilli, the Odlings' house in Kalimpong (where he had stayed before Everest with Pamela Freston),[8] on the Ranjit

---

[5] An interesting character, fluent in Urdu and Tibetan, Morris was a link to the expeditions of the 1920s, having also served as transport officer on the second Everest expedition in 1922. Wounded at Gommecourt Wood on the Somme, he transferred into the Indian Army in 1917, became an officer in a Gurkha regiment and fought all along the North West Frontier, witnessing scenes of medieval brutality. He was homosexual, and the ready availability of boys was one factor that kept him in the East.

[6] For more on which see Patrick French's fine, quirky and adroit biography *Younghusband* (HarperCollins, 1994).

[7] If you're looking for this on a map, it lies north-east of the Hispar Pass on the watershed between the Hispar and Biafo glaciers, and the official modern name is Lukpe Lawo.

[8] To dispel any possible impression of Glen Rilli being a house of sexual licence, Norman and Bunty Odling were respectively son-in-law and daughter of Dr John Anderson Graham, a Scottish minister and missionary worker who had set up the St Andrew's Colonial Homes to educate and train Anglo-Indian children (the

river east of Darjeeling. Here he waited for the call to join Major Gordon Osmaston's Nanda Devi survey team, and whilst doing so set to poring over the few not entirely reliable maps that existed of approaches to the Karakoram, familiarising himself with the geography of these immense mountains with their complex inter-weaving of glaciers, reading the accounts of exploration in the massif, pondering problems and access routes and costs:

> At this stage my plans were necessarily vague, but I was fas-cinated by the idea of penetrating into the little-known region of the Karakoram. As I studied the maps, one thing about them captured my imagination. The ridges and valleys which led up from Baltistan became increasingly high and steep as they merged into the maze of peaks and glaciers of the Karakoram, and then suddenly ended in an empty blank space. Across this blank space was written one challenging word, 'Unexplored'.[9]

About what came from this single, thrilling word he was to write that 'of all my expeditions, I still look back with most delight to the season I spent in the Shaksgam filling in all those blanks on the map on the northern side of K2'.[10] The outline for an exploratory journey was already formulated before he left India in 1936. He approached Indian government authorities in Simla as early as July – a bold and interesting move. The Surveyor General gave his blessing in principle to a skeleton proposal for the project as one that was much

---

progeny of relationships between English colonists and Indian women, against whom there was considerable prejudice) in the early years of the twentieth century. A thoroughly worthy man, Dr Graham was friend and associate of Mahatma Gandhi and Rabindranath Tagore, who both visited here. The house of Bunty and Norman Odling (the latter had lost a leg in the Great War) throughout the 1930s remained closely associated with the children's training and educational establishment, and also became a haven of hospitality for travellers on their way to Tibet. A high moral and religious tone prevailed (on his retirement in 1931 Dr Graham, who still lived in Kalimpong, was appointed Moderator of the General Assembly of the Church of Scotland – a representative appointment of a year's duration). The drainpipe ascents pre-Everest would of necessity have been very discreet, particularly in view of Mrs Freston's marital status. A final point here is that Norman Odling was a Reuters correspondent – a fact that was to cause trouble and embarrassment in 1938, when he filed reports that arrived earlier than those to the official contracted outlet.

[9] Eric Shipton, *Blank on the Map* (Hodder & Stoughton, 1938), p.2.
[10] Letter to Charles Houston, August 1954.

needed (and no doubt in doing so he made sure that intelligence agencies were notified about its potential usefulness). After him, there was the External Affairs Department to be placated about the risks of kidnapping and banditry, and reassured on the advantages to be derived from a closer knowledge of the regions stretching out from British India towards China and the USSR. Over thirty years on, Shipton could talk a little more freely about how 'at that time mounting tension in that Chinese province due to Soviet intrigue was causing the Government of India much concern', adding that 'they were reluctant to allow travellers to approach the area.'[11] His previous accounts had been much more guarded, but here he gives the gist of the matter and alludes obliquely to his own coming role in Central Asian diplomacy and administration. As early as September of that year, as he was setting out to guide the Osmaston party into the Nanda Devi Sanctuary, he had received official permission to go ahead with his Shaksgam journey. The unprecedented rapidity of this approval – an official response within weeks – for what was initially a venture the detail of which was unconfirmed into a piece of very sensitive territory was astonishing.

So why was it given so readily?

With this projected expedition, Shipton – perhaps unwittingly at first, though I doubt it, given the range of contacts he had already built up in India and London – was positioning himself as a player in a current phase of the Great Game,[12] and the implications for his

---

[11] Eric Shipton, *That Untravelled World* (Hodder & Stoughton, 1969), pp.100–1.
[12] The Great Game, briefly, was the struggle between Russia and the British Empire for supremacy in Central Asia. The term originated with Captain Arthur Conolly, beheaded in Bokhara in 1842, and was popularised in Rudyard Kipling's picaresque masterpiece of 1901, *Kim* (with which marvellous novel Shipton was well acquainted). Its crucial period was during Victoria's reign, though it entered a second phase after the Russian Revolution which lasted to the end of the colonial years and saw Shipton in consular service at several highly sensitive listening-posts along the borders of empire. His appointment to these becomes more understandable when you consider his exploratory activities at the end of the 1930s in the lead-up to the Second World War. As to the frequently-posed question of whether Shipton was ever a spy, well – it depends what you mean by a spy? *Pravda* certainly believed he was, and referred to him as 'the well-known English spy'. What is very clear is that his anxiety about capture by the Chinese during the Cho Oyu expedition of 1952, which contributed to its failure and was a strong factor in his removal from the leadership of 1953 Everest, was thoroughly justified. Had he fallen into Chinese hands, his position would have been invidious – interrogation and a bullet in the back of the head its likely outcome. A Great Game indeed..! Peter Hopkirk's 1990 book of the same title is the essential reading here, exemplary in its research

future both professionally and as a mountaineer were to be of very considerable significance. He was also, quite modestly but with a certain exploratory competence to draw on now, offering to sort out problems in a strategic area the surveying of which over forty years had descended into utter cartographic confusion.

Once back in London in December he set to canvassing his acquaintance for more impressions of and information about the region. Longstaff and Bruce told him that the Karakoram – the range of remote high peaks, the highest concentration of the world's 8,000-metre giants among them, at the western end of the Himalaya between the valleys of the Indus and the Yarkand rivers, the plains of Chinese Turkestan beyond – surpassed description or imagination, its colossal scale and drama something he would only appreciate by seeing it for himself. He had immediately alerted the man who was still his first-choice companion, Tilman, to the idea, suggesting to him a small party consisting of the two of them together with Fazal Elahi from the Osmaston team, the speed and efficiency of whose mapping work in the Sanctuary had impressed him; another young Indian surveyor of growing reputation, Inayat Khan, to assist Fazal; and their usual band of Sherpas for a lightweight trip. The two Indian surveyors would work from a base camp to produce 'a nucleus of accurate work to which we could attach our long, less detailed traverses'.[13] Tilman of course, possible 'Bugger you' telegram notwithstanding, responded positively and with alacrity, by which point Shipton, safely ensconced in Lexham Gardens again under his mother's chaste and potentially disapproving[14] eye, with the research facilities of the Royal Geographical Society just down the road, had begun to concentrate rather more closely on the matter in hand.

He soon realised that there were attendant difficulties, and these were far from minor. The logistical problems of keeping a party provisioned in a landscape vastly larger, more barren and

---

and narrative sweep, dramatically written and thoroughly compelling.
[13] Eric Shipton, 'The Shaksgam Expedition, 1937' (*Geographical Journal*, April 1938), p.313.
[14] I.e. where his liaisons were concerned. Mrs Freston, a married woman with a child, would have been far beyond the pale for Mrs Haly, which fact the former sensed and endlessly fretted about in her correspondence with Shipton. This was probably a factor in the quite-rapid cooling of their relationship, which ended early in 1939 though a lifelong friendship endured, as it seems to have done with the majority of Shipton's liaisons.

inhospitable than those of Garhwal where most of their explorations
had taken place were considerable, involving an exponential
increase in the scale of provisioning, rendering 'lightweight' in this
instance a relative term – not an Everest siege trip by any means,
but still, two tons of flour and the hundred or more porters needed
to carry it! Problematical too was the question of access. The only
feasible route, given constraints of time and season, was to cross the
main Karakoram range from the Baltoro glacier. This, truly, was to
venture into the throne-room of the mountain gods, and to catch
the right conditions it would mean reaching the glacier – itself a
considerable journey – by the end of May. Thereafter they would
head on over the Karakoram watershed, possibly by Younghusband's
Old Muztagh Pass twelve miles to the west of K2, used in 1887 and
again in the reverse direction by Ardito Desio's party of 1929, when
it had become an even more formidable obstacle through glacier
shrinkage; or perhaps by an unknown col to its west observed by
Desio which seemed to offer hope of an easier passage over to the
Sarpo Laggo glacier.

They would have to carry sufficient food and supplies to maintain
them for a hundred days through excursions from a base camp
and cache beyond the snout of the Sarpo Laggo glacier, near the
confluence of the valley below with that coming down from the
Crevasse glacier, which huge ice stream led up twenty-five miles
westwards into the glacier complex north-east of the Hispar-
Biafo glacial axis – beyond which again lay the fabled Snow Lake,
first described and named, despite only having been seen from its
southern periphery, on the expedition led by Martin Conway in
1892. General Bruce and the Pen-y-Pass pioneer Oscar Eckenstein,
who is credited with the invention of crampons, were also members
of this team, which succeeded in making a very decent sketch map
survey of two thousand square miles of the Karakoram that year –
an achievement that earned Conway his knighthood of 1895. Seven
years later Snow Lake was transformed by the power of imagination
into the permanent ice cap of William Hunter Workman and Fanny
Bullock Workman's surmise. [15] So Shipton's group would be entering

---

[15] Dr William Hunter Workman and his wife Fanny Bullock were American
mountain explorers active in the Himalaya, and particularly the Karakoram,
before the Great War. Though admirable in many respects – Fanny in particular
having become iconic within women's studies in recent years – their survey work
was delegated and tended to the slipshod, inattentive and exaggerated, and their

here the most complex and extensive – and in the main unreliably charted and reported – region of ice in the Himalaya. Peter Mott, surveyor on Shipton's major projected survey expedition of 1939–1940, sums up the existing state of mapping as follows: 'Before Shipton's expedition the only maps of the region were based on sketch surveys by Conway and, later, the Bullock Workmans, which provided only a hesitant outline (often wildly in error) of this vastly complicated terrain.'[16]

From the projected Sarpo Laggo/Crevasse glacier junction base camp they planned to cross the Shaksgam river and push on into the Aghil range to the north-east. After exploring and surveying here for as long as could be risked before summer floods consequent on glacier melt rendered the Shaksgam river impassable, they would return to the Sarpo Laggo base camp around mid July. Once safely back across the major barrier of the Shaksgam, they hoped to locate and investigate the mysterious course of a river described by Colonel Kenneth Mason on a Survey of India expedition in 1926 and named by him the Zug (or false) Shaksgam, which had acted as barrier against his attempt to explore the Aghil range and find Younghusband's Aghil pass of 1887. All this with luck and reasonable conditions having been accomplished, they hoped next to investigate the purportedly peculiar glacial phenomena – particularly the Snow Lake, and also the Cornice glacier – that had been anomalously described by the exploratory party led by the Bullock Workmans during the years around the turn of the century in the area forty miles to the west and north-west of the world's second-highest mountain, K2, and which had been the subject of intense and at times acrimonious debate within the RGS, of which Fanny was one of the first female members.

The scale of this proposal for an itinerary of many months through remote, inhospitable, ice-bound and unexplored country is a clear index to the confidence his 1934 and 1935 explorations, with their success and their flattering reception, had bred in Shipton. Now

responses when challenged on this to vituperation (an invariable clue to insecurity and guilt). Sir Martin Conway, most important of early Karakoram explorers, bore the brunt of their slanders after daring to question certain outlandish conclusions at which they had arrived, notably with regard to the Snow Lake and the Cornice glacier.
[16] P.G. Mott, 'Karakoram Survey, 1939: A New Map' (*Geographical Journal,* July–September 1950), p.89.

in his thirtieth year, and Britain's most celebrated young mountain adventurer (Frank Smythe's growing backlist and the unexpected success of Tilman on Nanda Devi notwithstanding), not only was he immensely personable and perhaps a little mysterious, he was also schooling himself to be very capable in his chosen field of mountain travel, cartography and survey. For all the famous dialectical insistence on back-of-an-envelope planning, he was much more meticulous than that. And it became apparent to him that this undertaking required more than the usual happy-go-lucky, Tilman-and-himself-and-a-trio-of-their-blokes formula to bring back the kind of worthwhile results that would meet with the approval of his paymasters – for this trip would certainly not be possible on their former shoestring of £143 each. In fact, he calculated it out to a budget total of £855, still exceptional value for the area to be covered and the amount of work it was intended to produce. This money – not an inconsiderable sum at the time – Shipton managed to raise, again with unusual rapidity, through grants from the RGS, the Royal Society and the Survey of India.

So having titillated Tilman with the prospect of another grand adventure into the unknown wild with just himself and their 'blokes' for company, he now started to disappoint him again by shaping and adding to the party. The Indian surveyors were dropped, the Darjeeling middlemen were cut out for once and Ang Tharkay himself – a sign of his growing stature and influence – was directly delegated to recruit half a dozen Sherpas under his sirdar-ship. In this task he performed as reliably as ever: Sen Tenzing ('The Foreign Sportsman'), Lhakpa Tenzing, Lobsang, Ila, Nukku and Ang Tenzing were a good balance of experience and youthful strength and enthusiasm. First among the Europeans after Tilman, sensibly and usefully, there was Shipton's London near-neighbour and increasingly warm acquaintance Michael Spender, always up for an adventure, even one like this of several months' duration, and, by a stroke of luck and the good offices of a Leverhulme scholarship which he planned to use for research into new geographical surveying techniques, available for the whole of 1937.

Spender's presence on this trip established a strong and con-tinuing inflection in the Shipton/Tilman expeditionary style, for all the latter's resistance to it. Exploration and mapping now took precedence over mountaineering. This was to provide a widening target for those opponents and critics that success always breeds through the malignant agency of Kleinian Envy (and to whom the internet now gives unbridled scope for carping expression and vicious mendacity. Small wonder Tilman in the main avoided humanity). Another poet's elder brother and mountaineer with some alpine and Himalayan experience, John Auden (he had been of the same Cambridge generation as Jack Longland), who was employed by the Geological Survey of India, proved to be ready, willing and already stationed out in India, so a steamer fare was saved and another ingredient of expertise added into the exploratory mix. Auden was acquainted with the Karakoram, having made a trip to the Biafo glacier on the west side of K2 in 1933, and his guidance in planning the first stages of the journey and advice about porters in the region would prove valuable, as did the 6.5 x 54 mm. Männlicher-Schoenauer hunting rifle he brought with him, though his character as the journey progressed proved less than amenable. In one of his expedition accounts Shipton notes enigmatically that 'cutting ourselves off . . . for a period of three-and-a-half months placed a considerable strain on the party'.[17] To be fair to Auden, it should be recorded that his own later accounts of his fellow-expeditioners were models of courtesy and balance, and quite devoid of openly expressed rancour, though hints were there for those ready to pick them up.

The element developing here of London cultural society stepping out on the roof of the world is marked. That Lexham Gardens base was proving its worth, and affording Shipton entrée to an influential, bohemian and tangled cultural coterie. Michael Spender, who soon became perhaps his closest friend, was eventually to begin an affair with the wife of the artist William Coldstream (she was herself an artist, working under her maiden name of Nancy Sharp, and Coldstream's many life studies make her appeal perfectly clear). She and Coldstream, by whom she had two daughters, would be divorced during the war years, and Spender – with whom she had a son, Philip – married her two years before his death in a flying accident in 1945. Michael Spender's predecessor as her lover had been the major Irish poet Louis MacNeice, two of whose best poems, 'Leaving Barra' and 'Autumn Journal', were addressed to Mrs Coldstream as she then was ('. . . I am glad/ That life contains her with her moods and moments/More shifting

[17] *G.J.* April 1938, p.323.

and more transient than I had/Yet thought of as being integral to beauty;/Whose mind is like the wind on a sea of wheat,/Whose eyes are candour . . .').[18] Further complications in this introverted circle were Mrs Coldstream's attraction to John Auden's younger brother Wystan Hugh, whom she remembered from his time in 1935 working at the GPO with her husband (the well-known short film 'Night Mail' was one result of this collaboration): 'I loved him dearly,' she confessed – though she added that he was 'barely house-trained'. She also found him sexually desirable, but 'I knew he was queer'. For his part, Auden told his elder brother John that he and Nancy had been on the point of having an affair, 'but just in time I remembered that all women are destructive'. He may have had a point on this occasion – most men reading the relevant sections of 'Autumn Journal' would quail.

This metro-centricity does occasionally surface in *Blank on the Map* (1938), Shipton's book about the 1937 Shaksgam explorations, most notably when the author confides that 'the stake for all our bets was a meal at Simpson's. Though since our return none of us seems to have had enough spare cash to honour his debts.'[19] It also raises the question of how excluded the taciturn and austere member for Wallasey, whose pawky humour was a distinctly subtle and exotic ingredient in the expeditionary mix and for whom the notion of a dinner at Simpson's would scarcely have set the pulse racing, might have felt among his fellow team members.

There is a certain amount of contradictory evidence about the interpersonal dynamics of this team. In an early letter to his sister Adeline, written from Ladakh, Tilman states that 'we are getting on very well', before going on to mention that Spender 'harps a good deal on food'. Shipton lets the cat out of this particular bag (or rather, to mix our animal metaphors, gives us a clue as to the identity of the team's scapegoat) in the second of the chapters he devotes to the expedition in *Upon That Mountain*. His account of relations within the group, though given in general terms, is well

---

[18] From 'Autumn Journal' – one of the best long poems of the 1930s, which contains some very fine and understated erotic passages, their perceptions suffused with a post-coital glow – in Louis MacNeice *Selected Poems* (Faber, 1988, p.48.)

[19] Shipton, *Blank on the Map*, p.95. Simpson's was (and is) the famous restaurant close to the Savoy Hotel on the Strand. In its heyday in the 1930s, its sirloins of beef and saddles of mutton were the subject of copious expeditionary daydreams and salivations – particularly for those on Shipton/Tilman rations.

worth examining in detail. He begins the chapter by stating the
premise of how difficult it is to preserve harmony between members
on prolonged mountaineering or exploratory trips, mentions the
manner in which this was generally glossed over in the standard
accounts, and proceeds to suggest that 'sufficient of the inner history
of the classic expeditions has leaked out' to hint at an exigent rather
than a romantic reality. His own more honest epoch allows of
greater frankness around this issue: 'All manner of things, great and
small, are liable to promote discord. Garrulity is notoriously hard
to bear; silence can be no less trying. Even an unconscious display
of virtue can be as intolerable as any vice . . .'

From laying out general principles (in which a coded element
is already present and obvious), he moves on to describe incidents
and delineate traits which would have been clearly and personally
applicable: 'I remember once that someone became very angry when
I playfully threw an egg at his face; it was not that at the time there
was any scarcity of eggs, nor was the egg particularly bad. There is
no limit to people's unreasonableness.'

Shipton is in his vein of light mockery here of course, the
incident referred to one from the 1935 Everest reconnaissance trip.
He proceeds to a humorous sketch, suitably generalised though
immediately recognisable, of his own and Tilman's expedition
character traits: 'I know several travellers, most delightful people,
who admit quite frankly that they cannot stand having a companion
on their journey. Very wisely they travel alone. Others, of course,
are equally incapable of enduring their own exclusive company for
long, though they quarrel with all who share it.'[20]

There is playful teasing going on here, and we will come to the
response to it shortly. Before doing so, the same chapter abandons
generalities and works round to some quite sharp criticisms: 'I often
find that I get on well with men who are given to making wild
statements providing they support them with intelligent argument.
I consider that people who never say anything unless they are
perfectly sure of their ground become most irritating.'

He could hardly have given a clearer indication than this for
his shift in emotional allegiance from Tilman to Spender, and he
confirms the identification in the very next paragraph, whilst at the
same time defusing any potential offence: 'It would be difficult to

---

[20] Shipton, *Upon That Mountain*, pp.207–8.

find two people less alike in their intellectual make-up than Tilman and Spender. Yet I regard each in his way as the best companion I could wish for.' He goes on to talk of the Tilman–Spender relationship, suggesting that behind the appearance of not taking each other seriously was a 'strong mutual esteem'. Next to come under scrutiny was the tension between Spender and Auden (having I suspect, particularly after seeing group photographs, commented earlier on the way the latter 'wears his hat, or the silly manner in which his beard has grown'): 'Far more inflammable was the contact between the two scientists, and it was generally prudent to keep them separated as much as possible.'

In the chapter Tilman contributed to *Blank on the Map*, a confirmatory alternative perspective is provided on this observation. He and Auden, on their exit journeys, have climbed to the top of an easy peak overlooking a col on the watershed between the Nobande Sobande and Braldu glaciers:

> From the top there was a remarkable view, but Auden was ungrateful, because there was no concrete bed, or its equivalent, for the legs of the wretched theodolite, and the sky was rapidly clouding over. He explained at some length, and with great warmth, that readings taken as the theodolite sank slowly into the snow might be accepted by nit-wits like myself, but certainly by nobody else, and that observations should have been made lower down, when the visibility was good. Stunned though I was by this verbal storm, it was impossible not to enjoy the view which I, at any rate, had come for, and which was all the better for not being looked at upside down through the telescope of a theodolite.[21]

It does sound here as though Lawrence Wager picked the wrong scapegoat, and that Shipton and Tilman have appointed his fellow geologist to the role instead of Spender. I was given a late insight into the dynamics of a Tilman expedition by none other than Tilman himself. It came in the form of an anecdote related in the course of one of those winter-quarters fireside conversations at Bodowen, on this occasion early in 1977. I had asked him how many of the stories which had grown up around him were apocryphal. He knew perfectly well what I meant, having had to contend with mockery of his perceived traits from the 1930s onwards (to the extent, even, of the satirical novel *The Ascent of Rum Doodle*, which parodies Tilman's Nanda Devi book). So he paused to fill his pipe, and with his face creased in good humour, delivered the following perfectly balanced *ex tempore* periods in response, which I copied down studiously into my notebook immediately on leaving – having imbibed the due quota of potent pre-lunch home-brew – an hour or so later:

> By far the greater number, but there is one which is substantially true. It was on an expedition in the thirties. We embarked at Tilbury, and I am said to have stayed on deck until we rounded the North Foreland, whereupon I was heard to mutter the words, 'H'm, sea!' After this I went below decks and was not seen again until we hove in sight of Bombay. I then came on deck once more and was duly heard to utter the words, 'H'm, land!' It is asserted that these were the only words I spoke on the entire voyage, which is more or less the truth of the matter, and the reason, quite simply, is that I could not stand the other chaps on that trip.

At this point he dissolved into alcoholic chuckles, and then studied me very carefully to see what effect had registered. I've been pondering this story for over thirty years and am still, to a degree, perplexed by it. For many years I looked on it as a kind of parable, setting forth his moral relationship with the world: being below decks; seeing sea; seeing land; above all shunning the company of his fellow men. Latterly I've been attempting to square that with a more literal interpretation.[22] The first point to be made from that direction is that the voyage referred to is identifiable, and the only one on which he sailed from Tilbury to Bombay. It was on the new P&O liner *Strathmore* – quite a large and elegant boat of 23,500 tons that served on the Orient run from 1935 to 1963 (after which by a neat irony it became a Greek-owned pilgrim ship carrying

---

[22] There is of course another very obvious way of looking at this, and a simpler one too – that he was making fun of both of us, me and himself, and testing my sense of humour in doing so. I was a keen climber in those days, so the humour bypass would have been no doubt firmly in place and I might not have picked up on this. It *is* more complex than that, though, and all these views are relevant.

the devout on their way to Mecca). Shipton and his mother, along with Tilman and Spender, travelled out on her to Bombay from Tilbury. Would he have behaved in the manner he describes given that in their peculiar way he and Shipton were fixed in a distant orbit of friendship; that Tilman had received hospitality from Isobel Haly at Lexham Gardens; that he was anyway courteous and old-fashioned to a fault in the company of 'family' women, and the most punctilious of men;[23] that Spender he knew from the 1935 Everest reconnaissance trip, and his work would have been both interesting and comprehensible to a degree from his gunnery days, however much he might recoil from Spender's garrulity, and gripe about his weighty equipment and devotion to food? The answer to all of these questions must surely be a firm 'no'.

Whatever else the story may be, it is not one to be taken at face value. Is that echo of Shipton's tease against him in *Upon That Mountain* ('cannot stand having a companion') significant? I think when you take into consideration the longest-running and most public of all the teases between these two – the one about the Yeti, which has occasioned so much huffing and puffing from certain po-faced observers and commentators in recent years (see the epilogue for more on this – where *has* mountaineering's sense of fun disappeared to of late?) – you have to conclude that it is so. Having accepted that, you're thus given a clue as to how this friendship operated, several idiomatic phrases being useful here: mickey-taking, leg-pulling and so on. But you also have to take into account that this is humour, particularly on Tilman's side – Shipton is distinctly more sly and deft – of a pretty sardonic and astringent variety, and that, in the best Freudian manner,[24] it is likely to contain several grains of sour truth. You might remember here too just how acerbic the Tilman brand of humour became, particularly after his second period of war service – the statement, for example, that 'there is a good case to be made for dropping bombs on civilians

---

[23] He was outraged, for example, when his Italian resistance friends in a visit by him to Belluno after the war attempted to install him and his accompanying favourite niece Pam Davis in a double bedroom, on the very Italian-male assumption that Pam was his mistress. 'But she *is* my niece!' he insisted furiously. Pam, meanwhile, not remotely offended, was having to turn away and hide her face in her handkerchief to suppress fits of the giggles.

[24] Sigmund Freud, *Jokes and their Relation to the Unconscious* (Harmondsworth, 1976) is the relevant text here.

because so very few of them can be described as inoffensive', which
is comic misanthropy on a Swiftian scale, laughter used as agent of
accommodation to a deep-seated dislike-in-principle of the human
race, at least in its Western manifestation. All this should alert us to
how very careful we need to be around interpretation of either of
our subjects' verbal sallies.

The voyage out, 'an interlude between a life and a life',[25] may
or may not have been passed sociably and happily in throwing
medicine balls around and paying court to Mrs Haly each evening
in the tourist-class dining room. It certainly ended with a jolt and a
clatter on 22 April 1937 when the *Strathmore* collided heavily with
the Ballard Pier while docking in Bombay, damaging her bow and
consigning her to dry dock for the next couple of years. Whatever
the soothsayers clustered around the Gateway to India may have
predicted, no symbolic significance seems to have been placed on
this by the expeditioners. They transferred their equipment on to
the Frontier Mail due to depart from Ballard Pier Mole, and clacked
away by a roundabout route to Karachi and Rawalpindi, which
they reached four days later, Tilman and Spender having travelled
second class in a grubby, crowded carriage whilst Shipton and
his mother, through the good offices of 'friends at court', relaxed
in a 'gleaming white-and-chromium special coach' – the first air-
conditioned carriage on Indian railways. In Rawalpindi the social
divisions widened further. Shipton, along with the coolly elegant
Mrs Haly, was whisked off to the colonial-period luxuries of a
private saloon at Government House, to consultative meetings,
briefings, baths and a bed and lavish hospitality. After a comfortable
night's rest he donned his best suit and breakfasted sumptuously
on bacon, eggs poached or better still scrambled with Gentleman's
Relish, muffins and devilled lamb's kidneys, toast and coffee and
Oxford marmalade, before sauntering down to the nearby railway
platform, where he located his two fellow expeditioners: '. . . soot-
blackened ruffians, their unshaven faces streaming with grimy
sweat, their tired eyes regarding me with incredulous loathing . . .
I asked them how they had slept, and made some remark about it
being surprisingly cool in the Sind desert for the time of year.'[26]

Clearly this was a diplomat in the making. He returned to

---

[25] Shipton, *Blank on the Map*, p.15.
[26] Ibid. p.16.

Government House, changed into more suitable attire, arranged for the charter of a lorry to take them the two hundred miles to Srinagar, and they settled down to wait for the Sherpas to arrive from Darjeeling. Ang Tharkay and his band turned up apparently out of nowhere, with not a train in sight, at three the next morning, and all spent the next twenty-four hours being bounced around in the back of a lorry. Astonishingly, Mrs Haly accompanied them, though no doubt she had a seat in the cab. This lady's incessant travelling, often as now in company with her son to some jumping-off point for his expeditions, or to the south of India or Ceylon to visit her daughter, or into China purely for herself, or to Budapest or Bratislava to follow her European cultural interests, comes across as both profoundly impressive and at the same time pathologically driven. It contributed to her early death in a London hospital of tropical sprue – a miserable cause of demise, and endemic in the subcontinent, where she surely contracted it – which occurred within a year of Shipton's December 1942 marriage to Diana Channer at Lyme Regis. The degrees of connection between these two events seem obvious, and scarcely need commenting upon here. Throughout the writing of this book Isobel Haly has felt omnipresent and watchful. To my mind, comments made about her by Shipton's biographer, and by her daughter-in-law, have been a little unkind – taking into account neither the positive effect she had on her son's life; nor the unusual closeness, for all its apparent lack of intimacy, of the relationship between them; nor the sterling and enterprising character she so clearly possessed, aspects of which were passed on to her son. Certainly there appears to have been distance and reserve – no bad things, surely? – but to balance those there were other qualities: concern for her children, resourcefulness, intelligence, culture, an adventurous spirit, and great physical beauty, which all too often produces adverse and envious reactions. There is far more to Isobel Haly than the two-dimensional caricature tag of ice maiden allows. I wonder what a sympathetic and competent biographer like Claire Tomalin might make of her as a woman of her time?

The lorry ground its way up from the valley of the Indus through Abbottabad and Baramula, and on to the cool lakeside setting of Srinagar. Here they organised themselves over the space of a week, camping on the governmental lawns whilst Mrs Haly stayed with Sir Peter and Lady Clutterbuck in the official mansion, and left by car – or lorry in the case of the Sherpas – on 5 May for the roadhead at Woyil Bridge, where Shipton said goodbye to his mother and Lady Clutterbuck. From here began the march up the Sind valley, beyond which they had to cross the 11,500-foot Zoji La into Baltistan, heading for the valley of the Indus. In the first days they found the country they were journeying through 'wonderfully easy to live off. Eggs, chickens, butter and milk are plentiful and cheap',[27] and they supplemented the contents of a grand hamper of luxuries, plum cake among them, bestowed by Lady Clutterbuck. Shipton notes in his journal the Sherpas' enthusiasm for cards, which 'are produced whenever there is the slightest opportunity of playing', and records that he himself is 'suffering from my usual tiredness, foot-fatigue and despondency with which I start these shows'. A 'wonderful roast chicken . . . preceded by a very good soup and followed by excellent coffee by Spender' and rounded off with a cigar bought on the ship raised his spirits. Porters were taken on at Baltal, 'a typically Alpine village at the head of the valley . . . set in deep woods of silver birch and tall firs', amid bizarre scenes – 'several fine battles raged in various quarters of the compound – Bill in fits of laughter and Auden rushing about trying to get photos'.

With twenty-five Balti porters they crossed the Zoji La by night, starting at 2 a.m. with a single glacier lantern, because of deep snow and the risk of avalanches. 'Tilman gloated over the opportunity of waking us early. At 2 a.m. I heard him clumping about self-righteously. There was no hope of sulkily defying his onslaught.'[28] To lighten his own mood, Shipton snaffled the lantern and led the way over the pass, Tilman as last man profiting little from its dim illumination. Beyond the pass they came across a sad little scene where a pack pony in a caravan going in the opposite direction had fallen into the river and its owners, without taking off its burden, were attempting to drag it out. Shipton records how Tilman without a second thought leapt fully clothed into the swift, icy water, took off the pony's load and succeeded in floating the animal out into midstream, but it was paralysed with the cold and snow overhung the banks of the river to prevent its exit: 'Eventually the wretched

---

[27] There are two small black notebooks written in pencil describing the Shaksgam expedition. All unattributed quotations from here to the end of the chapter are from these.
[28] Shipton, *Blank on the Map*, pp.27–8.

thing drowned and was left in mid-stream. Owner said it had broken its back. Doubt this.'

They came across women and children gathering baskets of a small aromatic herb, admired the fantastic pinnacles all around, and watched a snow avalanche pour over the cliffs above. 'Bill made some very good scones this afternoon. Half of these Kashmiri coolies have blue eyes.' The route descended into bleak desert country devoid of vegetation. Tilman panned for gold by a river and found nothing but concentrates, whilst Ang Tharkay and Lhakpa Tenzing were dispatched to Kargil and returned in the evening with 'three chickens, two dozen eggs, two pounds of meat and a bottle of "arrak".[29] They had drunk a whole bottle themselves in spite of which they didn't think much of Kargil. Arrak good stuff and makes this desert seem a much pleasanter place.' Moving on along a skilfully engineered path across the cliff face two hundred feet above the water they amused themselves by levering off large rocks and listening for the percussive report as they dropped into an 'oily river rolling so quietly but with such strength'.

Can hear places it goes over rapids for miles, Bathed in pool of side river. Lovely sunbathing after it. I dropped my watch which now won't go. <u>Bloody</u> nuisance! One gets ridiculously reliant on a watch. I suppose one will get used to it as one gets used to having no trousers to change into! We are camped in an apricot grove on grass. Ang Tharkay has made new culinary effort – chicken, green veg. and maize flour – very good. Spender finished up the coffee with excellent brew. Wish we had more of it. Never had such good coffee on expedition before – and seldom in 'civilisation'!

The latter was being left well behind:

Path kept very high up the craggy hillside and we entered the Indus valley about 1,000 feet above the river and then descended steeply to it. As usual the two streams appeared no bigger after they had joined than either before the junction. It was fun being in the Indus valley. Utterly bleak and forbidding. Just like surroundings of Aden. At intervals there were the

---

[29] In this region, a potent rice brandy.

amazingly green oases of apricot trees, poplars, and the brilliant, terraced corn fields with their few stone huts.

At Tarkati the villagers boiled them eggs and told them the Balti names for things, many of them now of Tibetan origin. A little beyond, in the heat of the day, they came to a grand two-hundred-foot waterfall and another of those recurrent Shiptonian moments of glorious visionary regression ensued:

> Bill and I stripped and climbed up some great boulders standing right in front of where the water landed throwing up clouds of spray. Very cold but incredible sight. A brilliant rainbow formed all around us, expanding and contracting as density of spray increased or decreased. <u>Wonderful</u> sight. Later went (still naked) to prowl in enchanting caverns full of moss and spray and lit by own personal rainbow. Put on shorts and marched on feeling cool and full of energy to enjoy the weird country. Bill bathed four times in all today.

Beyond the oases the country became increasingly barren and dry. At one village the inhabitants boiled fifteen eggs for the three of them to eat (Auden had taken a lower path and missed the treat). They walked on 'talking about beer and feeling that nothing else in the world we wanted as much'. At Tolti, the next village along their route, the local raja and his servant turned up and cadged cigarettes from Spender before demanding to see their rifle and setting up a target. Tilman was appointed by the others as marksman, being ex-military and a gunner at that. After taking careful aim he just missed, firing too high, whilst the servant, waving the gun around somewhere in the region of his midriff, blew the target to bits, bowling himself over with the recoil in the process. They were challenged to a chukka of polo, so left hurriedly before more damage was done. From another village they bought 'three dozen eggs and some butter which we made into a huge rumble tumble in a native pot, fashioned spoons out of wood and all ate out of pot to vast entertainment of natives'.

On 18 May they reached Skardu in Baltistan after a thirteen-day trek enlivened by continual porter politics, frequent skirmishes between them and the warrior band of Sherpas, and 'geology very interesting with Auden to explain things to us.' Shipton took the opportunity to write to his mother to describe their adventures and journey so far.

'My Darling Mum,
    We got here yesterday and I found your letter waiting. Thank you so much for it and also for the lovely parcel of chocolate which, as you can imagine, is <u>most</u> welcome. Also thank you for the snaps; the ones you took at the bridge are very good and the Sherpas loved having the enlargements of themselves.
    The march here has been most interesting since I wrote. First a long one of 20 odd miles through very barren country – like a large edition of Aden. But as we got further down into the Indus river basin, every few miles we came to glorious little oases where an ancient alluvial terrace had been left and is now irrigated and cultivated and supporting a village. The corn is just growing and is an amazing green, and higher up, where the apricot trees are in blossom these oases are shaded by a blanket of pink. Imagine chunks of spring Kent dumped in the midst of Aden hills. It makes one realise how true it is that contrast is the real spice of life. But the country is fascinating too, geographically and geologically. It is vast fun following these enormous rivers and having their whole past history spread before one. I have enjoyed it very much and so have the others. Bill bathes four times a day and occasionally induces me to do the same, while Auden spends his time happily hammering away at rocks, and must quite have changed the face of the scenery! We used to halt about half way through each march at some village and collect as many eggs as the inhabitants could produce (generally from two to three dozen) and boil or scramble them to the vast entertainment of the villagers, who meanwhile manufacture wooden spoons to help us deal with the eggs.

After describing to his mother their proposed itinerary for the next few months, he comments that 'it will be very exciting to see all the ranges, rivers and glaciers we have been talking about so much without having any idea what they really look [like]'. He ends on a very personal note:

I hope you are having a good trip to Ceylon and are finding

things OK there. I am very sad that I shall not be able to hear
from you as you go East. I will always be thinking about you
and wondering where you have got to. It is fun that your and
my taste are so much the same; though the necessity of making
some sort of career and doing some sort of work makes me do
this rather than what you are doing. But they are both exactly
the same really.[30]

In Skardu they were visited by the town's doctor, who told them
that though there was no cholera or dysentery in the area, there
was a lot of typhoid and smallpox in the water. He had vaccinated
30,000 people in the region, and wanted to add the expeditioners
to his list. They declined, which may have been a mistake. From
the bazaar they took on supplies of tsampa, ghee, rice, sugar, salt,
paraffin and blankets for the porters, and arranged for two tons
of flour to be waiting for them in Askole, five days' march ahead.
In the course of this march they were given their introductions
to the means and terrors of Karakoram river crossings (that of
the Indus was on a huge barge reputedly in use since the days
of Alexander the Great). Terror of icy rivers apart, there was the
pleasure of hot sulphur springs, 'in which Bill and I wallowed for a
goodish time and washed ourselves with soap. Rather like bathing
in soda water. Huge knot of queer hollow-sounding crusted stuff
formed by sulphur deposits. Marched on naked to get dry until
forced hurriedly to dress by approach of Balti maidens.' In the
village from which the latter came, a major battle was taking
place between the Sherpas and the villagers that caused Shipton
to recall Ang Tharkay's indiscretions of 1935 and Rinzing's at
Shekar in 1936. It necessitated the payment of compensation and
brought a few degrees of frost into the vital relationship with the
locals on whom they were going to be dependent for food and
porterage.

It is very marked how good is the material from the two Shaksgam
notebooks from which much of the above is taken, and how directly
and in little altered form it finds its way into *Blank on the Map*.
Most of the strongest passages in the book are taken more or less
verbatim from this source. In his Shipton biography Peter Steele
suggests that Pamela Freston, to whom *Blank on the Map* bears a

dedication,[31] had a strong improving effect on Shipton as a writer. He cites as evidence for this view her influence on his reading matter (*Gone With The Wind* apparently – Tilman observes laconically his friend's proclivity for carrying, on lightweight expeditions, 'the longest novel that has been published in recent years'.[32] Whether Shipton ever read it is unclear, but it appeared time and again, grew increasingly dog-eared as trips went by and its spine finally gave way so it was relegated to use as toilet paper);[33] and also a 'very heavily edited – you might almost say re-written' typescript for *Blank on the Map*. Of the latter, Steele quotes from a letter of 3 March 1938 in which he suggests that 'Shipton whines to Pamela, "I am terribly sorry it is so bad".'[34] It is quite clear, reading through the source notebooks and comparing them with published accounts, that the editorial interventions, whoever's they may have been, in the main come in the form of intrusive and awkward explanations of technical terms which a non-mountaineer and lay reader wholly devoid of both imagination and a dictionary or glossary might just on a very few occasions find difficult to understand. The Shipton diffidence is at work here, and a word needs to be offered on his behalf. At his best, he is a delightfully evocative, humorous and precise descriptive writer who can handle narrative, action and character and blend them into a compelling and persuasive story. There is also the quirky and endlessly curious cast of his mind, which in itself appeals – somewhat in the manner of the definition of John Donne's attraction for us that Mario Praz gives in *The Romantic Agony*: 'It is the rhythm of thought itself that attracts, by virtue of its own peculiar convolutions.'

Shipton was certainly insecure about his writing – as most good writers are – and that surely stemmed from his early and unfortunate educational experiences at the Gifford academy, which affected him lifelong and were perhaps compounded into a kind of inferiority complex (of which the tentative self-diagnosis of 'word

---

[31] 'To Pamela Freston, without whose help the book would not have been written' – a standard and quite cool courtesy from an author towards a sexual partner, surely?

[32] 'Mount Everest, 1938' (*Alpine Journal*, 1939), p.7.

[33] Tilman was the source of this information – as you may gather, he did not approve.

[34] Peter Steele, *Everest and Beyond*, p.89. Having seen the letter, I would not have characterised it in this manner.

blindness' was an expression) by his avoidance tactics around the opportunity of reading for a Cambridge degree. One point by which I would swear, having studied the source texts, is that the quality of his writing is entirely his own, and not dependent in any way on essentially uninformed editorial input. Aileen Fisher-Rowe, the Wiltshire friend in whose house he died in 1977, vouchsafes that Mrs Freston essentially did no more than 'dot the Is and cross the Ts'.

As further support for the case I'm putting forward here, there is a consensus on Shipton's two best books being his first, *Nanda Devi*, and his last, *That Untravelled World*. (A case needs also to be made for the long influence of *Blank on the Map*, based on some very strong individual passages, the intrinsic interest of its subject matter, and its original photography, though in terms of narrative structure the book is an appealing shambles – one that needed, in fact, a good editor. Stephen Venables rightly points out in a lucid and authoritative foreword to the 2010 edition of *The Six Mountain Travel Books*, that 'It was Eric Shipton's 1937 photos of the Latok peaks, the Ogre and Uli Biaho that inspired the new generation[35].' Most of these are to be found in *Blank on the Map*, though several impressive ones – a particularly striking one of the Trango Tower for example, and a beautiful study of Rakaposhi – were included in *Upon That Mountain*.)[36] *Nanda Devi* is the clear Shiptonian voice, youthful and very romanticised at times, but already possessed of great suppleness, expressive power and control. From the holograph material I have seen, I would conclude that it was very little changed on the way to publication. *That Untravelled World* by contrast passed through the hands of Hodder's long-time, universally loved mountain-books editor Margaret Body, a skilful professional who possessed the inestimable editorial virtue of knowing when to leave well alone – a technique to which an almost entirely unmarked final typescript prepared from an identical manuscript attests. The text was left exactly as it had been written – a dignified late meditation on a life well and bravely lived. These two are Shipton's masterpieces and his other books are lesser work in which his imagination was

---

[35] Eric Shipton, *The Six Mountain Travel Books* (paperback edition, Baton Wicks 2010).
[36] As too were a couple of rather silly snaps captioned as ice-climbing on Everest that were actually taken on the Nobande Sobande glacier in 1937. So much for some editors!

not so fully engaged. Of them, I am quite willing to believe that they may have been edited.[37] They do not seem to me the better for it. None of this is to dismiss the likely helpful influence of Mrs Freston, which Shipton as her lover would tend generously to overrate. It is merely to argue that Peter Steele's assertions are no more than that, unsubstantiated, and the proof is lacking that she augmented the quality of an extant and considerable natural talent;[38] and to note further that her assistance clearly was useful in the messy business of dealing with publishers, marking up typescripts and checking proofs for publication – the necessary foot-slogging at which most writers, being idle drones in the common view, baulk, and for any help with which they are abjectly, or even whiningly, grateful.

Finally, on this complex and difficult subject – which demands considerably more space than this narrative can afford – it puzzles me that no one has picked up on the psychological parallel between the lack of an assertive self-belief with regard to his writing, and the manner in which the same quality manifested in many of his statements concerned with, and stances taken around, the 1953 leadership issue, which led to the disgraceful manner of his removal after having been appointed to that position[39]. But more (though not much more – the subject was already tedious and the conclusions to be drawn from it obvious in 1953) on this in the epilogue.

The caravan duly arrived at Askole, and in the course of a 'bloody day and stupidly busy one' Tilman and Shipton bagged up fifty maunds[40] of *atta*, which 'came in silly driblets which kept one busy

---

[37] *Upon That Mountain* (1943) I think must stand outside these judgements, because of the unique difficulties attendant on its production in wartime, with Shipton at such a remove in Kashgar. Like *Blank on the Map*, though perhaps even more so, it is a notably uneven book that you treasure for certain outstanding passages. More on the editing of this in the epilogue.

[38] Peter Steele argues that 'Pamela got him to use the active mood instead of endless passives that fudge his earlier writing'. (*Everest and Beyond*, pp.89–90). He provides no supporting quotation or specific manuscript evidence for this assertion. The notebooks vigorously and predominantly employ active verbs, and their accounts are assimilated wholesale and little-changed into the published books.

[39] As an aside here – and this is not the place to elaborate, but I would hope that a future Shipton biographer would explore the issue in depth – the relevance of attachment theory, and particularly John Bowlby's work, to Shipton's life is very marked.

[40] A variable quantity, this, throughout India, though its official weight is given – variously! – as 82.3lb or 82.6lb.

doing very little', into sixty-pound loads and recruited 104 porters from surrounding villages to carry it, whilst Auden and Spender went off to resurvey the snout of the Baltoro glacier that Auden had visited four years before. The whole huge light-as-could-be-but-scarcely-lightweight caravan of Shipton and Tilman, Sherpas and porters moved out of Askole on 26 May. The adventure had begun in earnest, the first serious section lay immediately ahead, and everything now depended on crossing a high and difficult watershed with sufficient supplies to see them through the next three months and more. They had the accounts of their predecessors to rely on in the crossing to the Shaksgam, but Shipton, in his intelligently questioning way, was unconvinced by them, arguing in line with current theory that though the previous explorers 'all agree that the old passes have become impracticable because of the increased glaciation, it is probable, in my opinion, that this theory is incorrect, and that the present blocking of the passes is in most cases due to the disintegration of the glaciers: not to increased glaciation, but to the breaking up of the ice. In the earlier days there may have been easy snow-covered ice-slopes leading up to the passes, which in the gradual deterioration of the glaciers have become jagged, steep and impassable.'[41]

Even before they had reached the difficult stages of the crossing, he was weighing and analysing the evidence, considering carefully the difficulty of conveying supplies across the range and also the responsibility of taking a large number of ill-clad and ill-equipped porters into as cold and unwelcoming territory as exists on the planet, and one intersected by 'the rivers of the Karakoram . . . the most dangerous and the most difficult to deal with I have ever met'.[42] Which is surely saying something! To add to the unwelcoming aspect, heavy rain now drenched down on them continually, causing concern particularly for the flour which was to be their mainstay. On the evening of the 27th, two days' march out from Askole, they reached Paiju, two miles from the snout of the Baltoro glacier, with its shepherds' huts, willow-thickets and grasslands. Here they made camp, and a further difficulty arose – Tilman and Sen Tenzing both fell ill: 'Bill was no better this morning, with a temperature of 101.6. Very difficult to know what to do . . .'

[41] Shipton, *Blank on the Map*, p.57.
[42] Ibid. p.67.

In an astonishing and crucial passage from *Upon That Mountain*, Shipton reflects on the nature of leadership. It's necessary to give it in full at this juncture not only for the glimpse it provides into the exceptional leadership he displayed – whilst giving the impression that he was doing no such thing – on the Shaksgam expedition, and particularly at this point where his loyal adjutant was incapacitated and a dangerous and unknown crossing lay ahead; but also for the way in which it naturally follows on from the discussion above of his diffidence about his writing, and the further instances we will be coming to of his impish refusal ever to take himself too seriously, in which admirable stance he had found the perfect foil in Tilman (you might also consider the latter's refusal of promotion towards the end of the Great War in this context). Here's the passage:

> In my opinion far too much emphasis has been laid on leader-ship in connection with mountaineering and exploratory expeditions, for this led to an exaggerated notion of the importance of the leader and the difficulty of his task. How often does one hear the word 'brilliant' applied in this connection, when in fact all that was called for was the exercise of a little tact and common sense? In ordinary mountaineering the man who has had most experience on the particular type of ground to be covered generally assumes tacit charge of the party; the more evenly experience and skill are distributed among the members, the less obvious is this assumption of charge.

The applicability of this to his now long-standing relationship with Tilman is obvious. He continues:

> Anyone who tries to play the dictator in the lower valleys is likely to become very unpopular. As far as possible the same principle should be applied to the whole conduct of an expedition. A leader should make his position as inconspicuous as he can, and he should certainly avoid the appearance of taking his responsibilities too seriously.

The last phrase is central, and sums up what is at the core of the Shipton expeditionary style. Be very clear, though, about the significance and resonance of that word 'appearance'. In no way does it imply that the responsibilities themselves are to be taken at a deep level with anything other than the utmost seriousness:

> His primary task is the selection of his party. In the field his
> main function is to see that every man is placed in a position
> which gives him the widest scope for his particular job and
> for the use of his own initiative. Heavy military discipline,
> obviously necessary when vast armies are involved, is wholly
> out of place when dealing with a handful of carefully selected
> and thoroughly competent specialists. When it ceases to be
> laughable, it becomes intolerably irksome.[43]

The challenges here to the hierarchical values not just of
mountaineering society are striking, the whole passage a powerful
and reasoned refutation of militaristic values ever being valid in a
mountain context. This was and is revolutionary thinking, and it has
been the manifesto to all that is most to be admired in mountain
achievement over the last sixty years. For the moment, in Paiju, he
was still faced with the dilemma of what to do. To his notebook, he
presents the situation, and the practical conclusion he reaches about
how best to resolve it: 'Could not stop with bandobast of 103 porters[44]
in full swing – cost too much in food and cash. Decided to leave
Auden to cope with any situation that may arise. Very unsatisfactory
but the only thing to do. One can only hope that it is nothing serious.'

The fear, of course, after the earlier conversation with the doctor
in Skardu, was that the two men had gone down with typhoid – a
view which Tilman's near-obsessive addiction to bathing (remember
in this context his use in recalling his Great War experiences of
the Ancient Mariner quotation, 'And a thousand, thousand slimy
things/Lived on, and so did I', and consider the psychological
dimension of the habit – consider too his own later transmutation
into a version of the Ancient Mariner)[45] rendered likely. Possibly

---

[43] Shipton, *Upon That Mountain*, p.210.

[44] There is no discrepancy in the figure here – just a reflection of the manner in
which porters dropped out regularly throughout the crossing.

[45] The fine old Quaker, educationalist and mountaineer Robin Hodgkin (1916–
2003) alerted me thirty years ago to the necessity to consider the later image of
the water-snakes along with this, Coleridge's great axis of forgiveness turning
between the two. That it is relevant to do so with Tilman seems to me unarguable.
Remember here the post-war letter to the Alpine Club in support of Paul Bauer
previously mentioned.

they were suffering from a mild attack, the sickness following a characteristic phasal course over weeks in Tilman's case. Resolving to press on, and return by himself if no news had reached him by the time the base camp had been established and provisioned in the valley below the Sarpo Laggo glacier, with Spender, six Sherpas and Shipton at the head the long caravan was set in motion, climbing up on to the Baltoro glacier, 'the host of mankind,/A feeble wavering line./Where are they tending?'[46]

The answer to the last was that they did not exactly know, and the porters sensed they did not know – a situation ripe for mutiny, and it came close to that. On their first night along the Baltoro, they happened upon a grassy plain in an angle between the main glacier and a smaller ice stream flowing in to join it, and here, on 30 May, they camped. Spender talked that evening, after a 'big plateful of rice and very curried but very good mutton soup', of what it would now be like in an English spring landscape, and set Shipton, who had not seen an English spring in a decade, in a mood of yearning remembrance, for the delicate translucencies of the young beech leaves, and the croziers of bracken uncurling in the woods. The scale of this glaciated landscape was beyond anything he had previously encountered on Everest, in Sikkim, in Garhwal. His palpably awed response added to the porters' already present mood of anxiety and likely mutiny. This was particularly so when, after 'a very long and anxious day coaxing them over the desolate intricacies of the Trango glacier', Spender and Shipton returned unable to conceal their despondency from a fruitless examination of the hoped-for exit at the head of a right-hand branch they had chosen to reconnoitre beyond a fork.

That night they had to take off the porters' boots for them, light their campfires and instruct them in making snow shelters. The situation appeared hopeless; but the morning dawned fine, cold and clear, the snow was in good condition, and the whole party, its leaders convinced of the route now by a process of elimination, set out up the left-hand branch, along which they discovered a further side glacier rising gently to a col which had every appearance of being on the main divide of the range. Though it was only 9.30, they decided the col was out of reach for that day. Another freezing

---

[46] From 'Rugby Chapel' in *The Poems of Matthew Arnold*, ed. Kenneth Allott (Longman, 1965), p.451.

night was spent on a 'bleak, comfortless ledge' and the following morning Shipton, Spender and the Sherpas took it in turns to thrash through soft, crusted snow, followed by a handful of tougher characters from Skardu who had kept up all along. They reached the col, only to find that it was a false summit. 'Two miles off we saw another and lot higher one – devastating discovery.' The true crest was on the farther side of a wide snow basin. Rather than wait for the porters to arrive, see, and turn tail, the two Europeans 'plunged down into basin between – vile snow'. They were halted halfway across the basin by furious screams from behind. A stand-off ensued, the porters behind unwilling to take another step, the Europeans – with the Sherpas and Skardu men – desperate to coax every extra yard out of them to shorten the relay down to the Sarpo Laggo glacier beyond the col.

The trump card was in Shipton's hand and he knew it – he had the cash, and was not going to take one backward step in order to pay off the men. After an hour and a half of shouting, begrudgingly the Baltis filed across, dumped their loads, had silver rupees counted out into their palms and with remarkable alacrity and renewed energy now fled for home. The seventeen men of Skardu agreed to stay on and the diminished party reconnoitred the descent to the Sarpo Laggo, over the next twelve days moving all the loads down through temporary camps to the base camp, where they were rejoined by the – still intermittently sick – invalids from Paiju. They paid off the remaining Skardu men, and Spender immediately set to with the task of surveying. The crossing of the main Karakoram watershed had been accomplished, and as a piece of man-management in the harshest conditions and terrain it had been – out of respect I'll not use the word brilliant – exemplary. The crucial objective was reached, and now the work of the expedition could begin.

Time, however, was pressing upon them in ways redolent of their situation in the Nanda Devi Sanctuary. It was already mid June, and their next objective was to explore towards the Aghil pass, to the north-east beyond the Shaksgam river. If they found themselves trapped there by the swollen rivers on every side – Shaksgam to the south and west in its great curve round to join the Yarkand; the latter a huge obstacle to the north; the unknown imponderable of the Zug Shaksgam that had stopped Kenneth Mason thundering through its gorges to the east, and the Surukwat pouring down from below the Aghil pass – islanded within raging waters, their survival would be in jeopardy. There would be no way out. They set a latest-possible date by which all the party would need to be back on the south-west side of the Shaksgam – 10 July, and even that proved in the event to be cutting it dangerously fine. Yet what came to them in this place was the curious peace that danger carries as its concomitant to the aware and the attuned. The senses are sharpened, appreciation the more acute. And in these desert landscapes, the beauty of the intimate was amplified, as here in describing an oasis three miles to the north-east of their base camp on the way to the Shaksgam, close to the mouth of the valley coming down from K2 and its glacier:

> Suget Jangal was a perfect resting-place, for it had a quality of serene peace, rare in this country of stern severity. Some tall shrubs which grew beside the shallow blue pools were now covered with pink blossom. The song of small birds, the splash of a brook which welled from a crystal spring, the young hares running shyly across the meadows . . .[47]

For Shipton, there was something else in his response to this landscape that goes deeper than the conventional arcadianism of the above passage. It's the recurrent motif that stretches right back to the days in Wardour Vale – 'which I love best of all English country'[48] – of adolescence. It's the Richard Jefferies tradition of quietism and nature-mysticism that finds one of its clearest and best expressions during the exploration of the Aghil range, at the point where they have all but solved the geographical problem of Mason's Zug Shaksgam river, and the pieces in the landscape at which they have been quizzing and probing away have started to click into place. The passage is well worth quoting again, being key to an understanding of Shipton's response to nature:

> . . . we settled down on a comfortable bed of sand, and watched the approach of night transform the wild desert mountains into phantoms of soft unreality. How satisfying it was to be travelling with such simplicity. I lay awaiting the approach of sleep, watching the constellations swing across the sky. Did

---

[47] Shipton, *Blank on the Map*, p.139
[48] Writing from his wife Diana's parents' house in Warminster to Pamela Freston, Christmas Day 1944.

I sleep that night or was I caught up for a moment into the ceaseless rhythm of space?[49]

Note there the 'travelling with such simplicity', as being a point entirely crucial to the process of natural attunement. It is in passages like this, emotionally complex despite their apparent accessibility, that we can best appreciate how the rigorous simplicity of the Shipton/Tilman style satisfied in both men a deep emotional need. These are the Desert Fathers in mountaineering dress, seeking to expiate the savage effect upon themselves of so-called civilisation. Had they confessed themselves such to the climbing society of their time, and distanced themselves from it by so doing, then as now they would have been laughed to scorn. As it was, they provoked unease, and a readiness to criticise and mock.

Tilman had by now recovered from the bouts of fever from which he had been suffering recurrently for six weeks, and that 'ceaseless rhythm' collocation in the above quotation aptly sums up their restless activity throughout the remaining two months of the expedition. The whole party made it back south of the Shaksgam by 10 July – a little anxiously, and with the separate units into which they had divided to work most effectively on their individual projects arriving back at different times, and communicating their activities through notes left at base camp. Auden, as befitted the name, wrote his in verse.

> No news from Aghil Heights,
> No news from Zug Shaksgam,
> Only snow and wind at nights,
> And dreams of Birmingham.
>
> Small and worthless though I am,
> If peaks are part of Heaven,
> My Belly calls insistently
> For Delicatessen.
>
> All pervading deity,
> Ah yes! I recognise.
> To food I bend the knee,
> To food before mine eyes.

---

[49] Shipton, *Blank on the Map*, p.123.

> All is figment of the mind,
> And food we can invent,
> And wind is wind indeed
> If blown from fundament.

The family facility for light verse is obvious – not often a mountaineering book can boast of a newly discovered Auden poem. The flatulent effect of their diet, incidentally, is much commented on elsewhere, the Sherpas in particular finding huge amusement in the incessant and prodigious expulsions of wind. No doubt explanation lies here of their preference for sleeping in the open air and out of tents as often as possible. Tilman makes veiled allusion to this in his comment about Sen Tenzing: 'He is not a good sleeping companion – singing far into the night is his least offensive habit.'[50]

The long-established Shipton response to landscape was certainly as strongly present as ever on the Shaksgam explorations. Here, for example, he describes his feelings just before they cross the Shaksgam river to begin exploration in the Aghil range. He and Spender have climbed a ridge above Suget Jangal, looking up the valley to K2 and its glacier, and have spent the day making a series of high survey stations: 'It was fascinating work getting to know the features of the country and speculating how the individual pieces would fit into the whole intriguing puzzle which new country always presents.'[51]

For all the familiarity of the mental habit here, it is the task of surveying that has become the different and dominant inflection now. One incident, wryly described, indicates that this was not entirely consensual. It happened in the course of a five-thousand-foot descent on rotten rock of a gully near the Zug Shaksgam: 'The theodolite nearly came to grief. It was dropped ten feet on to a ledge while the load of survey equipment was being lowered over a difficult place. Tilman, who was not very fond of the theodolite, and was standing where it landed, showed great self-restraint in not encouraging it to fall the rest of the way.'[52] The suggested resentment here was real enough, and would find its voice, just as the language and concepts of surveying became dominant in Shipton's writing from the expedition: 'Using a Wild theodolite, subtense-bar and

---

[50] Shipton, *Blank on the Map*, p.219.
[51] Ibid. p.103.
[52] Ibid. p.127.

plane-table, [Spender] had laid out a base and fixed the relative positions of a large number of prominent peaks in the district, which formed a network of fixed points for a plane-table survey . . .'[53]

For Shipton, the interest by this time had firmly shifted away from mountain-climbing to mountain exploration, and he made this wholly explicit in his submission to the evening meeting of the Royal Geographical Society on 10 January 1938, after their return home. Having given a narrative account of the expedition, and told of how it had completed a survey of five hundred square miles, carrying an accurate system of heights throughout that entire region, and including seventy-five square miles on the unknown northern side of the Asiatic watershed, almost as an afterthought he came to its mountaineering content. What he said that night is the clearest expression of this major shift in his interest. From 1937 onwards we keep company not with Shipton the mountaineer, endlessly energetic, continually prospecting for the new and exciting line of ascent; but with Shipton the mountain explorer, technically well equipped for his task. Lawrence Wager, his tutor and progenitor in this new line of approach, would have good reason to be proud of his young friend and student's dedication and aptitude:

> With such a vast area of unknown mountains to explore, the climbing of any of the countless peaks one sees offers little interest compared with the enthralling business of finding one's way about the country, and crossing passes which lead from one region of mystery to another. Incidentally this occupation provides all the mountaineering one could wish for. In the course of our travels about half a dozen peaks were climbed, but all for the old-fashioned reason of wishing to see the view.
>
> We discovered and crossed seven major passes, four of which led across the main Asiatic watershed, and also four minor passes such as that which led from the Surukwat to the Zug Shaksgam, and that which led from the head of the Biafo to the Cornice glacier.

His conclusion to what must have seemed a remarkable and unexpected peroration, coming as it did from a man acclaimed as

---

[53] Shipton, *Blank on the Map*, p.91.

one of the outstanding British mountaineers of his time, was yet more radical in 'suggesting to mountaineers who have the opportunity of visiting the Himalaya that it is not by climbing its great peaks that we can most enjoy this great range. We have now the opportunity to see the Himalaya as de Saussure saw the Alps. When the country is known, we shall enjoy it by climbing its peaks; and, when all the peaks are climbed, we shall look for more difficult routes by which to climb them, in order to recapture the feel of adventure and to demonstrate our modern superiority.'[54]

Gradualism and conquest are mutually opposed concepts, and less refined mountaineers would hold to the latter for many years yet. The tradition to which Shipton and Tilman now held, by contrast, was that older, more relaxed and exploratory one of 'Peaks, Passes and Glaciers'.[55] The perspective that Michael Spender, the expedition surveyor, brought to all this was that the Shaksgam venture 'involved for Shipton and Tilman a definite sacrifice'. Tilman himself saw it slightly differently. On the way out from their base-camp, heading back towards Skardu and Srinagar with Ila and Sen Tenzing, with his health restored and in the Sherpa company he loved best, he soon recovered his good humour.

In the course of his formidable journey he managed to rubbish the established belief about the extent of the Snow Lake, which he investigated thoroughly and reduced to the more modest proportions of a mere series of contiguous mountain-surrounded snow basins, chief source of the Biafo glacier, stretching over thirty square miles rather than a fully fledged ice cap occupying three hundred. He also – this against his inclination, since he was a Romantic and a Luddite at heart, and had previously argued, albeit with the habitual tongue in cheek, at the RGS for its possibility – had proved conclusively that the Bullock Workmans' Cornice glacier (now known as the Sokhal glacier), far from being 'that startling topographical phenomenon, a glacier with no outlet', was a perfectly conventional member of the species, the head of a known and mapped glacier, and should have been recognised as behaving thus normally from the outset. Fanny

---

[54] Shipton, 'Shaksgam Expedition', pp.330–1.
[55] The two series of the journal published under this title and subtitled 'Excursions by Members of the Alpine Club' went out in 1858 and 1862. They were the precursors to the *Alpine Journal*.

being thirteen years dead, and her husband having passed on the preceding year, the only vitriol heading in Tilman's direction from his demolition of what he fondly termed 'Fanny's Fantasy' would have been in ectoplasmic form. His own acid stockpile from the expedition leaked out in diluted rivulets of his customary pawkiness and acerbity.

> I was never quite at home on this trip, for there was a man to whom slide rules and trigonometry are as intelligible as Chinese, making one of a party who thought in angles, talked in tangents, and read log tables for amusement – all this, by the way, in the metric system, so that if any height or distance was under discussion, pencil and paper were necessary to reduce it to intelligible terms. Shipton, of whom I hoped better, was the chief offender, and proved to be a confirmed 'theodoliter' – a word I have coined and patented to denote worshippers of the theodolite. True, in a moment of forgetfulness we did climb two peaks, and very good fun they were too, thanks, in the one case, to leaving the theodolite behind, and in the other, the rope.[56]

Very good fun too was the matter he also introduced into his brief presentation of *Homo Nivalis Abominibalis* as he playfully termed it in some contexts (elsewhere it is given as *Homo Nivis Odiosus*, which is correct but doesn't scan quite so well),[57] most notably by his own hearth where dog-Latin would pass muster, particularly in the conversations between Tilman and Toffee[58] – as it would not amid the high academic seriousness of the RGS, of course. The footprints of this putative patten-wearing[59] humanoid he and his Sherpas had come across in the vicinity of Snow Lake. Sen Tenzing, the flatulent and defrocked (it had gone with the wind) lama, assured him that it was the human-devouring variety, and

---

[56] Shipton, 'Shaksgam Expedition', p.337.
[57] E.g. *H. W. Tilman: The Seven Mountain Travel Books* (Diadem Books, 1983), pp.318–9.
[58] The aforementioned amiable little creature, short-legged and long-haired, of terrier type and indeterminate breed, who stuck to Tilman's heel as closely as the name implies.
[59] Though only when in Sikkim, apparently – *Yeticus peditatus nudus* (Linn.) elsewhere throughout the Himalaya, as I recall.

not its milder and larger cousin that subsisted on a diet of raw yak steaks and – showing ingenuity equal to that of its patten-inventing relative – had designed a wooden implement for removing the yak wool from its teeth. Both Shipton and Tilman, needless to say, were to have great fun with these beings and their shadowy putative existence over many years, and I think it fair to say that in Tilman's case, behind the play, there was some small degree of belief in their presence rather like that in God himself. We all need Yetis in our lives, wherever their supposed footprints may lead us.

In the paper Shipton read, he was characteristically generous about his friend's return itinerary and its results:

> Tilman's journey was a fine performance. In the space of three weeks allotted to him he covered a tremendous amount of ground. He managed to connect up the country we had been exploring and the unexplored head of the Biafo with the country round the Hispar pass, and also succeeded in unravelling the complicated glacier system to the south-west. In doing this he solved two interesting geographical problems, the nature of the Snow Lake, and the supposed phenomenon of the Cornice glacier.[60]

Which latter had now, in Tilman's words, 'gone the way of the lost continent of Atlantis'. Shipton's own journey from Shaksgam back to Srinagar, by way of Snow Lake, the Braldu glacier leading north, Chikar (from which a detour was made down the Braldu river and its lower valley to a confluence with the Shaksgam) and the Shimshal pass was a kind of ecstasy to him, described as such in *Blank on the Map*. Here he is in anticipation of it:

> I felt rather like a schoolboy, at last beginning a holiday full of exciting possibilities which had first begun to take shape months before, but which, as the term dragged on with maddening slowness, had receded to an unattainable but infinitely enticing dream. The Shimshal pass, the people of the lower Braldu valley, and the unknown ranges and glaciers that surrouded it, had been discussed by us for so long that it seemed impossible that we should ever get there. Now at

[60] Ibid. p.326.

last we were on the threshold of this region, ready to cross its passes and to grope our way through its unmapped valleys.[61]

After careful redeployment and repositioning of supplies, Shipton began his journey. Auden had gone off with the four remaining Baltis from Skardu. Shipton's team of Sherpas comprised Ang Tharkay, Lhakpa Tenzing, Lobsang, Nukku and Ang Tenzing. He wrote to his mother from Crevasse glacier on 8 August, entrusting the letter to Auden to post when he reached Askole. After lamenting to her at length about the lack of a trained archaeologist to accompany them and explain the wealth of ancient and more recent human habitation they had discovered, he moved on to tell her of his plans:

> Spender and I want to get into the country to the north-west. We have both found routes, but his being apparently the easier we propose to take it. It was <u>thrilling</u> looking from these passes and a great relief having found them. We have now reached the most exciting part of the show and I am itching to get across Spender's pass, but we have got to wait a bit (i) because the survey of this area is not quite completed (ii) because the weather has turned bad. Spender and I have got another 33 days food which should give us heaps of time. Both in the Aghil and this side of the Shaksgam I have shot a lot of bharal (two of them had very big heads, though we couldn't bring them with us) so until a fortnight ago we had masses of fresh meat. I hope we shall get some more beyond the pass, which should extend our food still further. I expect to reach Gilgit about September 26th, though if we can get any food in Shimshal we might be a bit later.

The insight here into the level at which his mother and he could communicate, and the interest in geography that is clearly shared, carries on in a gossipy vein that throws yet more light on their relationship, whilst at the same time affording glimpses into how cut off they had felt on this expedition, and the at times jokey attitude towards their sponsors:

---

[61] Shipton, *Blank on the Map*, p.228.

324   *Shipton and Tilman*

We have had no news of the outside world since we left you in Srinagar on May 5th. What ages ago that seems. Then we were talking about the bus strike,[62] the coronation, the Spanish War. People will have forgotten the results of these events by the time we get back – I expect – and England and Europe will be flooded with new crises (there are no Test Matches this year!). We have named one of our glaciers 'Coronation Glacier' and one of our peaks 'Jubilee Peak' (it being the 50th anniversary of Sir Francis Younghusband's famous crossing of Central Asia). It is very difficult to think of names for all these glaciers, peaks, passes, rivers, valleys etc. and they get ridiculous names such as 'Father Christmas', 'Cock-Eye', 'Bill's Folly' – names which I'm afraid the RGS wouldn't accept.

The letter's ending gives a strong sense of their affectionate closeness-in-distance:

I do so wonder where you are at this moment, as I have been wondering all along – how you have been getting on, on your wide travels. I only hope you have been enjoying yourself as much as I have. It will be tremendous fun when we can exchange experiences with each other. But I hope to have long accounts of your doings before then – when I get back to Srinagar . . . I am longing to hear all your news.
    Lots of love Darling, from Eric.

The letter having departed along with Auden and Tilman, Shipton was left on Crevasse glacier to finish the survey work with Michael Spender, about whom he would write, in summarising the trip, that 'There was no man in whose company I found more pleasure, or with whom I would rather have shared the deep and varied experience of an exploratory journey'. This was the same man against whom he had been warned (and then had thrust upon him through, it would seem, a dual and influential playful agency) by his great exploratory mentor Wager. There is an excerpt from

[62] The 1937 London bus strike lasted for four weeks, and inspired copycat actions throughout the country. It was defeated through the Transport and General Workers' Union head Ernest Bevin's refusal to involve trams and the London Underground to bring about a comprehensive stoppage of transport in the Metropolis – an act of apostasy for which he is still damned by the far left.

his journal that is most revealing about why his and Spender's bond was so strong, and the manner in which these two related to each other:

> September 2nd. Another fresh meat dinner last night. Very unselfish of the Sherpas to deny themselves in order to give us a second go – especially as they had shot the creatures [bharal – the expedition's staple supplementary food source, along with snow-cocks]. We started down the valley in a state of excitement, expecting to contact with humanity today. Worked up a great argument about the ethics of Empire which lasted until half the distance down the valley. It was not even checked by Michael falling into a muddy side-stream. The Braldu river caused us to keep up on alluvial fans. It appeared to be of terrific size – much bigger even than the Shaksgam in July. We had not expected this and now began to doubt whether we would get to our destination that day (or ever).

Straightforward, then – they were both consummate argumentarians, and there is nothing one of that breed likes better than to fall in or out with one of his own kind. His other great friend in this new grouping, Ang Tharkay, continued meanwhile to be an irrepressible and occasionally embarrassing source of diplomatic incidents.

> During our supper the tactless Ang Tharkay said that the presence of our escort was not necessary to us in finding our way down the valley. Poor Tweedledum [Shipton's pet name for one of their two escorts] was deeply hurt. With tears in his eyes he rose to his feet, picked up his few belongings, ordered his companion to follow him and stalked out into the night evidently intending to leave us to our own devices. However I managed to get him back and soothe him sufficiently by explaining that without their help not only would we fail to get down the valley but even if we did we would inevitably fall prey to the wolves of civilisation.

They were back among those soon enough, and in their most perfidious lair – London itself. Left to his own devices, Shipton would rather have stayed out in India and gone back to the Karakoram, particularly since, on his broken-booted[63] arrival in Srinagar, he had met a leggy young wild and barefoot seventeen-year-old girl by the name of Beatrice Weir, a colonel's daughter in Srinagar, who 'melted at the sight of him', became unofficially engaged to him two years later, and had sufficiently recovered her senses and dried her soppier parts by 1941 to marry instead someone of whom her parents could approve – this being Major James Rutherford Lumley of the 6th Gurkha Rifles (with whom in 1946 she had a daughter, Joanna). Brief charmed idyll aside, Shipton dutifully returned to London. He had promised Tilman he would be there to help with preparations for the 1938 Everest expedition: 'I had to remain content with a resolve to come back some day to this land of boundless promise with unlimited time before me.' He had become entranced 'by the country, its fantastic natural phenomena, its vastness and arid severity', and by the people too, with their 'vivid mode of living, their habit of wide travel'. For the moment, though, the old shibboleth of mountaineering militarism, 'the conquest of Everest', hung heavily over him once more.

Walt Unsworth, in his standard history of the mountain, with regard to Shipton and this expedition paints a picture of a man who 'had a burning ambition to be the first man up Everest'. What may have been true in 1933 was by 1938 no longer the case, as Shipton's own writings time and again confirm. He had moved on in his personal scheme of values, to a point where the ascent of Everest was not merely no longer of overriding importance, but had become in every way an unwelcome distraction from those plans about which he could become truly enthused, and for which the time in this decade of golden opportunities was fast running out. Nonetheless, he knew where his duty lay, and what was expected of him. He was heading back to Rongbuk once more, and this time it was under Tilman's leadership.

How this had come about is slightly obscure. Early in 1937 four men – Shipton, Tilman, Frank Smythe and Charles Warren – had been invited to the RGS by the Mount Everest Committee to discuss plans for an attempt on Everest in 1938. It would be fair to say that of these four, whatever their innermost thoughts

---

[63] The photograph of these, and the extreme condition of them, that appeared in *Blank on the Map* became – along with that of Michael Spender and the condition of his only shirt – iconic.

about the mountain Shipton and Smythe would still have been gratified by the honour of an invitation to *lead* the expedition. Of the remaining two, one would not have expected this, and one would not have wanted it. You'd not deserve a prize for guessing, after this summary, to whom it was offered. In the period prior to embarking at Tilbury on the SS *Strathmore* for Bombay and Shaksgam, Tilman was chosen ('It was with some diffidence that I accepted this responsible post, for amongst those whom I proposed to invite were men with a greater mountaineering experience than mine and particularly more experience of Everest').[64] So a fine pair of spectres trailed in the boat's wake. Not only had Shipton been beaten to Nanda Devi – he and Smythe had both been ousted from position of honour for the next trip to 'their' mountain. Writing to his mother at the beginning of March from Gangtok, on the now familiar march through Sikkim to Tibet, Shipton gives in passing some interesting glimpses into the social milieu in Kalimpong as well as into the ongoing expeditionary dialectic.

My Darling Mum,

We have started again. I had so much to do last winter and up to the time we left Kalimpong that it seems hardly credible that we really have left. Our two-and-a-half weeks at K'pong simply raced. I finished the book[65] on the morning of the day we left (3rd) . . . On Sunday Bill and I read the lessons at a service [in] Dr Graham's church. You will never guess who came to lunch that day – RUTH DRAPER.[66] It so happened that one of Bunty's house staff was marrying away one of his daughters and we were to share the wedding food. So we had a very amusing lunch of curry and rice which we ate off leaves with our fingers. Ruth Draper stayed the whole afternoon and after tea she did two sketches for us – 'to give those Everest boys something to think about when they're way up' as she put it. At my request she did the 'Garden' and at Christopher's she did 'The Italian Lesson' – have you seen either of those?

[64] Tilman, ibid. p.438.

[65] I.e. *Blank on the Map*, published by Hodder & Stoughton in the autumn of 1938.

[66] Ruth Draper (1884–1956) was a famous American actress and *diseuse* (monologist) – a close English parallel would be Joyce Grenfell, upon whom Draper was a significant influence. Shipton mentions a couple of her more famous monologues later in the letter.

It was amazing for me to see her acting for the first time, in a drawing room. She is amazing! And <u>so</u> charming in real life.

The poor boy sounds positively star-struck! He quickly moves on to more familiar ground:

It's been simply pouring with rain and is still at it. We left Kalimpong on Thursday. We stayed at the Residency. Gould, the P[olitical] O[fficer] is in hospital in Calcutta, but we were entertained by Rani Dorji, the wife of the Prime Minister of Bhutan. We had dinner with the Maharaja, which was as dull as usual. It would have been much better if we had been given a Tibetan meal. Yesterday we didn't start till the afternoon and ran down to Dirchu. Do you remember us starting in 1935? They have built a road now for the first four miles and we were given a lift as far as there. Ang Tharkay has begun by feeding us very well indeed. He really is a very good cook. Each evening . . . he has given us very good soup made from vegetables, lentils and bits of chicken, and roast chicken and huge piles of vegetables. Porridge and Bacon & Eggs in the morning. He also makes very good bread. It's a thousand times better than all that tinned nonsense. I can't think why it was so impossible to convince Hugh and others. I was amazed at what you said about Frank expecting to be starved. I wonder what he will bring with him?

It strikes me as very warm for the time of year, though we are still very low. It will be very interesting to see how things are when we get up into Tibet. I'm enclosing a few stamps that might interest M[arje]. Also two snaps; one of Bill and me in Calcutta; the other is the 'wedding lunch' at the Odlings. You will recognise Dr Graham on the right, next to him is Norman Odling, I am slightly behind him, then Bunty O. and Ruth Draper is standing with her back to the right-hand ivy-covered pillar – looking rather fatter than she really is.

<u>Later</u>. We are at Changtang now. It was beautifully fine this morning and we had a pleasant march but it's pelting again now. The peach blossom is out here and it is very lovely. Tomorrow we go to Lachen where I expect there will be a good deal of snow as it's nearly four thousand feet above here. It's a very pleasant party, and wonderfully peaceful after the

awful turmoil of a large expedition.[67]

Possible disappointment over the leadership aside, there was other acknowledgement for Shipton, and from a welcome and new direction. News of it came in the form of a letter from Arthur Hinks, secretary of the RGS, dated 24 March 1938, by which time its intended recipient was at Shekar Dzong on his way to Everest.

My dear Shipton,

I have today the great pleasure to inform you that His Majesty the King has signified his gracious approval of the Council's recommendation that you should receive this year The Patron's Medal[68] for your explorations around Nanda Devi and Mount Everest and your conduct of the Shaksgam Expedition of 1937.

The Medals are presented at the Annual General Meeting to be held this year on Monday June 20. By that time we may hope that you will have climbed Mount Everest, but can scarcely expect that you will be home again; but perhaps you will be able to designate someone to receive the Medal for you at the Meeting.

It gives me particular pleasure to be the channel by which this announcement comes to you, and I beg that you will accept my personal congratulations. '

It was a huge honour, particularly for a man of thirty, and the warmly personal tone of Hinks's letter makes plain how highly Shipton was regarded within RGS circles. He remained so – it was only within the mountaineering firmament that his star came to be viewed as no longer in the ascendant. Another acknowledgement of his contribution was through the style of expedition that the Mount Everest Committee had this time determined to send out, which was a clear endorsement of the sermon Shipton and his adjutant had

---

[67] Letter to Mrs Haly from Singhik, 5 March 1938.

[68] One of two Gold Medals (the other is the Founders' Medal) awarded annually by the RGS and the one usually given to mountaineers. Though in contradiction to that, Tilman received the Founders' Medal after the Second World War for his immense solo Asian journeys described in *Two Mountains and a River* (1949) and *China to Chitral* (1951) – two of the outright classics of British travel writing, and incomprehensibly undervalued; and Longstaff was its recipient in 1928.

by now been preaching – echoing the example of their predecessor
Tom Longstaff – throughout the 1930s, and ever more insistently
since the overweight expeditionary debacles of 1933 and 1936 –
trips which even the leader of them, the likeable and principled
Hugh Ruttledge, wished had been other.

As it happened, the outcome of the 1938 trip was far from other –
it was exactly the same. Though when they first saw it the mountain
was clear of snow, at that time temperatures on its slopes were simply
too cold for climbing to take place. Tilman sets the scene:

> I had been warned by General Norton from his own
> experience in 1924 against committing the party too early,
> with the possible result of putting most of us out of action
> with frostbite, and at that time conditions were such as to
> render this less a possibility than a certainty . . . The wind and
> cold continued unabated until May 5, when snow fell heavily
> and continued to fall daily for the next week. After that date
> the mountain was never in climbable condition, and the lull on
> which everything depends between the cessation of wind and
> the first monsoon snow never occurred.[69]

Nor were the climbers in much better condition than the mountain.
In his dispatch to *The Times* published on 4 July, Tilman observes that
'a casual observer might have taken us for a party of consumptives
enjoying a cold air cure.'[70]

The monsoon had definitely arrived early in May. There was
immense danger of avalanche in the approach to the Chang La
(North Col) from the head of the East Rongbuk glacier, just as there
had been in 1935 and 1936. When they switched to approaching the
col by following the main Rongbuk glacier round beneath Changtse
and climbing its western flank, they found that approach, though
it was the one they chose to use, was on hard ice and perilous for
heavily laden porters. Deep powder snow on the section of the north
ridge route below the crest itself and leading up to the Yellow Band
brought them to a halt at 27,300 feet, with any further progress
impossibly risky. Two parties made it to this point from Camp Six
at 27,200 feet – Shipton and Smythe, and following them a day

---

[69] *A.J.* 1939, ibid. p.8.
[70] *Times*, 4 July 1938, p.15.

later Tilman and Peter Lloyd who two years before had been on the Nanda Devi expedition. Lloyd, an engineer and exact contemporary of Shipton (had the latter taken the proffered opportunity, they would have been at Cambridge together and would surely have made a formidable alpine partnership, particularly since they were well suited temperamentally), was conducting comparative tests on the two types of oxygen equipment then available for high-altitude climbing. In coming down strongly in favour of the open-circuit breathing system, which used ordinary air as well as cylinder oxygen, and recommending and advising upon this to what became Brigadier John Hunt's expedition of 1953, as well as effecting design changes to the equipment, he contributed significantly to the first ascent of the mountain.

In 1938, however, after the initial enthusiasm for its use in the 1920s, the subject of oxygen had become very controversial, and neither Shipton nor Tilman nor Smythe would personally avail themselves of it (opinion these days – the special case of commercial expeditions to Everest apart – has strongly turned against its use, providing yet another example of how prescient the purism of the Shipton/Tilman approach was.)[71] Lloyd stated his own opinion on

---

[71] A related point here concerns the likelihood of Mallory and Irvine's having reached the summit of Everest in 1924. Both men were wearing oxygen apparatus weighing in excess of 30lb – huge weights to carry when rock-climbing. Nonetheless, some Everest historians – among the straw-grasping, speculative ranks of whom non-climbers are legion – expect us to believe that, carrying this burden and at a height of 28,000 feet, Mallory managed to lead the overhanging crack pitch of the 200-foot-high Second Step (a pitch that in Snowdonia, for example, modern accounts give us to believe would receive a grade of 'Extremely Severe'). They expect us to believe this despite the fact that Mallory never remotely approached this level of rock-climbing competence even in rubber shoes on Welsh summer rock. With the discovery of his body clearly pointing to a fall from on or below the Second Step, it is surely time to consign this Romantic/Imperialist wishful thinking to the realms of 'never was' rather than 'might-have-been'. If any proponents of the fantasy remain unconvinced, they might wish to consider the ascent by Joe Brown – the most important, naturally gifted and prolific of all British rock-climbing pioneers – of the short rock pitch below the summit of Kanchenjunga in 1955, when he was at the height of his powers. This was at almost the exact altitude of the Second Step, though much shorter, and Joe found it desperate to lead, whilst his companion, George Band, had to be hauled up on a very tight rope. When asked to grade the pitch, Joe's terse response was 'It's about gritstone V. Diff.' – which doesn't, of course, make it entirely straightforward, as gritstone devotees will vouch, but it's still much easier than the Second Step would appear to be. And would surely also have stopped Mallory in his tracks.

their return to Britain that autumn with his habitual blend of tact, firmness and elegance – he was an enormously likeable personality, an honest broker of the climbing world for sixty years – and in winning the day with his argument, he effectively won the summit for Hunt's climbers fifteen years later: 'I have a lot of sympathy with the sentimental objection to its use, and would rather see the mountain climbed without it than with; but, on the other hand, I would rather see the mountain climbed with it than not climbed at all.'

As to Tilman, according to Shipton, the man who had so obviously failed to acclimatise at anything over 20,000 feet in 1935 'was going well' and there was no obvious difference between his performance and that of Lloyd with his oxygen. But like Shipton and Smythe, Tilman and Lloyd had no choice in the prevailing highly dangerous snow conditions but to turn round. On their descent a further problem awaited at Camp Four on the Chang La. Tilman's old friend from the 1934 explorations, Pasang Bhotia, lay in his tent paralysed on his right side and incapable of coherent speech. One terrifying photograph in a full-page broadsheet portfolio published in *The Times* on 28 July shows Pasang, supported by a Sherpa on each side and still carrying a great sack on his back, being helped into Camp Four on the Chang La, slumped heavily against his companions and with a clearly useless right leg trailing through deep snow.

He and Tenzing Norgay had performed magnificently in carrying loads up to the col and beyond it to Camp Five (25,800 feet) and Camp Six in dreadful conditions, thus enabling the lead-climbers to progress as far as they did. Now, superstititiously, the Sherpas thought to leave him here to die, believing that the mountain gods were claiming his life and if they were denied it, another's would be claimed instead. None of the other Sherpas were now willing to go near him anyway because he had, in the old-fashioned phrase, 'fouled his linen' and they would have felt polluted by the contact. Tilman soon set them in order ('One had not to be a great linguist to make them understand that the suggestion was unpalatable.')[72] and Pasang was dragged or lowered down the mountain and survived, later making a reasonable though not complete recovery from the paralysis.

After this came the inevitable abandonment of the attempt, the long, slow withdrawal from the mountain, and the habitual active

---

[72] *A.J.* 1939, ibid. p.15.

appendices to these dreary sequential failures. Shipton 'armed himself with a theodolite instead of an ice-axe' as his disapproving erstwhile leader observed, and made once more for the Nyönno Ri. For Tilman, there was a small unresolved issue for him from 1936 in the neighbourhood of Kanchenjunga which was the crossing of the Zemu Gap, between the Zemu and Tangshyong glaciers to the east of the mountain. For this he took with him two Sherpas from the expedition, Rinzing and Lhakpa, and approached in the reverse direction to the one he had attempted two years before. It proved hazardous and exciting in the descent. 'The gap was hairy, much more interesting than Everest,' he commented in a letter to his sister on 15 July. His method of crossing a crevasse at one point prompted Lhakpa to ask if he were intent on trying to kill him. But they succeeded, and even before doing so had made the first ascent of Lachsi, an attractive little 21,100-foot peak on which Marco Pallis and Freddie Spencer Chapman had failed pre-monsoon in 1936. They also met a collecting party with a German anthropologist in attendance who was immediately buttonholed by Tilman: 'I . . . earnestly besought him to spare no pains in tracking down the Abominable Snowman, urging him not to be discouraged by the croaking of the zoologist who would assuredly tell him that if he did succeed in tracking it down he would find no Abominable Snowman, no Snark, not even a Boojum, but a bear.'[73]

So the last pre-war Everest expedition ended as the first and all the rest had done in failure, and in his late autobiography Shipton dismisses it so cursorily that if you were to blink you would miss the bare mention of its having taken place. Here's all he has to say about it in that context: 'In 1938 Everest intervened once more – this time a light expedition led by Bill . . .'[74] In a letter to his mother from Rongbuk, dated 15 June 1938, he is significantly more revealing, and the long letter is worth quoting in its entirety not only for his account of events, but also as a very frank expression of his feelings towards the mountain.

My Darling Mum – Here we are back again – defeated. What a mountain it is! Much has happened since I last wrote – only a little over a fortnight ago. Frank and I went up the main

[73] H.W. Tilman, 'Lachsi and the Zemu Gap' (*Himalayan Journal*, 1939, pp.272–3.
[74] Shipton, *That Untravelled World*, p.117.

Rongbuk glacier picking up Peter Lloyd from Camp One on the way. Bill caught us up and made a fourth. We got to the West foot of the col on the 4th and climbed the thing (for the first time)[75] the next day with 16 Sherpas. It was a great deal more difficult than it looked and is not much of an alternative route to the other side. The following day we established Camp Five. F. and I were held up there a day by a gale of wind and on 8th, with seven Sherpas we put Camp Six at the top of the North East Ridge at 27,200 feet. It was heavy going and we took eight hours to do about 1,400 feet. I have never seen the Sherpas so completely done as when we got there. It was perfect weather and the views as you can imagine were glorious. But one is too half-conscious to appreciate anything of them. One is always falling asleep – rather as if one is under a dose of morphia – only not so pleasant. I had taken a small book, *Bridge of San Luis Rey*, up with me in case the night was tiresome.

Thornton Wilder's 1927 novel certainly weighed in at a lot less than *Gone With the Wind*, but it still proved to be excess baggage in the situation to which it was intended to bring relief:

It was frightfully difficult to read as all the words got muddled up with a sort of half-dream just like when one is falling asleep in bed. We started very early next morning but got so cold that we had to come back to the tent to warm up before starting properly. Our idea was to attempt the ridge and at least 'look at' the 2nd step. We started traversing the slabs towards the 1st step, and found what we knew already – that conditions were HOPELESS. We were up to our waists in powder snow, and the whole time we had to be very careful that it didn't all come away with us. Even clear of snow those slabs are quite tricky, but with all that powder . . .! One just can't climb Everest when it is like that – at least I can't. We know now that the mountain remains like that all through the monsoon. There was nothing for it but to turn our backs again. The mountain looked a real devil that day.

    When we got down to Camp Five we met Bill and Peter Lloyd, told them to try and get on to the shoulder at the extreme

---

[75] I.e. for the first time from the west side.

left, and went on down to the North Col in the evening in quite a fierce blizzard. Next day we intended to take our Camp Six men down. We started with that object early, but found that one of the seven, Pasang (my old Nanda Devi Pasang) had gone off his head and we could do nothing with him. We could not take him down the West side which is very exposed for nearly all the way. We spent that afternoon examining the East side, and digging out the fixed ropes. That night we were woken by shouts from the tent of Ondi, another of our seven. On investigation it was found that he had pneumonia. So we had him in our tent and administered oxygen for the rest of the night. Started early next morning with all hands, but we could not cope with Pasang as we now had Ondi to deal with, as well as the route on the east side to re-make. The slopes were not too good but eventually Charles [Warren], Frank and I got down with the remaining five and Ondi and reached Camp Three. The next day the whole lot got down including Bill and Peter Lloyd, who had got back down from above. Bill, Ang Tharkay and Kusang took up the rear with Pasang and lowered him down the vertical bits and dragged him across the traverses. By now the whole of his right side was paralysed – he had had a stroke. We all got down here yesterday and are waiting for transport to take us home. We want to fix up for another show next year. I don't think I will come again – four times is enough, and there is too much to do elsewhere, but I am keen to help to get the right party up. Lovely getting your letter. I'm delighted that they have asked you to receive the gold medal on 20th. I hope you make a pretty speech!

Lots of love Darling from Eric.

Everest '38 had been a curious, and in some ways controversial, experience, and not one without its positive aspects. The letter above and the incident with Pasang highlight the most crucial of these – the depth of active concern Shipton and Tilman had for their Sherpas, and the recognition they accorded them. This was formalised by Tilman on this expedition in enduring form through a system of bonuses ('Tigers' earned an additional eight annas[76] a day)

---

[76] There were sixteen annas to the rupee, so at a time when Sherpas earned one rupee a day, this was a fifty per cent pay rise.

and through what became the much-coveted 'Tiger' badges. On the climbing side, it certainly gave powerful support to the cheap and lightweight argument. At the time of planning for 1938 the Mount Everest Committee, after the Ruttledge extravaganzas with all their cases of quails in aspic and the like, was more or less broke. In January 1937 the committee account was overdrawn by £1,538. An advance from Hodder & Stoughton for the 1936 expedition book reduced that, and Tom Longstaff generously offered to underwrite the costs of a 1938 expedition so long as either Shipton or Tilman led it – he did not mind which and liked both, though he was rather wary around the former where his daughters were concerned (a perfect example of the universal principle that calumny is nothing other than projected guilt). So 1938 was, as Longstaff knew it would be, an economical expedition run with regard to cost and value – particularly since each member was desired to make a financial contribution according to his means.

Value it certainly gave. It put two assault teams high on the mountain, well supplied and at what was then the generally accepted right time. Unsworth asks the crucial question, and answers it to his own satisfaction:

> Supposing conditions had been good on the North Face [i.e. along the Norton Traverse], could Tilman's experiment have succeeded? There seems no reason to doubt it: Smythe and Shipton had never felt fitter, on their own admission, and though there was 1,800 feet to climb from Camp Six to the top, they stood at least as good a chance as their predecessors. Tilman had certainly proved his point.[77]

Other aspects were more debatable. The Shipton/Tilman diet proved unpopular, particularly with Noel Odell, who was used to better things and was particularly chagrined by Tilman's refusal of a sponsor's proffered case of champagne (he did accept a case of tinned tongue from the same source). Tilman's argument in essence was that food was merely fuel, better sourced locally than carried in; that everything tastes the same at altitude, when there is anyway no appetite; and that the chief critic of their rations 'has not yet finished criticising the food we ate on Nanda Devi in 1936', where,

---

[77] Walt Unsworth, *Everest*, p.222.

'in spite of his semi-starved condition,[he] succeeded in getting to the top.'[78] No doubt Odell, at whom this barb was aimed, was one of those who 'were mightily relieved to find at Rongbuk large quantities of stores left behind by the 1936 party, and considered that this windfall, consisting mostly of nourishing food like jam, pickles, and liver extract . . . alone saved the party from starvation'. I suspect a modern dietician on the whole would approve of the rations supplied, though she might jib at the amount of processed meat like pemmican and bacon. Tilman's final statement on the matter is pleasingly terse: '. . . we did ourselves pretty well; but much depends on a man's standards of living. If a man expects to have a choice of three or four kinds of marmalade for breakfast it is a disagreeable surprise to find none at all. There was ample food this year; the supply of candles may have been short, but we were never reduced to eating them.'[79]

Rest assured that the marmalade jibe was again aimed straight at the amiable academic and collegian geologist Noel Odell – a change from the usual shafts Tilman directed at Odell's ever-present and singularly weighty glacier drill. And none of this should induce you to doubt that Odell and Tilman, despite differences of opinion, were anything other than perfectly good friends. The same could not, perhaps, be said of post-expedition relations between Odell and Shipton, who fell out over a story the latter related in the course of a London lecture to the effect that on Everest in 1924 Odell had mistaken geological specimens gathered at height in his pocket for sandwiches, had tried to eat them, presumed they had become frozen and hence threw them away. This is clearly a joke directed against Odell's perceived obsession, and yet in some quarters, astounding though this may seem, it was taken literally. Which gives me opportunity to repeat my refrain about how it is a mistake ever to take either of our subjects – ironists and humorists that they are – too seriously, or too much at face value.

The matters of diet and of style inevitably lead in to that of Tilman's leadership. His examination of these two issues in his *Everest 1938* (not published until 1948) is so thorough and reasoned as to make this book the classic theoretical manifesto for lightweight style – I'm tempted by the irony of calling it a sort of mountaineering

Clausewitz. But as with his later thoroughly reasoned rebuttal of a complaint by a crew member on one of his immense southern-ocean voyages in *Mischief*, the first and best-loved in his series of three Bristol Channel pilot cutters, that they carried no life raft or distress flares, in the main it was either mocked or disregarded. On his leadership, we could accept his own assessment, which could hardly be categorised as self-glorifying:

> . . . with men like E. E. Shipton, F. S. Smythe, and N. E. Odell amongst the party, it would be my part to sit listening with becoming gravity to their words of wisdom, waking up occasionally to give an approving nod. In fact I should have a sinecure, as should be the case with any well-balanced climbing party. And so it was so far as making decisions on the mountain went, most of which were imposed on us, willy-nilly, by the weather.[80]

What his fellow climbers thought of his leadership is more straightforward than this comical self-effacement. At the RGS on their return to London, Peter Lloyd took to the podium and spoke up for him in public to warm and general applause: 'In appreciation of Tilman's leadership I would like to say that if ever I go to Everest again I very much hope it will be under his leadership.'[81] Shipton is more offhand in his private comments from correspondence to Mrs Freston, but even here there is respect and a degree of warmth from his mentor towards the man who had been his closest climbing associate, and by whom he had seemed so oddly and accidentally marginalised. 'Bill is shaping well as far as I can judge, and his exalted position does not seem to have affected him a bit. I suppose I am some moral support to him as he fusses rather about things.'

In the same letter he continues with an essentially favourable impression of the nature of the group: 'The contrast and the general atmosphere of simplicity and genuineness that prevails is helping me to take a better view of the show – which otherwise is a bloody bore, and wasting much valuable time. This is a bad thing to say, I suppose, but it's the fourth time I have set out on this journey.'[82]

---

[80] Ibid. p.438.
[81] *G.J.* December 1938
[82] Letter to Pamela Freston, 6 March 1938.

Three months later, even after an arduous and, in terms of achieving its objective, unsuccessful expedition, Shipton could still write the following testimonial for his old friend to Mrs Freston: 'Out of this party there is no one who would make as good a leader, except Peter Lloyd or myself. Bill has a number of silly faults, such as shyness in discussing plans and lack of mental flexibility, but he's got more guts than the rest of us put together.'[83]

Just how much guts and how clear a sense of duty he possessed were made very clear as he mulled over his future plans on returning from Everest – about which expedition the consensus was that it had been a valiant attempt, achieving as much as anyone could have expected in the prevailing dire conditions on the mountain, or indeed as any previous expedition had done – and 'for a tithe of the cost'. As Tilman knew all too well, mountains were the simple side of life, the hostility encountered upon them elemental, impersonal, entirely indifferent to individual human fate (though the Sherpas might have argued that point).

In Europe, however, the political situation was growing ever more complex and intense. Whilst the 1935 and 1936 Everest expeditions had been taking place, the forces of Benito Mussolini had invaded and conquered Abyssinia. In the latter year, as Tilman was crossing Longstaff's Col and Shipton was guiding the Osmaston party into the Nanda Devi Sanctuary, the Axis powers of Germany and Italy threw in their lot with the nationalist forces of General Franco as the Spanish Civil War began. The following April, planes from the Luftwaffe and the Aviazione Legionaria bombed the leftist and Basque Nationalist town of Guernica and in doing so inspired one of the masterpieces of modern art. Britain's tardy response to these disturbing developments in Europe was to send Neville Chamberlain to negotiate in Germany, from which he returned on 30 September 1938. Landing at Heston Aerodrome near the present-day Heathrow, the Prime Minister stepped from his plane waving a piece of paper in his hand, and that evening announced from the steps of 10 Downing Street, in the calm and orotund tones of the English upper middle classes: 'My good friends, this is the second time in our history[84] that there has come back from

---

[83] Letter to Pamela Freston, June 1938.
[84] The first occasion had been when Disraeli returned from the Congress of Berlin in 1878 and announced 'I have returned from Germany with peace in our time.'

Germany to Downing Street peace with honour. I believe it is peace for our time. We thank you from the bottom of our hearts. And now I recommend you to go home and sleep quietly in your beds.'

If anyone believed him then, their faith would have been shaken the following morning as news arrived of the German army having moved in to the Sudetenland.[85] Tilman was certainly not among the hordes of the credulous:

> I like to think I can see as far through a brick wall as most people, and in the latter part of 1938 it seemed clear to me, as to many others, that war was inevitable. This affected my plans for 1939. Shipton was returning to the Karakoram to continue the work which we had begun in 1937, and I should very much have liked to have joined him. But we should be extremely isolated, almost beyond recall in fact, and Shipton's plans necessitated staying out the following winter. I was not so abandoned yet as to consider being beyond recall an advantage. Moreover, the War Office, after twenty years of deep thought, had just remembered they had a Reserve of Officers, of which I was one, and had announced a scheme for their training. I decided therefore that by August 1939 I must be home. This ruled out the Karakoram, and my choice fell upon the Assam Himalaya as being the most accessible and the least known region for exploration.[86]

It was neither a good choice nor a lucky expedition. When Tilman wrote it up for the *Alpine Journal* it was under the title 'Assam Himalaya Unvisited', which sums up with remarkable brevity what was achieved. He had wanted to climb Namche Barwa (25,531 feet), a remote and dangerous mountain that remained unclimbed until 1992, at which time it was the world's highest unclimbed peak. The problem was that it was outside British territory, well over the border into Tibet, and Tilman had already prompted the Mount Everest Committee of which he was now a member to apply – on the grounds that in one of these years they must surely strike lucky with weather and snow conditions – for permission to send

---

[85] Along the borders of the present-day Czech Republic, the ethnic-German areas of Bohemia, Moravia and Silesia.
[86] Tilman, ibid. p.277.

out modestly sized Everest expeditions in 1940, 1941 and 1942. Sneaking in yet another application for a peak in a different and culturally sensitive area for 1939 would most likely have made the keenly separatist Tibetan authorities feel rather as the Czechs did when the Germans poured into the Sudetenland. It was too much of a bad thing, and the Indian government refused even to forward the request. 'For British mountaineering parties,' commented Tilman with feeling, 'most of the goodwill of Lhasa is exclusively needed for Everest expeditions.'

Nothing daunted, he set to planning a mountaineering trip to Assam anyway, with Kangto[87] (23,260 feet) as his new objective and Gori Chen (21,450 feet) and Nyegyi Kansang (23,120 feet) – three peaks in Arunchal Pradesh at the far eastern end of the Himalaya range, rising out of the remote forests above the headwaters of the Brahmaputra river – also in mind.

> I also hoped to make a map; not in the cause of pure science, but with a utilitarian notion of its possible usefulness to myself in future. And it is always well to have a secondary objective, preferably scientific, as we are urged to do on Mount Everest expeditions; for though a few misguided people climb for fun, many think that mountaineering by itself, particularly if unsuccessful, is a waste of time and money.'[88]

Seldom can *homo ludens* have expressed his Luddite and anti-rationalist sentiments more slyly. The teasing relevance here to Shipton's preoccupations of the last few years is transparent; but this is the lightly mocking commentary of a friend, and quite devoid of animus.

He was out in Darjeeling in April and recruited Wangdi, Nukku – one of his previous year's Everest party – and Thundu from the Sherpa community there to accompany him. The former two were known quantities, Wangdi having a Tiger's Badge. Thundu he had

---

[87] This peak, along with nearby Gori Chen, became significant oropolitically in the last decades of the twentieth century as tensions increased in the border areas between India and China where it lies – raising memories of the crassest oropolitical initiative of all: the planting of the nuclear-powered monitoring device on Nanda Devi to observe Chinese activity (see Chapter 7, note 14). The Great Game did all this kind of thing with far more panache.

[88] H. W. Tilman, 'Assam Himalaya Unvisited' (*Alpine Journal*), 1939, p.53.

never met before. It would have been better for all three of them had they not been available. For once, lightweight philosophy caused Tilman to come unstuck. The approach march began through low foothills only five hundred feet above sea level, the weather was hot and dry, the air swarmed with mosquitoes and the nights were purgatorial with heat and bites. Above a thousand feet a new pest, 'dimdams' or blister flies, appeared, raising blood blisters wherever it bit. For reasons of lightness, not thinking this uninhabited region would be malarial, between the four of them Tilman had only brought a hundred quinine tablets in his medicine chest (though the latter did contain ample quantities of cocaine, for treatment of snow-blindness in conjunction with castor oil). One by one they went down with the disease. Wangdi coped best, his malaria proving to be of a benign variety. The others had contracted the malignant tertiary form. They continued towards their objective over passes higher than 14,000 feet, intermittently feverish and spending days at a time in their beds. Tilman went up to a couple of stations at over 16,000 feet with the plane table before taking to his sleeping bag for a week. When he came round and was on his feet again, his first concern was for the Sherpas.

> Thundu seemed to be mending slowly, though he was very weak, but Nukku was unaccountably dull and lethargic. He would not go to bed but could do little work; Wangdi, who had everything to do, used to get very angry with him. He seemed not to have any fever and complained only of pains in the legs and shoulders. On the 19th [of May 1938], he, Wangdi, and myself carried loads to the upper camp where Wangdi and I remained.[89]

The fever returned and Tilman was bed-ridden again. Wangdi was sent down on the 24th to find out what Thundu and Nukku were doing. He came back that evening to report that Nukku had lost consciousness. He and Tilman descended to find both Sherpas lying in sleeping bags by an extinct fire, Nukku breathing stertorously. On the 26th, without regaining consciousness, he died of cerebral malaria. Wangdi and Tilman buried him and built a cairn in Sherpa fashion over his grave. Two days later the headman of the nearest

[89] Tilman, 'Assam Himalaya', p.60.

village, Dyuri, with six men and four *dzos*,[90] arrived to evacuate them. Thundu was carried on the men's backs, Tilman on a *dzo*, 'which gave me a safe and pleasant ride. It rained every day.' The three survivors, Thundu and Tilman being carried or riding the whole way, reached Charduar, the village from which their trek had begun, on 11 June, exactly two months after setting out, after what was perhaps Tilman's saddest and most unsuccessful venture of the whole decade, as well as its last:

> It is easy to be wise after the event. There are several precautions
> that might be taken, assuming of course that malaria is due, as
> some think, to a mosquito bite and not merely the result, like
> sore throat and influenza, piles and paralysis, of an 'unscientific
> diet,' which is the opinion of others. Our first camp, which
> seemed to be the worst source of infection, could be avoided
> by a long double march. Mosquito nets, trousers instead of
> shorts, bamber oil,[91] and heavier prophylactic doses of quinine,
> would all help to reduce the risks.[92]

This is Tilman at his most anti-scientifically obtuse. The link between mosquitoes and malaria had been established as long ago as 1897 by Sir Ronald Ross in Port Swettenham. We have to presume that he did not know of the malaria risk in this region of Assam, for in every other situation Tilman's concern for his 'blokes' invariably shines through. He was obviously caring and fond of them, preferring their company on the whole to that of his Western friends, fully prepared to undertake long journeys with them and to rely entirely on their help and resourcefulness as equal partners in any of the enterprises he undertook. There is a fascinating modern perspective on their relationship, from the other side. It was provided by Norbu, one of the Sherpas on the 1938 Everest expedition, to the journalist Alan Hankinson, who was accompanying the 1974 Anglo-Indian expedition led by Chris Bonington that made the first ascent of Changabang, the imposing rock spire on the rim of the Nanda Devi Sanctuary, a Himalayan version of the Petit Dru,

---

[90] A cross, always male, between a yak and a cow.
[91] An old-fashioned insect repellent made up of liquid paraffin, coconut oil and oil of citronella.
[92] Ibid. p.62.

which provided opportunity for several epoch-making ascents over a twenty-year period at the end of the last century.

Of all his many experiences, Norbu remembers none so vividly as those with H. W. Tilman. According to Norbu, Tilman was always away first in the morning, carrying a load in excess of the standard Sherpa load. He always arrived first at the day's destination – sometimes he'd run along parts of the route. He would have tea brewing by the time the rest of them caught up with him, and then he'd praise those who'd made good time and yell and scream at those he thought had been lazy or lacking in some way. On at least one rest day he made all his Sherpas a cake – Tashi, who was translating for me, was made to repeat this fact several times. He was always the first to cross turbulent streams, pass hard rocky sections, and shoulder awkward loads. He was obviously a born leader and Norbu, at any rate, was still very impressed.[93]

From Charduar Thundu was taken to hospital suffering not only from cerebral malaria but also black fever (visceral leishmaniasis) – the latter the world's second highest killer disease, and transmitted by sand-fly bites. He did eventually make a complete recovery, and found his way home to Darjeeling with the help of the political officer, Captain Lightfoot, in whose bungalow Tilman and Wangdi were given food, shelter and ample quinine and made their own recoveries before setting off on their respective homeward journeys. The trip had been neither happy nor successful, but it had taken Tilman into 'country which is more or less unknown, sparsely or not at all inhabited, inhospitable, difficult to move in, and of course mountainous'. He commented that it had been 'not easy to reach, but neither were Christian's Delectable Mountains, nor is any place that is worth reaching'.[94]

This particular Christian had experienced his last mountains of a decade rich in achievement and adventure. He was back in England by August, inducted on to a short course for officers from the Military Reserve, and on 1 September, two days before the outbreak of war, a grey-haired, upright, forty-one-year-old lieutenant with a

[93] Alan Hankinson, *Changabang* (Heinemann, 1975), pp.43–4.
[94] Tilman, ibid. p.304.

Military Cross and bar, he joined 32 Field Regiment of the Royal Artillery at their Brighton barracks ready to embark for France once more. The great phase of his mountaineering career – with all its philosophy, example, rigour and achievement the legacy of which resonate down through the history of mountain activity to the present day – was at an end.

As Tilman was sailing back to England, Shipton had already found another of those scenes of idyllic retrospect in which he so delighted. It was along the Barpu glacier, west of Hispar village and south-east of Baltit in the Hunza valley, at the western end of the Karakoram range: 'Along its right bank, almost to the head, there extends a wide ablation valley filled with willows and rose thickets and wild flowers. The roses were then in full bloom and for miles great banks of their gay blossom seemed to fill the valley.'[95]

The major expedition on which he was bound – the invitations to join which Tilman and Spender had in both cases so regretfully declined, the latter at the very last minute – had come about through ruminating on the 1937 Shaksgam explorations. He had concluded – a radical paradigm shift here – that further exploration into the 'blanks on the map' which now most interested him on either side of the Aghil pass (and as the boundary areas with Chinese Turkestan, these were of obvious and significant strategic interest to his pay-masters too) might best be pursued through the winter months, when the rivers would be low or better still frozen, hence easily crossed or even useable as highways into the heart of the remaining unknown tracts of country. On his way out to Everest in 1938, he had called on the Surveyor General of India and discussed his plans. His timing was immaculate. The Survey of India was going through a phase of upheaval and reassessment. To have someone of Shipton's capability, experience and enthusiasm, who was known to them not just through the seminal explorations of 1934, 1935 and 1937 but also through the laudatory testimonials of Gordon Osmaston, walk in able to offer his services was a godsend to those in charge.

The Surveyor General – a military man who was perfectly aware of the developing world situation and hence quite happy to keep his own men in reserve and delegate cartographic duties to a civilian – talked over with Shipton the topographical and cartographical confusions, chiefly emanating from the Bullock Workmans, that

---

[95] Eric Shipton, 'Karakoram, 1939' (*G.J.*, June 1940), p.412.

had become increasingly evident in the crucial zone around the Karakoram watershed – the northern boundary of Empire. He was acquainted with Shipton and Spender's work from 1937, and was particularly anxious to resolve and clarify the problems around the Biafo, Hispar and Panmah glaciers, all of which in an unsettled region during an unpredictable world situation offered unlikely but possible opportunity for surprise enemy infantry attack across to lightly garrisoned Gilgit and on down into Kashmir.

Thinking fast, Shipton realised how easily relief for the Surveyor General's unease could be obtained through his own half-formulated plans. He re-formulated them and submitted them straight away, backed up with detailed arguments and examples of already completed work. Nothing could have been better calculated to appeal to a military mind. Financial assistance, endorsement, permission and encouragement from the Indian Survey were immediately forthcoming for an expedition to be completed in four stages. The first would be to solve those nagging Hispar/Biafo problems to the Surveyor General's satisfaction during the summer of 1939. The ensuing winter would see the members of the team in the area to the east of the Shimshal pass, probing down the Braldu river again and crossing the Shaksgam river to approach Aghil from its unknown western side with the intention of venturing into the range to investigate the region to the north of that explored and mapped by Kenneth Mason in 1926. The position of this terrain in the shadow of the main Karakoram range gave the likelihood of lighter snowfall. They would take arctic gear to ensure their survival through the coldest months. With the arrival of spring, their journey in 1940 would be the one John Morris had suggested, along the Shaksgam river from Shimshal to Leh. As a planned itinerary the ambition was obvious – it was to be a reexamination conducted over a period of eighteen months of all the previous unfinished, partial or inadequate and erroneous survey work done in the region over more than fifty years. If he succeeded in his designs, Shipton's exploratory future was assured. To a man who had, for all his early promise and the high esteem in which he was held, suffered setbacks, it was a crucial throw of the dice.

Once back in England after Everest and the Nyönno Ri, he set to putting the expedition together in earnest. His team was chosen first. With Tilman unavailable and Spender uncertain, new faces were brought in. The first of them came on Dan Bryant's recommendation.

He was Robert Scott Russell, a twenty-six-year-old botanist at Imperial College with extensive climbing experience in the Southern Alps of New Zealand, to which country his parents had emigrated when he was a child. In 1938 he had been to Jan Mayen Island, four hundred miles north-east of Iceland within the Arctic Circle, where he had researched the effect of cold climate on plant metabolism – a topic he could continue to work on through a full cycle of Karakoram seasons. Whilst on Jan Mayen, he had also made the first ascent of its 7,470-foot-high dormant volcano, Beerenberg.[96] Without Tilman around to offer his usual iatrogenic[97] resistance (he had even been awkward about Charles Warren's presence on Everest in 1938, rightly considering physicians, bachelors of medicine and the whole panoply of body mechanics in almost every situation of life to be supernumerary), Shipton was free to take a medical man, and on his old friend Lawrence Wager's recommendation he chose Eadric Fountaine, who had Arctic and climbing experience, was also and usefully a reasonably competent surveyor, and would contribute to the expedition's research portfolios – then as now invaluable in raising grant assistance – by studying 'certain medical and ethnological aspects of the people of Shimshal'. To fill his own role as surveyor, when Spender definitely decided against joining the venture – which was not until early in 1939 – he proposed Peter Mott, also from Imperial College, with which Shipton was to have strong links over the years. (Of his expedition leader Mott recorded that 'Shipton assisted me greatly both by his profound knowledge of the country and a remarkable gift for recognising peaks from widely differing angles.')

These four were to be joined by the Indian surveyor with whom Shipton had been so impressed on the Osmaston trip into the Nanda Devi Sanctuary, Fazal Elahi, and by Fazal's younger colleague Inayat Khan. Of the former, Mott was later to write that:

it would have been difficult to find his equal for accuracy, speed and resourcefulness. His out-turn was quite remarkable and

---

[96] Coincidentally, Beerenberg had been Tilman's objective in 1968, when his first and best-loved boat *Mischief* – a name perfectly suited to Tilman's character – was wrecked off Jan Mayen Island. As to its dormancy, it did erupt in 1970, and still grumbles from time to time.

[97] I.e. resistance to the healers – an increasingly important stance in the leading of a healthy life.

can be gauged from the fact that in the course of three months' work he surveyed in great detail a total area of approximately 600 square miles, much of it above the snow line at 14,000 feet, and including the entire area of the Lukpe Lawo ('Snow Lake'), the whole of the Biafo glacier and two-thirds of the Hispar. Inayat Khan, although a younger and less experienced man, also produced some excellent work.[98]

Shipton added to the growing chorus of praise for Fazal, in the following terms about their time in Hispar: 'I was very glad to have the opportunity of being with Fazal Ellahi for a long time while he was at work. I was impressed by the skill with which he chose his stations, the speed and neatness with which he worked, the accuracy of his fixings, and the extraordinary energy he displayed.'[99]

Whilst they were together in 1939, incidentally, 'at the head of the Jutmaru [glacier] we followed for miles the tracks of some creature in the fresh snow. The tracks were a good deal bigger than those made by our boots, and though I suppose they must have been made by a bear they did not in the least resemble the bear tracks we had seen in the mud at the sides of the Biafo and Panmah glaciers. The difference was possibly due to the melting of the snow.'[100] The entertainment of a slight doubt here in the subtext of an ongoing interchange between Tilman and himself about the Yeti is a good lead-in to the final, outrageous tease in this saga – again, more of which in the epilogue.

Out in Darjeeling Ang Tharkay put together an habitual warlike and playful band of Sherpas, some of the customary faces missing now after the second tragedy on Nanga Parbat in 1937, when nine Sherpas were lost in an avalanche along with seven of their German sahibs. But several of the old characters Shipton had known throughout most of the 1930s were there: Kusang, Lobsang, Lakhpa Tenzing, as well as Ang Tharkay himself. With the composition of the team finalised, Shipton could now look to raising the finance required beyond the assistance offered by the Survey of India. The Royal Geographical Society the Royal Society, the Percy Sladen

---

[98] P. G. Mott, 'Karakoram Survey, 1939: A New Map' (*Geographical Journal*, July–September 1950), p.91.
[99] *G.J.* June, 1940, ibid. p.417.
[100] Ibid. p.418.

Memorial Fund of the Linnaean Society of London, the Royal Botanical Gardens at Kew and the Natural History Department of the British Museum as well as significant donations from R. W. Lloyd and Augustine Courtauld all contributed to what, because of the length of time they would be away and the special cold-weather equipment they would need, was going to be a very costly enterprise.

Before setting out again for the projected eighteen months away, in January 1939 Shipton went over to Switzerland, to work for six weeks with Michael Spender at the Wild-Heerbrugg factory near St Gallen. The two of them, together with the inventor Heinrich Wild, were engaged in refining the design of the Wild range of theodolites: 'The work is extremely interesting. The plotting instrument is an amazing affair and well worth coming all the way to see. The work is going ahead quite well and with luck we should be finished in time.'[101] Quite apart from his reason for being in Switzerland ('an excellent opportunity of studying survey, and it would be a pity to cut my stay shorter than necessary. I have got to get back anyway owing to my lecture in Blackpool on 18th Feb.'),[102] there were plenty of distractions on hand. He went skiing to Klosters, where he ran into Ella Maillart,[103] who 'came here to stay with us until she goes to Poland with her ski-team on Saturday. It is a nice opportunity of getting to know her well.'

By the middle of February Shipton was back in Britain, fulfilling his lecture obligations and making final preparations for his expedition. These having been completed, he and his mother headed off for a brief holiday in the south of France before she took the train to Italy and he went on board the P&O liner *Strathaird*.

---

[101] Letter to Mrs Haly, January 1939.

[102] Letter to Mrs Haly, 2 February 1939.

[103] Ella Maillart (1903–97) was one of the great twentieth-century female travellers and travel-writers, her journeys including one through Soviet Turkestan in 1932 and, notably, the seven-month 1935 odyssey from Beijing to Srinagar through civil-war-torn Chinese Turkestan with the *Times* journalist Peter Fleming, variously described in her *Forbidden Land* and his *News from Tartary*. Fleming was brother to the more famous Ian, creator of 'James Bond', and was also husband of the actress Celia Johnson, star of *Brief Encounter*. At the time of her meeting with Shipton, after her Polish trip Maillart was about to depart overland by car from Geneva to Kabul (hence the later elaborate practical joke involving Peter Mott in drag – see note 110 below). It's also worth noting that Maillart played a significant role in the promotion of the Swiss expedition to Everest in 1952 that came so very close to prising Coronation Everest out of the Imperial grasp.

This is a very dull ship – load of people, most of them Australians and nearly all the rest refugees from middle Europe. It appears that Hitler is paying their fares out to Australia to get rid of them. I shall be very glad when the voyage is over, as it is a bad ship and very crowded . . . There was a bit of a sensation on board . . . an old chap in the 1ˢᵗ class who disliked the band. He complained that it kept him awake at night. Of course they did not stop so he pitched all their instruments overboard – about £65-worth. We are due at Port Said tomorrow morning at 6 o'clock.[104]

For all the tedium of the voyage out, this major undertaking of his life-in-exploration so far started well. The expedition had assembled in Srinagar early in June and there was an immediate bonus for Shipton in the form (with the physical manifestation of which he very quickly became intimately acquainted) of a young woman who was staying in the house of the Clutterbucks, on whose lawn they camped. Her name was Diana Channer, and her father was an officer in the Indian Forest Service. Beatrice Weir having been placed in purdah by her mother, who disapproved of the crush she had on Shipton, Diana had the field to herself. Another child of nature, and respectably closer to Shipton's own age, she confided to her diary the growing attraction to him, the effect of those blue eyes, the flirtation, the timbre of his voice, the feel of his head in her lap, the bathing together and the lying naked in the sun to dry. Then, inevitably, came the parting, though delayed by Diana and Lady Clutterbuck walking with them for the first five days – an experience it is safe to say Tilman would not have been happy to share.

The march from Srinagar through the woods of Gurais with sun dappling through the branches, over the Burzil, Tragbal and Kamri passes, snow still lying and the great bulk of Nanga Parbat's tragic peak where Sherpa friends of his had died glistening in the west, enabled them in some degree to forget 'the ugly turmoil of the world we had left behind.' As they descended towards the Indus, the mulberries and apricots were sweet and ripe. Beyond Gilgit, the colossal scale of Rakaposhi, 'one of the most stupendous mountain faces in the world',[105] taunted their punier designs. They divided up

[104] Letter to Mrs Haly from SS *Strathaird*, 23 May 1939.
[105] Shipton, *Upon That Mountain*, p.219–20.

into small groups on 3 July and set to with their individual tasks. Fazal Elahi and Peter Mott progressed rapidly with the work required by the Surveyor General – the latter checking closely on the previous Bullock Workman survey results and finding that they had frequently estimated wildly on the high side for the Hispar and Lukpe Lawo peaks, at times by as much as 3,000 feet. In early September Shipton himself was travelling up the Choktoi glacier, ten miles north-east of the Biafo and parallel to it: 'When we entered the upper basin we were met by a stupendous view of the granite peaks of the Ogre group standing a sheer 7,000 feet above the glacier. As we rounded the corner, one after another of the ice spires crowning the knife-sharp ridges of the peaks flicked into view, brilliantly translucent in the afternoon sun.'[106] This was on 4 September. They carried on with their intense work, the various parties widely scattered, going about their individual tasks in solitary concentration, oblivious to each other in the efficient and happy manner Shipton had developed for maximising an expedition's effectiveness and opportunity. From time to time their paths would cross on the passes or glaciers, or notes be left at dumps and camps to maintain communication prior to their all meeting up again according to plan back in Gilgit in October, before the onset of winter.

Completely cut off from each other for the most part, and from the outside world entirely, their only contact with the latter was by means of a heavy battery radio weighing more than thirty pounds at the base camp in the Hispar valley where Scott Russell was doing most of his botanical research. One afternoon, against expedition protocols that forbade its frivolous use, he switched it on for entertainment.

Late in the evening of the 15th, Russell and two Sherpas arrived from across the Hispar pass, which was heavily covered by new snow. He brought news of the outbreak of war, which he had heard by wireless. The news, though not altogether unexpected, was a considerable shock. We had been in the field only a few months, but European politics already seemed very remote, and it was hard to realise the meaning of the disaster. It seemed obvious that we must abandon the expedition, but the party was too widely separated for immediate recall, and

[106] *G.J.* June, 1940, ibid. p.415.

as less than a month was necessary for the completion of our summer programme, I decided to carry on until we reassembled in Gilgit. First we had to wait for Fazal Elahi's party, so that we could make a combined crossing of the Hispar pass, which was likely to become difficult with further snowfalls. He was due back at the dump [on Snow Lake/Lukpe Lawo] on September 22nd.[107]

It was a month from the time Scott Russell brought them news of war when they all finally reassembled back in Gilgit.[108] By then some of them – Mott for example – had been out of contact with the rest of the team for over two months. Now they had to take the bitter step of abandoning a monumental enterprise that was to have been the summation of everything that Shipton had achieved over the last fifteen years. 'For all that', Shipton wrote, 'we are lucky to have been able to snatch a few more months of life from the wreck of the future.' A letter to his mother from Srinagar, dated 12 November 1939, gives an impression of the confusions and uncertainties of the time.

My Darling Mum,
    It is a long time since I wrote I'm afraid. I did not write from Gilgit as the mail was stopped owing to heavy snow on the passes. I think my last letter was from the Hispar glacier where I was supervising the work of one of the surveyors before I came down. When I got to Gilgit I found that all the others had been there for some time; all having come back by different routes . . . I had told Scott [Russell] to send off the wires I told you I was going to send to the RGS and the Government of India. The latter had not replied and the former told me to put our services at the disposal of the Government of India.[109]

---

[107] Ibid. pp.416–17.
[108] Scott Russell had been dispatched to Gilgit with telegrams requesting advice on their best course of action, and had arrived there to send them and await replies on 3 October.
[109] Letter to Mrs Haly from Srinagar, 12 November 1939. The letter continues as follows, and is worth giving here in its entirety as one of the few pieces of his writing that records this period of his life: 'We sent repeated wires through the Political Agent and we waited there [i.e. in Gilgit] a fortnight after I got there before we got a reply and it was most unsatisfactory. It was a very difficult thing to decide whether to go on or come back, but I thought I would be open to a lot

Catch 22! In *Upon That Mountain*, written during wartime from amid the relative peace of Kashgar on the fringes of the Taklamakan desert, Shipton records his feelings on first hearing from Scott Russell that hostilities had broken out between Britain and Germany. The passage reveals a good deal about the essential Shipton, and the manner in which his mind and spirit continually sought out and returned to the solace of natural beauty and a desired, optimistic, ideal world.

It was a strange, dreamlike experience hearing such news in those surroundings. I felt for the moment as though one of the crevasses had opened and that I was dropping into a bottomless pit. I passed the news on to Ang Tharkay, and for a timeless moment we stood motionless. Then we went on to meet the other party, relieved them of some of their loads, and made our way back to camp, where I listened to such realities

---

of criticism if I took the expedition besides the financial difficulties due to the war; although it seems impossible to get war jobs in the services either out here or at home. So I decided to come back. We had some difficulty getting over the Burzil Pass, which was under very heavy snow. I sent Scott and Peter ahead and Eadric and I got the stuff over after some delay. When we got here [to Srinagar] the Clutterbucks were still here having waited up purposely for us which was extraordinarily kind of them. They <u>had</u> to go on, however and we are now on a houseboat paying Rs.2/8 each per day all in and including servants – which is pretty good. The Resident asked us to put the boat in a place reserved for him which is nice.

'These are our plans as far as they go. Peter and I have got a month's work at Dehra Dun, but before that I want to go to Delhi to see some influential people there to get their advice on what to do. On the way to Delhi I will go to Peshawar to see a man there. So now I am waiting for a reply from Delhi to say when I can go there. Peter will go ahead to Dehra Dun . . .

'I had a letter from Bill Tilman who is fighting in France now. I wrote to him to get a further line on how things are. Now we must just bide our time and await events.

'We had a very pleasant time in Gilgit. The new PA is a most charming person – Major Crichton by name – married, with two little girls of 5 & 9 and a young Yugoslavian girl to look after them. The Battys had just gone and there was a new APA and wife and a new doctor. They entertained us a lot and gave us a very good time. On our last night we had dinner with the Crichtons who suggested that we should stay an extra day and they would give us a dance. From that we concocted a fine leg-pull on the whole station. The PA sent out a notice to say that he had just got word that Ella Maillart had crossed over from Afghanistan and would arrive the next day, and inviting everyone to come in for a few drinks to meet her. We dressed Peter up as a girl and the joke went marvellously. Everyone was completely taken in.'

as Russell was able to give. It was no dream, but a grim reality.

He moves on to ponder the implications of what he had just heard, comparing it as ever with his eternal point of reference in the mountain symbol.

> I suppose we must have been expecting it, but that did not seem to lessen the shock. It was hard to realise the meaning of the disaster. Perhaps even now the London where we had planned this very venture was a chaos of destruction and terror. How fantastic, how supremely ridiculous it seemed in our remote and lovely world of snow and ice.

The negative impact on his state of mind as ever produces one of those quietistic, hopeful moments of oneness with natural creation that had always been his way of coping with human evil, whether as a vulnerable child recovering from ill treatment at the hands of Mr Gifford or now as a free adult in the wild facing the threat and implications of Nazi world domination.

> As if to point the contrast the mists cleared and for a moment the glacier was bathed in a sunset glow reflected from the high peaks. The great granite spires of the Biafo stood black against a deep blue sky. At least this mountain world, to which I owed so much of life and happiness, would stand above the ruin of human hopes, the heritage of a saner generation of men.[110]

That seems to me one of the clearest statements of Shipton's outlook – an optimistic, heuristic ameliorism, that offers so strong a contrast to Tilman's continually witty and grinding pessimism and cynicism, which latter is again only exorcised by contact with natural creation and simple, hardy people. The vital clue here is that paradoxical one of humour, the exponents of which, from Aristophanes and Molière to Bob Dylan, have all been depressive moralists trying to put a shine on the bleak.

It's appropriate at this point to bring in some further perspectives, to play into our attempts to understand these two exceptional men. Shipton's turning at the age of thirty to his great project of

---

[110] Shipton, *Upon That Mountain*, p.221.

surveying and mapping wild landscapes, following on from the happy-go-lucky, seat-of-his-pants journeying through them, seems best explicable in terms of seeking from landscape as he approaches maturity some of the emotional certainty and definition denied him throughout childhood and adolescence. We are back with John Bowlby and attachment theory here – an apposite area of study (as also are the extensions from it into adult peer and romantic relationships by Cindy Hazan and Phillip Shaver).

For Tilman, conversely, within the secure and defined framework of his family there was a wholly different psychological mix; he had been subjected as a boy to John Hinkes Tilman's relatively benign tyrannies; had cleaved to the oppressed mother; was denied freedom of emotional expression firstly by public school and then by the strait-jacket of military discipline within the nightmarish environment of mud and carnage in Flanders; was physically scarred and suffered the extraordinary symbolism of that flesh wound in the thigh – remember here King Pellinor in the Arthurian quest-romances. His obsessive bathing seems as though to rid himself of the taint of those putrid battlefield-mangled corpses. Time and again there subtly manifests at a level never beyond faint suggestion something Tilman's admirers, of whom I am unequivocally one as well as having been a personal friend, have always been at pains to squirm away from and deny, but which is somehow insistently present: the slight and undemanding suggestion so ubiquitous among Great War survivors of homo-eroticism.[111] Let me make it absolutely plain here that I am not remotely suggesting Tilman was 'gay'. The modern sexual lexicon is wholly inapplicable to the chaste subtleties of affectionate relationships in the first half of the last century. Nor am I in any way referring to consummated physical homosexuality, which Tilman, knowing his *Leviticus*,[112] would have deemed 'an abomination', just as he would have found repugnant the prurient contemporary obsession with Bloomsbury buggery. A clear insight into his attitude comes from the time when he was fighting alongside the Italian Partisans' Gramsci Brigade in the Dolomites in 1944. He and Captain John Ross were sheltered by a farmer and given a

---

[111] Do not confuse this term with homosexuality – they are not remotely the same thing.

[112] *Leviticus* 18: 22, if you must – not a book that puts you much in sympathy with the Bible-bashers.

properly made-up double bed to share. Tilman was concerned that the farmer and his family would think them homosexual because they left only one impression on the sheets after each night. In fact, they took turns to sleep on the floor, it being more comfortable than the exceedingly lumpy mattress.[113]

What is at issue here, of course, is same-sex friendship (not 'platonic love', incidentally, which properly refers to a chaste spiritual affection for someone of the opposite sex – the exact opposite, in fact, of its origin as a synonym for *amor socraticus*, which was closest perhaps to pederasty). There is not the slightest suggestion from any source that Tilman was ever tempted to the physical expression and consummation of this. In fact, on occasion his physical appreciation of women is quite apparent, and decidedly un-'gay'. It is important to the understanding of many creative and dedicated people with the 'Victorian' stamp of personality to realise that their lives were often characterised by the successful sublimation of sexual energy into artistic or adventurous achievement. Modern insistence on annexation of historical figures – even modern historical figures like Tilman – into the realms of sexual politics can be doctrinaire and wrong-headed at times. The debate within feminist criticism as to whether or not Jane Austen – a woman whose biting sense of humour Tilman relished – was a lesbian is a good example. Had Tilman been prey to homosexual impulses, then feeling them to be wrong and knowing them to be illegal he would surely have mastered them through one of his favourite quotations: Dr Johnson's stern and to our age unpalatable maxim that 'To deny early and inflexibly, is the only art of checking the importunity of desire.'[114] What we are touching on here is one of the defining aspects of Great War literature. Read closely through the work of those druids of the broken body who wrote imaginatively on the battlefields and the trenches – Wilfred Owen's is an excellent example – and the erotic ache of appreciation, no more than that, comes through as surely as it does in Christian liturgy and art, with its wound-and-lance sado-masochistic symbolism. Whatever psychological accommodation Tilman made with all this tangled and conflicting matter was as private and personal as could possibly

---

[113] The anecdote comes from personal correspondence in 1983 with John Ross, who became, after the war, a much-loved consultant physician in Hereford.
[114] Dr. Johnson: *Idler* (April 14, 1759) paragraph 52.

be. He gave us not the slightest clue. We neither know, nor to my mind should even wish to know, and I now leave this defence of my subject against what he would have deemed a slur, and one far too casually levelled, before readers tire of it and decide that perhaps I protest too much.

What I can tell you with some certainty is that Tilman had a traditional belief in an interventionist God. He was a devout and formal Christian throughout his life. When home in Bodowen he would always attend Sunday service at the little church of Caerdeon (the Church in Wales building in exquisite position above the Mawddach estuary where his memorial service was held). To believe in God and witness horror and human barbarism enslaves you to paradox, from which humour offers the surest and perhaps easiest escape. And a degree also of containment and hard-won equanimity. People fuss around the self-contained, insisting on a need vital to their own cases for human connection and intimacy which is neither necessary, nor in some cases present. If Betsy Cowles imagined that Tilman was her Alceste and she his Célimène,[115] she was simply mistaken, though her feminine curiosity and admirable qualities of character ultimately won her his friendship. Shy, inhibited and withdrawn he may have been, but in no sense was Tilman emotionally cold. Charlie Houston, implicitly comparing Shipton and Tilman, comments on how 'Bill Tilman, curiously, was the one I came closest to over the next thirty years.'[116] My experience of Tilman too was of a man who was warm and welcoming, who was ready to engage both intellectually and in his own way emotionally (though the rations here were frugal – a handshake and a 'Nice to see you' were effusion enough for him), once the initial reserve had been thawed or circumvented.

Shipton was also profoundly religious in temperament, in an entirely different way. I have a sense that there was more of the Desert Father[117] in him, by contrast with Tilman's orthodox Pauline and disciplined believer. Shipton was the modest Gnostic; a believer

---

[115] Protagonists in Molière's *Le Misanthrope* – subtlest and most profound of all comedies.

[116] Eric Shipton and H. W. Tilman, *Nanda Devi: Exploration and Ascent* (The Mountaineers/Baton Wicks, 1999/2000), p.13.

[117] An entrancingly diverse group, the Desert Fathers, by no means necessarily as austere as the image the name evokes. For a wise and witty introduction, see Thomas Merton's illuminating commentary and anthology, *The Wisdom of the Desert* (New Directions, 1970), already quoted in the introduction.

in the oneness, and in the sustaining power of nature, as in the 'saner generation' passage quoted above that is the penultimate paragraph to *Upon That Mountain*. The fascination here is in the way the defining life passage – and for both of them their shared mountain activity in the first half of the 1930s was just that – arrived for each of them through the agency of their partnership, their keeping company and adventuring with the other. They were Hazard's Itinerants together, to use Geoffrey Hill's resonant collocation,[118] the energy and imagination of the one enthralling the loyal, adjutant and enabling affection of the other. It was the oddest of relationships, and Shipton could certainly gripe on occasion about its inadequacy to his social, intellectual and emotional needs (though I suspect nothing was ever adequate to the latter – François Truffaut's charming and poignant film *L'Homme qui aimait les Femmes* from 1977, the year Shipton died, might well be one of the best glosses on this).

That they little understood each other and remained both fascinated and slightly mystified to the last is made plain from one side in Tilman's baffled obituary for Shipton in the 1977 *Himalayan Journal* where, at the end of a skeletal catalogue of facts, he writes, 'It would need a readier pen than mine and someone with more discernment to assess his character; I must content myself with this slight tribute to the most outstanding mountaineer-explorer of our time.'[119] Tony Astill, in his affectionate retro-volume on the 1935 Everest reconnaissance, includes a telling anecdote from Shipton's younger son John, who had sailed with Tilman on his penultimate voyage in *Baroque*, that gives a clear view of the mutual mystification from the other side:

I saw my father for the last time in the summer of 1976, a year before he and Tilman died.[120] He was intensely curious as to what I made of Bill. Astonishingly Tilman remained an enigma to the man who should know him better than any other. I couldn't enlighten him very far, only that to us the old man was a hero who you could follow with total confidence.

[118] In *Clavics* (Enitharmon Press, 2011), p.12.
[119] *Himalayan Journal*, 1977, p.338.
[120] Shipton died at the end of March 1977, and Tilman was lost at sea in the autumn of that year.

I now know of course that my father, although so different in
character, also had the same quality.[121]

Perhaps it's the case that all too often we flatter ourselves with the
illusion that we really know our friends. Perhaps the modern stress on
intimacy insists too strongly that we should, and thus has the reverse
effect of rendering it fixed and commonplace. Or to take an even more
heterodox view, perhaps friendship, like love, exists and manifests
satisfactorily only in actions and not through words, in which case that
between Shipton and Tilman was proven true time and again beyond
all question, as was their mutual regard. Both seemed intuitively to
know that mere ambition is the weakness and the obsession of lesser
men, who sense their own worth to be slight. Both knew for certain,
viscerally, that in danger you are in the presence of the laughing and
the dancing gods, whose company and crucial formative influence
contemporary culture and 'civilisation' seek continually to traduce
and deny, to our children's detriment and loss.

It seems fitting to end this account of the greatest decade in
mountain exploration, and the central role in that of our two
protagonists, with a tribute to the man Tilman in that obituary
passage quoted above called 'the most outstanding mountaineer-
explorer of our time' from the man who became from 1935 onwards
Shipton's most frequent social companion and intimate friend, and
with whom he enjoyed a temperamental affinity that he had never
possessed with the reliable, watchful, austere and on occasion
slightly bumbling substitute-father-figure of Tilman. The tribute
was delivered at the Royal Geographical Society on 4 March 1940,
after Scott Russell had read Shipton's paper on their Karakoram
surveying in 1939 (Shipton himself was going through officer
training in southern India at the time). It emerged in the course
of the succeeding discussion, after contributions from Sir Francis
Younghusband, Professor Philip Mason, and Frank Kingdon-Ward
the botanist. The speaker, of course, was Michael Spender. He stood
up to extemporise, and his contribution ran as follows:

My principal feelings about this paper [of Shipton's] are of
pleasure and gratitude at seeing some pictures of mountains

---

[121] Tony Astill, *The Forgotten Adventure – Mount Everest: The Reconnaissance
1935* (privately published, 2005), p.29.

and thus being reminded that the mountains are still there. Nevertheless, I feel bound to enter into something which is dangerously near to being ponderous, because I should like to relate this expedition to the journeys of previous travellers in the same region. It was Conway who first ascended the Hispar; he made a very good survey indeed; but others came along later and in their efforts at map-making got surveys of the district into appalling confusion.

Thus the premise and the historical outline. Spender quickly proceeds to the qualities Shipton brought to the task.

What Shipton did was to tidy up in one fairly short expedition the work of several expeditions. He used his forces and disposed his food and Sherpas so that he did in the course of a short time an amount of work which would have taken an earlier expedition a great number of seasons. It is important that none of this was new work over new country. It was all done simply out of the feeling that it had got to be done; the surveys of this area had to be straightened out before he could get on to what he really wanted to do.

What he really wanted to do Spender then outlined in a summary paragraph remarkable in what it discloses of Shipton's intent and the sympathy and mutuality of interest that existed between himself and Spender.

Shipton likes going to new country; he likes exploration. When we finished in 1937 we left one or two fascinating problems unsolved. There was the great patch of country near the Aghil pass to which Sir Francis has just referred, which is still unexplored. Looking to left and right of that we saw a large area of country still to be spied out and put on the map. That was what Shipton was looking forward to going back to. He had planned to spend the summer of 1939 doing the duty part of the work, and to spend the winter doing the interesting part. That point was not brought out during the paper, so I hope you will forgive me for stressing it now. It is important to me and important, I am sure, to Shipton.

Having corrected his audience with regard to their possible mis-apprehension, and the absent writer of the paper for his omission, Spender shifts into encomiastic mode to give his own assessment of the remarkable qualities of his leader and friend.

> Shipton went to the mountains for their own sake. At a time when so many do things for the wrong reason – because they will get some *kudos* or promotion or because the newspapers will write about them – it is important that there should be those who insist on removing inessentials, on discarding what is unimportant to the job in hand. That is why Shipton has been a successful leader, a leader with whom it has always been and always will be a great inspiration to work. He spent the summer preparing and laying the foundations, so to speak, laying out his depots in more senses than one, anticipating an interesting winter's work. I want you, in judging the expedition, to realise that it was cut off before the main part had begun and after the foundations had been laid.[122]

This is a wonderfully apt and skilful panegyric, and I like Spender all the better for it. His judgement could stand both for Shipton and Tilman, and for what they achieved in a decade wholly without parallel in the annals of mountain exploration. It might be argued that few major summits were achieved – though Kamet and Nanda Devi were very significant ascents in their time, the latter particularly so given its remoteness and difficulty. You could certainly claim that far too much energy and time was allotted to reaching time and again more or less the same point on the north ridge or north face of Everest, but our subjects would anyway doubtless agree with you, and this would also be to ignore the forbidden status at that period of the kingdom of Nepal, which Tilman neatly sums up even at the late date of 1949 as follows:

> Nepal is an independent kingdom. Like Tibet it has always sought isolation and has secured it by excluding foreigners, of whom the most undesirable were white men. A man fortunate enough to have been admitted into Nepal is expected to be able to explain on general grounds the motives behind this

---
[122] *G.J.* June 1940, pp.426–7.

invidious policy and, on personal grounds, the reason for such an unaccountable exception. But now that the advantages of the Western way of life are becoming every day less obvious no explanation should be needed. Wise men traditionally come from the East, and it is probable that to them the West and its ways were suspect long before we ourselves began to have doubts.[123]

Characteristically bracing, and a good foretaste of the reasons for his eventually taking to the sea! The fact that Nepal effectively remained closed until after the Second World War should explain why so much effort was expended on the far more difficult north side. Had Mallory – who was, it needs to be stressed, not nearly so accomplished a rock-climber as some recent mountain historians[124] have tried to make out – approached from the south and found his way through the Khumbu ice fall and into the Western Cwm, given reasonable snow conditions there is every chance that he and Irvine would have made the summit, with relative ease compared to the trials endured on the difficult northern side. And that, as has been said so many times, would have enabled everyone to get back to the proper mountaineering again and allowed Mallory to be properly deified as Bloomsbury required. Probably, too, it would have allowed greater credence to be given to the Shipton/Tilman style, which had proven itself ethically and practically superior to the militaristic assault-and-conquest ethos that inevitably was reintroduced when the threat of another nation's claiming the prize – Switzerland, in this instance – grew ever more large.

Once the prize had been won, however, and the obsessive interest and chicaneries that it aroused were defused, mountaineering could return to the same value system Shipton and Tilman, and Longstaff before them, had defined, to which for sixty years the sport at its best has been enthusiastically referential. And yet, contemplating that influence, I'm left thinking that there was more to Shipton and Tilman than that. There was more to them than a style to which they gave their names. I'm continually reminded in thinking of them

---

[123] Tilman, *Seven Mountain Travel Books*, pp.745–6.
[124] Particularly Americans and Canadians prepared to accept without question G. W. Y.'s mythopoeic project and remain ignorant of the context of Mallory's early Welsh record, its cultural milieu and class and colonialist agendas – I write as a Welshman here, well versed in the history of my native hills.

about a late interview given by the Argentinian master writer (and Peronian chicken inspector – what we do to our great men and women!) Jorge Luis Borges. In it he made the following observation: 'When I was a young man I was always hunting for new metaphors. Then I found out that good metaphors are always the same. I mean you compare time to a road, death to sleeping, life to dreaming, and those are the great metaphors because they correspond to something essential.'

Somehow, for me, what Shipton and Tilman achieved jointly and individually throughout the 1930s also corresponds to that 'something essential'. It does so through the qualities they displayed: resourcefulness, obduracy, skill, courage, fortitude, loyalty, humour – add in your own abstractions at will, for many are applicable here. But it also resonates out from that into a typological, metonymic dimension, the dialectical insistencies giving it the nature of a moral quest, made wholly authentic through the rigours shared and endured. With these two men, the journey transcends its physical form and path. It becomes a state of being, that we might all aspire in some part to emulate or cultivate, whatever ways we choose in the leading of our own lives. And so, following their examples as seen throughout this defining decade, we enact so far as we are capable of it this state. We do so as fully as possible until, through war as in their case, or disability, psychological retreat or death, there is 'sport no more seen, /On the darkening Green.'[125]

And yes, thus, the mountains that Shipton and Tilman sought out as balm to their individual and early confusions, damage and pain will have produced a saner – and simpler – generation of humankind who may go on modestly to vindicate their great exemplars.

Perhaps already, dawn lightening a black night-sky in the mountains, the evidence begins to point that way, rising like a distant peak above the shimmer of doubt.

I hope so . . .

---

[125] See note 1 above.

Epilogue

Knuckling the Footprint

i) Leave-takings

In E.M. Forster's fine, railing-against-conformity novel of 1907, *The Longest Journey* (the third part of it set in a distinctly pagan Wiltshire – where fighting against the conventional is concerned, Bevis-land rules!), the author rids himself of one of his central characters in the most sudden and unexpected way: 'Gerald died that afternoon. He was broken up in the football match.'[1] I hope readers of this book will not feel that I've as summarily dispatched my two subjects. To end this narrative in 1939 is not gratuitous. It is done in order to emphasise the magnitude of their achievements through one exceptional decade. Matthew Hollis, in a perceptive and vivid recent book[2] on the last years of Edward Thomas, employs the same useful stratagem of keeping focus on the crucial phase of his subject's life in order to achieve a concentrated view through which we may better understand the whole.

Though the 1930s, and particularly the years between 1934 and 1938, had been the great phase of their friendship and exploratory achievement, Shipton and Tilman were to live on for the best part of four decades from the outbreak of the Second World War. These years were far from inactive, and saw both of them add to their already-outstanding records in exploration. Only a few of these post-war initiatives were undertaken together, and even those few were not characterised by any great ambition or success. The war had both changed and aged them, and the world beyond it into which they survived was a very different place to the one that witnessed their

---

[1] E. M. Forster, *The Longest Journey* (Harmondsworth, 1960) p.56.
[2] Matthew Hollis, *Now All Roads Lead to France* (Faber, 2011).

days of bold and sunny vagabondage in the company of similarly insouciant and humorous hill people.

Politics and economics wrought their changes too, and what had been possible and appealing in 1930 wore a different aspect in the second half of the 1940s and the austerity of the early 1950s. Nor were Shipton and Tilman's own priorities as they had been a decade and a half before. For Shipton, there was his marriage to Diana Channer in 1942 and the birth of their sons – Nick in 1945, and John in 1950. Tilman, too, entered a kind of marriage in 1954 – to his beloved *Mischief*, the Bristol Channel pilot cutter, only eight years younger than her new owner, in which he sailed 114,000 miles north and south before she was lost off Jan Mayen Island in 1968 (something for which he never forgave a good climbing friend of mine, Ian Duckworth,[3] who was on watch at the time she went on rocks and was holed). Two more pilot cutters came after *Mischief* – *Sea Breeze*, sunk in an east Greenland fjord in 1972, and *Baroque,* sold before he departed for his final voyage aboard Simon Richardson's *En Avant* in 1977, subsequently restored, and still afloat today. This was an entirely new saga of adventurous travel, one that was every bit as impressive as his mountaineering of the 1930s, and which won him a different band of admirers – as well as a few detractors among the phoney-adventurer and yacht-polishing fraternities. Taken in sum with his service record in both wars and the climbs and mountain-travelling between 1930 and 1950, his was one of the great adventurous lives – perhaps the most adventurous life – of the twentieth century, and one that still awaits an adequate and informed retelling.

To recount both men's life stories in detail from 1939 to their

---

[3] Ian felt that he was unfairly blamed for this, and that there were extenuating circumstances. His subsequent view of Tilman was that 'he's a bastard – an absolute bastard! But my God, he's a hard old bastard!' From Ian, no marshmallow himself, relieved of his commission in the Royal Marines for outrageous behaviour, there were no higher terms of praise. I remember being on the difficult top section of Joe Brown's great Winking Crack on the upper tier of Craig Gogarth on a very early ascent in 1968, shortly after Ian had returned from the Arctic. From the final insecure overhanging off-width – a fun piece of climbing! – I looked down a long arc of rope little punctuated by protection, saw the massive physique of Ian holding it on the tiny stance below, and felt even in that precarious position entirely safe. Some people have that effect. I imagine Shipton had a similar response to Tilman in their climbing days, and would probably have echoed that assessment of him as 'a hard old bastard'.

deaths seven months apart in 1977 – Shipton to cancer, Tilman lost at sea – would make of an already long book a vast and unwieldy one, as well as tipping it over from being the account of a peculiar kind of friendship through its significant decade into a dual biography; so I do not propose to recount the second halves of their lives in any more than outline – the detail is all there in the individual biographies, and both Anderson and Steele handle the later years of their subjects' lives with degrees of competence.

As far as my outline here is concerned, Tilman's war record deserves to be mentioned first. He fought in France during the first months of the Second World War and was evacuated from Dunkirk. Back in Britain he was promoted to major (a rank from which he carefully contrived never to be further promoted) in command of a battery, and was sent out to India and then Iraq. After the fall of Tobruk, he led a 'Jock column'[4] covering the retreat to the defences then being prepared at El Alamein and in the Western Desert. It was the same kind of warfare he had relished in the closing stages of the Great War – fast-moving, light, instinctive. And mortally dangerous. Victory at El Alamein and the defeat of Rommel rendered the Western Desert too quiet for his liking. He volunteered for parachute training, and was assigned to fight behind enemy lines on special operations firstly with the partisans in Albania, and later with the Italian resistance in the Dolomites. For his exploits there he was awarded the DSO and made a freeman of the city of Belluno[5] in 1945. Throughout the second half of the 1940s he took up the Himalayan and Central Asian mountain themes of the preceding decade, often with an even more solitary inflection now. Not always, though. From April to July of 1947 he was a member of a Swiss expedition attempting Rakaposhi (25,551 feet). Poor and dangerous snow and ice conditions on their various chosen lines ensured its defeat, though much useful reconnaissance work was done, and this was invaluable in assisting the eventual ascent of the mountain by

[4] A light motorised column of armoured cars and artillery used tactically to hit and run against advancing Italian and German forces. They were named after a soldier from Tilman's old regiment of the Royal Horse Artillery, Lieutenant Colonel Jock Campbell, VC, DSO and bar, MC (1894–1942). Campbell devised the strategy, the impact of which was crucial in the ultimate victory at the second battle of El Alamein in October 1942, the turning point of the North Africa campaign.

[5] One of only five men ever to have this honour conferred – Garibaldi was his most illustrious predecessor.

the Royal Marines team of Tom Patey and Mike Banks in 1958.

In the same year he met up with Shipton and Gyalgen, his Sherpa assistant in Kashgar, for an attempt on Muztagh Ata (24,757 feet), the high point of an isolated mountain group to the south of the Kun Lun range which itself forms the northern border of the Tibetan plateau. Bitter cold and deep snow forced them to retreat from a point estimated at four hundred feet below the summit. No technical problems lay ahead, but with Shipton suffering from frostbite, Tilman less severely so, and all three exhausted the only option was retreat. Tilman stayed for a while with Shipton and his new wife during Shipton's second spell on consular service in Kashgar. In her book about their life in Xinjiang, Diana is notably reticent about the visits – he came again in 1948 for attempts on Bogdo Ola (17,864 feet) and the impressive peak of Chakragil (22,178 feet), both of which, for various reasons, were unsuccessful; though Nick Shipton vouchsafes that she did not enjoy them very much and disliked Tilman intensely. As a young wife who had left her first child with foster-parents in order to be with her husband, she felt understandably aggrieved at his preferring to go off on trips with this surly stranger (who from his side too no doubt resented her presence, and showed it in all the little bridling ways that people will). In her memoir Diana records the aftermath of Muztagh Ata thus: 'Eric's bad foot [from frostbite] tied him to the house for a couple of months and completely spoilt his plans for small trips with Bill, during the latter's short stay in Kashgar, before he returned to England.'[6] You cannot but imagine a certain gleeful note in that. As to Tilman returning to England, in fact he came back to Wales and the newly-bought house of Bodowen on the northern side of the Mawddach estuary which he and his sister Adeline shared for the rest of her life, and where he stayed on after her death in 1974.

In 1948 he was once more in Xinjiang. The impressive travels of this period, humorously described in *Two Mountains and a River* (1949) and *China to Chitral* (1951) – two of the eccentric classics of British travel-writing – mark an interesting phase in Tilman's life, and were the journeys that brought him the RGS Founders' Medal. They also proved to be the last of their kind to be undertaken in the region. He was certainly testing the boundaries, and bravely so, of where it was possible to go in this time of tension between Russia,

---

[6] Diana Shipton, *The Antique Land* (Hodder & Stoughton, 1950), p.184.

China and Britain, and this led to his being arrested from time to time – for straying into Afghanistan, for example. That both he and Shipton were engaged in some form of intelligence-gathering for the British government is not, I think, to be doubted (particularly in view of Shipton's consular and other service in key strategic locations and Tilman's SOE war record), and it will be interesting to see what future biographers of both men can turn up about their activities from British official records.[7]

Tilman's mountaineering was by no means in abeyance. He passed through the Hindu Kush on his journey to Chitral, and in both 1949 and 1950 was in the Nepal Himalaya, which had been newly opened to Westerners – firstly on a survey expedition with a plump and prosperous Peter Lloyd, the botanist Oleg Polunin, and his old friend from the mid-1930s Tenzing Norgay; and in 1950 with Colonel Jimmy Roberts, Charles Evans and others on an expedition to the north side of Annapurna on which Annapurna 4 (24,688 feet) was attempted. In the same year, in company with Charlie Houston and Betsy Cowles, he trekked to Everest by way of the Sherpa homeland of Solukhumbu, which he had long desired to visit, and viewed the mountain to which he had led the last pre-war expedition from the slopes of Pumori. After this, one of his biographers mischievously suggests that – his fond eye cast on Mrs Cowles – Tilman decided to seek gainful employment with a view to being able to support a wife. I doubt it somehow – he was already well off financially both from his inheritance after his father's death, and from the sale during the war of the land at Kericho, which had gained in value through the discovery that tea prospered there better than coffee. He did find himself a job, though, as British consul at Maymyo (now Pyin U Lwin) in the Shan Highlands of Central Burma. Perhaps he had Kipling and all the romance of the road to Mandalay in mind?

> *Ship me somewheres east of Suez, where the best is like the worst,*
> *Where there aren't no Ten Commandments an' a man can raise a thirst;*

[7] F. H. Hinsley's *British Intelligence in the Second World War* (HMSO, four volumes [Vol. 3 in two parts, 1984–8], 1979–90) is the indispensable background reading here, and fascinating also in its account of the Enigma saga.

For the temple-bells are callin', an' it's there that I would be —
By the old Moulmein Pagoda, looking lazy at the sea;
On the road to Mandalay.

Whatever the reason, the experiment in conventional employment was not a resounding success. His contract was not renewed, and any tentative canvassings of the notion of matrimony from either side – if indeed there were any – came to nothing. By 1953 Tilman was home in Wales, and increasingly to be found on the water in small boats. The following year he bought *Mischief*, and the rest is a history of an entirely different kind, quite beyond the scope of this book and ending in the autumn of 1977 with his sailing away as ordinary crew member on the boat of a young friend, Simon Richardson, to meet his fate somewhere between Rio and Port Stanley in November and a season of storms.[8]

On Shipton's later years, we left him undecided as to what to do after the dissolution of his grand 1939 Karakoram venture in northern India, where he was still involved in writing up survey work at Dehra Dun. Without the requested direction from his contacts in England, early in 1940 he took matters in his own hands, enlisted in the Indian Army, and was sent off for officer training to Belgaum in the hills behind Goa. It was another "interesting interlude between a life and a life", and one in which Shipton's natural antipathy towards authority, institutions and conventions found its habitually resistant expression. The waves he made didn't quite wash him out of the training school. At the end of June he was commissioned as a second lieutenant and – his immediate superiors not quite sure what to do with this dreamily subversive specimen of human obduracy

---

[8] This last venture of Tilman's was finely recorded by Simon Richardson's mother Dorothy in *The Quest of Simon Richardson* (Gollancz, 1986). For anyone who still retains a memory of the implied slur that Tilman was a desperate old man who ultimately succeeded in drowning his entire young crew – a casual and ignorant misrepresentation and calumny repeated by well-known outdoor journalists in reputable English newspapers over recent years – I thoroughly recommend a reading of Mrs Richardson's book, to guard yourself against passages like this, from the *Sunday Times Magazine* in 1990: '. . . a devotee of lightweight expeditions, one of which ended his life. He had made several trips to Patagonia in small and unreliable boats and after embarking once again in 1978 he and seven companions were lost at sea . . . There was . . . an unattractive edge in Tilman's make-up.'

Not one of which I was aware – and I knew him much better than did this writer.

that was so entirely unsuited to military regimentation – a further training course was found for him.

It was in triangulation – a subject in which he had, through his exploratory work, already developed considerable expertise. Word had, however, found its way upstairs about the wasted resource of this potentially useful human oddity – and also, no doubt, about a sympathy that was, by those in day-to-day command, deemed almost tantamount to insubordination with his Indian co-cadets, but that by those more devious ones higher up the intelligence ladders may have been viewed as a useful strategic attribute for one required to gather information in a troubled and vulnerable region. In August the second lieutenant on his elementary training course received a telephone call from Simla and found himself recipient of an offer from the Viceroy of India's office there to take up the grandiose-sounding position of 'His Britannic Majesty's Consul General' at Kashgar in Xinjiang. An eight-week trek from Srinagar across the Karakoram; reputedly the farthest point from sea on the planet; the walled city at the edge of the Taklamakan desert that was redolent of names like Sven Hedin, Aurel Stein, George Macartney – a more romantic place and offer could scarcely have come his way.

'Every traveller in Central Asia knows (and blesses) the British Consulate-General at Kashgar, for it is a haven of comfort and a centre of hospitality to the European who elects to try his luck in Chinese Turkestan,' wrote Colonel Schomberg[9] of the diplomatic oasis created during the long years of Macartney's tenure here. This was one of the crucial – perhaps at this period *the* crucial – listening points along the outposts of empire, and one that was at a pivotal moment in its history. From 1933 to 1942 Xinjiang was, in Shipton's words, 'a police state on the Soviet model' from which 'all outside influence other than Russian was rigorously excluded . . . Indian traders were persecuted, maltreated and deported in large numbers, often in cruel circumstances; the British Consulate-General in Kashgar suffered a rigid boycott'.[10] Such was the post being offered to a diffidently obstreperous newly qualified second lieutenant. Someone in a position of influence obviously thought very well of Shipton's capacities!

---

[9] Quoted in Peter Hopkirk's enthralling *Foreign Devils on the Silk Road* (Oxford, 2006) p.73.
[10] Eric Shipton, *Mountains of Tartary* (Hodder & Stoughton, 1950), pp.52–3.

He accepted, of course, and was to end up serving two consular terms here, by the end of the first of which, in 1942, General Sheng Shih-t'sai had performed an extraordinary volte face and, instead of an anticipated merger with Russian Turkestan, realigned Xinjiang with Chiang Kai-shek's Kuomintang (the Chinese nationalist party) and by draconian means brought about a Russian withdrawal. For any sense of Shipton's role in this momentous turn of events, his writings give us only the most veiled hints. The return journey from the first spell of consular service in Xinjiang gave him the time to complete his early essay in autobiography, *Upon That Mountain*. In his foreword, Geoffrey Winthrop Young writes that Shipton 'returned last winter [i.e. that of 1942–43] for a few weeks, writing this book upon the journey; he married, surveyed the home field, left to his wife the publication of the book in intervals of her own work in the ATS, and again disappeared, upon a distant and responsible charge'.[11]

There is explanation here, in both confused circumstance and geographical distance, for the host of errors in *Upon That Mountain*; and there is also an interesting surviving correspondence between Diana Shipton and G.W.Y. that gives a good impression of the fierce temper of those times. Diana had asked on her husband's behalf if G.W.Y. would write the foreword, to which he had agreed, and in a later note she asked his advice about using as epigraph a quotation from W. H. Auden. The reply was sharp and immediate.

Cambridge. 6. 10.

Dear Mrs Shipton,

I am glad you mentioned in your letter the idea of putting in a quotation from W. B. Auden [*sic*] Eric cannot know that this unsavoury young man bolted to USA with his no less unsavoury friend, Isherwood, immediately before the war, in order to escape any form of Service, and since then has been successfully evading attempts by the Americans and ourselves to return him to his duty.

The mention of his name, or the citing of him, in a book intended to promote courage and enterprise would arouse derision in many quarters.

I think him a bad poet, with a facile trick of imitating many

---

[11] Eric Shipton, *Upon That Mountain* (Hodder & Stoughton, 1943), p.5.

styles; but that is only a matter of taste! – On the other ground, I could not seem to be lending my name to any book in the war which gave countenance to, by quoting, a renegade.

I am so sorry to bother you with the detail! But I feel certain Eric can have no idea of how he is regarded.

The master copy will be much the best way. I send you much sympathy in the heavy work additional to your own.

Yours sincerely,
G. Winthrop Young

In the event, Shelley provided the epigraph – a much more appropriate choice though also a renegade, albeit of different cast; G.W.Y. contributed an attentive and polished foreword ('. . . how, again, where even bamboo-shoots are wanting, to carry provisioning enough for oneself, even though it meant a schism between the Shipton and the Tilman schools – whether a second shirt is or is not a superfluity for a three months' rude travel');[12] and Hodder published in 1943.

After his second spell in Kashgar, from 1946 to 1948, and accompanied by Diana, between 1949 and 1951 Shipton served as consul in the important city of Kunming, capital of Yunnan province in south-west China. This was another intriguing appointment, and when taken in combination with an obscure period spent in Persia in 1943–4[13] adds strength to the notion of Shipton's involvement in some form of intelligence-gathering. (Both Persia, at one end of the Trans-Caspian Railway by which aid and armaments could get through to the USSR, and Kunming, at the end of the Burma Road and the crucial air link for CIA supply of the Kuomintang,

---

[12] Shipton, *Upon That Mountain*, p.7.
[13] Interestingly, Shipton wrote nothing about his deployment to Persia (G.W.Y.'s 'distant and responsible charge') or journey there through Soviet Central Asia at the height of the war years. The obvious conclusion here is that the silence is significant, and owed much to the Official Secrets Act. That imperial intelligence files had been kept on Shipton (and Tilman too) certainly from 1935 onwards, and perhaps even before then – what *was* that trip to Government House in Nairobi in the summer of 1930 about? – is surely beyond reasonable doubt. A close reading of Shipton's writing – *Mountains of Tartary*, and particularly Chapter Four on the political background, is the crucial text here – yields an interesting harvest of more than usually elliptical Shiptonian clues. And makes me think that an adequately informed and intelligent biography of Shipton's later years (remember here that he was only thirty-two years old at the outbreak of the Second World War) would be a fascinating volume.

were vital logistical points, on the one hand in the war against the German army in its eastward offensive, and on the other in the early stages of the Cold War and the fight by America and her allies against the spread of communism in Asia.)

With the tide turning against Chiang Kai-shek, and his army retreating towards Formosa, Shipton had to flee Kunming before the Revolutionary Army of Mao Tse-tung, having sent Diana and their two boys home early in 1951. He himself arrived back in Britain in June, and by August he was back in the Himalaya again as leader of the 1951 Mount Everest Reconnaissance expedition to study the possibilities of ascent from the south – a trip on which the young, fit, acclimatised Ed Hillary found himself extremely impressed by Shipton's natural fitness and enduring ability at altitude, and on which Shipton was delighted to be reunited with the now prosperous and cosmopolitan old friend from the 1930s, Ang Tharkay, as well as Tilman's jocular old chum of offensive habits and endless stories (especially about the Yeti), Sen Tenzing, 'The Foreign Sportsman'. He was in Nepal again in 1952, leading an attempt on Cho Oyu (26,906 feet) His leadership came under harsh scrutiny for his unwillingness to cross into heavily militarised Chinese territory in order to reach the most feasible line up the mountain, though no one at the time appears to have defended him by making the very obvious point that as a former British consul who had served in two highly important stations on their borders during the civil war period and been in sympathy with the Kuomintang, had he fallen into Chinese revolutionary hands he would immediately have been perceived as a spy, and would in all likelihood have been shot.[14]

Instead, he was appointed to leadership of the 1953 Everest expedition, and knifed in the back by factions within the English

---

[14] The Welsh mountaineer Sidney Wignall, in *Spy on the Roof of the World* (1997), recounts what happened to himself and two companions when they were captured by the Red Army during an attempt on the border peak of Gurla Mandhata in 1955 – beatings, torture, mock executions, eventual release at a location intended to ensure they did not survive the trek back to Nepal. Shipton's likely treatment, in view of his diplomatic record, would have been far worse. In fact, Wignall had been recruited by Indian intelligence before leaving London to report on Chinese troop movements – a fact he concealed until this second published account of the expedition. Intriguingly, he claims to have told his captors, among other stories intended to fob them off, of a nuclear-powered device placed on Everest to monitor Chinese military activity. This may have been a *post hoc* appropriation on Wignall's part (see Chapter Seven, note 14).

mountaineering establishment. Here's the account I gave in the introduction to the 1985 compendium volume of Shipton's mountain books. It raised hackles within the Alpine Club/Royal Geographical Society at the time of its publication, but was endorsed by Charles Evans, Jack Longland and Peter Lloyd – all three well placed to judge its accuracy – with a demur from the latter to the effect that a certain amount of rewriting of minutes was standard practice, and the insistence from both Longland and Lloyd that Claude Elliott, though a weak and malleable chairman, was also a scrupulously honest one.

What emerges, from close examination of relevant Himalayan Committee minutes and written submissions from some of its surviving members,[15] is a bizarre tale of fudge and mudge, allegations about the falsification of official minutes, unauthorised (and not easily retractable) invitations, and opportunistic and desperate last-minute seizures of initiative by a particular faction. It is a perfect illustration of the cock-up (as opposed to the conspiracy) theory of history, and little credit redounds from it upon the British mountaineering establishment of the time.

There are two main themes to be considered here. The first is the general climate of feeling surrounding Shipton's perceived aptitude for, and interest in, the leadership of an expedition which even in its planning stage was subject to a jingoistic insistence that Everest must be climbed by a British party (that this was not to be achieved for a further 22 years after the 1953 expedition scarcely mattered or was noticed in the event).

This climate of feeling willingly accepted some of Shipton's own statements at face value. In *Upon That Mountain*, for example, he had written that 'there are some, even among those who have themselves attempted to reach the summit, who nurse a secret hope that Mount Everest will never be climbed. I must confess to such feelings myself.' It also drew on more questionable evidence, particularly relating to the 1952 Cho Oyu expedition, where a combination of political circumstance and personal history undoubtedly affected Shipton's leadership.

A synthesis of these points suggested to one faction engaged

---

[15] I am indebted to the late Peter Lloyd for enabling my access to these documents.

in the expedition planning that Shipton lacked the urgency, thrust and killer instinct which would be necessary to 'conquer' Everest. The case was immeasurably strengthened by Shipton's own submission to the Himalayan Committee meeting of 28th July, 1952, in which he expressed doubts about his suitability for the 'job' on the grounds that, being out of work with a wife and two children to support, he needed to consider his own position; that he felt new blood was needed to undertake the task; and that his preference was for smaller parties, lightly equipped.

This was the characteristic Shiptonian self-effacement coming into play once again, and it did him – and the subsequent reputation of the Himalayan Committee – much immediate harm. The 1985 introduction continues:

> The second theme – aside from the question of Shipton's likely attitudes and commitment – is that of the manner in which members of the Himalayan Committee conducted themselves over the matter of the leadership. The first point to be made is that the Committee was very weakly chaired. Because of this, the pro-Shipton faction carried the day at the meeting of 28th July, when Shipton – chiefly through the efforts of Laurence Kirwan – was strongly prevailed upon to accept the leadership. The contention then rested with the question of the deputy leadership.
>
> There existed a faction within the Committee and headed by Basil Goodfellow and Colonel Tobin – both of whom had been absent from the 28th July meeting – which had its own preferred candidate for this post in the person of John Hunt, who was, in Goodfellow's quaint phrase, a 'terrific thruster', and one who would bring a necessary application to the task. Tobin and Goodfellow lobbied forcefully that the deputy – or assault – leadership should fall to Hunt. Inevitably this would compromise Shipton, whose choice as deputy was Charles Evans and to whom in that role Hunt was therefore unacceptable.
>
> The crucial committee meeting took place on 11th September. The pro-Hunt faction was present in force, well-prepared, and determined to reverse the decision of the previous meeting. The

more ardent Shiptonians – most notably Kirwan and Shipton's old friend Lawrence Wager – were absent. The choice of Hunt was imposed – and as joint rather than deputy leader. Shipton was effectively compromised and morally compelled to offer his resignation, which was promptly accepted.

The rest of this squalid and bloody little episode is history, apart from a few later ripples spreading out from the main controversy, such as the charge of subsequent falsification of minutes levelled by Tom Blakeney against Claude Elliott – in the words of one contemporary observer, 'as bad a chairman of committees as one could find; he was hopelessly indecisive and hesitant and was too easily swayed by anyone (like Kirwan) who held firm opinions, however wrong these might be'.

That account, even taking into account everything I have read subsequently on the matter and all the representations made to me from those involved, seems to me to have the gist of the controversy. And a controversy it remained. The sense of shock that it engendered at the time is well conveyed in a letter to Shipton from his old mentor Tom Longstaff in Achiltibuie:

Dear Eric,

Absolutely shocking. I am quite unable to understand that committee. But I don't even know who they all are. Elliott never has an opinion of his own.

Your letter from Wordie:- I should say sympathisers on <u>Council</u> [i.e. of the RGS] wished him to write and that Founders Medal was dragged in because <u>they</u> recalled that award to you: also that Wordie was trying not to damn the committee out of a sense of loyalty.

I repeat I am unable to understand the committee's action. But I can now understand the fury of the letter I got from Dan Lowndes; he mentioned a case, or cases, of resignations being under consideration; possibly the committee that is.

I can't understand John Hunt accepting leadership under these conditions – I mean if he knew what happened. In his case I should have refused . . . I've met him often and he <u>seemed</u> a decent chap . . .[16]

---

[16] Letter from Tom Longstaff to Eric Shipton, 12 November 1952.

Ed Hillary, in a telegram of 21 September, was even more terse: 'Consider change most unwise. New Zealand climbers owe you considerable debt of gratitude. Hillary.'

After the successful ascent, John Hunt wrote from the British Embassy in Nepal to Shipton at the Outward Bound school in Eskdale of which the latter had been appointed principal in May 1953, in the following terms: 'I suggested that the team should finish with a weekend in the Lakes, as we had started with one in Wales. I thought you might like to have the party up in Eskdale, as you have so many friends here, and would want to have the full story. I further thought I do not presume to include myself, as I rather sense that I would not be very welcome to you.'[17] The sense of guilt and shame at the means by which his supporting faction's end was achieved is palpable here. And rightly so. The party spirit Shipton, in company with Tilman, had brought to British mountaineering in the 1930s was thoroughly spoilt by the style of 1953 Everest.

I do not for a moment believe that Shipton, with the same personnel and with Charles Evans as his deputy, would have failed on Everest in 1953. Evans's subsequent achievements are firm support for that belief. His leadership on Kanchenjunga in 1955 was a magnificent effort in the Shipton/Tilman style, and in the informed mountaineering view far surpassed that of climbing Everest (Shipton's stated leadership philosophy from the 1930s is also relevant here – see Chapter Nine.)

John Hunt – a lesser mountaineer than Shipton – was a charmingly vain, ambitious man practised upon by machiavels. He was also, it should be emphasised, eminently decent and formidably efficient and he ultimately used the fame accrued from Everest tirelessly in the public good. His sense of shame, of having been compromised by others' schemings and his own inability to resist the blandishments of ambition, seems to me one of the saddest aspects of the whole establishment debacle. No blame should attach to John Hunt for something from which he too in some internal way suffered. With that, we can surely say enough and goodbye to one of the sorriest chapters in British mountaineering history. As Eric Shipton said goodbye, more or less, to his interest in mountaineering among the

---

[17] Letter from John Hunt to Eric Shipton, 17 June 1953.

Greater Ranges after 1952.[18] But not to mountain exploration. From
1957 onwards, his marriage having ended, he found a new focus
among the ranges of Patagonia and Tierra del Fuego, and made
nine expeditions there, the last of them in 1973, four years before
his death. Fame would have denied him these quiet opportunities.
At the end he found safe haven back in Bevis-land, at the Manor
House in Ansty,[19] and the tributes that flooded in after his death
from round the world make it evident in how much affection and
esteem this essentially mysterious man was held.

---

[18] He did make one more trip to the Karakoram on an Imperial College survey
expedition in 1958, as well as some minor tourist treks, in Bhutan for example,
towards the end.

[19] On his return from a trip to Bhutan at the end of 1976, on which he had been very
unwell, he was operated on for prostate cancer, which had already metastasised
and moved to his liver. He was living at the time in the gloomy lower-ground-floor
Tite Street flat of Phyllis Wint in Chelsea. Another old friend (and Nick Shipton's
favourite 'auntie'), Aileen Fisher-Rowe from Ansty, hearing he was ill visited him
there ('. . . some of his lady friends hovered around and pressed him to leave his
"dreary, dingy basement flat" and go to the country.' [Peter Steele, *Everest and
Beyond*, p.253] is how his biographer has it). She found him still in his pyjamas,
looking frail and dishevelled, with Mrs Wint withdrawn and not knowing what to
do. Mrs Fisher-Rowe persuaded him to dress and to come out for a walk along the
Embankment and past the Physic Gardens to Cheyne Walk. On their return, as he
rested, before leaving she suggested to Mrs Wint that if she needed a break from
caring Eric could come to her at the Manor House in Ansty. The next day Mrs
Wint phoned to take her up on the offer, and the day after she turned up at Ansty
with Eric in the car. He was very weak, but still took his daily walks around and
along the loved and familiar sights and paths of Wardour Vale, though he leant
increasingly now on Mrs Fisher-Rowe's arm. In her sitting room after dinner one
evening he told her, apologetically, that he did not think he had strength to climb
the stairs. With her help, they made it: 'He was too weak to go to the bathroom,
so I brought him a huge bath-towel and we giggled about his peeing into that. He
kept his good humour right to the last.'

Mrs Wint was phoned to ask if she wanted him back. She drove down from
Chelsea to Ansty next day, was shown upstairs, took one look from the doorway
into the room where he lay, and drove off. The day after, very peacefully, he died,
and as mentioned in chapter two, after cremation his ashes were scattered on the
hidden lake at Fonthill.

As to the relationship with Mrs Wint, thought odd by many, Nick Shipton gives
an interesting perspective on the asseverations in the Steele biography that Eric
professed love and offered marriage to her. He recounts that after his father's
death Mrs Wint went to a famous (and costly) spiritualist, who conveyed to her
Eric's assurance that she was the love of his life, as well as his posthumous regret
that he had not married her.

ii) The Yeti Delusion[20]

With both Shipton and Tilman, there is a clue to the mystery, to the essence of the man. It's through the prime quality they both shared – that of humour – and it focuses on a standing joke between them that was perpetuated over fifteen years at least. The joke begins in *Blank on the Map*, with the chapter Tilman wrote under the heading 'Legends'. I have touched on this in a previous chapter, and recounted the Yeti-footprints puzzle on the feeder glaciers to the Biafo, in the vicinity of Snow Lake/Lukpe Lawo, that he and his two Sherpas Sen Tenzing – of course! – and Ila came across in 1937:

> The Sherpas judged them to belong to the smaller type of Snowman, or Yeti, as they call them, of which there are apparently two varieties: the smaller, whose spoor we were following, which feeds on men, while his larger brother confines himself to a diet of yaks. My remark that no one had been here for nearly thirty years and that he must be devilish hungry did not amuse the Sherpas as much as I had expected! The jest was considered ill-timed, as perhaps it was, the three of us standing forlorn and alone in a great expanse of snow, looking at the strange tracks like so many Robinson Crusoes.[21]

Thus the initial humorous response, but Tilman was too acute an observer to let the matter rest at a little friendly joshing between himself and his Sherpa companions. His interest was aroused, and he went on to comment in more detail but similar tone on something for which he had no ready and rational explanation:

> They were not the tracks of one of the many species of bears which seem to haunt the Himalaya, either Isabillinus, Pruinosus,[22] or 'Bruinosus'; for naturalists, like stamp-collectors, are keen

---

[20] An appropriate nod here in the direction of Professor Dawkins, with whom I seldom find myself in agreement.

[21] Eric Shipton, *Blank on the Map* (Hodder & Stoughton, 1938), pp.202–3.

[22] *Ursus arctos pruinosus*, the Tibetan blue bear – a creature almost as rarely seen as the Yeti, though proof of its existence is a little more certain. When Sir Edmund Hillary went on his great Yeti hunt in 1960, two scraps from the pelt of this animal were passed off on to him as Yeti-fur, their real origin subsequently established by scientific means.

on variety. There was no game of any kind, nor grass, within fifteen miles, and the nearest village was forty miles away. A few days later, lower down the Cornice glacier, bear-tracks were common and were recognised as such by the Sherpas and myself. A one-legged carnivorous bird, weighing perhaps a ton, might make similar tracks, but it seems unnecessary to search for a new species when we have a perfectly satisfactory one at hand in the form of the Abominable Snowman – new perhaps to science but old in legend.

His account continues by alluding to a controversy, chiefly prolonged by Frank Smythe, who had come across animal tracks on a high pass in Garhwal, that had recently occupied many inches in the correspondence and feature columns of *The Times*:

> All respecters of tradition must have noticed with surprise and regret how a certain great newspaper allowed the hospitality of its columns to be used, or rather abused, by the iconoclasts for a determined attack upon the very existence of the Abominable Snowman. No great harm, however, was done. Bear-tracks (species not agreed) were in the course of a column and a half successfully proved to be made by bears; wolves and otters were found to make tracks after their kind, and when the dust had settled the Abominable Snowman remained to continue his evasive, mysterious, terrifying existence, unruffled as the snows he treads, unmoved as the mountains amongst which he dwells, uncaught, unspecified, and not unhonoured.[23]

Tilman the sceptic and ironist is gently and teasingly at play here, and I can't resist the temptation to join in the fun and mix metaphors with him. What had got his goat – and this is a crucial point in the whole long history of the gag – was the rationalist assault on the existence of the Yeti mounted by Frank Smythe, the logical obtuseness of which had offended Tilman's intelligence and sense of reason. An argument that would not have won Hume or Burke's approval would certainly not have elicited his. We had better get back to the goats:

---

[23] Shipton, *Blank on the Map*, p. 203.

Readers of Boswell's *Hebrides* may remember the incident when the Doctor, in a manner unworthy of a philosopher, began reviling the roughness of the way and the awkwardness of his nag. The man leading it, whom Boswell in his pleasant way labels a common, ignorant, Highland clown, hoping to divert the great mind from present evils, points out some goats on the hillside: 'See the pretty goats,' he cries, whistling to make them jump. Something of the kind may have happened here. Instead of goats there were by ill luck these tracks, and the Sherpas, finding their Sahib a little irritable in the heat of the day, drew his attention to them. Smythe was interested enough to ask what made them and the Sherpas reply 'Yeti,' experience having taught them that was what most Sahibs expected them to say. Fatal! Little did they foresee the result of their rash answer. Smythe, who probably knew as well as they did what the tracks were, photographed them and submitted the prints to the two rival repositories of brute creation dead and alive respectively. The Natural History Museum and the Zoo both declared the tracks were made by a bear. Whereupon Smythe in an article in *The Times* announced that a Himalayan mystery was solved and that any tracks seen in the snow hitherto or hereafter must be bear tracks – a piece of reasoning on all fours with that classic example of a *non sequitur*: 'No wonder they call this place Stony Stratford. I was never so bitten by fleas in all my life.'[24]

We have run ahead of ourselves a little here, and in doing so have leapfrogged the main events of the controversy, so we had better backtrack (and if you think metaphor and logic are beginning to look somewhat confused, well, that's only the start of it!) The passage above comes from Tilman's 1955 *Alpine Journal* article entitled 'Himalayan Apery'. You will recall the meaning of 'apery' – 'the practice of an aper; a silly action'. And for the moment keep it in reserve whilst considering three further important statements from Tilman on this subject which had first teased his imagination in 1937. The middle of the three comes from a BBC radio talk given in 1949: 'I am at a loss to express a definite opinion. I merely affirm that tracks for which no adequate explanation is forthcoming have been seen, and will no doubt continue to be seen, in the Himalaya, and until a better claimant is found we may as well attribute them to their rightful owner, the Abominable Snowman.'

Less straightforwardly, he offers elsewhere the following advice, drawn from the supposed circumstances of the death of Lakhpa Tensing in 1949: 'By running downhill, which is, of course, the only way a man can run at these heights, one can usually get away from these creatures whose long hair, falling over their eyes, hampers them; but the unfortunate Lakhpa had apparently tripped, and lying half-stunned by the fall became easy prey.'

Do we begin to detect the presence, the giveaway habitual syntactical structures and ironic cadences, of Tilman's revered Jonathan Swift in this? Or again here: 'In the course of conversation these herdsmen confirmed the existence, or rather the recent presence, of the Abominable Snowman in the Langtang, pointing us to a cave which had been his favourite haunt. Six years previously these beasts (whose existence is surely no longer a matter for conjecture) had been constant visitors, but had apparently migrated elsewhere. The small kind, the size of a child, they called "chumi", while the big fellow went by the name of "yilmu" . . .'[25]

Chumis and yilmus![26] And not a houyhnhnm or a yahoo in sight? It strikes me that linguistic and anthropological approaches might yield more promising results here than humble zoology, or even cryptozoology, can provide; but we'll return to this point shortly when we introduce a third joker to our pack. Before that, there is another crucial text for consideration. It's 'Appendix B' to Tilman's 1948 account of *Everest 1938*, and is subtitled 'Anthropology or Zoology with Particular Reference to the "Abominable Snowman"'. Even by Tilman's standards, the tone of this spoof-scientific paper is odd, and should alert us to something being *afoot*. He reassesses all the accounts, re-rubbishes Smythe's photographs, and introduces footprint photographs of his own, taken at Snow Lake in 1937, which suffered as unfortunate a fate as that of any projector at the Grand Academy of Lagado: 'I was short of film but considering

[25] H. W. Tilman: *The Seven Mountain Travel Books* (Diadem Books, 1983), p.795.
[26] Given Tilman's daily dedication and competence in the matter of the *Times* crossword – a more impressive trait then than in these tabloid/Murdoch days – you might suspect an anagram here ('1 across. M-u-u-ch is slimy. 12 letters'). I wish you luck and fun – and we'd better be careful lest the notion of dyslexia attaches to Tilman this time.

the subject and the suspicious nature of scientists I thought I could spare one. In fact I made two exposures but being less skilful than Mr Smythe made both on the same negative.'[27]

Really, Major Tilman? How very inept! He continues as follows:

'Balu's[28] blundering stupidity with his camera cannot be too much deplored, especially when we consider Mr Smythe's cool, efficient handling of a similar discovery. In default of the tracks he produced a sketch which roused the naturalists to start a fresh hare, or rather otter. One wrote suggesting that the tracks were those of an otter progressing in a series of leaps. 'The Indian otter (*Lutra lutra nair*),' he wrote, 'has already been reported from high altitudes in the Himalaya.' This hint was snapped up by one brother naturalist who endorsed it and added that he had used it himself some years before to dispose of the Loch Ness Monster; and it was snapped at by another who unkindly pointed out that the otter in question was *monticola* not *nair*, the former being found in the Himalaya, the latter only in Southern India and Ceylon.

Amidst the snarls of the zoologists it was pleasing to hear a modest pipe from one signing himself 'Foreign Sportsman' (strange pseudonym) who introduced yet another small piece of first-hand evidence. He wrote: 'Balu's contribution to the discussion was welcome. His spirited defence of the Abominable Snowman wilting under the combined attack of Mr Smythe and the Zoological Society reminded me of Kipling's lines:

Horrible, hairy, human, with paws like hands in prayer,
Making his supplication rose Adam-zad the Bear.[29]

Note the flagging up there of the Foreign Sportsman, and his collusion with 'Balu'; and register too the sustained tone of mockery, and the ingenious rhetorical device of seeming to build up a case whilst at the same time effectively undermining it. We can cut now to a different

---

[27] H. W. Tilman, *Everest 1938* (Cambridge, 1948), p.132. For some reason, Ken Wilson and I omitted to include this appendix in the Tilman compendium – in retrospect, a grave error of judgement on our part. Or perhaps a cosmic joke.
[28] The name given to Tilman by his Sherpas and porters in 1936 (see Chapter 8).
[29] Tilman, *Everest 1938*, p.132. The couplet is from Kipling's 1898 poem, 'The Truce of the Bear'.

source entirely – to W.H. Murray's *A.J.* account of the 1951 Everest Reconnaissance expedition. The main group is encamped below the Menlung La, east of Gauri Sankar and Menlungtse:

> On 8th November, leaving Ang Tharkay and half a dozen Sherpas to wait for Bourdillon and me, Shipton and Ward set off for the pass with Sen Tenzing and seven days' food. That same afternoon they reached the main glacier on the far side at 18,000 feet. Half an hour later they came on the tracks of the Abominable Snowman. Sen Tenzing recognised them at once.

Sen Tenzing, the Foreign Sportsman – that man again!

> They were *yetis'* tracks. At least two of them had left spoor. Shipton and Ward followed the tracks for more than a mile down the glacier, finally losing them on the lateral moraine. Some of the prints were particularly clear. Pad marks could be seen within the footprints, which were 12 inches long, and where the creature had jumped the smaller crevasses the scrabble marks of its toes could be seen on the farther side.[30]

This is evidently a straightforward report of the account given by the three men – or more likely by the two loquacious ones – on their return to camp. Murray's word is certainly not to be doubted – he was a scrupulous witness and a sound Scotsman, though perhaps not one noted for ready access to a sense of humour. Also – and this is where the recurrences really begin to chime – Shipton brought photographic evidence to back up his report, and he printed it in his published account,[31] the last two plates in which are of a line of footprints with Michael Ward standing by them, wild-haired and bemused; and more famously, a single impression captioned thus:

> Footprint of the 'Yeti' found on a glacier of the Menlung basin. In general the tracks were distorted and obviously enlarged by melting; but where, as in this case, the snow overlying

---

[30] W. H. Murray, 'The Reconnaissance of Mount Everest, 1951' (*Alpine Journal*, 1951), p.37.
[31] Eric Shipton, *The Mount Everest Reconnaissance Expedition 1951* (Hodder & Stoughton, 1952).

the glacier was thin, the imprint was very well preserved and the form of the foot could be seen in detail. When the tracks crossed a crevasse we could see clearly how the creature, in jumping across, had dug its toes in to prevent itself slipping back.[32]

The final section of the book's quite brief text expands upon this:

It was on one of the glaciers of the Menlung basin, at a height of about 19,000 feet, that, late one afternoon, we came across those curious footprints in the snow the report of which has caused a certain amount of public interest in this country.

And elsewhere, Mr Shipton, to this day.

We did not follow them further than was convenient, a mile or so, for we were carrying heavy loads at the time, and besides we had reached a particularly interesting stage in the exploration of the basin. I have in the past found many sets of these curious footprints and have tried to follow them, but have always lost them on the moraine or rocks at the side of the glacier. These particular ones seemed to be very fresh, probably not more than 24 hours old. When Murray and Bourdillon followed us a few days later the tracks had been almost obliterated by melting. Sen Tenzing, who had no doubt whatever that the creatures (for there had been at least two) that had made the tracks were 'Yetis' or wild men, told me that two years before, he and a number of other Sherpas had seen one of them at a distance of 25 yards at Thyangbochi. He described it as half man and half beast, standing about five feet six inches, with a tall pointed head, its body covered with reddish brown hair, but with a hairless face. When we reached Katmandu at the end of November, I had him cross-examined in Nepali (I conversed with him in Hindustani). He left no doubt as to his sincerity . . .[33]

The photograph of the single footprint, which oddly enough

[32] Eric Shipton, *The Mount Everest Reconnaissance Expedition*, p.127.
[33] Ibid. p.54.

does not remotely resemble those in the photograph of Ward standing beside the tracks, is most peculiar, and has been endlessly reproduced and speculated over. On the day that Indira Gandhi was assassinated in 1984, I recorded an interview with Ed Hillary at the Travellers' Club on Pall Mall. I had a copy of the reconnaissance book with me, and in his small and chaotic room, between fielding press calls about the Gandhi assassination, he worked up a head of steam about the footprint-photograph.

> What you've got to understand is that Eric was a joker. He was forever pulling practical jokes, fooling around in his quiet way. This footprint, see, he's gone round it with his knuckles, shaped the toe, pressed in the middle. There's no animal could walk with a foot like that! He made it up, and of course he was with Sen Tenzing who was as big a joker as Eric was. They pulled the trick, and Mike Ward just had to keep quiet and go along with it. We all knew, apart from Bill Murray maybe, but none of us could say, and Eric let it run and run. He just loved to wind people up that way.[34]

So there you have it – the Yeti was actually a hare set running by our two, or rather three, comedians, for Sen Tenzing was surely complicit all along.

Ten years after the Travellers' Club interview I had Michael Ward on the end of a rope on the upper cliff of Glyder Fawr. Michael was an immensely talented rock-climber in his day, and a sharply funny, formidably bright, socially principled man of striking appearance. Marlborough-educated (his housemaster there was Edwin Kempson), he spent his working life as consultant surgeon for the National Health Service in London's East End hospitals, and eschewed private practice. He'd wanted to see just how hard a climb was a variant first pitch to Menlove Edwards's 1932 Procrastination Cracks, up which he'd led Menlove in 1949. It was substantially difficult, an extremely thin piece of slab-climbing as hard as almost anything in Wales for its time, and we were both impressed by how good he had been – he particularly.

We carried on up the main route, which is strenuous and under

---

[34] Interview recorded with Sir Edmund Hillary at the Travellers' Club, 31 October 1984.

the conditions we encountered probably in the HVS/E1 grade. As I was leading it, the heavens opened and the rock was soon streaming with water. Leaning over from the good belay ledge on top as Michael followed the pitch, I spotted him tussling with a particularly recalcitrant section of vertical crack coated with green slime, and yelled down: 'So, Michael, about that photograph of the Yeti footprint . . .?' As I did so, I paid out six inches of slack on a rope which hitherto I'd kept snug and tight. His eyebrows disappeared under the rim of his helmet.

'Take in, you bastard,' he gasped, face ruckling into a smile. It told me everything.

Trace the threads here right through, and you see the composite joke between Shipton and Tilman, the winding each other up over many years, the motifs, the recurrences. Sen Tenzing is the most important of those, and is surely the source of the story. You need to review here just how close Shipton and Tilman had grown to their Sherpas in the 1930s; how much they relished their sense of humour. An academic paper on the Sherpa sense of fun might bring us closer to the Yeti than any cryptozoologist ever will.

The suggestion that Britain's two most outstanding mountain explorers might have a hint of levity about them, however, produces establishment outrage whenever it's advanced. Peter Gillman, a fine and distinguished mountaineering writer, early in 1990 had a feature published in the *Sunday Times Magazine* under the title 'A Most Abominable Hoaxer' that – whilst interesting, readable and containing some good research – had a distinctly offended tone to it, and made some deplorable and inaccurate statements about Tilman which served to demonstrate how little attuned Gillman was to his very sophisticated humour (I rest my case here on the widespread syndrome Mountaineers' Sense of Humour Bypass). It also roused the ire of Shipton's biographer Peter Steele – it's notable how people spring to Shipton's defence whenever he's perceived as being under attack. Here's Steele's account of the Gillman piece: 'Not long ago Peter Gillman . . . denounced Shipton as "The Most Abominable Hoaxer". It is difficult to take seriously, being so full of scurrilous invective. He describes Shipton as "mercurial and disrespectful of authority", "defiant, non-conformist, restless and embittered".' I'd say those terms in fact were precise and appropriate and actually come through quite strongly in Steele's own book, though the 'embittered' needs the qualification of 'temporarily'. With the exception of the last, I'd not take any of them as pejorative – more as hallmarks of individuality, and on the whole admirable. 'This churlish appraisal of Shipton,' Steele concludes, 'does little to further the story of the yeti nor to discredit the footprints. Perhaps these tracks will always remain a mystery because we just *want* to believe in them.'[35]

Quite close, that, to the apocalyptic conclusion, written at the height of the Cold War, of Odette Tchernine's authoritative synthesis of all the evidence for the Yeti:

> I may be verbally flayed for what I am about to say but perhaps after all we are not meant to discover the whole truth about the Snowman . . .
>
> Perhaps these are the primal rough and secret stock preserved to withstand and survive any final disaster, preserved and hidden as the raw material for a fresh start in evolution should we finally blow up our so-called civilisation.
>
> There is more to all living humanity than flesh and bones and potential 'spare parts'.
>
> The Spirit that always walked on the face of the waters remains.[36]

Just as there is some measure of agreement between the octogenarian Russian researcher, tiny and sparrow-like in her Bayswater bedsit, and the mountaineering doctor schussing the trails of his adoptive Yukon, so too, I think, is there a degree of congruence, of mutual bewilderment finding its expression in fun, between our two lightweight satirists – who would probably have held more to Kipling's verdict: 'There is no truce with Adam-zad, the Bear that looks like a Man!'

Gratitude and honour to the jokers of this world, then, and the rigorous examples they have set! And time now to claim them back from an Establishment within which they never truly belonged, and by which their best qualities have for too long been sadly unappreciated and undervalued. Wry, modest, self-concealing, slyly mocking at cant, judging – whether it be situations or people – not from hearsay but through their own discerning intelligence and

[35] Steele, *Everest and Beyond*, p.161.
[36] Odette Tchernine, *The Yeti* (Neville Spearman, 1970), p.172.

hard-won experience – they're the kind of human beings I like. They represent the great tradition within mountaineering of light-heartedness and play in the face of mortal danger.

These two, with their hardihood and comic sense, would have fitted well into counter cultural climbing groups like the Rock and Ice Club in 1950s Britain, the Vulgarians around the Shawangunks in 1960s America, or the Californian Stonemasters of the 1970s. Resilient and courageous, they were pranksters too. And theirs was the authentic response to elemental challenge, delighting in experience for its own sake rather than as a means to wealth, celebrity and all that egotistical reward.

I hope you the readers have enjoyed keeping company with them through these pages as much as I've enjoyed the writing of this book, and the living with their work and quality of example and mind over the greater part of my own life.

Ariège, Bastille Day 2012

Acknowledgements

Hard to know where to begin in rendering thanks for assistance with a book ruminated on for as many years as this. I have grown old and grey in its service and many of those who advised, helped and gave freely of time, friendship and information have now passed on, so perhaps it is appropriate to thank them first: Tony and Celia St. John Armitage, Jack Baines, George Band, Peter Biven, Peter Boardman, R.W. Clark, Dave Cook, David Cox, Brigadier Derek Davis, Diana Drummond, Ian Duckworth, Nick Estcourt, Sir Charles Evans, Andy Fanshawe, Kevin FitzGerald, Sir Edmund Hillary, Robin Hodgkin, Peter Hodgkiss, Guy Kirkus, Lord Hunt, Sandy and Mary Lee, Peter Livesey, Peter Lloyd, Sir Jack Longland, Alex MacIntyre, John Millar, Annette Mortlock, W.H. Murray, Nea Morin, Marco Pallis, Dr. Arnold Pines, Dr. David Pluth, Ioan Bowen Rees, Odette Tchernine, H.W. Tilman himself, Michael Ward, Michael Westmacott, Don Whillans, Phyllis Wint.

Among the living, I am greatly indebted to Eric Shipton's sons Nick and John, and to Tilman's niece Pam Davis, for permission to use extracts from Shipton's and Tilman's writing, and for the pleasure of their acquaintance. Nick Shipton in particular has been an enormous help in the writing of this book, and I thank him for its foreword as well as for his and his wife Naomi's company, friendship and hospitality. They have been a source of sustenance and delight. Ken Wilson's shared enthusiasm for my subjects has kept their names current over a period of three decades, and here is surely a proper place to acknowledge his enormous contribution to the promotion and preservation of so much good mountain writing over close on half a century as magazine editor and book publisher, as well as to remember innumerable climbs enlivened by his vital and disputatious character. Our British outdoor community would have been much the poorer without his presence throughout this period.

From among the varied and extensive worldwide mountaineering community and associated individuals, I need to thank Rosemary Allott, Al Alvarez, Tony and Elaine Astill, Malcolm Baxter, John Beatty, Martyn Berry, Polly Biven, Margaret Body, Chris Bonington, Bill and Honor Bowker, Martin and Maggie Boysen, John Brailsford (father to the more famous Sir Dave!), Hamish Brown, Joe Brown, Colleen Campbell, Mark Charlton, Mick Coffey, Ingrid Cranfield, Martin Crook, Jim Curran, Hywel and Glenda Davies, Bernice Davison, Johnny Dawes, Steve Dean, Leo Dickinson, Ed Douglas, John and Pauline Earle, Aileen Fisher-Rowe, Chris Fitzhugh, Mark Goodwin, Conor and Sarah Gregory, Niall Griffiths, M. John Harrison, Stevie Haston, Tony and Di Howard, Malcolm Howells, Marni Jackson, Eric Jones, Harish Kapadia, Jill Lawrence, Jan Levi, John Lumb, Bernadette Macdonald, Isobel MacLeod, Cameron MacNeish, Sian Melangell Dafydd, Colin Mortlock, Bernard and Janine Newman, The Reverend Mike Perrin, Tom Perrin, Tom Prentice, Paul Pritchard, Royal Robbins, David Roberts, Paul Ross, Audrey Salkeld, Doug Scott, Walt Unsworth, Stephen Venables, Mick Ward, Nick Walton, Jonathan Westaway, Ray Wood.

Tony Shaw, first met on a wild and drenching winter's day at Windgather Rocks when we were both young teenagers and not another soul was crazy enough to be out there, has been invaluable as ever in chasing down obscure journal articles and discussing approaches and interpretations – more collaborative friendship than assistance. For specialist help in the uncertain identification of the Sanctuary eggs described in Shipton's Rishi Ganga journal, I have to thank my good friend Mark Cocker, surely the finest of writers on ornithological themes, as well as Douglas Russell of the Natural History Museum and Pamela Rasmussen. The previous biographers of my subjects - J.R.L. Anderson, Tim Madge and Peter Steele - whilst I may not always agree with their views, approaches or analysis of facts, have been invaluable in providing alternative discourses to my own narrative, and I thank them sincerely for the solid foundations they laid for the present volume.

Three institutions – The Royal Geographical Society, The Alpine Club and the National Library of Wales – have all, in their different ways, calmly and efficiently produced and provided crucial material. The enabling role of three more institutions has been significant. Sioned Puw Rowlands and Catrin Ashton, slyly humorous enchantresses of *Wales Literature Exchange*, arranged for a writer's residency in St. Nazaire and Nantes in the course of which much work on the book was completed in a luminous penthouse overlooking the mouth of the Loire. The Banff Centre in Alberta, through the grant of a Fleck Fellowship at its *Centre for Mountain Culture* that was as generous as it was welcome, gave me the chance to work on the book in peerless mountain surroundings and the most eccentric of accommodation – a converted trawler on a cradle in the woods, with mule deer sheltering under it each frozen night, the owls calling, and cougars of the feline variety patrolling among the trees. I salute all my friends there, and the animals too! The *Writers' Centre for Wales* in Llanystumdwy was also crucial through contact with many fellow writers under the aegis of its remarkable long-term director, my close friend Sally Baker-Jones. The support given by her and members of her family throughout a very difficult passage of time has been as heart-warming as it is unforgettable and unreturnable. *Diolch o galon*!

Finally, Emma Mitchell at Random House is an unflagging source of enthusiasm and support; the calm guidance, temperate stance, and scrupulous attention to detail of my editor and friend Tony Whittome make working with him one of life's civilized pleasures; and my former agent Jessica Woollard, before she wisely departed at the head of a small tribe of young children for Mumbai, was indefatigable on my behalf. I wish to thank Darren Bennett for his excellent maps drawn specially for this book. It only remains to excuse myself on the grounds of failing memory if I have omitted to mention anyone in whose debt I stand: and to beg forgiveness of those dearest to me; and to one of them in particular whose name I am not prepared to give here - the world operating far too often *sub specie mali* in these unaccountable times of the internet, 'social networking' sites and a depraved popular press - for long months of distance and preoccupation on my part. Their forbearance and understanding is far from unappreciated. To all the above, I would say that this happy book has felt to me a conduit for all the inspiration and goodwill I have received from them. I offer it to them now with my heartfelt thanks, in the knowledge that any virtues it may possess are truly theirs, and its manifold flaws entirely my own.

INDEX

'ES' indicates Eric Earle Shipton; 'HWT' indicates Major Harold William Tilman.

Tennyson, Alfred, Lord: 'Ulysses' 58*n*10
Tensing Norgay (Tensing Bhotia)
    153*n*36, 368
  in 1935 Everest expedition 248, 261
  in 1938 Everest expedition 332
  appearance 248
  and friction among the Sherpa
    community 248*n*61
Terrace Wall Variant 95
Tharkay, Ang 5, 27*n*10
Theytaz, Theophile 93
Thiepval fortress, Somme 66
Thomas, Edward 29*n*13, 364
Thoreau, Henry David: *Walden* 115
Thunacar Knott 109
Thunderer 239
Thundu 341, 342, 343, 344
Tierra del Fuego xviii, 378
'Tiger' badges 335, 341
Tilman, Adeline (HWT's sister) *see*
    Moir, Adeline
Tilman, Adeline (née Rees; HWT's
    mother) 54, 55, 57, 58, 148, 355
Tilman, Major Harold William (Bill) 5
  accident on Dow Crag 147–48
  allotted land in British East Africa
    105
  appearance 23, 63, 181, 344
  ascent of Nanda Devi (1936) 14,
    271, 275–83, 286, 287, 294
  background 9, 59
  as 'Bill' 22, 24
  biographies of 15–16, 21–22, 52
  birth 57
  childhood differs from ES's 61–62
  cycling trip in Africa 150–51, 176
  devotee of naked bathing in
    mountain water 188
  a devout Christian 357–58
  drinking 55, 179
  education 43, 57, 58–62, 103, 355
  farming in BEA 107, 167
  first meets the author 23
  first real climb (Mount Kenya, 1930) 14
  First World War service 9, 64–73,
    231*n*36, 242, 261, 312, 313, 355,
    366
  gold prospecting 149–50
  health 212, 217, 234, 274, 312, 317,
    342, 367
  and 'homosexuality' 355–56
  honoured by RGS 329*n*68, 367

  joins Shaksgam Expedition 291
  last two exploratory voyages 176*n*19
  leader of Britain's last pre-war
    attempt on Everest (1938) 9, 326,
    327, 331–36
  Longstaff's influence 13
  lost at sea (1977) 63, 366
  meets ES 9, 122–25
  military honours 69, 72, 345, 366
  Mount Kenya climbed by West Ridge
    127–34
  mountaineering value system 362
  obituary on ES 24*n*6, 123, 176–77, 358
  penultimate exploratory voyage
    (1975) 22*n*3
  physical hardihood 55, 72, 124
  quartermaster for 1935 Everest
    expedition 246–47
  reaches Nanda Devi Sanctuary
    (1934) 14, 28, 202–3, 204–5, 222,
    238, 240
  relationship with ES 10, 16, 21, 24,
    53, 123–24, 129–30, 207–8, 225,
    279*n*115, 281–82, 297–98, 312,
    338–39, 358–59
  relationship with his father 57–58,
    110, 355
  resigns his commission (1919) 104
  retires from Himalayan
    mountaineering (early 1950s) 22*n*3
  at the Royal Military Academy,
    Woolwich 43, 133*n*51, 150
  sails to Mombasa 105
  in Second World War 63–64, 344–45,
    353*n*110, 355–56, 366
  Shaksgam and Karakoram venture
    (1937) 14
  SOE war record 368
  'Tilly' nickname 22–23
  tragic probe of Assam (1939) 14,
    341–44
  visits Longstaff 179–80
  Yeti joke 379–88
  character
    abruptness 72
    austerity 296
    celibacy 71
    competence 129
    conservatism 104*n*2
    courtesy 24
    empathy for animals 69
    formality 22, 24